THE
IMMEDIATE ORIGINS
OF THE WAR

THE
IMMEDIATE ORIGINS
OF THE WAR

(28th JUNE—4th AUGUST 1914)

BY

PIERRE RENOUVIN

TRANSLATED BY

THEODORE CARSWELL HUME

WITH A PREFACE BY CHARLES SEYMOUR

NEW YORK

Howard Fertig

1969

LA SOCIÉTÉ DE L'HISTOIRE DE LA GUERRE

This volume has been translated and reproduced by special permission of the French Society of War History, under whose auspices it was originally prepared, and of which a brief description is here given.

THE Society of War History was founded in Paris in 1918, upon the initiative of M. André Honnorat, a member of the French Senate, and former Minister of Education, who has acted as President of the Society since that time. It is a private association, whose aims are the following:

1. To publish critical works and collections of documents dealing with the history of the World War, its origins, and its immediate consequences, considering it not only in its diplomatic, military, and economic aspects, but also in regard to the repercussions which it has caused in the political and social life of the various nations.

2. To encourage the development of the War Library-Museum, a French Government institution, which has undertaken to gather material from many international sources bearing on the great events which have so transformed the world since 1914.

The work of the Society of War History is based upon scientific considerations, and has been carried on in a purely objective spirit. Ever since the close of the war, the promoters of the organization have felt convinced of the need for applying the methods of historical criticism to a study of the great conflict. With this end in view, they made it possible for the University of Paris to introduce at the Sorbonne a course entitled "A critical study of the sources of the history of the World War." This course, the first of its kind in Europe, was started in 1922.

Among the numerous publications which the Society has already authorized are the following:

1. *Critical historical works.* In addition to the present vol-

ume by M. Pierre Renouvin, these include the volume by M. Charles Appuhn, *La politique allemande pendant la guerre,* and that by M. Jules Isaac, *Joffre et Lanrezac.*

2. *Collections of Documents,* dealing in particular with the great problems of the peace settlement: *La question des réparations,* from 1919 to May 1921, by M. Germain Calmette, Librarian of the War Library-Museum; *La sécurité de la France* and *Le désarmement de l'Allemagne,* by André Honnorat; and, quite recently, *Les dettes interalliées,* by M. Germain Calmette.

3. *Bibliographical catalogues,* making the resources of the War Library-Museum available to the academic world. (Catalogue of German sources, in four volumes, of Italian sources, in one volume, of British and North American sources, now in course of publication.) These catalogues may be regarded as nearly exhaustive bibliographies.

Furthermore, the Society has since 1923 undertaken the quarterly publication of the *Revue d'histoire de la Guerre mondiale* (Director, M. Camille Bloch, director of the War Library-Museum; Editor in chief, M. Pierre Renouvin), which draws to a large extent upon foreign contributors, and which publishes articles, documents, and full information regarding current bibliography.

The Society of War History is thus attempting to stimulate and to direct, in a common quest for truth, an important line of research, in which it hopes for active coöperation by the intellectual leaders of every country, and especially of the United States. It would also like to collaborate with students of the subject outside of France who, acting as correspondents, would be willing to assist it in completing its collections, and in furnishing any additional documentary evidence which might prove of interest.

The permanent headquarters of the Society are in the *Pavillon de la Reine, Château de Vincennes* (Seine), France.

CONTENTS

PREFACE

BY CHARLES SEYMOUR

*Sterling Professor of History, Yale University, Curator
Edward M. House Collection*

THE literature dealing with the problem of responsibility for the World War is extensive. Much of it goes
back to the early days of the war itself, pamphlets
and books tinged with the bias that results from the emo-
tions of belligerency or from a propagandist purpose, and
reflecting an ignorance consequent upon the lack of historical materials. Since the war, the output has been stimulated
by the political aspect of the question; for the Versailles
Treaty, by appearing to link the question of responsibility
with the obligation to pay reparations, furnished an occasion
to argue Germany's innocence of the verdict brought in
against her and hence the moral injustice of the reparations
clauses. Furthermore, and not alone in Germany, the natural reaction against the more extravagant charges of German responsibility has led to strong counter-charges leveled
against the Entente statesmen, so that at times the resulting
controversy has threatened to generate more heat than light.

Fortunately serious historians have approached the problem in a scientific spirit, anxious to revise the war-time verdict of the Entente peoples in accordance with the newly
published documents, but equally solicitous that the pendu-
lum of historical judgment, which for a time swung too far
in one direction, should not swing back in the other any
farther than is justified by the evidence now available. M.
Pierre Renouvin belongs to this group of objective scholars
who have been able to cast on one side national prejudice and
war-time emotion and to approach the task of investigation
in a scientific frame of mind; his research is characterized by
strict adherence to the canons of historical scholarship and

his conclusions are framed with judicial care. It is notable that the critics of his work, whether among the advocates of the cause of the Entente or those of the cause of Germany, have confined their objections to details and have acknowledged their confidence in his capacity for handling diplomatic documents and in his desire to evaluate the evidence impartially. Equipped with these qualities, he has made a thorough study of the voluminous German, Austrian, Russian, and British official documents as well as of the great mass of memoirs and unofficial material relating to the war collected at the Musée de la Guerre. Although Renouvin's historical method is untainted by national sentiment, the vigor and the lucidity of his presentation are in accord with the best traditions of French historical writing; the dramatic values of the great catastrophe lose nothing in his treatment.

It is not likely that complete agreement will ever be reached regarding war responsibility, for so many moral factors are found in the problem that there must of necessity be differences in individual judgments. We may hope, however, to reach definite conclusions as to what happened in the crisis of 1914. M. Renouvin himself insists that any that are formed now upon the basis of available evidence must be regarded as provisional. Nevertheless his conclusions carry us so far, and in view of the quality of his scholarship are of such interest, that it seems important that his book should be made available for English readers. Hence this translation, which is the more desirable since it has permitted M. Renouvin to revise his earlier French edition in the light of the new *British Documents* published in the autumn of 1926. The work of translation has been undertaken by Theodore Carswell Hume, who as M. Renouvin's pupil in the University of Paris has been able very happily to accomplish it under the supervision of the author himself.

October 1, 1927

SERBO-CROAT ORTHOGRAPHY

c	ts in "lots"	nj	ni in "opinion"
č	ch in "church"	š	sh in "show"
ć	t in "tune"	vj	vi in "view"
gj	j in "June"	ž	s in "measure"
j	y in "yet"	dž	j in "jungle"
lj	li in "million"	u	oo in "room"

IMMEDIATE ORIGINS OF THE WAR

CHAPTER I

THE PROBLEM

THE problem of the immediate origins of the conflict of 1914 remains even today dominated by the war spirit. Among the numerous works which appeared some years ago, only a few take into account all aspects of the question, and consider with any degree of care the arguments brought up by both sides, for analysis and criticism. Some of them plead the cause of the nation whose recognized advocates they are. Others, in an attempt to be independent, end by systematically discounting all official statements which contain any traces of passion. It did not seem unreasonable to hope that, at least in countries whose governments were not directly involved in the crisis of July 1914, writers would approach the problem in a calmer frame of mind and would escape the charge of prejudice. But such has not been the case. The inquiry which was to have been undertaken by a "neutral" commission formed at The Hague has not led to any appreciable results. Even American opinion has become a prey to polemical writers,[1] whose works may be inspired by strong conviction, but are certainly not based upon an objective study of the documents themselves. Such controversial writings have, at least, given occasion for the real historians to present a more balanced point of view.[2] It is just such a balanced presentation of the documentary evidence that the present writer hopes to achieve.

[1] I refer in particular to the work of Harry Elmer Barnes, *The Genesis of the World War, an Introduction to the Problem of War Guilt,* 2nd ed., New York, Knopf, 1927.

[2] Among the American contributions to the historical study of the problem, those of Mr. Bernadotte Schmitt and of Mr. Sidney B. Fay have appeared to me to be the most suggestive.

I.

BUT even if it is possible to apply the methods of historical research to this question, who can be certain that he is approaching it in the spirit of a historian?

During the war, national interest kept the subject from being treated by itself, detached from political and national points of view; it was impossible to study it coolly. Historical research seldom produces those precise formulas, those absolute conclusions, which respond to the instinctive demands of public opinion, and are necessary to the spiritual vigor of a nation whose every energy must be bent toward action. Imagine presenting the public with a complicated picture of the situation, showing every shade of the truth, and emphasizing every uncertainty! The archives were closed, the historians were enlisted in the service of propaganda. The critical sense of the people was deadened.

Peace came, and the question of the responsibility for the war was precisely one of those which the defeated nations discussed with the utmost bitterness. The world as a whole admitted in 1919 that the Central Powers were solely responsible for the war. Governments were carried away by public opinion. They felt called upon to furnish a moral basis for the Peace Treaty, by compelling Germany and her allies to admit that they were guilty of *imposing* the war on the world. The German experts at Versailles tried to assemble the arguments and to present a reasonable view of their side of the case; they sought not so much to leave Germany "spotless" as to upset the orthodox idea of one-sided responsibility. Article 231 of the Treaty of Versailles pronounced final judgment: acting upon incomplete information, the statesmen undertook to establish an official conviction, to define a historical truth, which, by its very nature, fell short of scientific certainty.

To tell the truth, this verdict does not bear upon the

fundamental cause; it simply states that the war was provoked by "the aggression of Germany and her allies"; an obvious fact, provided the declaration of war is to be taken as the sign and proof of aggression. But a note sent by the Allies to the German delegation charges the Central Empires with the premeditation of the war. The German Government protested, but signed. The problem of the origins of the war has since become a problem of contemporary politics, and one of the important factors in the peace settlement.

Germany has steadily rebelled against the verdict. Political interest has urged her to continue to do so: since the Allies had tried to place the duty of paying reparations upon a moral basis, would it not be possible, by undermining this foundation, to escape from the obligations of the peace? "The campaign against war responsibility," wrote a German newspaper in 1921, "is the wedge which will allow us to force open the Treaty of Versailles." The archives were opened in Berlin and Vienna by the revolutionary governments; on the whole, the documents brought to light strengthened the official position of the victors; they also brought out, however, certain mitigating elements, certain changes in detail, which once more raised the whole question of responsibility. The publications of the Soviet Government raised the veil which masked the archives of the Entente; they contributed certain facts which led to a further revision of the historian's view of the matter. France and England, by keeping to themselves the secrets of their archives, had thus far laid themselves open to a campaign of criticism. The force of German propaganda then began to develop; the Germans have drawn up their brief and are pleading their case, appealing from the judgment of Versailles to that of an "impartial tribunal."

On such ground as this, one should not conceal the fact that historical research is difficult. At every step one is faced with a controversy, and cannot avoid taking sides in the matter. Is it not possible, however, to try to set aside all preconceived ideas? This I have attempted to do; I have tried to maintain a purely critical attitude in my study of the facts, before drawing any conclusion from them.

II.

But is it not a dangerous pretension to try to reach the truth when many elements in our understanding of the problem are as yet incomplete and may be open to question?

Since 1919 the conditions for historical inquiry have undoubtedly been modified. During the war, the diplomatic "books" published by the governments did not constitute an adequate basis for historical research. A "book" of that kind is always to a certain extent a work of propaganda, at least when published in the very midst of the conflict. A government, whatever its character, cannot, must not, tell everything. Its obvious preoccupation, even its duty, is to keep up the morale and to exalt the will of the nation. It is therefore compelled to present the facts in a simple and summary fashion which will leave no room for ambiguity. This government has its allies; a certain coherence must be maintained between the publications which it is preparing and those of its friends; certain details must therefore be passed over in silence which might disturb, not the allied government (which already knows them well), but the public opinion of the country which is shoulder to shoulder in the common struggle. Finally, there is no time to make a carefully reasoned choice among the documents; the publication is therefore always hasty and incomplete. All the diplomatic "books" published at the beginning of the war are open to these objections, the German *White Book* of August 1914 more so than any other. It was composed with extraordinary rapidity—in a single night, so one of the German experts tells us. Of more than eight hundred pieces of correspondence and official reports, it included about thirty; it was the

work of a clumsy imagination, and the documents were muti-
lated and falsified. The Austro-Hungarian *Red Book* and
the Russian *Orange Book*, while a little less incomplete, gave
no better idea of the exact negotiations which took place;
certain texts were pieced together from a number of documents. Even the French *Yellow Book* also contained deliberate omissions, transpositions, and additions.[3] Presented with
these diplomatic "books," it was nevertheless possible for the
historian by comparing them to trace the general character
of the negotiations, and to pick out their salient features.
But there were still a good many gaps and uncertainties.

The new documents, published since the close of the war,
have brought an answer to most of these questions. The
Diplomatic Papers, published in 1919 by the Austrian Republic, included the correspondence of the Ballplatz with the
chief embassies, at Berlin, Paris, St. Petersburg, London,
and Rome, and also the official minutes of the Council of
Ministers for the month of July 1914.[4] At Moscow, the
correspondence exchanged between M. Isvolsky, Ambassador
to France, and M. Sazonov, Minister for Foreign Affairs,
was published for the period from 1910 to 1914 under the
title, *Materialy po istorii franko-russkikh otnoshenï za 1910-
1914 gg.* (Materials for the History of Franco-Russian
Relations, 1910-1914); it was by the use of this collection
that the French edition of this correspondence was prepared.[5]
Using those documents, and profiting also by some newly
discovered papers, the German propaganda service published, in pamphlet form, *Die Fälschungen des russischen Or-*

---

[3] *Cf.* Aug. Bach, "Irreführung der öffentlichen Meinung durch das fran-
zösische Gelbbuch 1914," *Die Kriegsschuldfrage,* II, No. 5, May 1924, pp.
129-153.

[4] *Diplomatische Aktenstücke zur Vorgeschichte des Krieges 1914, Ergänzungen und Nachträge zum österreichisch-ungarischen Rotbuch,* Vienna,
Staatsdruckerei, 1919, 3 vols. There is an English translation, *Austrian Red
Book, Official Files pertaining to Pre-War History,* London, Allen & Unwin,
1920, 3 vols.

[5] *Un Livre Noir,* Paris, Librairie du Travail, 1922-1923, 2 vols.

angebuches.[6] Later, it was in Berlin that the most important texts appeared, in the large collection of *German Documents Relating to the Outbreak of the War*, which is intended to be a complete collection of the pertinent official documents preserved in the archives of the Wilhelmstrasse.[7] Aside from these essential documents, the diplomatic correspondence of the Bavarian Government, published in 1922 by P. Dirr, is of only secondary interest. The collection was especially aimed to discredit the revelations made in 1919 by Kurt Eisner; it actually showed that the Socialist leader had no idea of the requirements of historical criticism, but it did not appreciably modify the knowledge which had already been secured through other sources.[8] Finally, in London there appeared not long ago the first of a series of publications under the general title of *British Documents on the Origins of the War*, edited by Gooch and Temperley.[9] This publication, Volume XI of the series, consists of documents relating to the outbreak of the war, collected and arranged by Mr. J. W. Headlam-Morley, whose work admirably fulfills every requirement of historical research.[10]

To these collections there should be added the testimony of the statesmen and ambassadors, which has been published

[6] Romberg, ed., *Die Fälschungen des russischen Orangebuches,* Berlin and Leipzig, de Gruyter, 1922. There is an English translation, *Falsifications of the Russian Orange Book,* New York, Huebsch, 1923.

[7] Kautsky, collector, Montgelas and Schücking, editors, *Die deutschen Dokumente zum Kriegsausbruch,* Charlottenburg, Deutsche Verlagsgesellschaft für Politik und Geschichte, 1919, 4 vols. There is an English translation, *Outbreak of the World War,* Carnegie Endowment for International Peace, New York, Oxford University Press, 1924.

[8] Dirr, ed., *Bayerische Dokumente zum Kriegsausbruch und zum Versailler Schuldspruch,* 3rd ed., Munich and Berlin, Oldenbourg, 1925. The most important papers, those which emanated from the Bavarian Legation in Berlin, had already been published in the *German Documents.*

[9] Dr. Gooch has also presented a study of the materials relating to the outbreak of the war in his recent volume, *Recent Revelations of European Diplomacy,* London, Longmans, Green and Co., 1927.

[10] *Vol. XI, The Outbreak of War, Foreign Office Documents, June 28th-August 4th, 1914,* collected and arranged with introduction and notes by J. W. Headlam-Morley, London, H.M. Stationery Office, 1926.

in the form of "memoirs" and "souvenirs," and that which was assembled by the German Parliamentary Investigation Committee.[11] These were all biased, of course, each one trying to justify his own attitude and policy, while at the same time exposing himself as little as possible. A comparison of these varied utterances, however, and a study of the discussions they have aroused, have served a useful purpose.

These collections of official papers which I have just named are, then, the basis of historical work today.[12] But if the documents published thus far cover the archives in Berlin, Vienna, St. Petersburg, and London, they do not as yet cover those of Paris, where the government has only just announced its intention of issuing a similar publication.[13] This gap, it is true, is not quite so important as one would be tempted to think, for the correspondence of the Russian diplomats gives abundant information about the attitude of the French Government.

Furthermore, no collection of documents, whatever its nature, carries with it a guaranty of absolute accuracy. Who can be sure that the editors have really given the complete series of pertinent documents, as they claim to have done?

[11] Germany (Republic), Nationalversammlung, *Beilagen zu den Stenographischen Berichten über die öffentlichen Verhandlungen des Untersuchungsausschusses, I Unterausschuss, Zur Vorgeschichte des Weltkrieges, Heft 1, Schriftliche Auskünfte deutschen Staatsmänner, Heft 2, Militärische Rüstungen und Mobilmachungen*, Berlin, Norddeutschen Buchdruckerei und Verlagsanstalt, 1920 and 1921. There is an English translation of the first by the Carnegie Endowment for International Peace, *Report of the First Subcommittee of the Committee of Inquiry* in *Official German Documents Relating to the World War*, New York, Oxford University Press, 1923, I, pp. 1-120.

[12] Publications such as the *Krasnyĭ Arkhiv* and other texts of a similar kind should also be mentioned. I shall refer to them during the course of this work. In addition, the governments opened their archives immediately after the war to certain historians, who have quoted from unpublished documents in their works: in France, É. Bourgeois and G. Pagès, *Les origines et les responsabilités de la grande guerre, Preuves et aveux*, Paris, Hachette, 1921; in England, Oman, *The Outbreak of the War of 1914-18*, London, H.M. Stationery Office, 1919; in Austria, R. Gooss, *Das Wiener Kabinett und die Entstehung des Weltkrieges*, Vienna, Seidel, 1919.

[13] See M. Poincaré's statement to the Chambre des Députés, 11th February 1927.

Most of the time they have omitted telegrams which seem to be of only secondary interest, and would have encumbered their work. It is possible, however, that any one of these papers might, by a comparative study of the date and hour of its issuance, possess an importance which escaped the authors of the publication. One must, however, have faith in their competence and in their good intentions. The value of the work depends above all, therefore, upon the reputation of its authors in the world of historical science. Are they men who would let themselves be guided by political interest, or cover a deliberate omission with their names? When one is presented with a publication prepared for some local political purpose, such as the collection of *Bavarian Documents,* one's doubts are justified; they are also admissible when the editor is closely linked with the fortunes of a government which is accustomed to dictating the official truths which concern it.[14] The editor may have reproduced the text in an incomplete manner, to avoid a troublesome detail. This all goes to show what suspicions cluster around any publication of this kind, when it is a work of propaganda.

The collection of *German Documents* is free from this reproach. Immediately after the Revolution, the Independent Socialist Kautsky was asked to assemble and classify all the documents covering the diplomatic correspondence for the period just before the start of the war. The work was lengthy; before it was completed, the Independent Socialists were relegated to second place in the political struggle, and the publication was entrusted to a jurist, Professor Schücking, and to a staff officer, Count Montgelas. But Kautsky was not entirely thrown aside. He has placed his name on the volume, along with those of Montgelas and

14 It is in this respect that the works of Pokrovsky have often been under suspicion. I must say, however, that the comparison made by my colleague and friend, M. Charles Appuhn, between three important papers published by Pokrovsky and the minutes preserved at the former Russian Embassy in Paris, showed that the documents were correctly reproduced.

Schücking. Now, for us in the field of history, the name of Kautsky is a guarantee; he was not easy on the Emperor; he was certainly not anxious to spare the old German diplomacy. He wrote the most heated indictment of them both in his famous book, *Wie der Weltkrieg entstand*. We therefore have every reason to think that he published *all* the documents of interest, without discarding those which might have been unfavorable to the German policy before the war. That is what gives such historical value to the work. And yet, even in this case, we must guard against conclusions which are too final. Kautsky certainly published all that the papers contained at the moment when he had them in his hands. But some may have been destroyed before he took possession of the archives; someone may have seen to the disappearance of a few very compromising papers. During the Fechenbach-Cossman case, which was heard in Munich in April 1922, a former diplomat, when called to the witness stand, testified that he had seen three important documents destroyed at the very moment of the first revolutionary outbreaks.[15] Without exaggerating the significance of these revelations, it must nevertheless be admitted that the destruction of documents may have been even more extensive than is realized.

The path is therefore full of snares. The diplomatic documents cannot merit absolute confidence; sometimes the historian actually knows that certain papers exist which he has never seen, and perhaps never will. The most positive testimony is often biased, or is the result of partisanship. While this is true, it may also happen that some experience or other may lead to a hypertrophy of the historian's critical sense, a result that is equally unfair, for he should not systematically distrust the use of all documents in general. With this uncertain and incomplete material, however, he should not pretend to reach conclusions which are anything more than

15 Herr von Lözl. *Cf. Münchener Post*, 28th May 1922.

provisional. Is that any reason for abandoning the work? I certainly do not think so. The question of the causes of the war is not one which can be left to the future; each new inquiry may bring about some reconciliation or some discussion which will bring us a step nearer to the truth. Today is the very time, while the witnesses and actors in the great drama are for the most part still here, for a historical investigation which will help in reaching precise conclusions, or in discovering proofs of guilt. A critical study, however imperfect, has no other purpose than to contribute its share to that investigation.

III.

In limiting this work to the diplomatic crisis between 28th June and 4th August, 1914, which led Europe into the war, I lay myself open to another objection. Is it possible to separate these events from all the crises which preceded them?

The two groups of Powers which were drawn up on opposing sides in 1914 had been in rivalry for some years. The German victory of 1871 had placed Europe under a hegemony which was destined in the end to provoke a reaction; the formation of the Entente Cordiale in 1904, the Anglo-Russian reconciliation in 1907, and the Anglo-French conferences in 1912, were the chief manifestations of this resistance. The statesmen in Berlin saw in them the threat of a general "encircling." The Moroccan crises between 1905 and 1911 had aroused the old Franco-German antagonism, and had stimulated parallel efforts for the development of effective military forces. The Balkan crisis in 1912-1913, after the one in 1908-1909, had ranged face to face the interests of Austria and those of Russia, and had already manifested the general character of the one which was to open the war in 1914. Finally, the Treaty of Bucharest had been a setback to the policy of the Central Powers. The military and civil leaders of Austria had firmly resolved not to accept its conclusions. Germany, who had not encouraged Austria to the point of a rupture during this earlier quarrel, was nevertheless conscious that her position had been weakened. Russia, on the other hand, after the experiences of 1908 and 1912, had developed her program of armament and had defined more narrowly the terms of the Franco-Russian military pact. She seemed to feel a determination and firmness on the part of the French Government, of which she had not been quite sure up to this time.

The idea of an inevitable war tended to spread. The state of European politics, the race for armaments, the growing rivalry of the two groups of Powers, seemed to be leading toward it unavoidably. People were actually waiting for the conflict to begin. When a statesman reaches this conviction, he reasons and acts as though the current were invincible. He must make the necessary preparations for the conflict, without actually believing that it is coming. How can the stream of Destiny be turned aside?

This was the moral situation which dominated the decisions of the statesmen in July 1914, and which explains the development of the crisis.[16]

The diplomatic negotiations of July 1914, however, form a complete whole which it is legitimate to study separately. A number of crises since 1904 might have led to the war, but were ended by reaching a compromise. A war delayed is often a war saved. If the germs of a conflict already existed in Europe, was there not someone who struck the spark? This is why it has seemed legitimate to me to confine this work to the immediate causes of the conflict.[17]

[16] It does not, however, constitute an excuse for Germany, whose attitude had resulted in the forming of a "moral coalition" against herself, and who believed that the various governments were mutually suspicious.

[17] Taken as a whole, this volume comprises simply the material of the course taught at the Sorbonne in 1922-1923, as the first year of a research devoted to "a critical study of the sources of the World War," and founded upon the initiative of the Société de l'Histoire de la Guerre.

CHAPTER II

THE SARAJEVO CRIME[1]

ON 28th June 1914, Archduke Franz Ferdinand, heir to the Austrian throne, who had come to Bosnia to supervise the army maneuvers, was making an official visit to the town of Sarajevo, accompanied by his wife, Sophia Chotek, Duchess of Hohenberg. As he was driving to the City Hall in an automobile, a hand grenade was hurled across his path; it missed its mark and wounded an officer in another car. At the command of the Archduke, the procession halted a moment and then went on its way, while the police arrested the would-be assassin, Čabrinović. The call at the City Hall went ahead as planned. As the party was leaving, the Archduke spoke rather angrily to General Potiorek, Military Governor of Bosnia, who replied that no measures of safety would be able to prevent another attack. He therefore suggested that the official visit should be discontinued. The Archduke agreed, but wished to stop and see how the wounded officer was getting along. The procession then started off on the same route along which it had come, following the Quai de la Drina, where the traffic was lightest.

[1] *Der Prozess gegen die Attentäter von Sarajewo nach dem amtlichen Stenogramm der Gerichtsverhandlung aktenmässig dargestellt von Professor Pharos und einer Einleitung von Josef Kohler,* Berlin, R. von Decker, 1918, gives such information as was gathered during the official inquiry. For the new facts which have been learned since 1918 see, first of all, *The Serajevo Crime,* by M. Edith Durham, London, 1925 (violently anti-Serbian); "The Murder at Sarajevo," by R. W. Seton-Watson, an article in *Foreign Affairs* (New York), April 1925, pp. 489-509, and *Sarajevo, a Study in the Origins of the Great War,* by the same author, London, Hutchinson, 1926 (both more favorable to the Serbian side of the case); finally, an article by Wegerer, "Der Anlass zum Weltkrieg," in *Die Kriegsschuldfrage* for June 1925, pp. 353-405, who reviews and summarizes all the testimony, with a view to reaching certain conclusions which are favorable to Germany. Detailed references will be given during the course of this chapter.

Due to an error on the part of the driver, the car slowed down as it reached the corner of the Franz Joseph Strasse, where a young Bosnian, Princip, leaped out and fired a revolver point-blank at the Archduke and his wife, both of whom died a quarter of an hour later.[2] Along with the assassins, the police arrested a number of other armed men who were waiting, in different parts of the town, for the official procession to pass by.[3]

Princip and Čabrinović were Austrian subjects, but both of them came from Belgrade, where one had been studying for two years and the other was a typographer. The weapons which were found upon them came from Serbia, and the hand grenades bore the mark of the arsenal at Kragujevac.

I. *The Nature of the Crime.*

In order to appreciate the true nature of the crime, one must bear in mind the state of Austro-Serbian politics at the time when it was committed.[4] Ever since the annexation of Bosnia-Herzegovina by the Austrian Government in 1908, the spirit of irredentism had been growing in the two provinces. The Serbs of Sarajevo looked longingly across the border to Belgrade, where the Serbs in "the kingdom" were stretching out cordial hands. The control of Bosnia-Herzegovina by Austria-Hungary was therefore a constant source of trouble between Austria and Serbia. Nationalistic and Pan-Serbian propaganda was disturbing the Austro-Hungarian officials, for it had frankly espoused the cause of

[2] For the account of the crime, see the testimony quoted by "Pharos," the report made by General Potiorek, printed in *Der Tag,* 28th June 1924, and the article in the *Berliner Tageblatt,* 28th June 1924, by L. Adelt, who received the details from Colonel Manussi, the Archduke's aide-de-camp.

[3] Upon this point, see the information given by the Serbian journalist, Boriveje Jevtić, which has been summarized by A. Mousset in an article, "L'Attentat de Serajevo," in the *Revue d'histoire diplomatique,* 1925, I, 44-68.

[4] *Cf.* Denis, *La grande Serbie,* Paris, Delagrave, 1915; Seton-Watson, *German, Slav and Magyar, a Study in the Origins of the Great War,* London, Williams and Norgate, 1916; Wendel, *Die Habsburger und die Südslawenfrage,* Belgrade, G. Kohn, 1924.

separatism. Any increase in Serbian power thus appeared dangerous to the eyes of Vienna. Now, the Balkan Crisis of 1912-1913 had resulted in the enlargement of the Serbian Kingdom, and in the growth of nationalistic feeling among the South Slavs. Austria had stirred up new hatred against herself at that time by refusing to allow Serbia access to the Adriatic. More than once already had Austria thought of war as a means of ridding herself of this menace.

The Sarajevo crime, committed by two Serbs from Bosnia, seemed to be directly connected with this significant and deep-rooted movement. It has given rise, however, to many discussions, and to a number of different explanations.

The theory of the "police plot" is one which has often been favorably received among the peoples of the Entente. This is the sole reason for which it deserves a moment's critical consideration. In its most extreme form, such as that given by M. Jules Chopin,[5] it implicates even the Archduke's own personal police. Franz Ferdinand, it is claimed, had reasons for hoping that some incident might take place at this time which would compromise the position of Serbia. Čabrinović was acting under the supervision of the Archduke's own agents, and it was taken for granted that the hand grenade would not reach its mark. The gesture made by Čabrinović then incited Princip to commit his crime, which thus had nothing to do with the original frame-up! This fanciful interpretation is contradicted by the authoritative documents in every essential detail.[6]

The idea that the crime was "Hungarian" in origin has been put forward by Rudolph Bartulić, a Croat who was employed in the Austrian espionage service during the war.[7]

[5] *Le Complot de Sarajevo*, Paris, Bossard, 1918.

[6] M. Chopin is forced to deny flatly the most important and official records of the whole incident. He does not even seem familiar with the account of the various discussions, published by "Pharos."

[7] M. Bartulić's memoirs have been edited by Gottfried Beck, *Ungarns Rolle im Weltkrieg*, Lausanne, Payot, 1917, pp. 215 and ff.

It appears that the author was taken into the confidence of a police officer, who had received anonymous letters, while on duty at Agram shortly before the crime, to the effect that the Archduke was in danger. The officer had communicated this information to Budapest, but had received no reply. It is going a bit far to say at once, as Bartulić did, "The Hungarians and the Austrian Serbs have assassinated the heir to the throne, Franz Ferdinand, by common consent." It is true that the Archduke was the enemy of the Magyars. As Czernin said, he had a deep-seated antipathy for everything Hungarian, and he did wish "to crush Hungarian hegemony" by supporting the claims of the smaller nationalities. But there is nothing to justify the belief that the Budapest police had any complicity whatever in the crime.

The suggestion brought forward by Mr. Wickham Steed, then director of the foreign political department of the *London Times*, rests upon a much firmer basis.[8] One can hardly believe, he says, that the Austro-Hungarian authorities were wholly unaware of the plot. Now, they did not take the necessary measures of precaution, and he hints at a suspicion: "Several members of the royal imperial family had strong reasons for not wishing the Archduke to accede to the throne."

There was no doubt whatever about the hostility which certain elements at court bore toward the Archduke. His marriage to Sophia Chotek, and his avowed intention of making his wife the first lady of the Empire if he succeeded to the throne, were intolerable to Austrian aristocracy. By the brusqueness of his nature and his conduct, Franz Ferdinand had aroused much personal animosity against himself, all of which combined to bring him "the great unpopularity which he enjoyed."[9] The old Emperor had but little sympa-

[8] *Cf. Edinburgh Review,* October 1915, and *Nineteenth Century and After,* February 1916.

[9] Margutti, *Vom alten Kaiser,* Vienna, Leonhardt-Verlag, 1921, pp. 47 and 221. *Cf.* also Czernin, *Im Weltkriege,* Berlin, Ullstein, 1919, pp. 50-60.

thy for his appointed successor. "A great gulf yawned between them, which could not be bridged over."

On the very eve of the crime, the preparations for the trip to Sarajevo had created quite a stir in court circles, for Franz Ferdinand had adopted the very same form of ceremony as was customary for the Emperor. "It is terrible! See what we have come to!" exclaimed the Adjutant-General, who was the Emperor's confidant. Franz Joseph did not dare to protest, but he left Vienna earlier than usual, to avoid receiving his nephew when he should return from Bosnia.

These little incidents show something of the attitude which was felt quite generally at court when the news of the crime reached Vienna. "The death of the Archduke," writes Kanner, "had the effect of a great deliverance in political and official circles, except in the group which was closely attached to him. The old Emperor is breathing more easily."[10] If we may believe the word of General Margutti,[11] Franz Joseph's only remarks, on hearing the news, were: "Terrible! The Almighty allows no one to challenge Him! A Higher Power has restored the order which I was unfortunately incapable of maintaining!"

But is this testimony sufficient to warrant the suspicion which Mr. Steed implies? Even admitting that the court at Vienna was pleased by the elimination of the Archduke as the candidate for the throne, can anyone show that the Austrian aristocracy actually wished for his death? No one has thus far produced the slightest proof of such a fact.

In all this, however, there is one detail to be kept in mind, namely, the attitude of the responsible authorities. Count Tisza remarked the following week, before the Council of Ministers at Vienna, that "the state of affairs in the police department must have been indescribable to make it possible that six or seven individuals, known to the police, could have

---

[10] Kanner, *Kaiserliche Katastrophenpolitik,* Leipzig, Tal, 1922, p. 192. The author was director of the *Zeit.*
[11] Margutti, p. 148.

posted themselves, on the day of the assassination, along the route of the murdered heir to the throne, armed with bombs and revolvers, without the police observing or driving away a single one of them." And this negligence is all the more astonishing when we realize that the higher officials were aware of the danger. The Archduke's trip to Bosnia was frankly political in character; it was hoped that his presence might encourage the elements that were loyal to Austria, and counteract to some extent the nationalistic agitation. The news of his coming had caused great excitement among the Serbs in Sarajevo. Franz Ferdinand had received threatening letters, and the Army Staff knew perfectly well that the heir to the throne was taking his life in his hands. What explanation can be given for the fact that General Potiorek, Military Governor of Bosnia, did not take more adequate measures of protection?

This fact certainly confirms the remarks which Tisza made in Vienna. The idea of a "police plot" was, of course, the product of sheer imagination, but the negligence of the police and the inertia of the higher officials were astonishing, to say the least.

If we may judge by the foregoing facts, then, the murder at Sarajevo appears to have been a political crime. Whatever may have been said to the contrary,[12] it had all the characteristics of such a crime, for it was intended to alter existing conditions, to change a given system of government. "I detested the heir apparent," said Čabrinović during the trial, "because he was the enemy of the Serbs." "I killed him, and I am not sorry," said Princip, "for he was an enemy of the Slavs."

Was this hatred well-founded?[13] From what we can learn

12 Cf. Morhardt, Les Preuves. Le Crime de Droit Commun. Le Crime Diplomatique, Paris, Librairie du Travail, 1924, pp. 16-18.

13 To tell the truth, the question is only secondary. It was quite sufficient that, in the fanatical group among whom the murderers lived, the Archduke was reputed, whether rightly or wrongly, to be unfriendly to the Slavs.

of his political ideas, Franz Ferdinand was the confirmed opponent of the dualistic system. His own scheme was based upon the federal idea.[14] "The Czechs," he had told Margutti,[15] "should be autonomous and separated from the Germans of Bohemia, and, in the same way, the Croats, Slovenes and Serbs of Hungary." But, if all these statements are true, as everything seems to indicate,[16] why did this man loom up as an enemy in the minds of the South Slavs? The reason was that he wished to solve the Jugo-Slav problem *within the limits of the Dual Monarchy.* When the Serbs of Austria-Hungary had received the liberal institutions which the Archduke proposed to grant them, they would exercise, "by the very force of numbers, such an attraction upon the Serbs 'of the Kingdom,' that the latter would seek for union in a centripetal direction—that is to say, towards the Dual Monarchy—and not in a centrifugal direction, by the union of our South Slavs with the Serbs 'of the Kingdom.' " This would be all the more true, he added, "because our South Slavs are markedly superior to the Serbs and Montenegrins in respect of civilization." This proposal which he mentioned to General Margutti gave evidence, not of a complete and precise program, but of certain well-defined tendencies which were an open secret in political circles. Bethmann-Hollweg, for example, was quite aware of them.[17] Now, these plans ran directly counter to the Jugo-Slav idea, such as the Pan-Serbian propaganda had steadily proclaimed it to be.[18] The assassins took the opportunity to allude to these plans of the

14 Upon this subject, see the important article on "L'archiduc François Ferdinand," by Seton-Watson in *Le Monde Slave,* April 1925, pp. 1-18.

15 Margutti, p. 137.

16 *Cf.* Szilassy, *Der Untergang der Donau-Monarchie,* Berlin, Neues Vaterland, 1921, p. 259, based upon an interview with the Archduke.

17 *Betrachtungen zum Weltkriege,* Berlin, R. Hobbing, 1919-21, 2 vols., I, p. 117.

18 Furthermore, they doubtless corresponded, in the Archduke's mind, with certain preoccupations of a religious character, namely, to look for support to the Catholic elements among the South Slavs, and not to the Orthodox elements.

Archduke's. "We were told," so Čabrinović declared, "that he wished to found a federal monarchy, calling for the annexation of the Serbs." And Princip added: ". . . As the future sovereign, he would have carried out certain ideas which stood in our way."

Neither the old Emperor nor the other political groups shared these ideas, which appeared to them as dangerous. They feared that the plans of Franz Ferdinand and the violence of his methods might turn out to be disastrous for the Monarchy.

When the young Bosnians murdered the Archduke, it was thus a whole political system which they were overthrowing, or thought they were overthrowing.

II. *The Preparation of the Crime.*

THE assassins steadily claimed, of course, that their "undertaking" was "absolutely personal." The very earliest inquiry, however, proved that they had accomplices both in Serbia and in Bosnia. It was in Belgrade that they had obtained the means necessary to carry out the crime, and practised the use of the revolver. The weapons and money were furnished by Ciganović, a railway employé of Bosnian origin, who, in turn, had secured them from Tankosić, a Serbian officer. In making their way across the frontier, at Sabać, they were assisted by Major Popović, a Serbian customs official. They received guidance and help from friends at each stage of their journey, at Pribož, and at Tugla; finally, at Sarajevo itself, they were welcomed by a Bosnian teacher, Danilo Ilić, who told them exactly where to go, and recruited, on the spot, a number of men ready to forswear the conspirators if necessary. The ease with which the assassins eluded the Austrian police would lead one to infer the existence of a permanent organization. All the men who were arrested made some allusion to "the tunnel from Belgrade to Sarajevo." From the very first, it was thus evi-

dent that the murder of the Archduke was not an isolated
act, but that it had been prepared for a long time, and had
been carefully planned to the last detail. The Austrian investigation traced throughout these plans the influence of
the *Narodna Odbrana*, a Serbian nationalistic society, which
centered in Belgrade, but was active among Serbian groups
in Austria-Hungary.

These early conclusions were incomplete and partially
incorrect. It took nearly ten years for them to be rectified
in the light of new discoveries. The following is the account of
the preparation of the crime based upon the most recent testimony.[19]

The scheme originated in Bosnia. It was conceived by a
group of young men belonging to a patriotic and revolutionary society, the *Mlada Bosna* (Young Bosnia), some of
whom lived on Austrian territory, in Sarajevo, and others
"outside," in Serbia, Switzerland, and France. The most active spirit in this group was a student twenty-four years old,
Vladimir Gačinović, whose hope for the political emancipa-
tion of Bosnia-Herzegovina was inseparably linked with that
of a social revolution. He was in touch with a number of
Russian revolutionists who had been forced to emigrate to
Switzerland.[20] It was in January 1914, in Toulouse, in a
hotel on the Rue St. Jérome, that three members of the
Mlada Bosna—Gačinović, Golubić, and Mehmedbašić—decided upon the assassination of the Archduke. Neither the

---

[19] Upon this subject, see "La vérité sur l'attentat de Sarajevo," by Victor
Serge, *Clarté,* May 1925, based upon the account which the author received
from two of the conspirators, Golubić and Bastaić; "The Murder at Sarajevo," by Seton-Watson, *Foreign Affairs* (New York), April 1925, in which
the author presents certain information which he secured during a recent
inquiry in Bosnia; "Nouvelles dépositions concernant l'attentat de Sarajevo," by Bogičević, *Die Kriegsschuldfrage,* January 1926, which criticizes and
corrects certain points in the preceding article, basing his statements on the
same testimony as Victor Serge; "The Black Hand Plot that Led to the
World War," by Sidney B. Fay, *Current History,* November 1925, pp.
196-208.

[20] Gačinović died in 1917.

place nor the date for the crime was yet decided upon, for Franz Ferdinand's trip to Bosnia was only being considered in official circles in Austria-Hungary, and had not been publicly announced. The three conspirators then informed Princip, another member of their organization, whom they had summoned to Lausanne to ask whether he would be willing to undertake the deed. For the completion of their plans, they might count upon the personal influence of Danilo Ilić, the leader of the *Mlada Bosna*, who would also help them to secure the necessary accomplices.

Once this decision was reached, the young Bosnians approached, not the *Narodna Odbrana*, but a Serbian secret society, which collaborated directly in the preparation of the crime. This society, called "Union or Death," was better known by the name of the "Black Hand." Founded in 1911, its purpose was to bring about by force the union of all the Serbs, the Serbs "of the Kingdom," and those of Austria-Hungary and Macedonia.[21] The members of the Society were mostly army officers, headed by Colonel Dimitrijević, then chief of the intelligence service of the Serbian General Staff, who had been one of the organizers of the plot against King Alexander in 1903. He was an expert in political crime. Major Tankosić served as secret agent to Dimitrijević. It is quite probable that the "Black Hand" had a number of adherents within Bosnian territory, and it appears that Gačinović was one of them.

Major Tankosić and Colonel Dimitrijević helped the members of the *Mlada Bosna* to arrange the details of their plan, and assemble the means to carry it into execution. The intermediary agent was Ciganović, the railway employé whose complicity was proved during the inquiry made by the

[21] For the organization and the statutes of the "Black Hand," see the information given by M. Edith Durham, pp. 45-51, which draws upon a Serbian book entitled *Tajna Prevratna Organizacija* (The Secret Revolutionary Society), published in Saloniki in 1918, following the trial in which the leaders of the "Black Hand" were condemned.

Austrian police in July 1914. The information recently published by the Serbian historian, Stanojević,[22] leaves almost no doubt in my mind about the important rôle played throughout by the leaders of the "Black Hand."[23] When the date and the place for the crime were fixed upon, in May 1914, it was by agreement with his chief that Tankosić delivered the weapons and money to the conspirators. On 15th June, Dimitrijević himself called together the executive committee of the Society, to inform them of the decisions he had made. He met with unexpected opposition, and it appears that he countermanded the crime. But the assassins had already crossed the frontier and were in Sarajevo. Did the word reach them too late? Or did the young Bosnians refuse to take notice of it when it came? In any case, according to M. Stanojević, an effort was apparently made at the last minute to avoid the crime.

Was Dimitrijević, in lending his support to the undertaking, acting on his own initiative and his own responsibility? It has been suggested that he had opportunities for contact with certain Russian groups. But the testimony cited is far from decisive.

If Dimitrijević decided to organize the plans for the crime, says Stanojević, it was because he had received word from

22 *Die Ermordung des Erzherzogs Franz Ferdinand,* German translation of the Serbian manuscript. Frankfurt, Frankfurter Societäts-Druckerei, 1923. This is the book which brought to light the active part played by Dimitrijević.

23 It must be kept in mind that the discussion centering about this incident is linked up with the domestic politics of Serbia. Dimitrijević was condemned to death in 1917, in Saloniki, for a plot against the Serbian Prince-Regent. This was the outcome of a struggle which the government had been waging against the "Black Hand." In order to prevent a Franco-British intervention on behalf of the condemned, M. Pašić appears to have sent word to Paris and London that Dimitrijević was responsible for the Sarajevo crime. Thus the complicity of the "Black Hand" with the *Mlada Bosna* became one of tenets of the Radical party in Serbia, for whom M. Stanojević seems to have been a kind of spokesman. It must also be pointed out, however, that M. Stanojević's statements have been confirmed by other testimony, such as that of Colonel Simić.

Russia about certain plans which it was believed had been worked out by the Archduke and the German Emperor, at the time of their interview at Konopiště. According to this information, Franz Ferdinand had outlined the plans for an attack upon Serbia. It may, perhaps, have been no more than a rumor, but the chief of the "Black Hand" took it for the truth, and acted accordingly! It is hardly possible, however, to believe this account, for the interview took place on 13th June. How, then, could the decisive information have reached Belgrade by way of Russia as early as the fifteenth? Furthermore, it appears that Dimitrijević had already reached a decision in his own mind some weeks before he communicated it to the executive committee of his society.

According to certain other accounts,[24] Dimitrijević had been in touch with Artamanov, Russian Military Attaché, whom he had informed of the plot. After thinking the matter over for some days, the Attaché had encouraged the leader of the "Black Hand" to proceed with his plans: "Go ahead! If you are attacked, you will not be alone!" Can any degree of confidence be placed in this account? It comes from three different sources, all of them indirect, and between which there are considerable divergences, amounting in one case to an absolute contradiction of the accepted facts. And, as this whole discussion has not escaped the influence of politics, it becomes all the more necessary to learn precisely the names and the character of the witnesses whom each writer has quoted.[25] Until this is done, it will be difficult to consider these statements as real proof of the facts.[26]

[24] See articles by Mandl, in the N. Wiener 8 Uhr Blatt, 1st July 1924; by Nevadović, in La Fédération balkanique, 1st December 1924; and V. Serge, in Clarté, May 1925.

[25] Nevadović and Mandl do not give the names of the witnesses from whom they claim to have obtained their information. Victor Serge, on the other hand, reproduces an account given by Colonel Simić, but, as the latter was a friend of Dimitrijević, his testimony must be subject to caution.

[26] It has been asked whether Artamanov informed his government of the

The support and coöperation which the members of the
Mlada Bosna found in Belgrade thus extended to certain
groups on the General Staff, but no farther. The leaders of
the "Black Hand," although employed in an official capacity,
had been on bad terms with the Government ever since the
end of the second Balkan war. They had just been making
serious trouble for the Government, with regard to the administration of the newly acquired Serbian territory. They
were openly hostile to the Minister of the Interior, who had
considered closing up all military "clubs" during the spring
of 1914. The friends of Dimitrijević constituted a powerful
and dangerous group in the army, a group which had got
beyond the control of the civil authorities. The Government
was not strong enough to break up the "Black Hand" organization.

III. *The Attitude of the Serbian Government.*

THE complicity of Dimitrijević and his friends therefore
does not prove that the Serbian Government had any part
whatever in the preparation of the crime. There is nothing
among the known documents to justify the belief that the
plot was inspired in Serbian official circles.

Did the Serbian Government, however, not know in advance of the plan?

According to M. Ljuba Jovanović, a Serb who was active in political life, and who in 1914 was Minister of Public

proposal which Dimitrijević had made to him. The diplomatic correspondence published by the Soviet Government contains no reference to anything of the sort. Certain writers, however (Bogičević, in *Die Kriegsschuldfrage*, July 1925, p. 441), call attention to a proposal which M. Sazonov
apparently received, shortly before the crime, during a trip in Rumania.
Reference was evidently made in this proposal to the time when Archduke
Franz Ferdinand should be "out of the way." It is therefore assumed that
the Russian Minister knew of Dimitrijević's plan. But the testimony on
which these assumptions are based, namely that of the diplomat Schelking,
is subject at least to caution. Furthermore, the phrase used may have been
no more than a reference to the poor condition of the Archduke's health.

Education in the Radical Cabinet, the Government had received certain information about it.

"I forget whether it was at the end of May or the beginning of June," writes Jovanović, "that Pašić told us one day (he usually discussed such questions with Stojan Protić, Minister of the Interior, but he also told the rest of us quite a few things) that certain preparations had been made for a trip to Sarajevo, to assassinate Franz Ferdinand, who was to be there for an official reception. I later learned that the crime had been prepared by the secret organizations and the Bosnian students of Belgrade."

As a consequence, Jovanović was somewhat distressed, but not in the least surprised, when the news of the crime reached him on 28th June.[27]

Pašić, it is true, flatly denied the truth of these revelations. Jovanović has further developed them in long articles, in which he diminishes their importance by his comments, but does not withdraw his original statements.[28] But the more detailed explanation which the former announced that he would make, and the publication of certain documents which he continued to promise had not been forthcoming at the time of his death. It need hardly be said that the belief in Jovanović's testimony became more firmly established with each week of the prolonged silence.

Now, if the government circles in Serbia had received even vague hints about the preparation of the crime, did they

---

[27] The article by Ljuba Jovanović appeared in Belgrade in 1924, in a collection entitled *Krv Sloventsva* (The Blood of Slavdom). It was translated into German in *Die Kriegsschuldfrage*, February 1925, pp. 68-82. The author, one of the important members of the Radical party, had a disagreement with Pašić, and recently, in April 1926, was read out of the party. This rivalry is another element which the critic should keep in mind.

[28] Pašić told a correspondent of the *New York Herald:* "If the fact of a plot against the Archduke and the Duchess of Hohenberg had been known to us, we should certainly have warned the Austro-Hungarian Government." On 25th April 1926, he repeated this denial even more forcefully. *Cf. Politika,* Belgrade, 28th April 1926.

make any efforts, during the month of June, to prevent its execution?

From the very first, says Jovanović, the Serbian Cabinet was agreed that orders should be sent to the frontier authorities to intercept the conspirators. The official records of the frontier post at Loznica contain a copy of this order, which fell into the hands of the Austrians at the beginning of the war.[29] But the officers of the frontier guard were members of the "Black Hand." They did not carry out the instructions which they received, and replied that the orders had reached them too late, as the young Bosnians had already crossed the frontier. The truth of this account appears quite probable to anyone who knows what the attitude of the secret societies to the Government must have been, and who realizes the impotence of the Government to command obedience from the "Black Hand."

On the other hand, certain writers claim that the Serbian Cabinet actually did warn the Austro-Hungarian Government of the dangers which Archduke Franz Ferdinand would run by coming to Sarajevo, and made an effort to have the plans for the visit canceled.[30] But was this warning ever really sent? And if so, what was its precise nature? The Serbian *Blue Book* for 1914 does not contain the slightest reference to it, and the most recent testimony is if anything unfavorable.[31]

The members of the former Serbian Legation in Vienna

[29] Jovanović published this information, together with the name of the officer who was in command of the post, in the Serbian newspaper, *Politika*, 12th April 1925. *Cf. Die Kriegsschuldfrage*, June 1925, p. 395. But he did not give the text of the order, which it would have been helpful to see.

[30] Ernest Denis, in his *La grande Serbie*, p. 277, was the first to call attention to this point. In July 1914, M. Pašić told the Skupčina, in reply to a question from one of the deputies, that he had warned Vienna of the possibility of a violent demonstration.

[31] This testimony has been reproduced, in large part, in an article by Wegerer, in *Die Kriegsschuldfrage*, June 1925, p. 398. For further criticism, see the works of M. E. Durham, Seton-Watson, and Bogičević.

declare that an effort was made to warn the Austro-Hungarian Government, but they do not agree about the circumstances and the nature of this communication. According to Josimović, Counselor to the Legation,[32] the Serbian Government sent instructions on 18th June that steps should be taken in this direction, and the warning was communicated to Bilinski, Joint Minister of Finance, on the twenty-first. But Joca Jovanović, who was Serbian Minister in Vienna at the time, does not corroborate the statements made by his subordinate.[33] He insists that he did not receive the instructions in question from Belgrade. He did warn Herr Bilinski, but that was on 5th June, and on his own initiative. He had said at that time that the army maneuvers which were to take place in the presence of the Archduke would be interpreted as a provocation by the nationalistic groups in Bosnia. "It is possible that some Serbian youth may slip a cartridge into his rifle or his revolver, a loaded cartridge, not a blank, and fire it." Jovanović thus pointed out the danger of a possible attack on the part of a Bosnian soldier; he made no reference to any preparations for a conspiracy. Some days after this first *démarche*, he again called upon the Minister of Finance about the same matter. He soon learned, however, that the Archduke intended to carry out his trip whatever the danger.

The information was thus communicated, in one form or another, to Bilinski, and not to Count Berchtold, Minister for Foreign Affairs. This is no cause for surprise, for the personal relations between the Serbian Minister and the Minister for Foreign Affairs were not of the most cordial nature, and M. Jovanović was in the habit of discussing cer-

---

[32] *Wiener Sonn und Montagszeitung,* 23rd June 1924.

[33] *Neues Wiener Tageblatt,* 28th June 1924. Furthermore, Jovanović took the occasion to repeat his statement in a formal way to Mr. Seton-Watson, *Foreign Affairs,* April 1925, to the effect that he did not receive from Belgrade the instructions to which Josimović refers.

tain questions with the Minister of Finance, who was charged with the administration of Bosnia-Herzegovina.[34]

These declarations of the Serbian Minister have not been contradicted by anyone in Austria. Bilinski makes no reference in his memoirs to Jovanović's call, but he certainly does not deny that it took place.[35] Baron Rummerskirsch, the Archduke's Master of Ceremonies,[36] declares that he had no knowledge of the "warning." But Flandrek, head of the Press section of the Ministry of Finance, confirms the truth of the *démarche*.[37] When the plans for the Archduke's trip were made public, he says, in May 1914, Jovanović drew the attention of Bilinski to the trouble which might easily result. He warned him of the danger which would attend any manifestations on the part of the Bosnians, and referred to the unusual spirit of agitation among the Serbian nationalists. Bilinski, in turn, who considered the Archduke's trip as extremely ill-timed, at once told his colleague of his conversation with Jovanović, but, according to Flandrek, he did not take it upon himself to warn Count Berchtold or the Emperor.[38]

Is there no documentary evidence whatever on the matter? According to the Austrians, there is absolutely nothing. The Serbian historian, Stanojević, has felt justified in stating that there is a paper among the Austrian archives entitled, "Serbian communication regarding the possibility

[34] *Cf.* Mandl, *Die Kriegsschuldfrage,* April 1924, p. 108; and Flandrek, in the *Neues Wiener Tageblatt,* 26th May 1925.

[35] *Wspomnienia i Dokumenty* (Memoirs and Papers), Warsaw, 1924–1925, Vol. I, p. 273. Upon a request from Mandl for further information, Bilinski replied that he preferred not to discuss the subject, which he hoped "would pass into oblivion."

[36] *Cf.* Wiesner, in *D. Neue Reich,* 2nd August 1924, p. 973.

[37] *Neues Wiener Tageblatt,* 26th May 1925.

[38] Bilinski makes no allusion to this conversation, but he gives it to be understood that he considered the whole affair none of his business: "I had no reason to concern myself over this *military* visit." His attitude shows that he was on anything but friendly terms with Potiorek, Military Governor of Bosnia-Herzegovina.

of an attack upon the heir-apparent," and he even gives
the number of the document. The Keeper of the Archives
in Vienna replies that there is no such number. But might
the document not still be there under another number? The
Austrian administration has not thus far shown any willingness to allow further researches.[39]

In the face of all this contradictory evidence, this reticence on the part of the leading men in question, and this
cautious attitude on the part of both the Vienna and the
Belgrade governments, there is one fact, at least, which may
be considered as certain. The Serbian Minister, acting in his
personal capacity, did try to have the Archduke's trip canceled, but he did not disclose any precise information, nor
did he reveal the existence of a conspiracy. The warning
therefore failed to have the significance which it might have
had.

Would any more precise information, however, have been
more apt to command the attention of the Vienna Government? It is very doubtful whether it would; the Austro-
Hungarian government officials did not wish to give up the
plans for the trip, because they would thus have acknowledged their fear of the nationalistic movement. Besides, they
already had information, through their intelligence service,
about the activities of the groups of Bosnian refugees in
Belgrade, and about the risks which the Archduke was running by going to Sarajevo. "Intelligence posts along the
Serbian frontier were sending back daily reports, secret and
otherwise, which did not leave the slightest doubt," writes a
direct witness.[40] One cannot help wondering exactly what the

[39] This, at least, is as far as Wegerer's account of the matter goes, in
Die Kriegsschuldfrage, May 1925, p. 290. The Austrian publicist Kanner, who
asked for access to the Archives in order to make this research, has not
received the necessary authorization.

[40] General August Urbański von Ostrymiecz, then chief of the Evidenz-
Büro of the Austrian General Staff. He wrote a short article, entitled
"Mein Beitrag zur Kriegsschuldfrage," which appeared in Die Kriegsschuld-
frage, February 1926, pp. 70-87.

nature of these reports must have been. The Austrian General Staff may even have had, perhaps, more complete information about the conspiracy itself than is generally supposed.

*   *   *   *   *   *   *

If we are to appreciate the true position of the Austrian Government immediately after the crime, we must, of course, exclude all of these details which were not known until long afterward, and consider the precise nature of the information gathered by the Austro-Hungarian police at the time.

The *Diplomatic Papers*, published in 1919 by the Austrian Government, include the report made by Wiesner, the regional adviser, who gave an account of the initial results of his inquiry up to 13th July 1914.[41] Wiesner did not believe that the Belgrade Government was directly responsible: "The complicity of the Serbian Government in arranging the crime, by preparing or delivering the arms intended for the assassins, is entirely without proof, and should not even be assumed. On the contrary, there are grounds for believing it quite impossible," he wrote. On the other hand, the complicity of Ciganović and of Tankosić was established from the outset, as also that of the frontier guards. The bombs did come from a Serbian military storehouse, but, as Wiesner added, "there is no proof that they were taken from the storehouse at the time of the crime, and with that specific intention, for the bombs may have come from the supplies of munitions dating back to the recent war."

This aspect of the inquiry was comparatively free from political influence.

41 *Dipl. Pap.* I, 17. Wiesner was attached to the division of international law at the Ballplatz. After studying the papers in Vienna, he spent two days in Sarajevo to clear up certain details. He wished, so he tells us today (*Das Neue Reich,* 2nd August 1924, No. 44, p. 973), to limit his report to *indisputable* facts. General Potiorek, who was anxious for war, steadily protested, after 13th July, against the conclusions of the Wiesner report, which he claimed were too moderate. See his letter, in Conrad's book, *Aus meiner Dienstzeit,* Vienna, Rikola, 1924, IV, p. 83.

On the other hand, the *indirect* responsibility of the Serbian Government was also involved. The Austrian officials in Sarajevo were convinced that the Pan-Serbian propaganda brought into Bosnia "by societies and other organizations" was being directed from Belgrade, "with the knowledge and consent of the Serbian Government." Of course, the information gathered during the course of the investigation furnished no proof that the government had "encouraged" the propaganda, but certain documents, "rather uncertain documents, to be sure," might be taken to indicate that the propaganda had been "tolerated." With this idea in mind, then, it was necessary to investigate the organization and the work of the *Narodna Odbrana,* which might furnish "precious material."

The Wiesner report thus arrived at very moderate conclusions which were, taken as a whole, quite true.[42] Even today, in the light of the more recent inquiries, the direct complicity of the Serbian Government is out of the question. The attitude taken by the Cabinet at Belgrade, however, did lay it open to criticism and complaint on the part of the Austrian Government. It had "allowed a public campaign to be carried on with a view to fomenting subversive activities among subjects of Austria-Hungary." It had not prevented its own officials and representatives from taking part in this campaign. Perhaps it had not had the strength to do so, even if it had wished to.

The very form of the report shows the spirit in which the Ballplatz set out to conduct the inquiry immediately after the crime. It was trying to gather, not support for a preconceived belief, but a series of official papers which it might present to the rest of Europe. When, however, it communicated its celebrated memorandum to the various Powers a few days later, the "probabilities" indicated by

[42] The reproaches which he directed against the *Narodna* applied much more directly to the "Black Hand."

Wiesner had become "certainties." The new statement was to the effect that the secret societies had carried on their campaign of hatred against Austria "under the patronage of the Serbian Government." The fact must not be lost sight of that the rejoicings of public opinion in Serbia just after the crime, the general tone of the Serbian newspapers, the passivity of Pašić's government in the presence of these manifestations, and the systematic lethargy of the Belgrade police in making its inquiries,[43] were all of such a character as to aggravate the grievances which Austria was already cherishing.

[43] The Serbian authorities allowed Ciganović, the railway employé who had furnished the assassins with their weapons, to make his escape, and may even have aided him in his flight.

CHAPTER III

THE INTERVIEWS AT POTSDAM
(5th and 6th July)

FROM the very day after the crime, the Austrian Government was disposed to undertake some kind of political action against Serbia, but it could do nothing without the preliminary assent of Germany. It was during the 5th and 6th days of July that the policy of the Central Powers took definite shape. This particular moment in the negotiations is of capital importance in the history of the immediate causes of the war. The accounts of it have for a long time been adorned with inexact details, which have suffered at the hands of many a critic. Today the documents are precise enough to permit certain definite conclusions to be established.[1]

I. *The Austrian Program.*

THE Cabinet in Vienna had decided, even before the crime, to make an effort to strengthen Austria's position in the Balkans, and to counteract the effects of the Treaty of Bucharest. The program which it had worked out was of a diplomatic nature.[2] Rumania, who was wavering in spite

[1] Besides the diplomatic correspondence, one must take into account the testimony of two Germans, Bethmann and Jagow. The Chief of the Cabinet under Berchtold, Count Hoyos, was also directly concerned in the negotiations of 5th and 6th July. He has made a few brief allusions to them in a small book entitled, *Der deutsch-englische Gegensatz und sein Einfluss auf d. Balkanpolitik Österreich-Ungarns,* Berlin, Vereinigung wissenchaftlicher Verleger, 1922, p. 105. Finally, the German Parliamentary Investigation Committee has devoted a part of its work to these events.

[2] This program was set forth in a memorandum, upon which the Ballplatz had been working since the month of May. The text was completed on 24th June. For this preparatory work, see Gooss, *Das Wiener Kabinett und die Enstehung des Weltkrieges.* Vienna, Seidel, 1919, Ch. I.

of the treaty, must be drawn into close relations with the Triple Alliance. Bulgaria and Turkey might well be reconciled. It would thus be possible to reconstitute a Balkan League under the protection of the Central Powers. Serbia would be weakened by her isolation, and Russia would lose the preponderant position she had attained in 1913.

The murder of the Archduke enabled the Austro-Hungarian Government to replace this more gradual program by a plan of immediate action. Instead of resorting to indirect diplomatic action against Serbia, it would now be possible to take her in hand directly, since she had given cause for grievance.

The crime at Sarajevo thus furnished the Ballplatz with the opportunity for an energetic move which would correspond with its interests, and would be the means of realizing by a more rapid method a plan which it had decided upon long before. The Austrian documents leave no room for doubt on this point. Count Berchtold told the Chief of Staff, Conrad von Hötzendorf, on 29th June, that the time had come to settle the Serbian question once for all.[3] He also announced to Count Tisza "his intention of taking advantage of the crime at Sarajevo to square his account with Serbia."[4]

The decision of the Minister for Foreign Affairs was made on the very day after the assassination. Certain "considerations of domestic policy" urged him to act vigorously, namely, the resistance which the Austro-Hungarian control had met with in Bosnia-Herzegovina; and the ill effects which repeated mobilizations had brought upon national finance and even upon economic life.[5] The feelings aroused by the crime had created, for the moment, a rare spirit of unanimity in public opinion. General conditions thus appeared quite favorable.

[3] Conrad, *Aus meiner Dienstzeit*, IV, p. 34.
[4] *Diplomatic Papers*, I, 2.
[5] Hoyos, p. 82.

Berchtold's resolute purpose met with opposition from the President of the Hungarian Council, Count Tisza. To be sure, Tisza was not bothered by any scruples in the matter. "It would be the least of my worries," he wrote, "to find a suitable *casus belli*." But he believed that any *immediate* action would be ill-timed, because the diplomatic situation did not impress him as favorable, and because the hostility of Russia would have to be counted upon. His advice was therefore to seek *first* for the support of Bucharest and Sofia. These alliances would make it possible to settle the Serbian question *a little later*.[6]

Faced with such opposition, the essential thing was to learn the point of view of the German Government. The Chief of Staff, Conrad, remarked to Berchtold on 1st July: "We must above all ask Germany whether or not she is willing to guarantee us against Russia."[7] Austria was not in a position to undertake anything alone. It would therefore be up to Berlin to choose between the policy of immediate action, on the one hand, and that of delayed action, on the other, prepared by the work of the diplomatists.

In order to make up its own mind, and to feel out the situation, the government at Vienna first made use of the ordinary intermediaries which were at its disposal. It commissioned its Ambassador at Berlin, Szögyény, to secure what information he could from the German Ministry of Foreign Affairs. At the same time, in Vienna, it asked a number of questions of the German Ambassador, Tschirschky.

After a conversation with the Under-Secretary of State for Foreign Affairs, Szögyény wrote on 4th July: "Herr Zimmermann assures me that he considers it quite natural that the Monarchy, which has the sympathy of the whole

6 Tisza's report to the Emperor, 1st July 1914, *Dipl. Pap.*, I, 2. For the interpretation of this attitude, see A. Weber, *Die Kriegsschuldfrage*, December 1925, pp. 818-826.

7 Conrad, IV, p. 34.

civilized world, should undertake energetic action against Serbia. But he recommended great prudence in the matter, and advised against imposing demands which would be too humiliating for Serbia."[8]

In Vienna the German Ambassador called upon Count Berchtold and upon Emperor Franz Joseph. He agreed with the Austrian Government about the need for "energetic action" against Serbia. It was true that in the past Berlin had not always given Vienna very active support, but that was only because the Austrian Government had not formulated a clearly-defined plan of action.[9] According to Tschirschky, "it would have to be determined very carefully just how far one wished or would have to go . . . and the general political situation should be considered." But Austria "could count absolutely on finding Germany solidly behind the Monarchy whenever it came to the point of defending one of the latter's vital interests."[10]

Although Tschirschky had spoken "in a strictly private capacity," the Austrian Government might consider these remarks as an invitation to present its program, especially as the Ambassador had sent more energetic advice to the Ballplatz through the medium of a secret agent.[11] On the evening of 4th July, Count Hoyos, the Chief of the Cabinet under Berchtold, left Vienna to carry to William II the "memorandum" prepared before the crime; but this memo-

---

8 Szögyény to Berchtold, *Dipl. Pap.*, I. 5.

9 Daily report of Count Berchtold, *Dipl. Pap.*, I, 5.

10 Tschirschky to Bethmann-Hollweg. Account of his conversation with Franz Joseph. *Germ. Doc.*, 11, p. 66. The page references are to the English translation by the Carnegie Endowment for International Peace, *Outbreak of the World War, German Documents Collected by Karl Kautsky and edited by Max Montgelas and Walther Schücking,* New York, Oxford University Press, 1924.

11 A "daily report" of 4th July, No. 3117, published in part by Gooss, p. 40, mentions the message given by Tschirschky to "a secret agent," with the apparent intention of having this message transmitted to the Ballplatz. "Germany will support the Monarchy against the winds and tides. . . . The sooner Austria-Hungary acts, the better it will be. Yesterday would have been better than today, but today is better than tomorrow."

randum had been added to, and was accompanied by a personal letter from Franz Joseph. The letter from the Emperor indicated a possible plan of diplomatic action which would bring about the "humiliation" of Serbia.

The efforts of my government must in the future be directed toward the isolation and diminution of Serbia. The first stage of this journey should be accomplished by the strengthening of the present position of the Bulgarian Government, in order that Bulgaria, whose real interests coincide with our own, may be preserved from a relapse into Russophilism.

When it is recognized in Bucharest that the Triple Alliance is determined not to forego a union with Bulgaria, but would, nevertheless, be willing to persuade Bulgaria to go into partnership with Roumania, and guarantee the latter's integrity, perhaps they will retrace there the perilous step to which they have been driven through friendship to Serbia and by the *rapprochement* to Russia.

If this effort should prove successful, we might further attempt to reconcile Greece to Bulgaria and to Turkey; thus there would develop under the patronage of the Triple Alliance a new Balkan alliance, whose aim would be to put an end to the advance of the Pan-Slavic flood, and to assure peace to our countries.

His plan thus corresponded to the method and principle advocated by Count Tisza. But the letter also added:

This can, however, be possible only when Serbia, which at present constitutes the pivot of the Pan-Slavic policy, is eliminated as a factor of political power in the Balkans.[12]

The conclusion of the memorandum itself was also quite firm:

So much the more imperious becomes the necessity for the

[12] *Dipl. Pap.*, I, 1; *Germ. Doc.*, 13, p. 69. The text of the Emperor's letter was shown to Tisza, who would have liked to see the conclusion softened down. The words, "eliminated as a factor of political power," seemed a bit excessive. But this opinion did not reach Count Berchtold until after Count Hoyos had left for Berlin. *Cf.* Gooss, p. 82.

Monarchy to destroy with a determined hand the net which its enemies are attempting to throw about its head.[13]

While the Austrian *démarche* did not declare in so many words the idea of an immediate war against Serbia, it did hint at it.

In the minds of the statesmen at Vienna, what had been determined upon was some vigorous action and a general policy of force, if only Germany should give her consent: "If the reply is that Germany is on our side," Conrad von Hötzendorf asked the Emperor, "shall we declare war against Serbia?" And the Emperor replied, "In that case, yes." The General was still uncertain: "If Germany does not give us *this* reply, what shall we do?" That is to say, the Government at Vienna felt itself at the mercy of the decisions of Berlin.[14]

Count Hoyos repeated the same idea: "Count Berchtold was prepared to lay aside all the fundamental arguments in favor of war, and take a stand against the public opinion of all Austria-Hungary, supporting a program which would abandon squaring the account with Serbia, if Berlin should advise such a policy, in reply to the questions which had been sent."[15]

II. *The Mission of Count Hoyos.*

As soon as Count Hoyos reached Berlin, the Austrian Ambassador, Szögyény, who was charged with delivering the message, requested an audience with the Emperor, and was invited to take lunch at Potsdam. The Ambassador sent an account of this interview to Vienna that same evening.

After carefully reading over the letter and the memorandum, the Emperor declared that Austria might count on

---

13 *Dipl. Pap.*, I, 1; and *Germ. Doc.*, 14, p. 77.

14 Conrad, IV, pp. 36-37.

15 Hoyos, p. 79. This hesitancy was shared by certain members of the General Staff. At the time of the interview at Konopište, the Kaiser is said to have avoided answering a question from the Archduke about possible support from Germany in case of war.

"the whole-hearted support of Germany"; he was of the opinion that she should act without any delay. According to Szögyény, William II outlined the possible consequences of a possible Austro-Serbian conflict as follows:

The attitude of Russia would be hostile in every respect, but he had been expecting that for years, and even if war should occur between Austria-Hungary and Russia, we might be assured that Germany would side with us, with her traditional loyalty to the Alliance.

Besides, in the present condition of affairs, Russia would be totally unprepared for war, and would certainly think twice before issuing a call to arms. But she would be sure to stir up the other Powers of the Triple Entente against us, and to fan the flame in the Balkans.

He understood very well that His Apostolic Majesty, with his known love of peace, would find it difficult to march his troops into Serbia, but, if we had really decided upon the necessity for military action against Serbia, he [Emperor William] would be sorry if we did not profit by the existing situation, which was so favorable for us.[16]

That very afternoon the Emperor summoned the Chancellor and Under-Secretary of State Zimmermann. (The Secretary of State, Jagow, was on his vacation.) The following morning, Bethmann-Hollweg, in turn, received the Austrian Ambassador to explain the point of view of the German Government.

He was quite prepared, so he said, to initiate diplomatic action to bring about the entry of Bulgaria into the Triple Alliance, and to negotiate at Bucharest for the strengthening of the Austro-Rumanian alliance. He could also promise, "without interfering in the dispute now going on," that Germany would "faithfully" stand by Austria-Hungary, "as is required by the obligations of their alliance and their ancient friendship."

16 Szögyény to Berchtold. *Dipl. Pap.,* I, 6.

These statements were repeated by the Chancellor in almost the same words in a telegram which he sent that day to Tschirschky, and by the Austrian Ambassador in the report which he dispatched immediately to his Government.[17]

But was Bethmann-Hollweg satisfied with making these general promises?

If we are to believe the word of Count Szögyény, he added two extremely important remarks. The support which he promised in the name of Germany was unreserved and unconditional:

Concerning our relations with Serbia, the attitude of the German Government is that it is for *us* to judge what should be done to clear up this situation; whatever our decision in the matter, we may have the absolute assurance that Germany will back up the Monarchy as our ally and friend.

In fact, in the first draft of the telegram sent to Herr von Tschirschky, there appeared quite clearly the words, "under all circumstances," which the Chancellor finally decided to leave out.[18] He may have realized that he had gone too far, and preferred to strike out the traces of a statement which he regretted having made.

In the second place, according to Szögyény's report, the Chancellor encouraged Austria, as the Emperor had done, to act *without any delay:*

During the course of the interview, I noticed that the Imperial Chancellor, as well as the Emperor, felt that immediate action against Serbia on our part was at once the most radical and the best solution of our difficulties in the Balkans. From the international point of view, he thought the present moment more favorable than a later occasion might be.[19]

[17] *Germ. Doc.*, 15, p. 79; and *Dipl. Pap.*, I, 7.

[18] *Germ. Doc.*, 15, p. 79, note 2.

[19] *Dipl. Pap.*, I, 7. On the eighth, Szögyény further commented as follows: "I have had an opportunity yesterday and today of hearing the Under-Secretary of State and other competent persons express the opinion that our decision is being impatiently awaited here. It is felt that now is

This was another point which Bethmann-Hollweg failed to record in his official instructions to Vienna. Did the Austrian Ambassador put words into his mouth which he never spoke? It hardly seems probable. As a matter of fact, there was another Austrian witness at Berlin, besides the Ambassador, namely, Count Hoyos, the secret agent of Count Berchtold. Count Hoyos' memoirs entirely confirm the statements made by Szögyény:

"I feel it my duty to declare," he writes, "that both Count Szögyény and I received the impression at Berlin that the German Government was in favor of *immediate* offensive action against Serbia on our part, although it clearly realized that a world war might be the result."[20]

A study of the texts thus allows us to conclude the accuracy of Count Szögyény's report.[21] The Government at Berlin had pronounced itself in favor of immediate political action, and had urged its ally to make some move, without asking either what it wanted or where it was heading. It had promised its support in case of a quarrel. This is the sense in which the Bavarian Chargé d'Affaires at Berlin alluded on 18th July to "the blank power of full authority," given to Austria by Germany.[22]

It would have been very natural to ask Count Berchtold what he was expecting to do, how he expected to settle the Serbian question, and what general result he hoped to attain. But not at all! The Chancellor asked no questions. It was only to Under-Secretary of State Zimmermann that Count Hoyos said, in confidence, "Austria ought to dismem-

the very moment—a moment which will not recur under such favorable conditions—to march energetically against Serbia." Text published by Montgelas, *Leitfaden zur Kriegsschuldfrage*, Berlin, De Gruyter & Co., 1923, p. 174.

[20] Hoyos, p. 80. Szögyény said, in a dispatch of 12th July, that Germany had encouraged Austria "with the most eager insistence." *Dipl. Pap.*, I, 15.

[21] Tschirschky considered that Szögyény's reports "correspond exactly" with the words of the Chancellor. *Germ. Doc.*, 18, p. 81.

[22] *Germ. Doc.*, Supp. IV, 2, p. 617.

ber Serbia completely"; but it appears that this opinion was purely "personal."[23] And Bethmann allowed himself to be satisfied, without trying to clarify the meaning of this attitude of reserve. This was the very policy which he meant to continue.

III. *The Interviews between William II and the Military Leaders.*

THE Emperor and the Chancellor thus gave their entire support, on 5th and 6th July, to the Austrian policy. But did the German Government make preparations from that moment on for a general war? Did the Emperor, before leaving for his Norwegian cruise, take any steps, or give any orders? What advice did he receive from military circles?

It is important to consider what took place at Potsdam immediately after the conference between William II, the Austrian Ambassador, and the representatives of the Wilhelmstrasse.

I. According to certain accounts, which were accepted at first without any hesitation or reserve, the Emperor called together a Crown Council at the New Palace, at which certain extremely grave decisions were made.

Three documents have been quoted most frequently as proving the fact that this Council actually met:

Dr. Mühlon, one of the Krupp directors, who was not in Berlin on 5th July, but who happened to go there on the seventeenth, heard something about "a conference with the Austrians," which took place on the eve of the Emperor's departure for the North Sea. The Kaiser, according to what Mühlon heard, "had told the Austrians that this time he was going to go through with them, against wind and tide. . . . The Austrian Government was thus given *carte blanche*."[24]

---

[23] *Germ Doc.*, 18, p. 81. As a matter of fact, the Council of Ministers was considering this dismemberment. *Cf.* below, pp. 56-57.

[24] *Die Verheerung Europas*, Zurich, Füssli, 1918, p. 17.

This account does not mention a council of war, in which the chiefs of the General Staff took part. It simply alludes to the presence of certain Austrian statesmen, doubtless including Berchtold. Now, there was no Austrian minister in Berlin on the 5th of July. It is not surprising, however, that an indirect report of this kind should contain such an error. A casual remark by a waiter in a hotel at Potsdam appears to have been the origin of the rumor.[25]

The second document is of considerably greater importance. Baron von dem Bussche, who was, in 1917, Under-Secretary of State for Foreign Affairs, wrote the following note at that time and left it in the Archives of the Wilhelmstrasse:

On the same day, after the Austro-Hungarian Ambassador had presented to His Majesty the Emperor the letter of Emperor Franz Joseph brought by Count Hoyos, in the month of July, 1914, and after the Imperial Chancellor, von Bethmann-Hollweg, and Under-Secretary of State Zimmermann had been received in Potsdam, a conference of military authorities took place at Potsdam with His Majesty. There took part: His Excellency Capelle for Tirpitz, Captain Zenker for the Admiralty Staff, representatives of the Ministry of War and of the General Staff. It was decided in any case to take preparatory measures for a war. Appropriate orders were thereupon issued. Source absolutely reliable.[26]

But even this is not direct testimony. The author was not a member of the Government in July 1914. He simply picked up a rumor. From whom? When asked, he could not give a definite answer, and said, "Perhaps from Admiral von Müller." The Admiral, formerly Chief of the Navy Cabinet under William II, has flatly denied it.

Finally, there is a third testimony, also quite indirect,

[25] For details, cf. Montgelas, pp. 170-172.

[26] *Germ. Doc.*, Supp. VIII, p. 651. The note was not dated, but it was recorded at the Wilhelmstrasse on 30th August 1917.

which has often been referred to: that of the American Ambassador at Constantinople, Morgenthau. The Ambassador happened to receive confidential word, in August 1914, from his German colleague, Wangenheim, which he has reproduced in his memoirs.[27]

Wangenheim had been hastily called to Germany, at the beginning of July. He had been present at a Grand Council on the 5th, to which had been summoned, along with the important ambassadors, the great bankers, industrial heads, and high military authorities. The Kaiser had asked each one, in turn: "Are you prepared for war?" All had replied in the affirmative save the financiers, who had asked for a delay of fifteen days to arrange about their foreign holdings. The delay was granted. Every one then went back to his post, and "Bethmann-Hollweg went off for a rest."

This is the account which Morgenthau attributes to Wangenheim, without, however, reproducing the actual words of the conversation, other than in the two short sentences mentioned.

But the American Ambassador—as anyone can see by looking through his memoirs—was habitually facile about accepting statements without verifying them as carefully as he should have done. Moreover, his admiration for his German colleague was unbounded. Wangenheim may have taken pleasure in astonishing his colleague; or, conscious of his influence over this novice in the world of diplomacy, perhaps he wished to show himself in a still better light, and to pose as one who was always called to the Emperor's secret conferences. Morgenthau's testimony can therefore hardly be considered as anything conclusive in the way of proof.

Now, all the known facts contradict the German Ambassador's "confidential statements." His wife has testified that he was neither in Berlin nor in Potsdam at the time when the

[27] *Ambassador Morgenthau's Story,* Garden City, Doubleday, Page & Co., 1918, pp. 84-85.

Crown Council is supposed to have taken place. Furthermore, the diplomatic correspondence shows that during the following weeks he had no definite information whatever about the policy adopted by his Government.[28] Besides this, all the details of the account were purely imaginary, for neither Secretary of State Jagow, nor the most important ambassadors, nor the Chief of Staff, were with the Emperor on the date mentioned.[29]

Thus we are led to discard all the testimony which would allow us to believe that there was any grand "Potsdam Council." Bethmann-Hollweg tells us in his memoirs[30] that there was no meeting of the Crown Council, and upon this point he was apparently right.

II. But if there was not a formal consultation of the whole group in a solemn gathering, it is nevertheless true that the Emperor did receive the chief military authorities, after studying over the general situation with the Chancellor. Some of these interviews took place on the evening of the 5th, and others early on the morning of the 6th.

To tell the truth, General von Lyncker, Chief of the Emperor's Military Cabinet, would be glad to have us think that he knew nothing at all about these interviews. He claims to have no recollection of them, and "I certainly should have, had such events taken place, and had I been present." But the Investigation Committee, set up in 1919 by the German Parliament to gather all the testimony about the causes of the war, has questioned various people mentioned in the note

[28] See, for example, below, Ch. XVII, p. 320, note 27.

[29] In an article entitled "Herrn Morgenthaus Legende vom Potsdamer Kriegsrat," which appeared in *Die Kriegsschuldfrage* for February 1925, pp. 82-88, and in English translation under the title "Mr. Morgenthau's Legend of the Potsdam Council," in the May 1925 number of *Die Kriegsschuldfrage*, pp. 309-315, Mr. Sidney B. Fay has shown that there is not the slightest trace on the records of the New York Stock Exchange of any shift in prices brought about, according to Morgenthau's story, by the sale of foreign securities on the part of the German banks.

[30] Bethman-Hollweg, I, pp. 135-136.

left by Baron von dem Bussche. The following are the results given in the minutes of the Committee, which have
been only partially reproduced in the *German Documents*.[31]

Captain Zenker, head of the tactical division of the Navy
Staff, was called to Potsdam on the 5th, toward the end of
the afternoon. He represented the Chief of Staff, who was
away on his vacation.

"His Majesty the Emperor," he said, "informed me, to
be passed on to my official superiors, that at noon on the 5th
of July the Austrian Chargé d'Affaires had inquired of him
whether Germany would fulfil the obligations of her alliance
in the event of an Austro-Hungarian conflict with Serbia and
the strained relations with Russia that might perhaps result.
His Majesty had promised this, but did not believe that Russia would enter the lists for Serbia, which had stained itself
by an assassination. France, too, would scarcely let it come
to war, as it lacked the heavy artillery for the field armies.
Yet, though a war against Russia-France was not probable, nevertheless the possibility of such a war must be borne
in mind from a military point of view."[32]

Admiral von Capelle, who was in charge of the Navy
Office in the absence of Admiral von Tirpitz, who was on
his vacation, was summoned on the sixth, between seven and
eight o'clock in the morning.

I met the Emperor in the garden,[33] all ready to begin his
journey to the Northland. The Emperor walked up and down
with me for a short while and told me briefly of the circum-

[31] Germany (Republic), Nationalversammlung, *Beilagen zu den Steno-
graphischen Berichten über die öffentlichen Verhandlungen des Untersuchungsausschusses, I Unterausschuss, Zur Vorgeschichte des Weltkrieges, Heft
I, Schriftliche Auskünfte deutscher Staatsmänner*, Berlin, Norddeutschen
Buchdruckerei und Verlagsanstalt, 1920. There is an English translation by
the Carnegie Endowment for International Peace, *Report of the First
Subcommittee of the Committee of Inquiry* in *Official German Documents
Relating to the World War*, New York, Oxford University Press, 1923, I,
pp. 1-120. Page references are to this English translation.

[32] *Germ. Doc.*, Preliminary Remarks, p. 49.

[33] *Germ. Doc.*, Prel. Rem., p. 47.

stances of the day before, Sunday. He added, according to my recollection, something of approximately the following tenor (private or official memoranda on the subject made at that period are probably not available).[34] He did not believe in serious warlike developments. According to his view, the Czar would not in this case place himself on the side of the regicides. Besides that, Russia and France were not prepared for war. (The Emperor did not mention England.) On the advice of the Imperial Chancellor, he was going to start on the journey to the Northland, in order not to create any uneasiness. Nevertheless, he wanted to give me information of the strained situation, in order that I might consider what was to follow.

According to what precedes, no conference of military authorities took place in Potsdam on the 6th of July, as the Emperor started on his journey to Kiel immediately after the talk with me.

The testimony of General von Bertrab, representing the Army Staff in the absence of its chief, was almost identical.

From all this testimony, which is based entirely upon recollections five years old, one would be tempted to believe that an Austro-Serbian war would probably not bring on a general European war. But General Falkenhayn, Minister of War, also took part in these conferences. His testimony, soberly and carefully given, sounds quite a different note:

His Majesty the Emperor and King summoned me to the New Palace, on the afternoon of July 5th, by telephone, if I am not mistaken, and received me as soon as I arrived. Besides myself, there were also Colonel General von Plessen and General von Lyncker. His Majesty read me some portions of the well-known letter from Emperor Franz Joseph, together with part of the memorandum from the Austro-Hungarian Government. He pointed out that, as Austria-Hungary was apparently firm in her determination to put an end to all propaganda favoring a

[34] This phrase is a curious one. It is hardly probable that no report of this interview was sent to the leading navy chiefs then absent from Berlin. It may not, however, have been preserved in the Archives. Perhaps that is the meaning which Admiral von Capelle wished to convey here.

Greater Serbia, certain *very serious* consequences might follow, and he ended by asking me whether the army was prepared for any emergency.

According to my conviction, I answered "Yes," quite unreservedly and briefly. I then turned to ask whether any specific preparations were needed. His Majesty answered "No," also quite laconically, and dismissed me.

Other than the usual forms of greeting and leave-taking, not another word was spoken during our interview.[35]

It is true that Falkenhayn did not feel at that time that war would come about immediately. He wrote to Moltke[36] that when he read the memorandum and the personal letter, he was not convinced of "any firm decision on the part of the Vienna Government," since they did not specifically mention any "warlike intentions." "Surely," he wrote, "no decision will be made, in any case, in the weeks just ahead."

But, even if Falkenhayn personally did not believe in the "likelihood" or the "imminence" of a crisis, this does not imply that his testimony was inaccurate. When the Emperor told him of the "very serious consequences" which might ensue, he did not say that they would occur immediately.

In spite of all these inconsistencies in detail, the testimony taken as a whole allows us to conclude at least this much, that the Emperor did not himself give the order to start preparations for war.

But if he did not do so, the forces of the whole Empire were nevertheless prepared to answer any call.

". . . There was nothing to initiate as a result of General von Bertrab's audience at Potsdam. The regular mobilization work had been concluded on the 31st of March 1914. The

[35] Letter to the Parliamentary Investigation Committee, 1919. Bears no date. *Official German Documents Relating to the World War*, I, p. 64. This testimony was not printed in the *German Documents*, Preliminary Remarks.

[36] Document quoted by Montgelas, p. 196, based upon the Archives of the Reich.

army was, as always, ready."[37] Thus spoke Count Waldersee, Assistant Chief of Staff.

Furthermore, the Navy Staff sent out orders at this time to distant waters for "precautionary measures" which were extremely significant. On 9th July it notified Admiral von Spee, in charge of the Asiatic squadron, that war between Austria and Serbia was "possible." "It is not impossible that the Triple Alliance will become involved," said the telegram, and the next day England was mentioned as "a possible enemy," in case a general war should come.[38]

*   *   *   *   *   *   *

The German Emperor and his Government, when called upon by Austria, were thus anxious to take advantage of the existing circumstances to restore the prestige of the Double Monarchy, by firm action against Serbia, and by immediate diplomatic or military success. They did not wish to attack Russia. They were willing to attain their result by indirect methods. A general war does not appear to have been a definite part of the program adopted on 5th July, but it might easily follow as the consequence of such a program. This risk the Central Powers clearly accepted.[39]

[37] Letter from Count Waldersee, formerly Assistant Chief of Staff, to the Investigation Committee. *Germ. Doc.*, Prel. Rem., p. 48.

[38] *Cf.* the documents quoted by the official publication of the Navy Archives. *Der Krieg zur See, 1914-1918, Der Kreuzerkrieg in den ausländischen Gewässern*, Berlin, Mittler & Sohn, Vol. I (1922), p. 62. It was also on 9th July that the *Goeben*, which was heading back to Germany for repairs, hastily put in for repairs at the Austrian port of Pola.

[39] Was it, in their opinion, *probable*, or only *possible?* This question will be discussed later.

CHAPTER IV

THE PREPARATION OF THE AUSTRIAN NOTE

THE decisions made at Potsdam were, from now on, to dominate the course of events. The choice of methods still lay with the Vienna Government. Energetic and immediate action was called for, but, with the chronic hesitancy of the Ballplatz, the preliminary measures dragged on for eighteen days.

I. *The Decisions Made by Austria-Hungary.*

IMMEDIATELY upon the return of Count Hoyos and the arrival of the first telegrams from Szögyény, the Council of Ministers met in Vienna on 7th July.[1] The time had come, said Berchtold, to take action against Serbia in order to check a movement which was menacing the very existence of the Danubian Kingdom. Germany had promised her support. Doubtless the hostility of Russia would have to be reckoned with,[2] but any delay would be an admission of weakness which might worry the great ally. The situation could not be cleared up by anything but "vigorous action."

It was now that Count Tisza's objections made themselves felt. Was Austria to hurl herself against Serbia "without giving warning"? It was impossible to make any move without first taking diplomatic action. To do otherwise would be to invite the hostility of all the other Balkan states except Bulgaria. The Ballplatz must state its conditions: if Serbia rejected them, war would follow.

[1] *Dipl. Pap.*, I, 8.

[2] The official minutes quote him as follows: "It is clear that war with Russia would be very probable after our entry into Serbia." Berchtold corrected this statement to read: ". . . might bring about war with Russia as a consequence." *Cf.* Gooss, p. 52.

In the eyes of the Council, the question of form was secondary. There was no objection to the use of an ultimatum, provided they were quite sure of coming to blows by that method. To get around that difficulty was simple; the conditions imposed upon Serbia should be drawn up so that it would be virtually impossible for her to accept them.[3]

But Tisza opposed the idea.[4] Immediate war was not imminent; for the moment, at least, it was not "an absolute necessity." Russia might possibly, in the years to come, be distracted from the Balkans by "Asiatic complications"; Austria would have plenty of time to secure the alliance with Bulgaria, and to reconcile her with Rumania; finally, the military strength of the Central Empires would be increased, thanks to the rapid growth of the German population. Why drive Serbia to the necessity of fighting? They ought to offer her the means to avoid it, at the price of a diplomatic defeat. Austria ought to make demands which should be very harsh, but yet possible of acceptance. She should be satisfied by having Serbia submit to them.

No! that would be labor in vain, was Berchtold's reply: "A diplomatic success would be of no value at all." All the members of the Council shared his opinion. The Serbian

[3] The corrected minutes read: "As a consequence, demands must be made upon Serbia which are so excessive that we may count on their being refused, and thus open the way for a more radical solution by military intervention." The original words reported were: ". . . wholly unacceptable demands." Cf. also *Germ. Doc.*, 29, p. 93. Berchtold told Tschirschky on 10th July that if Serbia should accept, it would prove a solution which would be "very disagreeable" to him, and that he was still considering "what demands could be put that it would be wholly impossible for Serbia to accept." It is true that Musulin, *Das Haus am Ballplatz*, Munich, Verlag für Kulturpolitik, 1924, p. 225, declares that later on they did not adhere quite so rigidly to their purpose, and did not try to make the note unacceptable. But the documents do not bear out his statement. As a matter of fact, Berchtold wrote to the Emperor on the 14th, "the contents of the note to be addressed to Belgrade, which were completed today, are of such a character that we must count on the probability of an armed conflict."

[4] He threatened, if they did not take into consideration his point of view, "to withdraw from the consequences of their action with respect to his own person."

problem would soon present itself again, and delay would only aggravate Austria's position. Tisza had referred to the possible alliance with Bulgaria, and to the support of Rumania, but these were not sure of being obtained. How much easier it would be to secure them after Serbia had already been crushed! Tisza was counting on the increase in Germany's military forces. But was the Russian population not also growing? "The equilibrium of forces," said von Stürgkh, Minister of War, "is changing unfavorably for us."

The discussion continued without any result. While Berchtold was visiting at Ischl to explain the majority point of view to the Emperor, the President of the Hungarian Council wrote a long letter to Franz Joseph, in which he reviewed all his arguments.[5] ". . . A war provoked by us," he concluded, "would be undertaken at a very unfavorable time, whereas to delay squaring our account until later would result in a much better apportionment of strength, if we made the proper use of the diplomatic situation at that time." And he repeated: "I am unable to accept an exclusively warlike and aggressive solution."

The following week brought an end to the opposition. In a new conference on the fourteenth, "a perfect agreement was reached as to the conditions to be demanded of Serbia." The note was to be composed at once. Berchtold made one concession; he admitted the possibility that Serbia might accept the ultimatum, but, "that would mean a profound humiliation for this Kingdom," and Austria would be satisfied with that. Tisza, on the other hand, conceded that this outcome should be made very improbable; "the contents of the note are such that we must count upon the probability of an armed conflict."[6]

Why did the Hungarian statesman give in? "I showed

[5] *Dipl. Pap.*, I, 12.

[6] *Dipl. Pap.*, I, 19; the report which Count Berchtold sent immediately to the Emperor. The Count had at first written ". . . that a war with Serbia appeared very likely." Gooss, p. 87, note 1.

him," Berchtold tells us, "the military difficulties which would be caused by a delay." The Chief of Staff, Conrad von Hötzendorf, sent word to avoid "all procrastination, all diplomatic action by fits and starts."[7] It is quite possible that Tisza became aware of these factors, but it is also certain that Berchtold used other arguments as well. He had referred to the impatience of the great ally. "In Germany they would not understand our letting this chance go by without striking a blow. If we should compromise with Serbia, they would accuse us of weakness, which would sensibly affect our position in the Triple Alliance, and the future policy of Germany."[8]

At a further meeting of the Council, on the nineteenth, the Austro-Hungarian ministers completed the final draft of the ultimatum,[9] and then attempted to outline the probable results of the impending war.[10] "The Monarchy does not wish to annex any part of Serbia"—such was Tisza's program, based upon what he thought to be the best interests of the Empire. To tell the truth, the Magyars did not want to endanger their position in the Government by increasing the number of Slavs within the Monarchy. That is the true reason for the "territorial disinterestedness" which the Austrian Government was soon going to proclaim. But the discussions on 19th July showed very clearly what the real intentions of the Ballplatz were. The annexation of Serbian territory was not a matter of great importance for the moment, but it might become so at any time if Russia should succeed in winning over Bulgaria to her side.[11] In any case,

---

[7] Dipl. Pap., I, 14. Conrad to Berchtold.

[8] Dipl. Pap., I, 10. Berchtold to Tisza. Berchtold said that this summed up the impression he had received from a conversation with Tschirschky.

[9] Musulin, who was charged with drawing up the note, shows that there were three separate drafts, each more severe than the last. Loc. cit., pp. 223-224. They were carefully considered in several conferences, in which the two presiding ministers, Count Berchtold, and the Chief of Staff took part.

[10] Dipl. Pap., I, 26.

[11] Conrad, IV, 91. The Chief of Staff was firmly opposed to any declaration regarding Serbian integrity. At the close of the Council meeting Berchtold said to him: "We shall see! Before the Balkan war, all the

the Belgrade Kingdom should be crushed and put out of commission. The peace treaty should place it "in a position of dependence upon the Monarchy." A military pact should be imposed upon it, and the ruling dynasty should be changed. These were the views of Count Stürgkh. Besides, Serbian territory should be given to Bulgaria, Greece, Albania, and even Rumania. These were Berchtold's proposals. The Council unanimously decided "that, as soon as the war started, a declaration should be issued to the foreign Powers saying that the Monarchy was not waging a war of conquest, and did not contemplate the annexation of the Kingdom"; but "this declaration would not exclude certain adjustments of the frontier for strategic reasons,[12] nor the reduction of Serbia for the benefit of other states, nor the temporary occupation of Serbian territory which might be necessary."

On the following evening, Berchtold went to Ischl to submit to the Emperor the text of the note which had been prepared, which Franz Joseph approved on the 21st "without modification."[13] To tell the truth, Baron Macchio, of the Ministry of Foreign Affairs, had not even waited for this approval before sending instructions to Baron Giesl, Austrian Minister in Belgrade. The terms of the ultimatum had been forwarded to him on the evening of the twentieth.[14] The note was not to be handed to the Serbian Government until 5 P.M. on the twenty-third.

It had thus been almost four weeks since the crime had taken place at Sarajevo, and more than two weeks since Germany's approval had been obtained. The temporary disagreement between Tisza and Berchtold, and the ordinary

Powers talked about the *status quo* too; after the war, no one gave it a thought."

12 Conrad, IV, 91, refers, in this regard, to the occupation of the Sabać and Belgrade bridgeheads.

13 *Germ. Doc.*, 88, p. 143, and *Dipl. Pap.*, I, 46.

14 *Dipl. Pap.*, I, 27 and 28.

slowness of the diplomatic machinery, were not enough to explain such a long delay. There were two other reasons. The Vienna Government wished first of all to wait until certain preparations had been completed. These measures, declared Berchtold on 11th July, "would permit a smoother mobilization, and would avoid great economic losses."[15] Most important of all, he wished to delay until after the harvest. It appears that the date of the ultimatum was approximately fixed, in the Count's mind, as early as 8th July.[16] Berchtold told Conrad on that day: "In two weeks, on July 22nd." According to Tschirschky, it is true, Berchtold declared on the 13th that he was convinced "that the quickest action was required,"[17] and he seemed to be planning to send the note on the 16th. But that was only an apparent concession to the desires of Germany, since at that time he had not yet reached an agreement with Tisza.[18] In any case, the Government stated the next day that it was impossible to hasten the preparation of the note, "in respect to its technical details."

The Minister had been strengthened in his decision by an argument of a diplomatic nature: M. Poincaré was about to pay a visit to the Tsar. Since the ultimatum could not be delivered *before* the trip, it would be better to wait until the head of the French Government had left St. Petersburg, to avoid having the French and Russian Governments deliberate together at once upon the action which they should take.

II. *The Rôle of Germany.*

HAD Germany been a stranger to all these discussions and decisions?

The lengthy deliberations of the Vienna Government had irritated her, according to Dr. von Schoen, the young Chargé

---

[15] Tschirschky to Jagow, *Official German Documents Relating to the World War*, I, p. 119.
[16] Conrad, IV, 61.
[17] *Germ. Doc.*, 40, p. 101.
[18] See also *Dipl. Pap.*, I, 16.

d'Affaires of the Bavarian Legation at Berlin, and she was beginning to be somewhat impatient.[19] "Mr. Zimmermann has the impression that it is almost embarrassing to the always timid and undecided authorities at Vienna not to be admonished by Germany to caution and self-restraint." Herr von Jagow had not concealed the fact that he regretted the delay; he wished the note had been sent when the public opinion of Europe was still suffering from the first shock of the crime.[20]

Emperor William showed his contempt for the methods and conduct of Count Tisza on 11th July.[21] He was of the opinion that "very determined, very concrete demands should be leveled at Serbia." But these imperial sentiments were not transmitted to Vienna, at least not through any official channels. Secretary of State Jagow intended to keep Germany out of the detailed decisions. "We can take no hand in the formulation of the demands on Serbia, as that is Austria's affair."[22]

At the same time, the German Government was not unaware of what the Austrian Ministry was doing. If it did not wish to give advice, it was anxious at least to be kept in touch with the deliberations. In fact, it learned the essential points of the ultimatum as fast as they were composed. There is abundant documentary evidence to show how close the relations were.

From 11th July on, the German Ambassador, Tschirschky, was in confidential communication with Berchtold. "The principal demands leveled at Serbia will consist of the following, in so far as it is possible to tell today: The King will be requested to declare officially and publicly that Serbia

19 *Germ. Doc.*, Supp. IV, p. 617, 18th July.

20 Szögyény to Berchtold, 16th July, *Dipl. Pap.*, I, 23.

21 *Germ. Doc.*, 29, p. 93. Besides, after reading a telegram from Vienna on 11th July, William II recalled the famous words of Frederick the Great: "I am all against councils of war and conferences, since the more timid party always has the upper hand."

22 To Tschirschky, *Germ. Doc.*, 31, p. 95.

abandons all policy tending toward Pan-Slavism, and, secondly, a body representing the Austro-Hungarian Government will be set up to see that this promise is strictly carried out."[23] The following week Stolberg, the Counselor of
the German Embassy at Vienna, outlined the proposals of
the Chief of the Cabinet: "Hoyos has just told me that the
demands were really of such a nature that no nation that
still possessed self-respect and dignity could possibly accept them." And, if Serbia should yield on both points,
Berchtold definitely intended "to exercise considerable latitude in the practical execution of the separate postulates."[24]
Thus the conflict would become inevitable in any case.

This confidential information appeared of sufficient importance to the Secretary of State to communicate it to
certain other officials. Grand Admiral von Tirpitz, who was
on his vacation at Tarasp, knew about it. He knew that
Austria would demand that a high Austrian official should
take part in the inquiry into the Sarajevo crime, and that
she would demand "the dismissal and punishment" of all the
officers and government officials whose complicity should
be proved.[25] The Bavarian Chargé d'Affaires at Berlin
communicated nearly the same information to his Government. He had received it from Under-Secretary of State Zimmermann on 18th July. "It is perfectly plain that Serbia
cannot accept any such demands, which are incompatible
with her dignity as a sovereign state, and thus the result
would be war."[26]

Even before the Council had completed the final text of
the ultimatum on the nineteenth, Germany was thus familiar

[23] Private letter from Tschirschky to Jagow, 11th July, *Official German
Documents Relating to the World War*, I, 119.

[24] Stolberg to Jagow, personal letter, *Germ. Doc.*, 87, p. 141.

[25] Tirpitz, *Erinnerungen*, Leipzig, Koehler, 1920, pp. 211-212.

[26] *Germ. Doc.*, Supp. IV, No. 2, p. 616. Schoen learned elsewhere that
Austria was going to demand a declaration from the King of Serbia
repudiating all the Pan-Serbian agitation.

with the contents of the document in as great detail as was possible at the moment.[27]

But Austria was not so prompt about informing Germany as to the actual details of the note in its final form. It was not until the evening of the 21st, forty-eight hours after the Council meeting, that Tschirschky received the document and sent it to Berlin.[28] And as the Ambassador sent the document by mail, instead of entrusting it to a telegram,[29]— whether because he was afraid of giving away the secret of the code, or whether because he feared it would take too long to encipher and decipher so long a message—[30] it did not reach Berlin until 22nd July, late in the afternoon. Secretary of State Jagow had not yet even read it when, about seven o'clock, he received Count Szögyény, who brought the same text. In the absence of the Chancellor, who was still at his estate at Hohenfinow,[31] the Secretary of State studied the document. "After reading it over," he recounted to the Investigation Committee,[32] "I told the Ambassador that the note appeared too harsh to me, both as to form and content. As I remember, I pointed out with particular emphasis that the large number of the conditions seemed unfortunate. The Ambassador replied that there was nothing to do. The note had just been sent to Belgrade, and would be delivered the following day—the next morning, so he said by mistake. I expressed my very profound regret to the Ambassador that word had reached Berlin so late, and that no chance was left for us to express an opinion one way or the other. We could not help remarking that it would no longer be of any use to send our impressions to Vienna, and that consequently any step which we might take would be in vain." This same point

---

[27] The Entente Powers, too, had been able to secure fairly precise information for themselves. *Cf. Yellow Book,* 14.

[28] *Germ. Doc.,* 106, p. 152.

[29] *Germ. Doc.,* Supp. IX, p. 652, note from Count Wedel.

[30] *Official German Documents Relating to the World War,* I, p. 30.

[31] Bethmann had been away since 7th July.

[32] *Official German Documents Relating to the World War,* I, p. 30.

was made by the Chancellor: "Those are the facts," he wrote, after describing the conversation between Szögyény and Jagow. "They give the lie to the statements made on every hand, according to which we collaborated in the preparation of the ultimatum, were aware of its harsh tone, and in any case saw the text in time to influence its content or its form. There is not a word of truth in any of that."

The character of these denials, however, is not very convincing.[33] Germany did not try to modify the terms of the note, for neither Jagow nor Bethmann even telegraphed to Tschirschky to express their reaction to it.[34] But was it really too late? The Wilhelmstrasse knew that the note would not be delivered until the following *afternoon*.[35] There were therefore nearly twenty-four hours left to take some step. If Germany had wished to take the initiative, to demand, for instance, the suppression of a certain clause, or of certain details of a demand, was there not still time for it? The Vienna Government could have been notified on the morning of the twenty-third, and, even if a meeting of the Council of Ministers had been necessary to approve the amendment, Baron Giesl in Belgrade could still have received the order to strike out a given part of the note before the appointed hour.

But Germany did not limit herself to this passive assistance only. On at least two occasions she had a more direct part in preparing the path, by taking steps which would assure success.

On 19th July the Serbian Chargé d'Affaires in Berlin read a "*note verbale*" to Jagow. According to this note, Serbia knew that she was menaced with intervention by

---

[33] It is even doubtful whether Jagow made any active protest, for Szögyény stated, in his report to Vienna, "that the German Government is entirely in agreement with the tenor of the note." *Dipl. Pap.*, II, 6.

[34] There is no telegram in the *German Documents* from Berlin to Vienna on the evening of the twenty-second or the morning of the twenty-third.

[35] *Cf. Germ. Doc.*, 112, p. 155. Szögyény's mistake was therefore not a matter of any importance.

Austria, but she could not tell "in what direction, nor under what form" it would be. But the discussions which had taken place in the Hungarian Parliament enabled her to judge the probable nature of the steps to be taken.[36] Serbia would like to anticipate these steps. The Serbian Government was therefore prepared "to prosecute any Serbian subject whose complicity in the crime should be proved," even though no demand of this kind had yet been made. It would undertake "to oppose energetically every effort made in Serbian territory with the object of disturbing the peace and security of the neighboring Monarchy." On the other hand, it would not comply with such demands as were inconsistent with its "dignity" and its "independence." What would be the attitude of the Secretary of State? He evaded the question: Serbia in the past had failed to maintain the attitude she should have maintained. He could well understand it, therefore, if Austria should now take "more energetic measures."[37] Obviously this reply was consistent with the engagements contracted on 5th July, but its result was to announce to Europe the complete solidarity of Germany and Austria three days before the ultimatum.

The Wilhelmstrasse was even more closely implicated. On 11th July, Count Berchtold had sent word that the ultimatum would not be delivered during the visit which the President of the French Republic was about to make to St. Petersburg. Germany had acquiesced. The date and the hour of the delivery of the ultimatum at Belgrade was therefore fixed with that idea in mind. Jagow, who was more precise than his Austrian colleague, set about ascertaining the exact moment when M. Poincaré was to leave St. Peters-

---

[36] Tisza had made some statements at Budapest on the fifteenth which "partly raised the veil."

[37] *Germ. Doc.*, 91, p. 144. Jagow sent Tschirschky an account of the interview. In the report which Tschirschky immediately made to Count Forgách, *Dipl. Pap.*, I, 38, the words of the Secretary of State were a little twisted: ". . . It would be only very natural for the Cabinet at Vienna to speak in a *very* energetic tone."

burg. Through a wire from Pourtalès he learned that the departure was arranged for Thursday evening, the twenty-third, at eleven o'clock, that is to say, at ten o'clock by Central European time. He immediately notified Vienna: "If *démarche* is made in Belgrade tomorrow afternoon at five o'clock, it would become known while Poincaré is still in St. Petersburg!" Immediately Count Berchtold, after sending "warmest thanks" to Jagow, instructed Giesl to postpone the delivery of the ultimatum for at least one hour. It was therefore not until six o'clock that he was to make the move.[38]

It goes without saying that these details were not known until after the German Revolution. At the time of the actual crisis in 1914, the German Government, when giving its approval to the ultimatum, declared that it had not been kept in touch with Vienna during the course of its preparation. It held to this attitude throughout the whole war, although the truth began to come out after 1917.[39]

III. *The Ultimatum.*

ON 23rd July, at six o'clock in the afternoon, the Austrian

[38] *Germ. Doc.,* 108, p. 153; 112, p. 155; 127, p. 166, and *Dipl. Pap.,* I, 62, Berchtold to Giesl.

[39] The American journalist W. C. Bullitt interviewed both Tisza and Jagow in September 1916. After the United States entered the war, Bullitt communicated the information he had received to the State Department. Acting upon this information, the State Department issued a statement to the effect that the German Government had seen the Austrian ultimatum fourteen hours before its presentation in Belgrade. The press correspondents mistakenly declared that Zimmermann was the author of the statement, and this it was easy for the Wilhelmstrasse to deny. *Germ. Doc.,* Supp. VII, p. 650. Bullitt then decided to publish a full account of his conversations in the Philadelphia *Public Ledger* for 5th August 1917. He there contends that Jagow made the following statement: "I saw the Note for the first time at eight o'clock the night before it was presented in Belgrade, where it was delivered at ten o'clock the next morning." Jagow's statement is incidentally incorrect, as regards the time of the delivery of the ultimatum.

I am indebted to Professor Seymour for the details of the incident centering about the Bullitt interviews.

representative at Belgrade delivered the Note from his Government.[40]

The preamble recalled the fact that in 1909 Serbia, "in accepting the advice of the Great Powers," had promised to desist from her attitude of "protest and opposition" against the annexation of Bosnia-Herzegovina, and to live henceforth "on the footing of friendly and neighborly relations" with Austria. She had not kept her word; she had tolerated within her boundaries an active and "unhealthy" propaganda directed against the Dual Monarchy. She had allowed a subversive movement to take root, "whose object it is to separate certain portions of its territory from the Austro-Hungarian Monarchy." The crime on 28th June, prepared at Belgrade with the collaboration of Serbian government officials, had exhibited to the whole world the dreadful consequences of the Serbian attitude.

In order to bring this state of affairs to an end, the Austrian Government enumerated the conditions which it intended to impose. The Serbian Government was to publish, on the first page of its *Official Journal*, a disavowal of all propaganda, and was to express its regrets in the terms which should be dictated. It was to pledge itself to take steps against "every publication which shall incite to hatred and contempt of the Monarchy," against those societies which were given to political propaganda, and against all officials guilty of taking part in their activities. They were to be suppressed, dissolved, and repudiated. Point 2 of the Note specifically demanded the dissolution of the *Narodna Odbrana*, and the confiscation of all of its means of propaganda. Finally, the events of 28th June were to be the object of a judicial inquiry: Serbia was to arrest Tankosić and Ciganović, punish the customs officials who had

---

[40] The text was in French. For the first drafts, which were in German, see Gooss, pp. 94-95, and Musulin, pp. 223-225. *Cf.* also above, Ch. IV, p. 56, note 9.

facilitated the trip of the assassins, and make an explanation concerning "the unjustifiable utterances of high Serbian functionaries," who, after the crime, had not hesitated to express their hostile sentiments toward Austria-Hungary. Points 5 and 6 demanded that Serbia should agree to the institution of "organs of the Imperial and Royal Government" upon her territory, who should collaborate in searching out the guilty parties and in "the suppression of the subversive movement."

Finally, the Note indicated that the Serbian reply would be expected within forty-eight hours, that is to say, at 6 P.M. on 25th July, at the very latest. The Austrian representative had been instructed to say that, unless he received "consent without any reservations" to the demands, diplomatic relations would be severed immediately. Count Berchtold had taken pains to send Baron Giesl very precise instructions: "We cannot consent to any negotiation whatever with Serbia about our demands." He must avoid "all discussion about the contents of the Note," and must refuse to prolong the time-limit, even if the Serbian Government should ask for "more detailed information about the scope or the meaning of some of the demands."[41] Everything was arranged so that Vienna might learn the result of the *démarche* immediately by telephone and by telegram. If the reply was not such as Austria demanded, Baron Giesl was to leave Belgrade within half an hour.[42]

*   *   *   *   *   *   *

The ultimatum had been so worded that acceptance would be practically impossible. In the opinion of the Austrian Government, the demands constituted a blow at the dignity and the pride of Serbia; they went far beyond what was permitted by international law. So much can hardly be ques-

[41] *Dipl. Pap.,* I, 28.
[42] *Dipl. Pap.,* II, 1.

tioned.[43] Had Serbia by chance yielded, Count Berchtold would have been greatly disappointed and would have proceeded to carry out the demands with uncompromising rigor. The war with Serbia was deliberately provoked and anticipated.

Germany approved of this plan. It is true that she did not take a hand in the composition of the ultimatum, and that she did not suggest its terms, but she was constantly in touch with Austria's intentions and she was acquainted with the text of the Note in time to have taken steps to soften its tone. She said that she considered the form of the Note too harsh, but she allowed it to go through. More than that, she declared to Europe that she gave her approval to the ultimatum.[44]

These facts are clearly proved and beyond all question. But have we not a right to go still further and try to reach the bottom of the affair? Did Germany give Austria *secret* counsel? Upon this point there is still room for discussion.

The German side of the case claims that the Berlin Government remained nothing more than a mere spectator, hoping thus to be able to act as mediator between Vienna and St. Petersburg later on. On the face of it, it may seem unbelievable that the Wilhelmstrasse did not take the whole matter in hand, that she really gave up all "supervision" and all control over the situation. This is, however, the absolute truth. Germany allowed Austria a free hand, and Austria abused her privilege.[45]

The spokesmen of the Austrian Government, on the other hand, reply:[46] "We should never have taken such action if

[43] Upon this last point, see Schücking, *Die völkerrechtliche Lehre des Weltkrieges*, Leipzig, Veit, 1918, pp. 27-51.

[44] See below, Ch. V, p. 73.

[45] *Cf.* the position taken by Delbrück, *Glocke*, 18th December 1922. Delbrück was a friend of the Chancellor's, and has undertaken to defend him.

[46] Berchtold, statement made to the *Neue Freie Presse*, 28th September and 5th October 1919.

Germany had not encouraged us to do so." But whom do
they mean by Germany? Technically, her Ambassador in
Vienna, Tschirschky. He had declared to Berchtold that
Germany would not understand any hesitation on Austria's
part. He thus played the part of an *instigator*. Whether
or not the declarations made by Tschirschky were confirmed
by instructions received from his Government, the influence
which he exerted was exerted in the name of Germany. And
this influence proved decisive.

The "Tschirschky problem" has continued to arouse discussion ever since 1919. The German Parliamentary Investigation Committee has questioned the Ambassador's former
assistants. These witnesses defend the memory of their chief:
he was loyal, he was irreproachable, he had done nothing to
encourage Austria to take violent steps.

But, on the other hand, Berchtold's statements have been
confirmed by the word of certain Austro-Hungarian statesmen, and in particular by Count Czernin.

The discussion centers directly upon one point. It is
claimed that Tschirschky gave Berchtold definite encouragement on 8th July, and that he said Germany would be unable to understand why Austria-Hungary had let this chance
pass without aiming a blow at Serbia.[47] The Ambassador had
acted upon the authority of a telegram from Berlin, in which
the Emperor had instructed him to take "most energetic
steps" with regard to the Austrian Government.

Tschirschky's supposed statements are not recorded any-
where, however, except in a letter from Berchtold to Tisza,
and it is therefore possible that the Austrian Minister for
Foreign Affairs distorted the remarks which the Ambassador
really made. To what extent do his impressions of Tschirschky's attitude correspond with the other information we
possess?

[47] *Dipl. Pap.*, I, 10. See also Berchtold's statements to the *Neue Freie
Presse*, 28th September and 5th October 1919.

It is quite possible that Berchtold's impressions were justified. The conduct of the German Ambassador was undergoing a curious evolution just at this time. Immediately after the Sarajevo crime, he was inclined at first to calm down the impatience of his Austrian friends, "to advise quietly but very impressively and seriously against too hasty steps."[48] He later recognized the need for "energetic action,"[49] and finally, after the return of the Hoyos Mission from Berlin, he emphasized the necessity of reaching a decision at the earliest possible moment, "in order to put an end to the intolerable conditions in Serbia."[50] Was this change simply one of his own personal point of view? Certainly not. He was quite consciously representing the views of his Government—"our opinion," as he wrote Jagow.

The statements attributed to him by Berchtold, however, are certainly more extreme than the instructions which he had received from Berlin on 7th July. The official attitude of the German Government, as expressed by Bethmann, was that it lay with Austria to make the decision, now that Germany had pledged her support, and the only stipulation was that the decision should be made at once. In Vienna, however, Tschirschky is reported to have exerted direct and vigorous pressure to stimulate the Vienna Government to act in the most brutal manner! This was certainly a bold initiative to take, and at first sight it appears unaccountable.

Just here, however, is where another important element comes in: The evolution in Tschirschky's attitude was not spontaneous. If, after carefully trying to restrain the impatience of the Austrians, he was now inciting them to vio-

---

[48] *Germ. Doc.*, 7, p. 61.

[49] See above, Ch. III, p. 38.

[50] *Germ. Doc.*, 29, p. 92, Interview between Berchtold and Tschirschky: "His Majesty, the Emperor Franz Joseph, . . . stated that he was quite of our opinion that it was necessary *now* to come to some *determination*, in order to put an end to the intolerable conditions in connection with Serbia."

lent action, he doubtless had good reasons for doing so. On 4th July the Emperor had read and commented on a telegram in which Tschirschky reported the advice which he had given Count Berchtold, favoring prudence and deliberation. "Who authorized him to act that way?", William jotted down in the margin of the telegram.[51] "That is very stupid! It is none of his business, as it is solely the affair of Austria, what she plans to do in this case. Later, if plans go wrong, it will be said that Germany did not want it! Let Tschirschky be good enough to drop this nonsense! The Serbs must be disposed of, and *that right soon!*" It is entirely probable that the Ambassador heard echoes of these comments, perhaps in a private letter from the Wilhelmstrasse.[52] And this is doubtless the reason for his *interpreting* the official instructions of 7th July in the way that he did, and for his carrying out the *démarche* in the manner which he thought would correspond to the Emperor's intentions.

If this explanation be accepted, there is still at least one point in Berchtold's letter over which we must pause. To which telegram from the Emperor is Tschirschky supposed to have referred? The archives of the Wilhelmstrasse and of the Embassy certainly contain no traces of such a document.[53] The Ambassador's personal papers do not include any *official* documents of this kind.[54] But may not Tschirschky, in appealing to the authority of the Emperor, simply have had in mind the marginal notes? This might explain his

[51] *Germ. Doc.,* 7, p. 61.

[52] Szögyény learned, on 8th July, in the Ministry of Foreign Affairs in Berlin, that Tschirschky had been "reprimanded." See Montgelas, p. 174. It is true that the *German Documents* contain no proof that the Emperor's comments were officially communicated to Tschirschky. But it is hard to believe that the Ambassador was not informed through private sources of the observations made by William II.

[53] Montgelas, pp. 172-175.

[54] This statement was made by Tschirschky's son-in-law, Prince Hatzfeld. *Die Kriegsschuldfrage,* October 1924, p. 427. The word *official,* of course, still leaves the question open. Was there not perhaps a private letter bearing on this matter? See note above.

saying that he had received the decisive instructions *from Berlin* (that is to say, from the Wilhelmstrasse), and not from Potsdam, where the Emperor was residing.

This interpretation, suggested by the documents which we now possess, would thus attribute to Germany a large share of the influence which determined Austria's policy.

CHAPTER V

THE LOCALIZATION OF THE WAR

THE Austrian ultimatum became known to Europe on the morning of 24th July. During the day, the German Ambassadors in Paris, London, and St. Petersburg, acting upon the instructions of their Government, made identical moves.[1]

The text of these instructions was prepared on the evening of the twenty-first, even before Germany could have received the final text of the Austrian note. It was not modified after Berlin had seen the note. The German Government declared that the Austrian demands were "moderate and proper."

The purpose of this diplomatic move was to express the official attitude of the Wilhelmstrasse. The clauses of the ultimatum would be enforced "if necessary by recourse to military measures." It was to Austria alone that the choice of means must be left. Europe must not interfere. "The problem under discussion is one which it is solely for Austria-Hungary and Serbia to solve, and one which it should be the earnest endeavor of the Powers to confine to the two immediate participants. We urgently desire the localization of the conflict, as the intervention of any other Power would, as a result of the various alliance obligations, bring about inestimable consequences."

The attitude of the Central Powers thus implied a threat: "Hands off, or beware!" Russia must be persuaded to abandon her Balkan allies and resign herself to a loss of prestige. Thus a general war would be averted. Such was the policy of "localization," following logically upon the decisions of 5th July.

[1] *Germ. Doc.,* 100, p. 149.

I. *The Views of the German Government.*

DID Germany really believe that the war could be localized? Did the official attitude of her diplomats represent the honest conviction of those statesmen, or was it simply a bluff? She had accepted the risk of a general war. Was it, in their opinion, a probability or only a possibility? In order to answer this question we must pause for a moment over the conjectures which were being made in Berlin just before the presentation of the ultimatum.

On 18th July Dr. von Schoen, Bavarian Chargé d'Affaires in Berlin, outlined the attitude of the Wilhelmstrasse as follows: "In the interest of the localization of the war, the Imperial Government will, immediately upon the presentation of the Austrian note at Belgrade, initiate diplomatic action with the Powers. It will claim that the Austrian action has been just as much of a surprise to it as to the other Powers, pointing out the fact that the Emperor is on his northern journey and that the Prussian Minister of War, as well as the Chief of Staff, are away on leave of absence. . . . It will make use of its influence to get all the Powers to take the view that the settlement between Austria and Serbia is a matter concerning those two nations alone.

"The attitude of Russia will, above all else, determine the question whether the attempt to localize the war will succeed. . . . Mr. Zimmermann assumes that both England and France, to neither of whom a war would be acceptable at the present moment, will try to exert a pacifying influence on Russia; besides that, he is counting on the fact that 'bluffing' constitutes one of the most favored requisites of Russian policy, and that while the Russian likes to threaten with his sword, he still does not like so very much to draw it in behalf of others at the critical moment."[2]

2 *Germ. Doc.,* Supp. IV, 2, pp. 617-618.

On the same day Secretary of State Jagow wrote a letter to Prince Lichnowsky, German Ambassador in London, informing the Ambassador of the imminence of a conflict between Austria and Serbia:

"Austria is now going to come to an understanding with Serbia, and has told us so. . . . We neither could nor should hold her back. If we should do that, Austria would have the right to reproach us (and we ourselves) with having deprived her of her last chance of political rehabilitation." The Austrian alliance was doubtless far from ideal, said Jagow, but he added: "I say with the poet—Busch, I think it was—'If no longer you like your company, look for another, if any there be.' " Germany must try in any case to localize the present Austro-Serbian conflict. "As a matter of fact, Russia is not ready to strike at present, nor will France or England be anxious for war at the present time."[3]

These remarks are borne out by a telegram which Szögyény sent to Berchtold: Germany, according to the Ambassador,[4] did not believe that Russia was in any condition to make war, and it was therefore doubtful whether she would intervene on Serbia's behalf. Besides, England would probably stand aside, even though the Balkan affair should lead to a European conflict. Was she not already quite embarrassed, for that matter, with the way things were going in Ireland?[5] Thus it was that Jagow asked Herr Ballin, direc-

[3] *Germ. Doc.*, 72, p. 131. In an interview with Admiral von Behncke, Acting Chief of Staff, Jagow also expressed the opinion that England, in case of a general war, would maintain a waiting attitude, and would not decide until she saw what turn the events were taking. *Cf. Der Krieg zur See, 1914-1918, Der Krieg in der Nordsee*, Berlin, Mittler & Sohn, Vol. I (1920), p. 7.

[4] *Dipl. Pap.*, I, 15.

[5] Upon this point *cf. Germ. Doc.*, 254, p. 41, *in fine*. Also Churchill, *The World Crisis, 1911-1914*, London, Butterworth, 1923, I, p. 192, showing how much the British Cabinet was preoccupied at the time with affairs in Ireland, which were discussed with some bitterness up until the evening of 24th July.

tor of the Hamburg-American Line, to go at once to London, to "sound out" the various English statesmen.[6]

And how about France? The debate which had taken place in the Senate on 15th July on the subject of heavy artillery showed very clearly the faults and weaknesses in her military preparation. There was every reason to believe that she would hesitate before taking part in the conflict.[7]

It goes without saying that if these conjectures should prove wrong, Germany would carry out her decisions in any case. "If we cannot attain localization (of the conflict), and Russia attacks Austria, a *casus foederis* will then arise; we could not throw Austria over then."[8]

Although Germany accepted this risk of a general war of her own free will, the Wilhelmstrasse would apparently have preferred a simple diplomatic triumph. It hoped for capitulation rather than resistance on Russia's part. It did look upon localization as a possibility, even as a probability.

The situation was extremely delicate. Germany must avoid giving any alarm, and must maintain a calm exterior, in order to reassure the Entente Powers, and to allay their uneasiness. The incident relating to the Crown Prince, on 20th July, showed that this idea was uppermost in the Chancellor's mind. The heir to the throne, as was his custom, had indulged in certain "public utterances." He had sent telegrams of "very warm approval" to a certain Pan-Germanist, author of a pamphlet entitled *Das Deutschen Reiches Schicksalstunde*, and to a university professor who had praised Bismarck in glowing terms and violently attacked his successors. These demonstrations on the part of the Crown Prince were a disturbing sign, and might easily ruin the whole policy of localization. Bethmann-Hollweg had written

[6] Huldermann, *Albert Ballin*, Berlin, Stalling, 1922, pp. 299-302.
[7] Conrad, IV, 80.
[8] From the above-mentioned letter from Jagow to Lichnowsky.

to the Prince asking him to be more discreet, but he felt it the part of wisdom to approach the Emperor as well. "I am very much more afraid," he wrote to William II on 20th July, "that His Imperial Highness may, as soon as the Austrian ultimatum to Serbia is made public, come out with statements which, in the light of all that has passed, will be regarded by our opponents as wilful war-baiting." And he most humbly requested "that His Majesty should graciously command His Imperial Highness by an immediate telegraphic order to refrain from any political intervention of this kind." The Emperor sent the Chancellor's telegram to the Prince on the next day. The Crown Prince acquiesced two days later, and wired his father simply, "Your orders will be obeyed." And to the Chancellor, he sent the following message, in an ironical tone, "The contents of the telegram which Your Excellency sent to His Majesty in the matter you know of interested me greatly."[9]

One is tempted to wonder whether the opinions of the Chancellor and the Secretary of State were shared in all the official circles.

The Emperor himself does not seem at this time to have entertained any serious belief that the conflict could remain strictly limited. We may follow, from the marginal notes which he jotted down as he read the telegrams, the consecutive evolution of his thoughts as he cruised along the coast of Norway.[10] The details of these notes leave no doubt upon the point. On 20th July, three days before the ultimatum, William II, who had just learned of the "particular points" in the Austrian note, sent a telegraphic order to the Fleet

---

[9] *Germ. Doc.,* 84, pp. 138-139; 132 and 133, p. 169. Tirpitz declares in his memoirs that Bethmann-Hollweg sincerely believed that localization was possible. *Cf.* also Clemens von Delbrück's volume, *Die Wirtschaftliche Mobilmachung in Deutschland,* Munich, Verlag für Kulturpolitik, 1924. This was published by Joachim von Delbrück, who based it upon his father's personal papers. It also shows why the Chancellor wished "to avoid everything which might give the impression" that Germany was preparing for war.

[10] Kanner, pp. 228-231.

to remain concentrated until the twenty-fifth. He held to this order throughout the ensuing days, in spite of the observations made by the Secretary of State for Foreign Affairs and the Chancellor.[11] On the same day, he advised Bethmann-Hollweg to send confidential information to the directors of the large steamship lines about the possible complications, so that they in turn might warn their ships which were in distant waters. On the twenty-third he made the following note on the margin of a telegram from the Ambassador at Constantinople: "The thing to do now is to get hold of every gun in readiness in the Balkans to shoot against the Slavs for Austria."[12] And on the twenty-fifth, in a telegram to the Chancellor, he already spoke of putting "the confidential question" to Sweden. From one end of his cruise to the other, the Emperor did not seem to consider for a single moment that the war might really remain localized.

The opinion of the General Staff was not sensibly different. Waldersee, Assistant Chief of the General Staff, who had left Berlin on 8th July, after the conference at Potsdam, was on leave of absence. He declared in 1919, before the German Parliamentary Investigation Committee, that he had given no orders with a view to preparation of any kind before leaving for his vacation. Here was evidently a man quite unconcerned, who did not seem to be thinking about European complications, and yet, on the seventeenth, he wrote a personal letter to Secretary of State Jagow, in which he said: "I shall remain here ready to jump. We are all prepared here at the General Staff. In the meantime there is nothing for us to do."[13]

[11] *Germ. Doc.*, 82, p. 137; 101, p. 150; 115, p. 156. The Navy Staff was also somewhat surprised at this imperial decision, for, after all, the *exact* contents of the Austrian note were not yet known. *Der Krieg zur See: Der Krieg in der Nordsee*, I, 5-6.

[12] *Germ. Doc.*, 117, p. 158.

[13] *Germ. Doc.*, 74, p. 134.

Admiral von Tirpitz was also away on his vacation. On 13th July, ten days before the delivery of the ultimatum, he learned of the principal points which the Austrian note was to contain: "When I received this communication, my first impression was that the ultimatum would be unacceptable to Serbia, and might easily bring about a general war. I had as little hope of localizing an armed conflict between Austria and Serbia, with respect to Russia, as of the neutrality of England in a continental war."[14]

And when the Prussian Minister of the Interior, Clemens von Delbrück, learned, on 10th July, that an ultimatum was to be sent to Serbia, his first thought was: "That means war!" Bethmann and Jagow doubtless tried to reassure him, but they took the trouble to keep him within reach by telephone. Direct communications were established between the Prussian Ministry and the station in Thuringia where Delbrück had gone for a few days. The men in immediate contact with the Minister were convinced that war was imminent.[15]

II. *The Official Notes of Warning.*

THE feelings of the Emperor and of the military group may not have been shared at the start by the Wilhelmstrasse. But we must remember that on the very eve of the ultimatum, on 22nd and 23rd July, the diplomats in Berlin received communications from London and St. Petersburg which no longer allowed them to believe that Europe's attitude might be a passive one. The Vienna Government also received a direct warning.

The first word which reached them was from St. Petersburg. M. Poincaré and M. Viviani had arrived in Russia on 20th July. It was a visit which had been planned for some

[14] Tirpitz, *Erinnerungen,* p. 212.
[15] The facts bearing upon this point, which appeared in the book by J. von Delbrück, quoted above, Ch. V, p. 77, note 9, were summarized by M. Lajusan, in an interesting article in the *Revue d'histoire de la guerre mondiale,* April 1926, pp. 141-143.

time, but now that it was taking place under these particular circumstances, at a time of great uneasiness, it assumed very great importance indeed. Berlin and Vienna were intensely concerned with what was taking place at St. Petersburg.

The welcome accorded M. Poincaré did not on the whole impress the German Ambassador, Count Pourtalès, who remarked upon the "striking indifference" apparently exhibited by the general public. "There was," so he said, "no sort of enthusiasm."[16] In the statements issued to the press on the last day of the visit, the Russian and French Governments had been careful to avoid any expressions which might accentuate the known opposition between the groups of great Powers, and which might serve as the pretext for a grievance.[17]

One detail in the visit at St. Petersburg, however, greatly struck the Central Powers, and caused no little comment in Vienna and Berlin. On Tuesday, 21st July, at about four o'clock, M. Poincaré received the members of the diplomatic corps, and had, in particular, a brief conversation with Szápáry, the Austrian Ambassador. We have two accounts of this interview, which are almost identical. According to M. Paléologue, M. Poincaré made some allusion to the investigation undertaken at Vienna with regard to the assassination of Archduke Franz Ferdinand. He recalled the fact that such investigations in the past had usually led to tension in diplomatic circles. "With a little good will," he concluded, "this Serbian affair will be easy to settle, but it could also quite easily lead to quite serious trouble. Serbia has very warm friends in the Russian people, and Russia has an important ally, France. What complications there are to worry about!"[18]

16 *Germ. Doc.*, 203, p. 211.
17 On this subject, see the account by M. Paléologue, *La Russie des Tsars*, Paris, Plon, 1921, I, 17.
18 Paléologue, I, p. 10.

This account from M. Paléologue is almost identical with that given by Count Szápáry himself: M. Poincaré had asked the Ambassador what demands it was intended to make of Serbia. He had furthermore remarked that, in order to show that a government was responsible for a crime, proof of a very "concrete and definite nature" was necessary. He had ended by saying that it must not be forgotten that Serbia had friends, and that a situation might arise which would endanger the peace of the continent.[19]

These remarks had an irritating effect in Berlin and Vienna. Count Szápáry felt that they implied a threat, almost a challenge. There is another document, however, which is important as throwing some light on the situation. M. Poincaré knew, when he spoke to the Ambassador, that Austria was preparing a note to deliver to Serbia. He seemed to think that it would prove something of a surprise.[20]

On 16th July, Marquis Carlotti, Italian Ambassador at St. Petersburg, pointed out in an interview with Baron Schilling, Chief of the Cabinet under Sazonov that if Russia had decided not to allow any attack upon the independence or integrity of Serbia, "she would have to declare herself to Vienna on this subject without any ambiguity." The Ambassador was "under the impression that Austria might easily take irrevocable steps against Serbia, counting on the fact that Russia would enter a protest, but would not

[19] *Dipl. Pap.*, I, 45.

[20] The French Government had learned, through its secret agents, several of the conditions which the note was to contain. *Yellow Book,* 14. But this news, sent from Vienna to Paris on 20th July, could not possibly have reached Poincaré at St. Petersburg by the twenty-first. The English Government appears to have known only of the rather vague statements given in the *Neue Freie Presse* on the twenty-first. *British Documents on the Origins of the War,* edited by Gooch and Temperley, *Vol XI, The Outbreak of War, Foreign Office Documents, June 28th-August 4th 1914,* edited by J. W. Headlam-Morley, London, H.M. Stationery Office, 1926, 88, p. 72.

decide to protect Serbia by force against an attack by Austria."[21]

The Italian diplomat had added that if Austria were obliged to reckon with a certain rupture with Russia, "in all probability she would reflect a bit upon the consequences of too energetic an anti-Serbian policy."

The remarks which M. Poincaré made to Count Szápáry seemed to bear out Carlotti's advice and opinion. The important thing, as M. Viviani telegraphed a little later to M. Dumaine, was "to prevent a request for an explanation, or some *mise en demeure* which would be equivalent to intervention in the internal affairs of Serbia, of such a kind that Serbia might consider it as an attack upon her sovereignty and independence."[22]

Now, Poincaré's statement was known in Vienna on the morning of the twenty-third, at the very latest.[23]

M. Sazonov also took it upon himself to warn Austria. At about 4 A.M on the morning of the twenty-second,[24] he sent the following instructions to his representative in Vienna: "According to rumors which we have heard, the Austrian Government appears to be on the point of making certain demands at Belgrade with regard to the event at

[21] *How the War Began in 1914, Being the Diary of the Russian Foreign Office from the 3rd to the 20th (Old Style) of July 1914*, London, Allen & Unwin, 1925, p. 25. This is an English translation of "Nachalo voïny 1914 g., Podennaïa zapis' b. Ministerstva inostrannykh del," which appeared in *Krasnyï Arkhiv*, 1923, IV, pp. 3-62. Page references are to the English translation which is cited as the Journal of Baron Schilling or the *Journal*.

[22] The Reval telegram, 24th July at 1 A.M., *Yellow Book*, 22.

[23] *Germ. Doc.*, 131, p. 169. As for M. Dumaine, according to Gooss, p. 129, he had made a *démarche* at the Ballplatz on the twenty-second with a view to drawing the attention of the Austrian Government to the dangers of an Austro-Serbian conflict, but he had added that, in his opinion, Russia would not intervene by force of arms.

[24] Telegram No. 1475, *Journal*, Appendix I, pp. 85-86. This telegram has also been published in *Livre Noir*, II, p. 275. According to a recently published document (*Journal*, p. 38), this telegram did not reach Vienna until 3 P.M. on the twenty-third, and even then Kudashev was unable to see the Minister at once, as the latter was at the meeting of the Council. He was not received until the morning of the twenty-fourth.

Sarajevo. Draw the attention of the Minister for Foreign Affairs in a friendly but energetic way to the dangerous consequences of such action, in case this action is incompatible with the dignity of Serbia. From my conversation with the French Minister for Foreign Affairs, it seems that France is also following with great interest the relations between Austria and Serbia, and is not disposed to tolerate any humiliation which is not justified by the circumstances."

The Minister also had an interview with the German Ambassador, doubtless on the twenty-first, in which he denounced at length "the dangerous policy" which Austria-Hungary was pursuing at the moment. He even went so far as to say that the Serbian Government "was behaving itself with entire propriety." Austria must not forget, he added, that "Russia could not look on with indifference at a move at Belgrade which aimed at the humiliation of Serbia. . . . In no case should there be any talk of an ultimatum."[25]

Finally, on the twenty-third, a message of almost equal importance arrived from London. Prince Lichnowsky ventured to approach Secretary of State Jagow to caution him against too bold a policy. Of course he did not think that Austria should be abandoned, but he thought that it would be dangerous to support her unreservedly: "It is not to our interest to support her in an active Balkan policy in which we have everything to lose and nothing to gain." Localization? It was an impossibility. "You will have to admit that such a localization, in the event of a passage at arms with Serbia, belongs in the realm of pious wishes."[26] In an earlier telegram he had already outlined the attitude of the English Government:[27] "I meet with the expectation that

[25] *Germ. Doc.*, 120, pp. 160-161.

[26] *Germ. Doc.*, 161, p. 188, 23rd July. Time of arrival unknown.

[27] *Germ. Doc.*, 121, p. 163, sent 9.17 P.M., 22nd July. Arrived 1.25 A.M., 23rd July. William II noted, on reading the telegram: "Real British reasoning and condescending way of giving orders, which I insist on having rebuffed!" Incidentally, it should be remarked that the Foreign Office

our influence at Vienna has been successful in suppressing demands that cannot be met. They are counting with certainty on the fact that we shall not identify ourselves with demands that are plainly intended to bring on war, and that we will not support any policy which makes use of the murder at Sarajevo merely as an excuse for carrying out Austrian desires in the Balkans, and for the annulment of the Peace of Bucharest."

Now, Bethmann-Hollweg learned the details of the Austrian demands on that very day. How could he have had any further illusions about the future development of the crisis, or have believed that Europe would calmly remain passive when confronted with a show of force by Austria?

Count Berchtold had also been warned. No doubt some of these warnings arrived at the very last minute. Although the ultimatum was finally sent without alteration, the later diplomatic conduct of the Central Powers was sensibly affected by the position of the Entente.

Both of these statesmen, it is true, unquestionably noticed the fact that England had nothing to do with the Franco-Russian *démarche* carried out in Vienna on 22nd July.

III. *Germany's Move on 24th July.*

THUS the situation stood on 24th July when the German Ambassadors in Paris, London, and St. Petersburg stated the official position of their Government.

In Paris von Schoen acted on the afternoon of the twenty-fourth. M. Viviani and M. Poincaré had just left St. Petersburg and, as they were in the middle of the Baltic, could communicate with Paris only by wireless. M. Bienvenu-Martin, Minister of Justice, was meanwhile in charge of foreign affairs, in collaboration with M. Philippe Berthe-

had learned of Russia's intention to send a warning to Vienna, and was not disposed to have any part in it. It was even felt that such a move would be injudicious. *Brit. Doc.*, 84, p. 69.

lot, Assistant Director for Political Affairs. Neither of them made the slightest comment to the German Ambassador upon the unwonted character of the note.[28] The Minister agreed that Austria was justified in demanding the punishment of the accomplices of the crime, but he felt that it would be wrong for her to insist upon the immediate execution of her demands, especially those "which it would be difficult to reconcile with Serbian sovereignty." He remarked to von Schoen that the German Government seemed to be considering only one possibility, namely, "the pure and simple acceptance or refusal of the Austrian note." But it was altogether possible that Serbia would accept the great majority of the demands which Vienna had made, without granting them all. In such a case, would Austria refuse to consider discussing the matter? Baron von Schoen answered rather vaguely "that personally he had no views in the matter, . . . but that hope was always possible."[29] One might have assumed from this, as the Russian Chargé d'Affaires in Paris said, that the step taken by Austria did not preclude all possibility of negotiations.

As soon as he returned to the Embassy, von Schoen sent an account of this interview to Berlin. The text of his wire has been reproduced in the *German Documents*, and it corresponds almost exactly with the observations which M. Bienvenu-Martin made in the *Yellow Book*. The two remarks made by the French Minister are quoted. The Ambassador, without mentioning his reply to the questions, emphasized the position of the French Cabinet: "The French Government sincerely shares the wish that the conflict remain localized, and will labor along this line in the interest of the maintenance of the peace of Europe." This was also the impression at the Wilhelmstrasse.[30]

[28] The nature of the communication was, however, emphasized by one newspaper, the *Echo de Paris*.

[29] *Yellow Book*, 28; *Livre Noir*, II, p. 275, telegram No. 184.

[30] *Dipl. Pap.*, II, 33.

Baron von Schoen returned to the Quai d'Orsay at noon on the twenty-fifth to protest against the interpretation which the *Echo de Paris* had placed upon the German note. "There was no threat," he said. M. Berthelot made a note of this statement, but not without remarking that the terms of Germany's communication indicated at least her willingness to intervene. He added that the *Echo de Paris* had received no information from the Ministry for Foreign Affairs, and that Germany's *démarche* had been learned "elsewhere than at the Quai d'Orsay, and quite independently of it." The German Ambassador made no further allusion to the incident.[31]

In a wire to M. Viviani on the twenty-seventh, M. Bienvenu-Martin interpreted Schoen's attitude in the following manner. If the Ambassador had tried, on the twenty-fifth, to minimize the importance of the step which he had taken the previous afternoon, and if he had protested because a newspaper attributed intentions to Germany which she did not harbor, it was simply because the anticipated effect had been produced. The Entente Powers had been surprised and had not had time to react.[32]

In London Prince Lichnowsky presented the German note to Sir Edward Grey, also on the twenty-fourth. The response of the Minister at once took on a more categorical tone. Sir Edward Grey declared that the Austrian note, according to his point of view, "exceeded anything he had ever seen of the sort before." He went on: "Any nation that accepted conditions like that would really cease to count as an independent nation." England, however, admitted the idea of "a localized quarrel between Austria and Serbia"; she had nothing to do with it. But "it would be quite a different matter should public opinion in Russia force the Government to proceed against Austria. . . . The danger of a European

31 *Yellow Book,* 36.
32 *Yellow Book,* 61.

war, should Austria invade Serbian territory, would become immediate." It was absolutely essential, Sir Edward Grey concluded, to try to reach some solution by negotiation. "The Minister is evidently endeavoring to do everything to avoid European complications"—such was the opinion of the German Ambassador.[33]

During the course of this interview Sir Edward Grey had suggested the idea of mediation, in case the conflict should lead to "dangerous tension" between Austria and Russia. In this case, he said, "the four Powers not immediately concerned: England, France, Germany, and Italy," might intervene between Russia and Austria.[34] This proposal of four-power mediation was based on "a clear distinction between the Austro-Serbian quarrel and an Austro-Russian conflict." This very fact showed that he was not opposed to the idea of localization.

The atmosphere in St. Petersburg was becoming tense. M. Sazonov, Minister for Foreign Affairs, appeared "nervous and irritable." It was impossible "to consider as actually established the facts stated in the Austrian note." Even if these facts were proved, Serbia would have to yield on the legal side of the question, but ought not to accept "the demands of a political character." This was the attitude of the Russian Government.[35] M. Sazonov refused to accept the idea of localization. "After the Bosnian crisis," he told the German Ambassador, "Serbia undertook obligations toward Europe. The question is therefore a European one, and it is Europe's business to conduct the inquiry." He did not even hesitate to conclude with the following words: "If Austria-Hungary devours Serbia, we shall make war upon her." And to Sir George Buchanan the Russian Minister declared:

---

[33] *Germ. Doc.*, 157, pp. 184–185.

[34] *Brit. Doc.*, 99, p. 78. 7.45 p.m.

[35] Sazonov put the matter very clearly to the Austrian Ambassador: "What you want is war, and you have burned your bridges behind you." *Dipl. Pap.*, II, 18.

"Russia cannot allow Austria to crush Serbia and become the predominant Power in the Balkans, and, secure of the support of France, she will face all the risks of war."[36] At the same time, when Count Pourtalès sent an account of this interview to Berlin, he stated that it was not a question of immediate intervention on Russia's part. "My general impression is that, in spite of the very excited mood in which Mr. Sazonoff finds himself, he wishes above all to temporize."[37]

Moreover, M. Sazonov appeared much more calm and conciliatory in a further interview on the following day. He declared "that nothing lay farther from Russia's mind than the desire for war; that, on the contrary, she was ready to exhaust every means to avoid it; that a way must absolutely be found, and he urgently entreated our assistance in finding it." Austria should receive satisfaction with regard to the prosecution of the authors of the assassination at Sarajevo, but she should modify the demands "which directly violated Serbian sovereignty." And the impression received by the Austrian Ambassador corresponded exactly with that of his German colleague: "The tactics of the Minister," he wrote, "tended obviously to avoid anything like a hasty or premature judgment."

The Entente Powers were thus very careful at the start not to assume any definite attitude toward the policy adopted at Berlin. The German Government was under the impression, however, that whereas Russia had vigorously rejected the idea of localization, the feelings of England and France were somewhat different. "Paris and London are working zealously to localize the conflict," Bethmann-Hollweg wired to the Emperor.[38] The Chancellor was thus not encountering as much immediate resistance as the "warnings" of 22nd

36 *Brit. Doc.,* 125, p. 94.
37 *Germ. Doc.,* 204, pp. 213-214.
38 *Germ. Doc.,* 191, p. 205.

and 23rd July might have led him to expect. Sir Edward Grey's proposal of four-power mediation was in harmony with the essential principles of Austro-German policy, as it did not imply intervention in the Austro-Serbian affair. Bethmann-Hollweg was quite prepared to accept it.

*   *   *   *   *   *   *

Thanks to the vigor of their action, the Central Powers had met with initial success. But if they were to profit by the tendencies which they had noticed in London and Paris, the Berlin and Vienna Governments had two essential facts to take into account:

The Western Powers, as well as Russia, wanted to know the true aims underlying the Austrian policy, and the territorial aspirations which that policy might imply.

The Bavarian Chargé d'Affaires was already conscious of this feeling on 18th July, for he wrote: "The attitude of the other Powers will chiefly depend on whether Austria will content herself with a chastisement of Serbia, or will also demand territorial compensation for herself. In the first case, it might be possible to localize the war; in the other case, however, serious complications would be inevitable."

In order to reassure the Powers, Austria must therefore make a more definite statement upon this point. Now, although Count Berchtold had said to the Russian Chargé d'Affaires on 24th July, "Austria will not lay the least claim to any Serbian territory,"[39] he was not anxious to have this statement repeated by his Ambassador in St. Petersburg.[40] He was not disposed to make any official promises. Besides, the declarations of the Austrian Government did not correspond with his own secret intentions. According to the Cabinet's decisions, Serbia must consent to the rectification of her frontier on the Austrian side, and must

---

[39] *Germ. Doc.*, 155, p. 182. Tschirschky to Jagow. William II noted: "Ass! She must take back the Sandjak."

[40] *Dipl. Pap.*, II, 40.

cede territory to Bulgaria and to Albania. That was what lay concealed, unknown even to Berlin, in the phrase "territorial disinterestedness" which had been used by the Ballplatz. There was thus a gross misapprehension, a double game, which hung like a cloud over all the ensuing negotiations.

In the second place, the Entente Powers were concerned about the political independence and the sovereign rights of Serbia. Just as Russia had protested against the "demands of a political character" contained in the ultimatum, so also Sir Edward Grey had declared that "any nation that accepted conditions like that would really cease to count as an independent nation," and M. Bienvenu-Martin had emphasized the importance of Serbian "sovereignty."

Upon this point Austria had refrained from making any declaration whatever.

CHAPTER VI

THE SERBIAN REPLY

THE Austrian Government discounted the importance of the interest which the other European governments were taking in the Serbian affair. What took place on 25th July showed the unwillingness of Count Berchtold to accept either any postponement or any discussion of the matter, and his determination to carry out the program in all its rigor.

I. *The Forty-eight-hour Time Limit.*

THE first concern of the Entente governments, in London as well as in St. Petersburg, was to secure a prolongation of the forty-eight-hour time limit which had been set by the ultimatum. Such a delay would have given time for the conferences which Sir Edward Grey was hoping for, and possibly even for a provisional Serbian reply to the Ballplatz, which might have been made through the good offices of a third party, before the official reply was sent. This of course did not fit in with the plan which Count Berchtold had in mind.

Sir Edward Grey had declared, in his interview with Prince Lichnowsky on the twenty-fourth, that he was prepared to intervene at Vienna with a view to obtaining this concession, "as it might perhaps be possible to reach a solution in this way." He had asked the Ambassador to communicate this proposal to Berlin, and it had reached there at one o'clock on the morning of 25th July. It was not until the early part of the afternoon that the Secretary of State for Foreign Affairs made a reply to the English proposal, and a negative reply at that. "As the ultimatum expires today and Count Berchtold, according to newspaper reports, is at Ischl, I believe that a prolongation of the time limit will no longer be possible."[1]

As a matter of fact, Jagow had not even communicated the suggestion to Vienna, in spite of the assurance which he gave during the morning to Sir Edward Goschen.[2] It was not until four o'clock (two hours before the expiration of the time limit) that he sent it, taking care to indicate what response had already been made to England. It is impossible to believe that this delay was the result of mere chance.

During the afternoon Bronevsky, Russian Chargé d'Affaires in Berlin, took similar steps, but with no greater success.

In Vienna Prince Kudashev called at the Ministry for Foreign Affairs. He was received by Baron Macchio, Chief of the Political Division. "The great Powers," he said, "have been caught unawares. They should be given an opportunity to consider the basis of the Austrian demands." The Austrian diplomat contented himself with the reply that the note addressed to the Powers had been sent "simply by way of information." "What we do concerns no one but ourselves and Serbia."[3] And Count Berchtold gave his entire approval to this declaration in a telegram on the same day.

At six o'clock on the evening of the twenty-fifth, when the time limit allowed the Belgrade Government by the Austrian ultimatum had expired, the German policy of "localization" had been maintained without a single concession. But the brusque methods of Austrian diplomacy had not prevented the Serbian Government from seeking and receiving counsel from the other Powers.

On the evening of the twenty-third the Serbian Minister for Foreign Affairs had informed his diplomatic representa-

1 Germ. Doc., 164, p. 190.
2 Germ. Doc., 171, p. 195.
3 Dipl. Pap., II, 29 and 30.

tives that the demands could not be accepted "in their entirety." Prince Alexander, heir apparent, had approached the Tsar to ask for his protection: "We are prepared to accept those of the Austro-Hungarian conditions which are compatible with the position of an independent State, as well as those to which Your Majesty may advise us to agree."[4] The representative of the Belgrade Government in St. Petersburg had had an interview with M. Sazonov on the evening of the twenty-fourth, and the latter had advised "the greatest moderation" in the reply to the ultimatum, according to the Journal of the Ministry for Foreign Affairs. But Russia did not feel that the reply could be favorable. On the same evening M. Sazonov sent word to the Serbian Government to make no resistance to an attack by Austria, since there could not be the slightest doubt about the outcome of such a struggle. He advised Serbia simply to make "an appeal to the Great Powers."[5]

M. Vesnić, Serbian Minister in Paris, had secured the opinion of M. Berthelot "from a purely personal standpoint." The French diplomat had made two suggestions: first, to try "to gain time." To accomplish this purpose, Serbia might offer immediate satisfaction upon all those points which did not affect her dignity and her sovereignty, and might request to know the result of the Austrian investigation, "in order to verify it with all speed." Secondly, to try "to escape from the direct grip of Austria," by appealing for mediation by the other Powers.[6] It is possible that this advice may have taken more definite form. It has even been

[4] Serbian *Blue Book*, 33 and 37.

[5] Baron Schilling's Journal, *How the War Began in 1914*, Appendix I, p. 86. According to a report made by the Belgian Chargé d'Affaires at St. Petersburg, published in the *Deutsche Allgemeine Zeitung* on 25th May 1919, the Russian Government made it plain to Serbia that she must not give way on those points which concerned her independence or her sovereignty. *Cf.* Bülow, *Die Krisis,* Berlin, Deutsche Verlagsgesellschaft für Politik und Geschichte, 3rd ed., 1922, p. 75.

[6] *Yellow Book,* 26.

suggested that M. Berthelot inspired the very terms of the Serbian reply.

Finally, in London, Sir Edward Grey was of the opinion that Serbia should apologize and express her regret for the conduct of her officials, thus giving entire satisfaction in this regard. "As for the rest, I can only say that the Serbian Government ought to reply in the manner which it feels is demanded by the best interests of Serbia."[7] The Secretary of State did not wish to give any further advice without coming to a full understanding with Russia and France. The English Chargé d'Affaires at Belgrade did not take any further steps because his colleagues of the Triple Entente had not received similar instructions.[8]

To what extent, then, was the Belgrade Government influenced by advice from Russia and France when it drew up its reply to Austria?

II. *The Text of the Reply.*

THE Serbian reply was delivered to the Austrian Minister by M. Pašić a few minutes before the expiration of the time limit. Its tone was moderate, in contrast with that of the Austrian note. It was cleverly composed.

The Serbian Government challenged the accusations bearing on its general attitude. It had not neglected the promises made in the declaration of 31st March 1909. It had made no attempt to modify "the political and legal state of affairs" in Bosnia-Herzegovina, and it had even had occasion, during the Balkan crisis, to make certain sacrifices in the interest of peace. Besides that, Austria-Hungary had had no grounds for any criticism since then, "except one concerning a school book"; upon that point she had re-

---

[7] On the afternoon of 24th July the German Ambassador told Sir Edward Grey that he thought the Serbian reply ought not to be negative, but ought to give, at least "on some points," sufficient satisfaction so that Austria might have an excuse for not taking action immediately. *Brit. Doc.*, 99, p. 78.

[8] Oman, *The Outbreak of the War of 1914-18*, London, H.M. Stationery Office, 1919, p. 40, Grey to Crackanthorpe.

ceived a satisfactory explanation. As for manifestations "of a private character," such as newspaper articles and the activities of certain societies, the Serbian Government had no control over them, and declined to assume even an indirect responsibility for them. In the formal declaration, which it agreed to publish in its *Official Journal*, it therefore replaced the words, "the propaganda directed against Austria-Hungary," by the following, "all propaganda which may be directed against Austria-Hungary."[9]

The note then took up the Austrian demands one by one. Some of them it accepted, including the dissolution of the *Narodna Odbrana* and "every other society which may be directing its efforts against Austria"; the arrest and punishment of the criminals; and the suppression of offensive publications. Each acceptance was accompanied by certain reservations: if the Government promised to dissolve the societies, it did not say that it would confiscate the organs of propaganda; if offenses in the press were to be punished, it would require the passing of a special law and the amending of the Constitution; finally, with regard to the criminals, Ciganović had fled: "It has not yet been possible to arrest him." The Austrian Government, however, came out ahead on all these points, so far as the principle was concerned.

On the other hand, the Serbian reply definitely rejected Point 6 of the ultimatum, namely, the participation of Austro-Hungarian representatives in the inquiry into the Sarajevo crime.[10] The collaboration of such agents in suppressing the "subversive movement" (Point 5) was not wholly discarded, but Serbia accepted it only in so far as it was compatible with "the principles of international law and the friendly relations of a neighbor state."

[9] It is true, however, that it left in the phrase: "sincerely deplores the baneful consequences of these criminal movements," which implied the existence of this propaganda.

[10] It proposed to communicate to Austrian agents, "in certain concrete instances," the results of the inquiry.

The remaining points of the ultimatum were accepted only with definite reserves. With regard to the elimination from the public schools of "everything which might serve to foment propaganda" (Point 3), the dismissal of all army officers guilty of acts hostile to the Dual Monarchy (Point 4), and the official explanation of the remarks made by certain government functionaries (Point 9)—the Serbian Government would wait until Austria had sent it the names and furnished "facts and proofs."

If this reply were not satisfactory, Serbia was prepared to accept "a pacific understanding," and suggested taking the whole matter before the International Tribunal at The Hague. The closing words of the note pointed out that it would be logical to entrust the whole affair to the "great Powers" who had had a share in the Declaration of 1909. Such was the appeal to Europe.

The Austrian Minister hardly took time enough to scan over the reply before declaring it to be unsatisfactory.[11] He left Belgrade at once. The attitude of the Austrian representative corresponded with the intentions at Vienna. Count Berchtold had demanded an acceptance without reserves. He had not obtained it, as Point 6 had been rejected. This fact alone was enough to indicate the move for Baron Giesl to make.

III. *The Nature of the Serbian Reply.*

THE Austro-Hungarian Government thus broke off diplomatic relations with Serbia. The Serbian statesmen had so few illusions upon the subject that they had ordered general mobilization two hours before sending back the reply, and had withdrawn the seat of the government from Belgrade to Niš. In Vienna, upon the arrival of Baron Giesl's tele-

[11] According to the Serbian *Blue Book,* 40 and 41, Baron Giesl received the Serbian reply at 5.45 P.M. and at six he signed the letter breaking off diplomatic relations.

gram, it was immediately decided to mobilize eight army corps.[12] It was no longer a question of referring the matter to The Hague!

The hastiness of these decisions made any attempt at compromise out of the question, but during the afternoon Sir Edward Grey offered a definite suggestion. He had received word from Belgrade that the Serbian reply was to be drawn up in "most conciliatory terms."[13] He hoped that if the note came up to these expectations the Austrian Government might give it a favorable welcome. This desire on the part of Sir Edward Grey was transmitted to the German Government by Lichnowsky[14] and was sent on to Vienna, without comment of any sort, on the night of the twenty-fifth. When the telegram finally reached Berchtold, it was superseded by the course of events.

In a long memorandum, which compared the text of the original note with that of the reply,[15] the Austrian Government attempted to justify its attitude of intransigency. It questioned the sincerity of the Serbian promises, recalled the "captious" formulas by which Serbia sought to reserve "its freedom of action for the future," and emphasized the evasive tone of certain phrases, together with the ingenious reticence of certain others. These arguments have been brought up again quite recently, even in France.[16] The Ser-

[12] With regard to Franz Joseph's attitude at this time, *cf.* Margutti, *Vom alten Kaiser*, Leipzig and Vienna, Leonhardt Verlag, 1921, pp. 402-404.

[13] *Germ. Doc.*, 191 A, p. 206. The information which reached Sir Edward Grey did not mention the rejection of Point 6.

[14] *Germ. Doc.*, 186, p. 203, sent from London 6.09 P.M., received in Berlin 9.25 P.M.

[15] *Dipl. Pap.*, II, 48. This memorandum was drawn up by Musulin, the same official who had prepared the ultimatum. He has given a detailed criticism of the Serbian reply in his book, quoted above, *Das Haus am Ballplatz*, pp. 241-245.

[16] *Cf.* Morhardt, *Les Preuves. Le Crime de Droit Commun. Le Crime Diplomatique*, Paris, Librairie du Travail, 1924, Ch. 5, in particular pp. 87-105. Morhardt goes even further than the Austrian Government went in 1914, and declares that "Serbia definitely rejected, one after the other, *all* the stipulations of the Austrian ultimatum." His bias is self-evident.

bian reply was thus "dilatory and derisory." It is very true
that a careful reading of the text brings out the conditions
and reserves which restrict one part of the note; it was carefully prepared and cleverly worded, and leaves one with a
somewhat different impression from that which comes from a
hasty first reading. But this was not sufficient ground to
justify its wholesale condemnation by the Austrian Government. In 1918 a celebrated German jurist showed how
much of the criticism was exaggerated.[17] When the Vienna
Government, referring to Paragraph 1 of the reply, com-
plained of not knowing how long it would take to pass the
law regarding the press, it was wrong. The Serbian note
clearly indicated that it would be at the next session of the
Skupčina. It could hardly offer more than that. When, in
regard to Point 2, Austria stated that she had received no
guarantee that the dissolved societies would not be formed
again, again she was mistaken, for the Serbian reply had
promised to dissolve any society which *might* work against
Austria. It was quite natural that Serbia should wish to
have definite proof before punishing her officials. Professor
Schücking's analysis proves that Austria ought, perhaps, to
have demanded further explanations, but that she had no
grounds for rejecting the reply outright. "The Hague Tribunal," he added, "might very well have judged the litigious
aspect of the ultimatum. It was a clever move for the Serbian
Government to ask to have the matter submitted for settlement by The Hague." Such is at least the legal view of the
matter.

But this retrospective discussion is really of very little
importance. What must be remembered, from the standpoint
of the evolution of the crisis, is the impression which the
Serbian reply made upon the various statesmen at the time.
Everyone was struck by the moderate character of the re-

---

[17] W. Schücking, *Die völkerrechtliche Lehre des Weltkrieges,* Leipzig,
Veit, 1918.

ply; everyone was astounded by Count Berchtold's intransigent attitude. This was even William II's reaction,[18] and that of his Chancellor was not sensibly different.[19]

The Vienna Government had probably been counting upon this reaction, for it waited as long as possible before sending on the text of the Serbian reply. It took more than forty-eight hours to decide to send it to Berlin.[20]

[18] *Germ. Doc.*, 271, p. 254.

[19] *Germ. Doc.*, 456, p. 380. Bethmann's declaration to the Council of Prussian Ministers on 30th July: ". . . It must be considered that the Serbian reply has been an actual consent to the Austro-Hungarian demands, except in unimportant points."

[20] *Germ. Doc.*, 246, p. 237, and 280, p. 262.

CHAPTER VII

THE FIRST ATTEMPTS AT CONCILIATION

THE nature of the Serbian reply, Austria's refusal to negotiate, and the diplomatic rupture and the mobilization of the two Powers—such were the new elements in the situation which the Entente Powers now had to consider. Should they accept without a protest the uncompromising attitude on the part of Vienna, which, if we may believe a certain document, had received the sanction of the Vatican?[1] Should they tolerate the "punitive expedition"? Should they ignore the appeal which had come to them from the Belgrade Government?

A number of diplomatic "conversations" took place on 26th and 27th July. There was a general exchange of notes, of calls and of suggestions, which crowded one upon the other and sometimes overlapped. One feature, however, was common to them all: whereas the Powers had received enough information about the Serbian reply to permit them to judge of its general tone and content, none of them had as yet actually seen the complete text, which did not arrive in London until noon on the twenty-seventh, nor in Berlin until

---

[1] Baron Ritter, Bavarian Chargé d'Affaires at the Vatican, wired to his Government on 24th July: "The Pope approves of a rigorous attitude toward Serbia on Austria's part. The Cardinal Secretary of State hopes that Austria-Hungary will take her chance this time. He wonders when she will ever be able to fight if she does not take advantage of this opportunity to cut short a movement which has come from the outside, which led to the murder of the Archduke, and which constitutes a real menace to the very existence of the Empire." And the diplomat considered that these statements showed "the fears of the Vatican with regard to Pan-Slavism." *Bayerische Dokumente*, 3rd edition, Appendix, p. 206. This document has been the object of no little discussion. Were these the exact words of the Secretary of State, or were they simply the impressions which Ritter received from his interviews at the Vatican? *Cf.* the correspondence from Rome, published in the Paris *Temps*, 28th September 1923.

that afternoon. This is an important detail which must be kept in mind if we are to understand Germany's attitude.

I. *The Idea of Franco-German Mediation.*

As soon as diplomatic relations were definitely broken off between Austria and Serbia, Germany directed her efforts toward neutralizing the potential influence of Russia, hoping to protect her ally from all outside intervention. With this purpose in mind, she made urgent advances to the French Government in the interest of localizing the conflict.

The Russian Government had addressed a note to the Powers, in which it had stated that "it could not maintain an indifferent attitude" toward the Austro-Serbian conflict.[2] Some action must therefore be taken at St. Petersburg if Germany wished to prevent an extension of the hostilities. This was the attitude of the Wilhelmstrasse which Baron von Schoen was asked to communicate to France on the twenty-sixth.[3]

The Ambassador presented himself at the Quai d'Orsay on that day at five o'clock, and was received by M. Bienvenu-Martin. Austria, he said, was not looking for "territorial acquisitions," nor was she harboring any "designs against the integrity of the Kingdom of Serbia."[4] Further developments of the crisis depended solely upon Russia. "Germany felt herself at one with France in the ardent desire that peace might be maintained," and she hoped that the French Government "would exercise a modifying influence at St. Petersburg."[5] According to Schoen,[6] the suggestion appealed to

2 Russian *Orange Book,* 1914, 10.

3 *Germ. Doc.,* 200, p. 209. Bethmann-Hollweg to Schoen: "The decision as to whether a European war is to take place depends at the present moment upon Russia's action."

4 See above, Ch. V, *in fine,* for the truth of this statement. But Germany did not know of Austria's *secret* intentions.

5 An account of this conversation is given in the *Yellow Book,* 56, and in the *Orange Book,* 28. Complete account in the *Livre Noir,* II, p. 278.

6 *Germ. Doc.,* 235, p. 229. It is also certain that M. Sazonov heard of these remarks and was greatly stirred up by them. See below, p. 106.

M. Bienvenu-Martin. "Speaking for himself, he would gladly be willing to have pacifying influences set to work at St. Petersburg, as soon as Austria gave assurance that no annexation was contemplated." He would of course have to get in touch first with the Premier. He also added that Germany ought "to take similar steps at Vienna," but Schoen refused because, as he said, "that would not appear to be conformable to our view that Austria and Serbia ought to be let alone." "Would Germany at least be willing to permit *concerted* action by the four disinterested Powers, *both* at Vienna and at St. Petersburg?" No, that would be no better, for "the place where influence ought to be exercised was St. Petersburg." The German proposal, when reduced to these terms, was no longer acceptable, and M. Bienvenu-Martin declined it. But Baron von Schoen, who seems to have carried away a pleasant impression of the conversation, did not tell his Government of this refusal. He thought that he noticed indications that France was drifting away from Russia, and he wrote: "M. Bienvenu-Martin confidentially admitted, in the course of the conversation, that Sazonoff's idea that only the Powers as a body were competent to pronounce judgment on Serbia's conduct, would be difficult to uphold legally." Here was another indication of the success of the idea of localization. France's acceptance of the English idea of four-power mediation was still another evidence, as the Russian Chargé d'Affaires was rather annoyed to see.

Baron von Schoen was apparently not discouraged by the first refusal which he had received from M. Bienvenu-Martin, and tried to take advantage of the friendly interest which the French diplomat had shown. He came that evening at seven o'clock to see M. Berthelot, Deputy Political Director of the Ministry for Foreign Affairs, to show him the text of a note intended for the press:[7]

[7] *Yellow Book*, 57.

During the afternoon the German Ambassador and the Minister for Foreign Affairs had a fresh interview, in the course of which, in the most amicable spirit, and acting in an identical spirit of peaceful coöperation, they examined the means which might be employed to maintain general peace.

For these rather "exaggerated" statements M. Berthelot substituted a more moderate form, which contained neither the word "amicable" nor a reference to Franco-German solidarity. Now, these were the very expressions which von Schoen was anxious to have accepted: "Note well the phrase 'in an identical spirit of peaceful co-operation.' This is not an idle phrase, but the sincere expression of the truth," he wrote to M. Berthelot the following morning in a personal letter.[8] He enclosed at the same time a note reproducing the instructions he had received from Berlin, almost word for word:

"The German Government is confident that the French Government, with which it feels at one in its intense desire to maintain the peace of Europe, will exercise all its influence with the Cabinet at St. Petersburg in the interest of peace." But why did Germany, on her side, refuse to exercise a conciliatory influence at Vienna? That was the one point on which M. Berthelot had insisted.[9] And then, too, it would be necessary to await the return of the Premier before making any final decision.

Baron von Schoen wired to Berlin: "I have gained the distinct impression that Viviani's answer will be that he will be willing to exert a pacifying influence at St. Petersburg if we are willing to counsel Vienna to moderation, since Serbia has agreed to almost all the demands."

The Ambassador made a final *démarche* at two o'clock on the twenty-seventh. This time he sent to M. Abel Ferry,

[8] *Yellow Book*, 62. The British Ambassador advised the Foreign Office to ask the French Government to give its formal adherence to the German formula. *Brit. Doc.*, 184, p. 127. The Foreign Office decided, however, that it was better not to interfere.

[9] *Germ. Doc.*, 241, p. 233.

Under-Secretary of State for Foreign Affairs, "a new proposal for Franco-German intervention between Russia and Austria-Hungary."[10] As far as he was concerned, he was prepared to make a concession to the French point of view; he would ask his Government "to join with France in making the same *démarche* with respect to both Vienna and St. Petersburg at the same time." It was thus a kind of Franco-German mediation which was now uppermost in von Schoen's mind. Would the Chancellor have followed the suggestion made by his representative in Paris, had the French Government been willing to accept the same principle? It is very doubtful, for such a step did not correspond with the intentions he had expressed the night before. Baron von Schoen knew this so well that he was careful, at the time, not to inform the Wilhelmstrasse of the interview and of his proposal. It was only when he published his memoirs that he referred to them.[11]

M. Abel Ferry replied simply "that it would be preferable to leave the matter of intervention to the four Powers."

The German proposal of 26th July did not therefore lead to any practical result, as M. Bienvenu-Martin postponed any decision until M. Viviani should return. As a matter of fact, von Schoen never received another reply. To postpone such a step, which could be useful only if taken immediately, was equivalent to declining it.

From the German point of view, the Paris Government was responsible for the failure of this attempt at conciliation, "by refusing to caution Russia against making a fatal venture."[12] Romberg, in a well-known booklet,[13] has written

[10] *Cf.* Schoen, *Erlebtes,* Stuttgart and Berlin, Deutsche Verlags-Anstalt, 1921, p. 167 and ff.

[11] Schoen, *Erlebtes,* p. 170, and *Livre Noir,* II, p. 202. According to Isvolsky, the *démarche* was made in the name of the German Government, but this is apparently not true, since the *German Documents* make no reference whatever to it.

[12] Schoen, *Erlebtes,* p. 170.

[13] Romberg, *Die Fälschungen des russischen Orangebuches,* Berlin, de Gruyter, 1922, p. xi of the Preface.

that all the blame should be laid on "the distrustful attitude of France." To tell the truth, M. Bienvenu-Martin did not place much confidence in the offer from Berlin. He felt that its main purpose was "to separate Russia and France," and also, beyond all question, "to shift the responsibility from the shoulders of Germany, who had thus made every effort to maintain peace."[14] Was he justified in this opinion?

It is certain that the first steps taken by the French Ministry for Foreign Affairs caused the Russian Government no little uneasiness. When M. Bienvenu-Martin seemed inclined to favor the idea of approaching the allied government, M. Sazonov protested vigorously, and referred to a possible "misunderstanding": "If it means that France will try to exert a moderating influence at St. Petersburg, we reject it in advance, since we adopted at the start an attitude from which we cannot change in the least," he wrote Isvolsky on 27th July.[15]

It is also certain that this very "reaction" was one of the things on which Germany had been counting. A few days before the Austrian ultimatum, Bethmann-Hollweg had issued significant instructions to Roedern, Secretary of State for Alsace-Lorraine. He asked him to avoid doing anything which might give cause for nationalistic agitation. He hoped that France, "burdened at the present time with all sorts of troubles,"[16] would prevent Russia from intervening in the Austro-Hungarian conflict. "If we are successful," he said, "not only in keeping France quiet, but in having St. Petersburg admonished to keep the peace, it would have what would be for us a most favorable effect on the Franco-Russian alliance."[17]

---

[14] Isvolsky to Sazonov, *Livre Noir*, II, p. 282, and *Yellow Book*, 62.

[15] *Orange Book*, 32, completed by Romberg. Incidentally, this telegram arrived too late to have had any influence in postponing the reply to the German offer.

[16] It was just at this time that Mme. Caillaux's trial was starting.

[17] *Germ. Doc.*, 58, p. 120, 16th July.

This note, in my opinion, discloses the true purpose behind the German offer of 26th July.

II. *The Proposal to Hold a Conference.*

AT the very moment that Germany was carrying out this fruitless *démarche*, England had just made a move which was of great importance in the evolution of the crisis. The London Government proposed, on the afternoon of the twenty-sixth, to call together a conference of the great European Powers not directly concerned in the Serbian affair, namely, Germany, France, England, and Italy.[18] A common move should be made at Belgrade, Vienna, and St. Petersburg, demanding that "all active military operations should be suspended pending the results of the conference."[19] In this way Austria would be sure to obtain full satisfaction, as the Foreign Office officials told Lichnowsky: "Serbia would be more apt to give in to the pressure of the Powers and to submit to their united will than to the threats of Austria." But it was absolutely essential "that Serbia's territory should remain unviolated until the question of a conference had been settled, as otherwise every effort would have been in vain, and the world war would be inevitable."[20]

This program indicated an undeniable change and evolution in Sir Edward Grey's mind. Two nights before, when he first took the initiative with his idea of four-power mediation, the British Minister for Foreign Affairs had been con-

---

[18] The decision to send out this note was made, in Sir Edward Grey's absence, by Under-Secretary of State Nicolson, but the note had been prepared in collaboration with the Minister, who had approved of the initiative taken by his subordinate. *Cf.* Grey, *Twenty-five Years, 1892-1916,* London, Hodder & Stoughton, 1925, 2 vols., I, 315.

[19] Grey to Bertie, Rumbold, and Rodd, 3 p.m. 26th July, *Brit. Doc.,* 140, p. 101. The British Government only demanded the suspension of *operations,* and not of *preparations.* In this regard, it should be noted that Austria had informed the Foreign Office, on the previous day, that the rupture with Serbia would mean the beginning of preparations, "not operations." *Brit. Doc.,* 105, p. 84.

[20] *Germ. Doc.,* 236, p. 230. Lichnowsky to Jagow, 26th July, 8.25 p.m., received at Berlin 12.17 p.m., 27th July.

sidering only the possibility of an *Austro-Russian* conflict; it was only with regard to that conflict that he had intended to bend his efforts at conciliation. It had not been a question of intervening between *Austria and Serbia*, and Germany had therefore been quite satisfied. But now things had taken quite a different turn: the Austro-Serbian conflict must be settled by immediate intervention, and the local war there must be prevented from spreading along the Danube and the Save. In a word, Austria should obtain diplomatic satisfaction, but must abandon all hope of military exploits. This new attitude on the part of the Foreign Office was "in direct opposition" to the German policy,[21] which undertook to forbid any interference by the Powers in the open quarrel between Vienna and Belgrade.

The thoughts that may have passed through Sir Edward Grey's mind and the suggestions which may have come to him between the twenty-fourth and the twenty-sixth thus leave considerable room for conjecture. M. Paul Cambon was away from London on the twenty-fifth and the twenty-sixth. Before leaving he had, it is true, spoken in favor of mediation *between Austria and Serbia*, but his advice had not been followed. The known documents record no further attempt on the part of the French Government to exert any influence whatever at this time upon the English Government.[22] Benckendorff, the Russian Ambassador, on the other hand, had

[21] Upon this point, *cf.* the interesting remarks of Veit Valentin, *Deutschlands Aussenpolitik von Bismarcks Abgang bis zum Ende des Weltkrieges,* Berlin, Deutsche Verlagsgesellschaft für Politik und Geschichte, 1921, p. 210.

[22] The reply of the French Government to the proposal made on the twenty-fourth, and sent to Paris on the twenty-fifth, was handed to Sir Francis Bertie only on the twenty-seventh, along with the reply to the new proposal for a conference. *Brit. Doc.,* 194 (enclosure), p. 135. The Minister for Foreign Affairs had meanwhile expressed himself in favor of the idea of common action toward Austria and Russia on the part of England, France, Germany, and Italy. With this end in view, he had sent instructions to M. Jules Cambon. These instructions have not been reproduced in the *Yellow Book,* which simply contains an expression of M. Bienvenu-Martin's approval of the idea. *Cf.* No. 50, 26th July.

not concealed his dislike of the offer of mediation, in the form in which Sir Edward Grey had proposed it on 24th July, but he had not succeeded in discouraging the English Minister.[23]

The Foreign Office did, however, attach considerable importance to a suggestion made by M. Sazonov. The Russian Minister for Foreign Affairs had pointed out to Sir George Buchanan on the twenty-fifth that the obligations assumed by Serbia after the Bosnian crisis in 1908 had been given to all the Powers as a group, and not to Austria alone. It was therefore right that the question should be discussed from an international point of view. "Were Serbia to appeal to the Powers," said M. Sazonov, "Russia would be quite ready to stand aside and leave the question in the hands of England, France, Italy, and Germany."[24] In acknowledging this telegram on the morning of the twenty-sixth, Sir Arthur Nicolson especially noted this proposal, and took the earliest opportunity to convey it to Sir Edward Grey, who was not then in London:

I think that the only hope of avoiding a general conflict would be for us to take advantage at once of the suggestion thrown out by Sazonoff in the second paragraph of Buchanan's telegram, No. 169, which you will receive this morning, and that you should telegraph to Berlin, Paris, and Rome, asking that they shall authorize their Ambassadors here to join you in a Conference to endeavor to find an issue to prevent complications, and that abstention on all sides from active military operations should be requested of Vienna, Serbia and St. Petersburg pending the results of this Conference.[25]

Sir Edward Grey sent word by telegram from his country

[23] *Livre Noir*, II, p. 330. "I have not succeeded in getting Grey to leave aside his mask," wrote Benckendorff. For the interview between Sir Edward Grey and the Ambassador, see *Brit. Doc.*, 132, p. 97.

[24] *Brit. Doc.*, 125, p. 93. Buchanan to Grey, 8 P.M., 25th July, arrived 10.30 P.M.

[25] *Brit. Doc.*, 139, p. 100.

home, giving his approval to Nicolson's plan, and the telegram prepared by the Under-Secretary was immediately communicated to the Powers.

A Russian suggestion thus lay at the origin of the proposal to hold a conference. Why was the suggestion so cordially received at the Foreign Office? Doubtless because the main points in the Serbian reply were now known in London and because the intransigency of Austria stood out so clearly. The hasty rupture of diplomatic relations might lead any day to an Austro-Serbian war; Russian intervention was imminent. In reporting M. Sazonov's proposal, Sir George Buchanan had also added that the Russian Government agreed to the *idea* of partial mobilization.[26] The general situation had thus become much more serious, now that Austria had rejected the Serbian reply. With the crisis taking on such a new aspect, quite a new policy was necessary, and the proposals to hold a conference were felt to answer the new need.

The English Government received unqualified acceptances from Rome and Paris on the twenty-seventh.[27] From St. Petersburg it received an acceptance of the principle which should not, however, take effect immediately. From Berlin there came an absolute refusal.

What Sazonov actually replied was "that he was ready to accept the British proposal or any other proposal of a kind that would bring about a favorable solution of the conflict," but that he preferred first of all to try, by "direct explanations," to find some common ground for negotiations with the Cabinet at Vienna. If these negotiations should fail, he would willingly accept the idea of a conference of the four Powers.[28]

The German Chancellor had already made up his mind

26 See below, Ch. IX, I.
27 *Blue Book*, 42 and 49.
28 *Blue Book*, 53, and *Orange Book*, 32. Corrected text in *Livre Noir*, II, p. 279.

without even consulting the Vienna Government.[29] He wired Lichnowsky at one o'clock on the twenty-seventh: "We could not take part in such a conference, as we should not be able to summon Austria before a European court of justice in her case with Serbia."[30] And he also wired: "We must hold fast to the contention that the Austro-Serbian conflict concerns those two nations alone. Therefore we cannot mediate in the conflict between Austria and Serbia, but possibly later between Austria and Russia."[31] This was the general tone of the reply made to the English Ambassador[32] by Secretary of State Jagow, who was in complete agreement with the Emperor.[33]

It is certain that the Chancellor suspected in advance the verdict which the Powers might render. "No one," wrote Bethmann,[34] "could think of our allowing a German representative to sit at the same conference table with France and England, who are swimming around in Russo-Serbian waters, and with Italy." The decision could not be impartial, and the whole affair would drag on long enough to allow Russia to complete her military preparation. "Such a compromise," he concluded, "appeared to me to be quite impossible."

This decision on Germany's part is far too important to pass over without a careful examination.

Was there any reason for the Chancellor to fear the "partiality" of such a conference? One's first impression is that he was right in guarding against it. An important element,

[29] Cf. Dipl. Pap., II, 84, and Gooss, p. 179.
[30] Germ. Doc., 248, p. 237.
[31] Germ. Doc., 247, p. 237.
[32] Brit. Doc., 185, p. 128, Goschen to Grey.
[33] Cf. the notes made by William II, Germ. Doc., 157, p. 185. ". . . I will not join in it unless Austria expressly asks me to, which is not likely. In vital questions and those of honor, one does not consult with others." This note was written with reference to the idea of four-power mediation, and thus applied a fortiori to the proposal of a conference. It reached Berlin at about midnight on the twenty-sixth.
[34] Betrachtungen, I, pp. 143-146.

however, should be taken into an account just here, namely, the Italian suggestion.

The Chancellor believed that at the Conference Germany would find herself alone, with *three* other states against her. The ill-will of Italy appeared to him almost as a certainty. Perhaps he had good reasons for distrusting the government at Rome. In any case, the Italian Minister for Foreign Affairs had a conference with the German Ambassador on the morning of this same day, 27th July. "Marquis di San Giuliano expresses some hope," wrote Flotow, "that it may yet be possible to prevent the conflict. According to his information—he does not go any further into details—Serbia would be willing to agree to the Austrian demands if they were presented by Europe."[35] By responding to the idea of a conference, the Italian Government thus admitted that common action by the Powers might lead to the satisfaction of all the Austrian demands. This was also the opinion of M. Barrère:[36] "The Marquis di San Giuliano," wrote the French Ambassador, "thinks that Serbia would have acted more wisely if she had accepted the note in its entirety; today he still thinks that this would be the only thing to do, being convinced that Austria will not withdraw any of her claims, and will maintain them, even at the risk of bringing about a general conflagration." Italy's attitude at the proposed conference would thus not have been necessarily unfavorable to the Austro-German point of view. It is true that this message from Flotow did not reach Berlin until early on the afternoon of the twenty-seventh, a few minutes *after* the Chancellor had sent London his telegram of refusal. But it appears that the Wilhelmstrasse did not attach the least importance to it when it did arrive. It was not followed up in any way. William II simply jotted down in the margin the single word, "Rot!"[37]

35 *Germ. Doc.*, 249, p. 239.
36 *Yellow Book,* 72. Sir R. Rodd had gained the same impression. *Blue Book,* 57.
37 England had informed St. Petersburg of the Italian suggestion. M.

But why did Bethmann-Hollweg overlook the dangers involved in such a refusal? Lichnowsky repeated to him over and over again that England would turn very definitely in the direction of the Entente if Germany should reject the attempts at mediation! The Chancellor paid no heed to this advice. He felt that Lichnowsky was echoing only the ideas of Sir Edward Grey, and that Sir Edward Grey was not the whole of England. As a matter of fact, he had just received two highly significant statements about the attitude of the British Government. The Kaiser's brother, Prince Henry, was in London at the time. He had seen King George and had carried away a very pleasant impression of their visit. The King had said to him: "We shall try all we can to keep out of this, and shall remain neutral."[38] This remark had been telegraphed to Berlin at once, on the twenty-sixth, by the Naval Attaché,[39] and it had given Bethmann-Hollweg the feeling that he was now free to act as he chose. Furthermore, Ballin had just returned from his confidential mission to England.[40] He had seen several members of the British Cabinet on the twenty-third and twenty-fourth, and had put the question up to them: "If Russia marches against Austria, then we must fight. If we fight, France must fight. What will England do?" He gave them to understand that Germany would be willing to promise not to annex any

Sazonov replied "that he would agree to anything arranged by the four Powers, provided it was acceptable to Serbia. He could not, he said, be more Serbian than Serbia. Some supplementary statement or explanations would, however, have to be made in order to tone down the sharpness of the ultimatum." *Blue Book,* 78.

[38] *Germ. Doc.,* 374, p. 328.

[39] *Germ. Doc.,* 207, p. 215. Reached Berlin on the afternoon of the twenty-sixth. "King of Great Britain said to Prince Henry of Prussia that England would maintain neutrality in case war should break out between continental Powers." In a second telegram, sent on the twenty-eighth, after the British Admiralty decided to keep the Grand Fleet concentrated, the Naval Attaché repeated the same remark, but added that in his opinion English neutrality would not be maintained when the German armies should become victorious on the continent. *Der Krieg zur See: Der Krieg in der Nordsee,* I, 15.

[40] See above, Ch. V, pp. 75-76.

French territory on the Continent, and would be satisfied with colonial annexations. The British Ministers had not shown themselves very cordial toward his proposals. The possibility of British intervention, thought Ballin, might therefore have to be faced in case of an "unprovoked" attack upon France, or if Belgium's neutrality were violated. The dispositions of the British Government, however, were certainly "very pacific." Had not Mr. Winston Churchill, First Lord of the Admiralty, said to Ballin, just as he was leaving: "My dear friend, don't let us go to war"?[41] Although they did not go quite as far as the statements quoted by the Naval Attaché, Ballin's impressions nevertheless served to reassure the German Government, and to encourage it in standing its ground.

"It may be considered that England is maintaining an attitude of watchful waiting," the Navy General Staff wired on 27th July to Admiral von Spee. This was a profound and significant statement to come from the chiefs of the German Fleet.[42]

Thus the English offer was rejected, but Sir Edward Grey did not feel that the idea had been permanently abandoned. If the situation was not yet ripe for it, he would be willing to wait. "I shall keep the idea in reserve," he wrote to Goschen on the twenty-eighth.[43] Following out the Russian suggestion, he would await the outcome of the direct negotiations between Vienna and St. Petersburg: "I entirely agree that a direct exchange of views between Austria and Russia is the most preferable method of all, and as long as there is a prospect of that taking place I would suspend every other suggestion."[44]

[41] With regard to the Ballin Mission, cf. Huldermann, *Albert Ballin*, Berlin, Stalling, 1922, pp. 299-302. Also Winston Churchill, *The World Crisis*, I, p. 196.

[42] *Der Krieg zur See, Kreuzerkrieg*, I, p. 63. The Navy Staff could never have been said to place much faith in England's neutrality.

[43] *Brit. Doc.*, 223, p. 150, note 44.

[44] *Brit. Doc.*, 218, p. 149.

III. *The Attempt at Direct Negotiation between Vienna and St. Petersburg.*

IT was M. Sazonov who took the initiative in the direct relations between Austria and Russia.[45] Although, immediately after the ultimatum, he had not concealed his uneasiness, he now took quite a different attitude. Pourtalès took pleasure in noting, on the twenty-sixth, that the Russian Government no longer seemed to be insisting that the results of the Austrian inquiry should be submitted to the European Powers.[46]

The news which had reached M. Sazonov from Paris and London probably had something to do with his change of mind. He knew that M. Bienvenu-Martin had accepted the principle of four-power mediation proposed by the British Foreign Office on the twenty-fourth.[47] He himself had twice seen Buchanan, the British Ambassador, who had not been encouraging.[48] How could the Russian Foreign Minister possibly maintain an uncompromising attitude under such conditions, with the western Powers apparently not disposed to back him up?[49]

The Minister extended a warm welcome to Szápáry, the Austrian Ambassador, on the afternoon of the twenty-sixth.[50] "He had not been as careful as he should have been,"

---

[45] But it appears that the suggestion had been made to him by the German Ambassador. *Brit. Doc.*, 271, p. 175.

[46] *Germ. Doc.*, 217, p. 220. See above, Chap. V, p. 88.

[47] *Yellow Book*, 50. See above, Ch. VII, p. 103.

[48] *Blue Book*, 17. *Cf.* also Buchanan, *My Mission to Russia and Other Diplomatic Memories*, London, Cassell, 1923, 2 vols., I, pp. 190-191.

[49] But the advice to enter into direct conversations with Vienna certainly did not come to him from London. The Foreign Office did not seem to place much hope in these negotiations, and was quite irritated by the frequent changes of front at St. Petersburg. *Cf. Brit. Doc.*, 179 (note), p. 126; 207 (note), p. 144; 239, p. 156.

[50] According to Gooss, p. 206, Szápáry made his report to Vienna on the twenty-seventh, and it was on that day that the interview took place. But, according to Pourtalès, *Germ. Doc.*, 238, p. 231, and Sazonov himself, *Orange Book*, 25, it was certainly on the twenty-sixth that they met.

he said, in their earlier conference of the twenty-fourth. He certainly had no great love for the Dual Monarchy, but neither had he any particular sympathy for the Slavs of the Balkans. It was not the aims of the Austro-Hungarian policy that he objected to, so much as the character of the step that had been taken. He therefore proposed that he and Szápáry should read the text of the ultimatum over again together. The only points which appeared wholly unacceptable to him were those "relative to the collaboration of certain dignitaries and officers," whom Austria was to choose at will—points which seemed rather extreme "in their present form." The parties concerned might still come to an agreement on these points, with possible recourse to personal mediation by the King of England or the King of Italy. In this first interview Sazonov did not discuss the terms of the Serbian note, the complete text of which he apparently had not yet seen.[51] The Austrian Ambassador simply made a note of these statements, and did not refer to the position of his Government. He was not authorized "either to discuss the text of the note, or to interpret it." Besides, were not events already progressing rather rapidly? Szápáry intentionally limited himself to vague and lifeless formulas. He was unwilling to assume the responsibility of going any further without consulting Count Berchtold.

But Sazonov knew very well that there was one way to speed up Austria's decisions. He got in touch with Count Pourtalès, informed him of what had taken place, and asked "whether he might be able to make some new proposition."[52] On the following day he insisted that what he really wanted was the coöperation of Germany to ensure the success of his attempt at conciliation. "There must be a way of giving Serbia her deserved lesson, at the same time sparing her

[51] *Brit. Doc.*, 210, p. 145.
[52] *Germ. Doc.*, 238, p. 232; 282, p. 263. On the same day, incidentally, Germany had refused in Paris to counsel Vienna to moderation.

sovereign rights." Count Pourtalès was careful not to make any promises. He knew that for the moment his Government was not inclined to intervene at Vienna. If Russia wished to discuss the question, she must approach Vienna directly.[53]

This offer was made at once. Sazonov now had the full text of the Serbian reply, which he considered satisfactory.[54] The Russian Ambassador in Vienna was instructed to declare that "the Serbian reply might serve as the point of departure for a common agreement," and that, with this end in view, Russia "willingly held out her hand" to Austria. Count Berchtold had already been forewarned by the report which he had received from Count Szápáry.[55]

The Austro-Hungarian Minister for Foreign Affairs immediately rejected the Russian offer. "No one in Austria," he told the Ambassador, "could understand or approve negotiations bearing on the terms of the Serbian reply, at the very moment when we have just declared it to be unacceptable." And he added: "It would be still less possible now, because of the way in which feeling has been rising both in Austria and in Hungary, and, furthermore, war has actually been declared today upon Serbia."[56]

* * * * * * *

The English proposal to hold a conference was thus rejected by Germany and was being held in reserve until the outcome of the direct Austro-Russian negotiations should be known. These negotiations had now come to naught because of Austria's position. Vienna and Berlin were holding firmly to their original idea: the conflict was a local one, which did not concern the rest of Europe.

[53] On the following day, the twenty-eighth, Count Pourtalès also declined the suggestion of the British Ambassador: "I cannot undertake to discuss in any way the actions of Austria." Buchanan, *My Mission to Russia*, I, 198.
[54] *Brit. Doc.*, 208 (note), p. 145. 27th July.
[55] We know of this Russian *démarche* from the account of it which Berchtold sent to Szápáry, *Dipl. Pap.*, II, 95.
[56] *Dipl. Pap.*, II, 95.

In order to mitigate the tone of his refusal, Count Berchtold had introduced a new argument. He now claimed that it was too late! How could the terms of the Serbian reply be discussed when war had actually begun?

Now, the Austrian documents prove that, far from being driven along by the course of events, it was Austria herself who precipitated them. When, on the twenty-fifth, she had issued the order for the mobilization of eight army corps against Serbia,[57] she had named the twenty-eighth as the first day of mobilization. At that time she was therefore not considering the immediate opening of hostilities, as she wanted to wait until her forces were well concentrated. Berchtold asked Conrad on the twenty-sixth: "When do you want us to declare war?" And the Chief of Staff replied that if they wished to have the declaration of war coincide with the opening of hostilities, they would have to wait until the 12th of August. This was too long to wait, in the opinion of the diplomats. As yet, however, there was no hurry. On the morning of the twenty-seventh Count Berchtold wrote to Szögyény: "We will declare war in a few days now."[58] And then the Vienna Government suddenly changed its plans without any warning. On the afternoon of the twenty-seventh, the German Ambassador, Tschirschky, learned that the declaration of war was imminent.[59] Berchtold went to see Emperor Franz Joseph and obtained authorization to send the decisive message the following morning, the twenty-eighth. Why was there such a hurry? Had the Serbs already opened hostilities? Austria would have liked to believe this, but the facts con-

[57] The two corps from Bosnia (XV and XVI), and those of Temesvar (VII), Agram (XIII), Budapest (IV), and Graz (III), besides the VIIIth and IXth from Bohemia, which had been mobilized as a special precaution, because a rising of the Czechs was feared. Two divisions of cavalry were also mobilized.

[58] *Dipl. Pap.*, II, 69.

[59] *Germ. Doc.*, 257, p. 243. Telegram sent at 3.20 P.M., 27th July.

tradicted it.[60] Now it was a question of confronting Europe with a *fait accompli* and "above all of preventing any attempt at intervention." Berchtold stated this to the Emperor very clearly: "I think that a further attempt by the Entente Powers to bring about a peaceful solution of the conflict remains possible only so long as a new situation has not been created by the declaration of war."[61]

When the Austrian Government sent word to the Russian Government that war had been *decided upon* before it had received the *official* offer of negotiation from the Russian Ambassador, it was stating the actual truth.[62] But it neglected to add that it had hastened the rupture with Serbia precisely to cut short any such attempts at conciliation, which Vienna anticipated and even knew of.[63]

Now—and this statement is of no little importance—the German Government did nothing whatever to delay an act that it was wishing for, and had even advised.

On 25th July the Austrian Ambassador at Berlin had wired to Vienna: "I ought to remark that it is generally considered certain here, if Serbia refuses the ultimatum, we will reply *at once* by a declaration of war and then the opening of hostilities."[64]

On the twenty-sixth Jagow received a telegram from his Ambassador informing him of the action of the Austrian Government, which had already been outlined in Berlin by

[60] The first draft of the declaration of war submitted to Franz Joseph alluded to an attack by Serbian troops, "near Temes-Kubin." But this phrase was struck out when the rumor of the attack "was not confirmed." *Cf. Dipl. Pap.* III, 26.

[61] Report to the Emperor, composed by Hoyos and presented by Berchtold on 27th July. *Dipl. Pap.*, II, 78.

[62] *Dipl. Pap.*, III, 16 and 20. Also see *Bayerische Dokumente*, 36.

[63] For it must be remembered that Szápáry's report, whatever Gooss may say, must have reached Vienna on the twenty-seventh, and that, besides, the Austrian Government had already learned of the English proposal through its Ambassador at London. *Dipl. Pap.*, II, 71.

[64] *Dipl. Pap.*, II, 42.

Szögyény.[65] Tschirschky had "warmly supported" the idea of prompt military action.

Finally, on the twenty-seventh, at 4.30 P.M. the Secretary of State was informed that the declaration of war would be sent "tomorrow, or the day after, at the latest."

The decision of the Vienna Government corresponded with the will of Berlin. It is therefore hardly surprising that, upon hearing this news, Germany did nothing to restrain Austria.[66] In the opinion of the British Foreign Office, on the other hand, Austria's action was a matter for grave concern. Abstention from all military operations whatsoever would have been, according to Sir Arthur Nicolson, the only way to avoid the conflict.[67]

[65] *Germ. Doc.*, 213, p. 219. Jagow made no protest, thus indicating that Szögyény had been justified in the impressions which he had sent to Vienna.

[66] The question may be raised whether, at 4.30 on the twenty-seventh, when Germany learned the intentions of the Austrian Government, she actually knew the details of the Serbian reply to the ultimatum. It is impossible to be sure, because, according to the *German Documents*, 270, note 3, p. 250, the hour at which the Serbian Legation in Berlin communicated this text to the German Government is not known. It is only known that this step was taken during the course of the afternoon. But Bethmann knew the general contents of the document, for he wrote to the Emperor, on the morning of the twenty-seventh: "Serbia's answer to the ultimatum, the text of which we have not yet been able to get hold of, is said to agree to nearly all the points."

[67] *Brit. Doc.*, 252 (note), p. 166.

CHAPTER VIII

GERMANY'S "REVERSAL OF POLICY"
(27th-29th July)

U P until the afternoon of the twenty-seventh, when the German Government rejected the English proposal to hold a conference, and when the Austrian Government decided to declare war upon Serbia, so as to cut short any attempt at diplomatic "conversations," the Central Powers had succeeded in holding their ground. They fully realized that the uncompromising manner in which they were carrying out their scheme might lead to intervention by Russia, but both Berlin and Vienna had their eyes fixed upon England. There they felt that they had a virtual promise of neutrality, based upon the declarations which Prince Henry of Prussia had attributed to King George.

On the evening of the twenty-seventh, however, the attitude of the German Government *seemed* to undergo a great change. Whereas it had been rejecting all ideas of negotiation, now it seemed prepared to consider them; whereas it had been jealously protecting Austria against any kind of intervention, now it seemed willing to adopt another point of view. It had said again and again that Austria needed no outsider's advice; now it did not seem quite so sure. The Wilhelmstrasse apparently realized that the scheme of "localization," as it had hoped to apply it, was becoming a dangerous game to play.

This transformation in the German point of view has of course been greatly emphasized by the German historians. There are many references to Germany's "reversal of policy." The events which constitute the early phase of this "reversal" extend over a very short period of time,—thirty-six hours, to be exact—from the evening of the twenty-seventh to the morning of the twenty-ninth. But they have formed the basis for considerable discussion.

I. *The New English Proposal.*

SIR EDWARD GREY had another interview with Prince Lichnowsky on the twenty-seventh, probably a little before noon.[1] The English statesman did not yet know how the Wilhelmstrasse had reacted to his proposal to hold a conference, but he had just seen the full text of the Serbian reply. After thinking the matter over, his opinion was as follows:

Serbia had agreed to the Austrian demands "to an extent such as he would never have believed possible." "It is plain," he went on, "that this compliance on the part of Serbia is to be attributed solely to the pressure exerted from St. Petersburg." It was therefore now Austria's turn to adopt a conciliatory attitude, and to consider the reply "either as entirely satisfactory, or as a foundation for peaceful negotiations." If she should proceed with military operations, and if she should now occupy Belgrade,[2] Russia would consider it as "a direct challenge," and the result would be "the most frightful war that Europe had ever seen." It now lay with Germany to bring pressure to bear upon the Austrian Government, and to see that her more moderate advice should be accepted.

In communicating these statements to Berlin, Lichnowsky devoted a part of his telegram to describing his personal impressions of the interview. "I found the Minister irritated for the first time," he said. "He spoke with great seriousness. . . . I am convinced that in case it should come to war after

[1] *Blue Book,* 46. Lichnowsky's report was wired to Berlin at 1.30 P.M. *Germ. Doc.,* 258, p. 243.
[2] Sir Edward Grey expressed this same opinion to Count Mensdorff, the Austrian Ambassador. *Dipl. Pap.,* II, 72.

all, we should no longer be able to count on British sympathy or British support, as every evidence of ill-will would be seen in Austria's procedure." The Ambassador pressed the point still further in a second telegram, sent a few hours later:[3] England wished above all to maintain "the balance of power by groups." If Austria really intended to crush Serbia, "England, I am certain, would place herself unconditionally by the side of France and Russia, in order to show that she is not willing to permit a moral, or perhaps a military defeat of her group." Furthermore, the British Cabinet had just decided that the Grand Fleet, which was to have been broken up on that very day at the conclusion of its maneuvers, should be kept concentrated, and that all the crews should remain intact. This was certainly an unmistakable sign of warning. Lichnowsky's first telegram, containing Sir Edward Grey's new suggestion, reached Berlin at 4.37 P.M., and the second one at 8.40 P.M. Allowing time for decoding, the Chancellor must have learned of the contents of the earlier one at about seven o'clock, and of the later one at about eleven.[4] Now, at 11.50 P.M. he issued new and significant instructions to Tschirschky, his Ambassador in Vienna. He quoted the statements which Sir Edward Grey had made, in the form in which Lichnowsky had sent them, and pointed out that it would be impossible to reject this new suggestion outright. "By refusing every proposition for mediation, we should be held responsible for the conflagration by the whole world, and be set forth as the original instigators of the war. That would also make our position impossible in our own country, where we must appear as having been forced into

---

[3] *Germ. Doc.*, 265, p. 247, sent at 5.08 P.M.

[4] It is always hard to know just how much time to allow for the work of decodification, which varies with the style of code used, as well as with the length of the message. It is also possible, as Delbrück points out, that Lichnowsky's *second* wire may not have been brought to the attention of the Chancellor by the time he signed the draft of the new instructions to Tschirschky. But he had learned of the *first* telegram some hours before signing it.

the war."[5] He therefore yielded to England's request, and
asked for "the opinion of Count Berchtold." At the same
time, he hastened to notify Lichnowsky: "We have at once
inaugurated a move for mediation at Vienna along the lines
desired by Sir Edward Grey."[6]

It is worth considering for a moment just what the value
of this "move for mediation" amounted to. That Germany
should consent at all to counsel Vienna to moderation was a
new fact and a significant one. Had she not refused, the very
night before, to make a similar move? But this new *démarche*
on Germany's part was indeed a curious one. At heart, Germany had not abandoned her theory of "localization," as
it was still taken for granted that neither Russia nor the
Triple Entente as a whole had any right to intervene between
Austria and Serbia.[7] Vienna and Belgrade were still to be
left at swords' points. For that matter, Germany knew that
Count Berchtold was going to declare war on Serbia the
next morning.[8] Now, the essential precondition of the English proposal was that there should be no military action
taken whatsoever, and yet Bethmann carefully avoided making the least effort to restrain Austria, to persuade her to
postpone definite action, or to advise her to leave her rifles
stacked. This alone makes us question the true motive of
the new *démarche*, which was certainly mild, one might almost say timid! The Chancellor kept strictly within the
limits of his function as mediator. He agreed "to submit
the English proposal to the consideration of the Vienna Cabi-

[5] *Germ. Doc.*, 277, p. 256. The German text reads: ". . . *wo wir als die
zum Kriege Gezwungenen dastehen müssen*."

[6] *Germ. Doc.*, 278, p. 257, 27th July, 11.50 P.M. The Foreign Office was
not, however, deceived as to the extent of this "move." Sir A. Nicolson knew
perfectly well that the German Government had simply passed on the
English proposal to Vienna, and had not added any moderating counsel of
its own. *Brit. Doc.*, 239, p. 157. Letter from Nicolson to Buchanan, 28th
July.

[7] *Germ. Doc.*, 279, p. 261. Bethmann to Lichnowsky, 2 A.M., 28th July.

[8] Tschirschky's telegram, giving this information, reached Berlin on the
twenty-seventh at 4.30 P.M. *Cf.* above, end of Ch. VII, p. 120.

net," but he did not feel called upon to urge its adoption. "Since we have already refused one English proposal for a conference, it is impossible for us to waive *a limine* this English suggestion also . . ." Bethmann's own telegram makes it quite clear that all he wanted was to give some tangible evidence of his good will toward England.

Now, Austria attached but very little importance to this change of front on Germany's part.[9] On the afternoon of the twenty-eighth she went so far as to take official notice of the *démarche*, postponing her reply until later. But she observed, so as to leave no doubt as to her intentions, that the English suggestion had arrived too late, "after the opening of hostilities on the part of Serbia[10] and the ensuing declaration of war."[11] Had she not deliberately precipitated the rupture in order to prevent such attempts at conciliation?

It was not until the following day, the twenty-ninth, that she formulated a definite refusal and sent it to Berlin. "To her great regret," she could not accept the British suggestion, for "the Serbian reply had been superseded already by other events."[12] And Count Berchtold stated even more definitely, in an interview with the British Ambassador,[13] that he could allow "no discussion on the basis of the Serbian note," and that the question would be settled "directly between the two parties immediately concerned."

II. *The Initiative Taken by William II.*

At the very moment when Bethmann-Hollweg, under pressure from England, was giving at least the appearance of

[9] See, below, the discussion bearing on "the Szögyény telegram."

[10] Count Berchtold based this statement on a rumor that the frontier had been violated by the Serbs, a rumor which was later proved to be false. *Cf.* above, Ch. VII, p. 119, note 60.

[11] Tschirschky to the Wilhelmstrasse, 4.55 P.M., 28th July, *Germ. Doc.,* 313, p. 283.

[12] *Germ. Doc.,* 400, p. 348.

[13] *Blue Book,* 62, and *Dipl. Pap.,* II, 90.

yielding to Sir Edward Grey's proposal, the Emperor returned to Germany from his cruise.[14] He did so upon his own initiative, and apparently contrary to the wishes of the Wilhelmstrasse, where it was feared that his return might arouse the suspicions of Europe.[15] The diplomats were doubtless even more apprehensive of the abrupt changes in the imperial temper, which the mere suggestion to keep calm was enough to irritate.[16] So far as we may judge from the *German Documents*, however, the Emperor's presence did not at first aggravate the tension in diplomatic circles. The idea of "localization" was now to fade into the background. To tell the truth, William had never placed much faith in it,[17] and now he apparently felt that the time when this fictitious idea might be of some use was past.

The Imperial Chancellery received a copy of the full text of the Serbian reply at about 9.30 on the evening of the twenty-seventh.[18] Lichnowsky's first telegram doubtless arrived at the same time, but it appears that the Emperor did not learn of these documents immediately.[19] At five o'clock the Chancellor sent a messenger to him with the text of the second telegram from the Ambassador in London.[20] When William II, later in the morning, read and annotated the Serbian reply, he was thus acquainted both with the suggestion of the English Government and with the pessimistic feelings of Lichnowsky.

[14] He arrived, according to Moltke, at 3 P.M. on the twenty-seventh. *Erinnerungen, Briefe, Dokumente, 1877-1916*, Stuttgart, Der Kommende Tag, 1922, p. 381.

[15] *Blue Book*, 33.

[16] *Cf.* William II's note on the margin of a telegram from the Chancellor, *Germ. Doc.*, 197, p. 208.

[17] *Cf.* above, Ch. V, pp. 77-78.

[18] *Germ. Doc.*, 270, p. 250, note 2. The text had been transmitted to the Chancellor by the Serbian Legation during the afternoon.

[19] According to the editors of the *German Documents*, this telegram was not submitted to the Emperor until the next morning.

[20] Jagow had hesitated before sending this document to the Emperor: "Shall this telegram be submitted to His Majesty? It ought hardly to be kept from His Majesty." *Germ. Doc.*, 283, p. 264, note 3.

And the surprising thing is that the Emperor reproached Austria for her uncompromising attitude! "A brilliant performance for a time-limit of only forty-eight hours. This is more than one might have expected!" he noted down in the margin of the Serbian document. "A great moral victory for Vienna, but with it every reason for war drops away, and Giesl might have remained quietly in Belgrade. On the strength of this, *I* should never have ordered mobilization." He at once wrote to Secretary of State Jagow:[21] "I am convinced that on the whole the wishes of the Danube Monarchy have been acceded to. The few reservations that Serbia makes in regard to individual points could, according to my opinion, be settled by negotiation. But it contains the announcement *orbi et urbi* of a capitulation of the most humiliating kind, and as a result every cause for war falls to the ground." The honor of Austria, however, must receive apparent satisfaction, and she must beware of any change in policy: "The Serbs are Orientals, therefore liars, tricksters and masters of evasion." She must therefore have some guaranties: "Austria should receive a hostage (Belgrade), as a guaranty for the enforcement and carrying out of the promises, and should hold it until the conditions had actually been complied with." On this basis, said the Emperor, "I am ready to mediate for peace with Austria. I should refuse any proposals or protests to the contrary by other nations."

William II's proposal was thus quite distinct, both as to spirit and detail, from the English suggestion made on the twenty-seventh, for it implied the occupation of Serbian territory, whereas the declaration made by Sir Edward Grey dismissed in most definite fashion all thought of any military operations. There was, nevertheless, a certain degree of similarity between the two plans. There is no doubt that reading over the Serbian reply played a large part in the Emperor's decision, but it is obvious that he was also influenced by the

[21] *Germ. Doc.*, 293, p. 273.

fear of what might be implied in the new English position.[22]

The Emperor's letter was certainly delivered to Jagow before noon on the twenty-eighth. It took all afternoon, however, to prepare the details of the proposed diplomatic move, to submit them to the Emperor for approval, and to draw up instructions for Ambassador Tschirschky.

Meanwhile the Chancellor received disturbing news about the situation in Austria.[23] The Austrian Government had proclaimed its "territorial disinterestedness" and had told the Powers that it did not wish to *annex* any Serbian territory.[24] And now Count Mensdorff, Austrian Ambassador in London, told his German colleague confidentially of the secret decisions made by the Austro-Hungarian Council of Ministers on 19th July. He admitted that it was Berchtold's intention to make a present of portions of Serbia to certain neighboring Balkan states! Bethmann-Hollweg had not been informed of any such plan as this: "This duplicity of Austria's is intolerable!" he noted on the margin of a telegram. "They refuse to give us information as to their program, and state expressly that Count Hoyos' statements, which alluded to a partition of Serbia, were a purely personal expression.[25] At St. Petersburg they are lambs with not a wicked thought in their hearts, and in London their embassy talks of giving away portions of Serbian territory to Bulgaria and Albania." The Vienna Government had plans of its own which

22 Although he made no allusion to it in his letter to Jagow, he had Lichnowsky's message before him, as we have seen. Furthermore, it was on the twenty-eighth that Berlin learned of the British Admiralty's decision to keep the Grand Fleet concentrated, instead of allowing it to disperse at the conclusion of the naval maneuvers. Now, official circles in Germany had been looking forward for some days to this strategic moment in the developments. They felt that the decision of the British Government in regard to this vital question would be an extremely significant indication as to British policy. *Der Krieg zur See: Der Krieg in der Nordsee*, I, pp. 8-9.

23 *Germ. Doc.*, 301, p. 276. It reached Berlin at 3.45 P.M. on 28th July.

24 This statement had been made to the Russian Chargé d'Affaires in Vienna on the twenty-fifth, but had not been repeated in St. Petersburg.

25 See above, Ch. III, p. 44.

it was concealing from its ally! Bethmann vented his rage on paper, but did not dare as yet to express it in the form of a telegram to Vienna.[26] But this incident was enough to keep him from being led along any longer "in tow of Austria," and from blindly supporting Count Berchtold's policy.

This was the spirit in which the Chancellor drew up the telegram to the Ambassador at Vienna, acting under orders from the Emperor:[27]

"The Austro-Hungarian Government," he said, "has left us in the dark concerning its intentions, despite repeated interrogations." Now, the position of Germany was becoming extraordinarily difficult, for, if Austria maintained "a completely uncompromising attitude," while Germany remained exposed to "the mediation and conference proposals of the other Cabinets," how would the Central Powers avoid the responsibility for incurring the conflict? The Vienna Government, renewing its promise not to make any territorial acquisitions in Serbia,[28] ought therefore to declare that it was going to proceed with "a temporary occupation of Belgrade and certain other localities on Serbian territory, in order to force the Serbian Government to a complete fulfilment of its demands." As soon as the Austrian demands should be complied with, evacuation would follow.

Nowhere in the message to Tschirschky was there any question of modifying the conditions imposed by the ultimatum, or of negotiating to induce Serbia to accept the clauses which she had at first rejected. The seizure of territory as a hostage would be "the act of force" which would bring about both Serbia's assent to the demands and her execution of them. Upon this point, Bethmann's démarche did not quite

26 See below, Ch. XVI, p. 305.

27 *Germ. Doc.*, 323, p. 288, 28th July, 10.15 P.M.

28 Here it should be noted that, in spite of the word which he had just received from London, Bethmann did not ask Austria to promise the *absolute territorial integrity* of Serbia, which would have involved giving up any intentions in regard to Bulgaria and Albania.

conform to the desires which William II had expressed that morning. It had but one purpose, namely, to check the nature and extent of the military operations to be undertaken by the army of the Dual Monarchy. Bethmann then took care to humor the ally whom he had just found it necessary to admonish. Germany, he explained, was not going back at all on the plan of action which she had promised to support. But the public opinion of Europe was a force which one could not afford to neglect. Now, if the Central Powers made no concession whatever, they would bring about an inevitable European war. Of course, even now they might not be able to prevent the extension of the conflict, but they should at least do everything in their power to have it come about under the most favorable conditions possible. "It is imperative that the responsibility for the eventual extension of the war among those nations not originally immediately concerned should, under all circumstances, fall on Russia." That was the chief advantage which the Ballplatz would secure by accepting the German point of view.

The Chancellor still feared that this explanation and these high-sounding formulas would not be enough to ensure the complete confidence of Austria. He dreaded the thought of disturbing the closeness of the alliance and of displeasing Count Berchtold. He therefore added a note asking Tschirschky to carry out his instructions with great prudence: "You will have to avoid very carefully giving rise to the impression that we wish to hold Austria back."[29]

But Austria had no intention of allowing herself to be "held back" so easily. Count Berchtold was quite prepared to make a formal declaration of "territorial disinterestedness"; but, "so far as the further declaration with reference to military measures is concerned," he said that he was "not

---

[29] But Bethmann notified Goschen of the move at once, without specifying what security or guaranty Austria might take. *Cf.* Oman, pp. 54-55; and *Brit. Doc.*, 249, p. 164.

in a position to give a reply at once."[30] In spite of his representations as to the urgency of the matter, up to the evening of the twenty-ninth Tschirschky had not succeeded in obtaining any further word from the Ballplatz.

III. *The Szögyény Telegram.*

REDUCED to these terms, the policy of the Central Powers seems quite clear: On two separate occasions the German Government tried to persuade Austria to yield to conciliation, first by communicating to her the English suggestion of 27th July, which implied the cessation of all military operations, and again by proposing on the following day, on its own initiative, the seizure of Serbian territory as a hostage. Despite the weak and feeble character of this counsel, and despite the obvious *arrière pensée*, which lay behind her strategic move, there can be no doubt that the attitude of the Wilhelmstrasse had undergone a change. The Vienna Government, on the contrary, persisted stubbornly in its uncompromising attitude. It rejected outright the terms of the first *démarche*, and it evaded the second. Such, then, were the relative positions of Austria and Germany up to the evening of 29th July.

Just here is where the famous "Szögyény telegram" comes in.

On 27th July, at 9.15 in the evening, Count Szögyény, Austrian Ambassador in Berlin, sent an account to Vienna of an interview which he had just had with Secretary of State Jagow, and which read in part as follows:[31]

The Secretary of State declared to me in strict confidence:

That the German Government had decided to acquaint Your Excellency shortly with English proposals looking toward possible conciliation.

30 *Germ. Doc.*, 388, p. 341.
31 The American Delegation to the Peace Conference, who revealed the existence of the telegram, published only the first two paragraphs at that time.

That the German Government explicitly assured us that it in no way identified itself with these proposals, that it was even quite opposed to the idea of our considering them, and that it was communicating them to us simply to comply with the request from the English that we should do so.

. . . That, furthermore, the German Government, presented with each new English proposal directed toward Vienna, would declare to her [to England] most formally that it did not in any way give its own support to these requests for intervention, and communicated them to Vienna only to comply with the wishes of England.

England would thus receive formal satisfaction, while at the same time the policy of the Central Powers would continue as unhampered as ever.

As a matter of fact, Jagow added, the German Government had had occasion to apply this very principle on the previous evening, by communicating to Tschirschky another English suggestion, which urged the modification of the ultimatum of the twenty-third, but the German Government had not recommended the adoption of the suggestion, nor even asked to have it sent to Berchtold.

"In this present case, in the same way, the communication of an English suggestion does not necessarily indicate a desire for conciliation on the part of Germany."

Such, then, are the essential passages of the Szögyény telegram, in its complete and authentic form.[32]

There are three important points to be noted in the document:

32 *Dipl. Pap.*, II, 68. The text of the fourth paragraph reads in German as follows: "*Die deutsche Regierung würde übrigens bei jedem einzelnen derartigen Verlangen Englands in Wien demselben auf das ausdrücklichste erklären . . .*"

The interpretation varies somewhat with the meaning given to the word *demselben.*

Now, in the *French* edition of the *Diplomatic Papers* (Vienna, Government Printing Office, 1919), the Austrian Government adopted the following version:

"*Que du reste le gouvernement allemand, en présentant des propositions*

1. Jagow advised the Austrian Government not to accept an English proposal which he was about to communicate to Vienna.

2. He declared that *in the future*, in a similar case, he would explain to the English Government that he did not support the proposal himself, even though he agreed to communicate it to Vienna.

3. He added, finally, that he had already had occasion to take this attitude *on the previous evening*.

Here indeed is evidence which seems rather serious. It was Germany, then, who urged Austria to continue in her uncompromising attitude, and who even went so far as to discourage all mediation.

The German historians have tried their best to destroy the value of this document. Count Szögyény, they say, was very old and mentally quite "feeble." No one, of course, questions the authenticity of the document, but the Ambassador probably did not understand the Secretary of State's remarks, and reported them in a vague and whimsical way. This is the position which they hold, and which they bring in considerable testimony to support. When examined by the Committee of four German experts, in connection with the Peace Conference, Bethmann and Jagow strenuously denied the statements which Szögyény attributed to them in the first two paragraphs of the telegram. But this denial can hardly be taken as final, especially as the Austrian Ambassador was not present to uphold his side of the case. The former Secretary of State now also claims that he had always had his own opinion of the real value of the old diplomat's

anglaises de ce genre à Vienna, accompagnerait chacune d'elles de la déclaration la plus formelle. . . ."

The word *demselben* was thus taken to mean "to Austria."

This is the interpretation which is usually accepted, even in Germany. But Count Montgelas, in the latest edition of his book, *Leitfaden zur Kriegsschuldfrage*, Part IV, Par. 4, has adopted a different version. In his opinion, the word *demselben* referred to *England*. This is the corrected form which has been used above.

intellectual ability: "It was difficult to talk to him, often quite exasperating. . . . Often it was a hard task to make a point clear to him. I wondered a good many times, not without uneasiness, what the old man might be sending back to Vienna in the way of reports." This was an opinion current in Berlin. The historian Hans Delbrück affirms the truth of it, upon the testimony of a number of people.[33]

But one must be careful about too readily accepting these arguments. If Szögyény was really the kind of man they made him out to be, how was it that the Austrian Government kept him at his post? It is perfectly true that his removal was being considered, and that his successor had even been named: he was to be Prince Hohenlohe.[34] But the arrival of the new ambassador had been postponed precisely for the purpose of tiding over the diplomatic crisis. Count Berchtold thus had absolute confidence in Szögyény as a man who could carry on difficult negotiations in a creditable manner.[35] If Jagow was of such a totally different opinion, and if he felt such apprehension, he is the guilty one for having allowed such a condition to continue. Would it not have been easy, had the German Government so desired, to neutralize the effect of Szögyény's presence by arranging for a special envoy, and thus to avoid the necessity of recalling Szögyény, with the disagreeable consequences which that would have involved?

But, say the German historians, the very text of the document itself confirms their view of the matter: its confused and complicated wording presents an incoherent mass of statements which are contradicted by the facts.

It is true that the wording is rather labored and confused,

[33] On this point, see the article by Hans Delbrück in *Preussische Jahrbücher*, June 1919, pp. 487-490.

[34] *Germ. Doc.*, 324, p. 289.

[35] Count Hoyos, as well, after his trip to Berlin on 5th July, did not have the slightest criticism to make of the competence of the Ambassador, whose point of view, he said, he thoroughly approved. *Cf.* Hoyos, p. 80.

and that certain passages do not give the effect of very precise thinking.[36] Szögyény appears to have committed other errors during the course of the crisis.[37] Taken as a whole, however, the document does correspond with the known facts.[38] The English proposal which Jagow advised him to reject was the suggestion made by Sir Edward Grey, which reached Berlin in the middle of the afternoon of the twenty-seventh, and which was sent to Vienna a little before midnight: "to enter upon negotiations on the basis of the Serbian reply."[39] The reference to an earlier proposal concerns the desire expressed by England on the afternoon of the 25th to have the Serbian reply considered as acceptable, in other words, to modify the demands of the ultimatum.[40] The expressed intention of informing London that Germany would not, in the future, lend her support to any efforts at mediation is no more than might be expected. It is certainly consistent with what we know of Jagow's attitude at the time.

There are thus no decisive reasons for accepting the arguments of the German historians, in spite of the doubts which may be raised by certain passages of the text. There is every reason to believe, on the contrary, that the Szögyény telegram did express the prevailing attitude at the Wilhelmstrasse at that time.

This document enables us to conclude that Germany's

[36] Here are two examples: a. Paragraph III indicates that Jagow was "absolutely opposed" to any concession whatever; the last paragraph, which supposedly repeats the preceding declaration, gives it only in a much milder form. b. The idea of sending a note to Tschirschky without giving him instructions to deliver it to Berchtold (Paragraph V) is absurd. England had an ambassador in Vienna!

[37] For instance, with regard to the negotiations with Italy. *Dipl. Pap.*, II, 65; *Germ. Doc.*, 443, p. 373.

[38] The criticism made by Delbrück would appear to be much more justifiable if the original interpretation were adhered to, with *demselben* referring to Austria.

[39] The instructions sent to Tschirschky on the evening of the twenty-seventh, quoted earlier in this chapter, are incidentally quite consistent with Jagow's alleged statements.

[40] See above, Ch. VI, p. 97.

"reversal of policy" had not yet begun on the twenty-seventh. Jagow declared himself opposed to Grey's suggestion, and announced his intention of adhering strictly to the principle of localizing the conflict. It was indeed the German Government which advised Austria to reject the English proposal.

An analysis of the telegram does not permit us to go any further. By the following morning Germany's position had begun to change. Are we justified in thinking that the Szögyény telegram encouraged Austria in her uncompromising attitude during the ensuing days, and that it helped to block the path to later compromises? I think not. The idea of the "seizure of hostage territory" was the basis of all the diplomatic work in Berlin and Vienna between 28th July and 31st July. Now, this idea originated in *Germany*, and was later endorsed by England. Jagow's remarks, on the other hand, concerned only future proposals which should come from *England*. Count Berchtold could not have misinterpreted that. Thus Jagow's advice did not apply to the "seizure of hostage territory" nor to the *"Halt im Belgrad."* The Szögyény telegram simply enables us to fix the exact date of Germany's "reversal."

*   *   *   *   *   *   *

Austria would not hear of any concession, and refused even to discuss the matter. She would not subject her military activity in Serbia to any restrictions or limits. Even the "seizure of hostage territory" apparently did not satisfy her. War was what she wanted, and yet she knew full well that Russia would never stay passive. It was not by an oversight that she declined to consider William II's proposal. Count Berchtold's stubbornness was thus the primary and fundamental fact which overshadowed everything else during these difficult days.

Germany, on the other hand, must be credited with making one move as evidence of her "reversal of policy," namely, the proposal put forward by William II. For the first time the Wilhelmstrasse really tried to reconcile its views with those of the British Foreign Office. For the first time Germany had proposed a solution.

This act on Germany's part was inadequate, however, because it was half-hearted and because it came too late. The *démarche* was made timidly, for fear of giving Austria the impression that Germany wished "to hold her back." The proposal came too late, for the German Government delayed long enough to let its ally declare war upon Serbia, and that was sure to provoke an immediate reply from St. Petersburg.

Germany announced, of course, first to London and later to Paris and St. Petersburg,[41] that she was trying to exert a conciliatory influence upon Vienna,—incidentally neglecting to mention the basis which she had proposed for a compromise. At the very same moment, however, the Powers learned of the Austrian declaration of war upon Serbia. How could they place any confidence in the all too vague promises of the German Government? Germany's actions certainly did not indicate any very sincere desire for peace on her part.

To tell the truth, that was by no means her chief concern. The Emperor's preoccupations were of a quite different nature. Germany was now conscious of a threat on the part of the English Government. Bethmann admits his fear that a general war would be fought under unfavorable conditions for the Central Powers, as it would now mean not only a struggle with the Franco-Russian alliance, but against the Triple Entente. What he hoped to find was some compromise which would satisfy England. If such a compromise should fail, Russia must be made to appear solely responsible.[42]

[41] *Germ. Doc.*, 315, p. 284.

[42] "It is of the greatest importance to put Russia in the position of the guilty party," Bethmann again said to the Prussian Council of Ministers on the thirtieth. *Germ. Doc.*, 456, p. 380.

CHAPTER IX

RUSSIA'S DECISIONS:[1] *PARTIAL MOBILIZATION*
(27th-29th July)

THE position of the Russian Government was quite clear. It had declared immediately after the ultimatum that it could not abandon the Slavs in the Balkans. From 26th July on, it proceeded with military preparations, as both Vienna and Berlin well knew.

I. *The First Steps in Preparation.*

THE conversion of the army from a peace footing to a war footing constituted a preliminary step in Russia, as also in Germany, which preceded actual mobilization. It amounted to a "period of preparation," or a period of "premobiliza-

[1] The following is a brief bibliography:

Dobrorolsky, "La mobilisation de l'armée russe en 1914," *Revue d'histoire de la guerre mondiale*, 1923, No. 1, pp. 53-69 and No. 2, pp. 144-165.

Paléologue, *La Russie des Tsars pendant la Grande Guerre*, Paris, Plon, 1921, Vol. I.

Sukhomlinov, *Erinnerungen*, Berlin, Hobbing, 1924.

Recouly, *Les heures tragiques d'avant-guerre*, Paris, La Renaissance du Livre, 1922.

Hoeniger, *Russlands Vorbereitung zum Weltkrieg auf Grund unveröffentlicher russischer Urkunden*, Berlin, Mittler und Sohn, 1919.

Frantz, *Russlands Eintritt in den Weltkrieg*, Berlin, Deutsche Verlagsgesellschaft für Politik und Geschichte, 1924.

Danilov, "La mobilisation russe en 1914," *Revue d'histoire de la guerre mondiale*, 1923, No. 3, pp. 259-266.

Rodzianko, "Krushenie Imperii, Zapiski predsi͡adatelia Russkoĭ gosudarstvennoĭ dumy," (The Break-up of the Empire, Memoirs of the President of the Russian Duma), *Arkhiv Russkoĭ Revoli͡utsii*, Berlin, Slowo-Verlag, Vol. XVII, 1926, pp. 5-169. There is an English translation, *The Reign of Rasputin: An Empire's Collapse*, London, Philpot, 1927.

Mention should also be made of the articles which have appeared in the magazine, *Die Kriegsschuldfrage*, April 1924, pp. 78-79, and July 1924, pp. 225-231, which contain new information secured from Dobrorolsky and Sukhomlinov. The findings of the Sukhomlinov trial upon this subject were

tion," somewhat analogous to the German *Kriegsgefahrzu-stand*, but wider in its scope.[2]

The army regulation of 2nd March 1913, had defined the steps in premobilization as follows:[3]

The measures under the *first* category included the institution of censorship in the territory governed by the ruling, the dispatch of sealed orders covering all the means of transportation and the appointment of military superintendents for all railway stations, and the setting in order of artillery parks and regimental trains. In addition, in districts close to the frontier, the reservists might be called out for a period of practice,—if the latter were possible within the regular army budget. All available men were kept under the colors, and those on leave were recalled. Each army corps was to buy enough horses to complete its effective strength, and finally the covering troops were to take their positions near the frontier, under pretext of carrying on maneuvers.

The measures under the *second* category included the protection of all railways in the territory. In the zone near the frontier, the reservists should be called out for periods of practice, even if the army budget had not made this possible earlier, and certain defensive measures should be carried out in the vicinity of the great fortresses. These were at least the most important decisions.

In any country most of the steps which have been indicated are quite separate from actual mobilization, and may be carried out *before* the latter is determined upon. Only one of these measures is an act of mobilization, namely, the calling

published in an article in the *Revue d'histoire de la guerre mondiale,* Vol. II, No. 2, 1924, pp. 49-69. Finally, Baron Schilling's Journal has been translated into English under the title, *How the War Began in 1914,* London, Allen & Unwin, 1925.

2 Such was the opinion of the German Military Attaché, Eggeling.

3 *Cf.* Frantz, "Die Kriegsvorbereitungsperiode in Russland," *Die Kriegsschuldfrage,* 2nd year, No. 4, April 1924, pp. 89-98, which gives the text of the regulation.

out of reservists *in excess of what the army budget will permit;*[4] even then, the reservists are called out only in the frontier districts.

Article 6 of the 1913 regulation provided that *premobilization* might be undertaken as a result of a special decision of the Government. "It rests with the Council of Ministers to decide whether, in addition to the measures already outlined, certain other measures ought to be executed during the period of premobilization."

As soon as the Austrian ultimatum was made public, the Russian Government began to consider the military steps which the diplomatic situation might require.

On the afternoon of 24th July, the Council of Ministers gathered at Krasnoe Selo to hear a statement by M. Sazonov.[5] If, as might be expected, Serbia should turn to Russia for advice and perhaps also for assistance, what would the Tsar's Government reply? Assuming that the Serbian Army did not consider its own strength to be adequate, Russia would advise the Belgrade Government not to oppose the invasion by means of armed resistance, but simply to appeal to the Powers. Russia thus did not plan to lend Serbia her immediate military support. The Council of Ministers realized, however, that military intervention might become necessary, and it therefore authorized the Ministries of War and of the Navy "to request His Majesty to consent, if events should require it,[6] to order the mobilization of the four military districts of Kiev, Odessa, Moscow and Kazan,"

[4] The wording of the regulation is as follows: ". . . the calling out of members of the reserve for practice, if these measures (because the regular budget for the current year for army practice and test mobilizations has been exhausted) have not been possible in the first period."

[5] A copy of the minutes of this meeting, belonging to the Archive Department of the Hoover War Library, was published by R. C. Binkley, in *Current History,* January 1926, pp. 531-533.

[6] Mobilization was to be ordered "if Austria should attempt to coerce Serbia by force of arms," according to a communication from St. Petersburg, of which M. Bienvenu-Martin had taken note. *Yellow Book,* 50.

as well as the Black Sea Fleet. This involved the placing on a war footing of the thirteen army corps destined "eventually" to operate against Austria-Hungary. It was, however, only a decision *in principle*, which was not yet to be carried out.[7]

The next morning the Tsar presided over a meeting of the ministers concerned with questions of national defense, having Grand Duke Nicholas with him at the time. The Tsar read the report from the Council through and approved it, after adding a word about the Baltic Fleet as well as the Black Sea Fleet. In addition, a further decision was made after this conference, to be carried out at once. Premobilization measures of the first and second categories were to come into force throughout the whole of European Russia (and not only in the four districts where it was expected that there would be partial mobilization later on). This order was actually given at 3.26 A.M. on 26th July, to be put into execution without a moment's delay. The troops encamped at Krasnoe Selo for maneuvering purposes were ordered to return to their respective cantonments on the evening of the twenty-fifth.[8] At the same time, the cities and governments of St. Petersburg and Moscow were declared to be in a state of siege.

The European Powers were notified of Russia's intentions, but in a slightly different manner in the different capitals. The French Government was informed on the twenty-seventh of the *eventuality* of partial mobilization on Russia's part; M. Paléologue had anticipated this the previous evening.[9] According to this information, as M. Bienvenu-Martin realized, M. Sazonov was still free to continue his negotiations,

---

[7] The Council also authorized the Minister of War to increase his stock of war materials.

[8] Dobrorolsky, *loc. cit.*, and also Hoeniger, pp. 80-81.

[9] The exact wording of the telegram is not known. Did Sukhomlinov tell Paléologue of the mobilization of four *army corps*, or of four *districts? Cf.* Bourgeois and Pagès, *Les origines et les responsabilités de la grande guerre,* Paris, Hachette, 121, pp. 39 and 137.

even if Belgrade should be occupied.[10] England knew that if Austria proceeded with military measures against the Serbs, "Russian mobilization would at any rate have to be carried out."[11] Through General von Chelius, special envoy to the Russian Court, the German Government knew pretty well the state of mind in Russian political circles.[12] It had been officially notified on the twenty-sixth of "certain military precautions" which were being taken. M. Sazonov had told Count Pourtalès that mobilization would follow only in case Austria should adopt "a hostile attitude toward Russia."[13]

"Premobilization" was actually carried out on the 26th, 27th, and 28th of July. German agents besieged their Government with telegrams upon the subject.[14] There were artillery movements at Kiev, the summoning of reservists at Moscow and Odessa, the embarkation of troops at Brest-Litovsk. The German Consul-General at Moscow sent word on the twenty-eighth regarding the transportation of troops on the Volga and the mobilization of aviators. Mines were being laid at the mouth of the Dvina. The Austro-Hungarian Consul at Odessa felt sure that orders for mobilization in the districts of Kiev, Odessa, and Warsaw had already been given, "although not yet published."

To the queries of the German Military Attaché, General Sukhomlinov, the Minister of War, replied with a flat denial that any mobilization had been started: "Not a single horse had been requisitioned, nor a single reservist called out," he declared on the evening of the twenty-sixth, giving his word of honor.[15]

As a matter of fact, the fragmentary and uncertain in-

10 *Yellow Book*, 50.
11 Buchanan to Grey, 24th July, *Blue Book*, 6.
12 *Germ. Doc.*, 291, p. 269.
13 *Germ. Doc.*, 230, p. 226.
14 *Germ. Doc.*, 216, 264, 274, 276, 295.
15 Eggeling, *Die russische Mobilmachung und der Kriegsausbruch*, Oldenburg, Stalling, 1919, p. 26.

formation which reached the ears of the German Government was hardly enough to justify the conclusion that mobilization was actually taking place. "Military reports concerning Russia so far known here only as rumors and not as yet confirmed," Bethmann-Hollweg wired to Vienna.[16] From Moscow as well as from St. Petersburg the German agents reported that the working classes were "strongly opposed" to mobilization, and "determined to obstruct it wherever possible."[17]

II. *The Discussion on 28th July.*

ON the afternoon of the twenty-eighth the news reached St. Petersburg that Austria had declared war upon Serbia. The German Ambassador noticed its immediate effect upon M. Sazonov.[18] At five o'clock the Russian Minister for Foreign Affairs, with his assistant, A. Neratov, called upon General Yanushkevich, Chief of the General Staff.[19] Had not the moment arrived to execute the decisions made on 25th July?

Then it was that the plans of the General Staff entered in. Its opinion was that general mobilization should be ordered at once. Partial mobilization of the thirteen army corps destined to operate against Austria was impossible for technical reasons. The organization of the railway transportation was not adapted for such an eventuality, and the reservists were classified in such a way that the quota for one military district often overlapped the corps of a neighboring district. Finally, the troops from the Moscow region were, in active campaign work, to contribute to the strength of an army which was to group around the corps from the Warsaw region. The whole plan of mobilization was based upon the solidarity of the territorial districts. How could a group of

---

16 *Germ. Doc.*, 299, p. 276.
17 *Germ. Doc.*, 291, p. 271; 295, p. 274.
18 Pourtalès, *Am Scheidewege zwischen Krieg und Frieden,* Charlottenburg, Deutsche Verlagsgesellschaft für Politik und Geschichte, 1919, p. 32.
19 Recouly, p. 158.

only four districts be detached from the whole? That would mean upsetting the whole mechanism. Now, as Austria-Hungary was bound to Germany by a formal treaty, general mobilization would probably follow in the next couple of days, and that would be badly disorganized by ordering only partial mobilization now. And a general war, already declared inevitable in military circles, would then be fought under most unfavorable conditions for the Russian army.[20]

But there were political arguments in favor of partial mobilization on Russia's part. Russia wished above all to prevent any action by Austria in an affair concerning the Balkans, and military measures might furnish just the necessary pressure which would make the Ballplatz consider negotiation, as it had thus far refused to do. In the conference on the twenty-fifth, Sazonov had used the phrase, "military demonstration." That was as far as the Council had, in principle, decided to go. General mobilization, however, would mean quite a different thing, and, besides, had not General Sukhomlinov told General von Chelius, on the previous evening, "in any case, we will not mobilize on the German frontier . . ."? And had not Herr von Jagow stated to M. Jules Cambon that Germany would certainly not take any immediate counter-steps, so long as the Russian preparations were restricted to the Austrian frontier zone? Russia must therefore be careful about placing the whole country upon a war footing! Even if a *general* war were now certain, as M. Sazonov no longer seemed to doubt, it was still important to proceed slowly, if only to keep from antagonizing public opinion in England.[21]

What weight did these various arguments carry during the conference of 28th July? The documents and testimony at

[20] These arguments are given in detail by General Dobrorolsky, at the time chief of the department of mobilization of the General Staff.

[21] Sazonov knew of the declaration which von Jagow had made to Jules Cambon. "It was for this reason," so he told Sir George Buchanan the next day, that he had opposed general mobilization, *Brit. Doc.*, 276, p. 176.

our disposal today do not permit us to know much in detail.[22] But there is no doubt that the two points of view clashed. It is even doubtful whether any agreement was reached at all, for if we may believe the identical testimony of Dobrorolsky and Sukhomlinov *two* mobilization *ukases* were prepared by the General Staff that very evening, one for partial and the other for general mobilization.[23]

The fact that both plans were prepared did not imply that the choice between them had to be made at once. The Tsar's signature had to be obtained, and also the countersignature of the Senate to which the *ukase* was addressed. In addition, the signatures of the Ministers of the Navy, of War, and of the Interior had to appear on the telegram announcing mobilization. Not until all these signatures were obtained could the order actually be sent out. "The signing of the telegram for mobilization did not yet mean the order for mobilization," wrote Sukhomlinov. "It was only the actual despatch of the telegram that brought the order into force."[24]

If such was the case, it is quite possible that *two ukases* were prepared, and both even signed by the Tsar and his ministers. The final choice between the two may have been made at the very last moment, in the light of the most recent news received.

III. *The Moment of Hesitation on 29th July.*

IF we may judge from circumstantial evidence, the two plans for *partial* mobilization and for *general* mobilization still continued for a time to develop side by side.

M. Sazonov now considered that *partial* mobilization, at

22 The best comments are those of Recouly, based upon information furnished by Basili and General Danilov.

23 Dobrorolsky, p. 145.

24 *Die Kriegsschuldfrage*, II, No. 7, July 1924, p. 228. *Cf.* also *Erinnerungen*, p. 361.

least, was a certainty, and he did not hesitate to notify his ambassadors in Paris, London, and Berlin to this effect. "As a consequence of the Austro-Hungarian declaration of war on Serbia, we shall publish tomorrow the mobilization of the army districts of Odessa, Kiev, Moscow and Kazan. . . . Point out the absence of any aggressive intention on Russia's part with regard to Germany. Our ambassador at Vienna has not, for the moment, been recalled." This telegram was sent on the evening of 28th July.[25] A second telegram authorized each of the ambassadors to convey this news to the respective governments where they were stationed.

On the following day, the twenty-ninth, Sazonov himself announced the plans for mobilization to the German and Austrian Ambassadors. Szápáry, who thought that he had noticed signs of hesitation on the part of the Russian Minister in an earlier interview,[26] soon learned "that a *ukase* would be signed that day, giving orders for quite an important mobilization." But, Sazonov was careful to add, these troops would remain "with rifles stacked" until Russia's interests in the Balkans should be threatened.[27] Count Pourtalès received the same assurance: "The Russian army would doubtless be able to remain under arms for weeks to come without crossing the frontier." It was officially announced that the orders for mobilization extended only "to the military districts on the Austrian frontier."[28]

Up until the middle of the afternoon Sazonov made no reference whatever to *general* mobilization.

At the actual moment that Sazonov made these statements, there was still a strong chance that they might turn out to be inaccurate, for throughout the twenty-ninth the

[25] *Livre Noir*, II, p. 283, No. 1539. It was communicated to the British Foreign Office on 29th July. *Brit. Doc.*, 258, p. 169.

[26] *Dipl. Pap.*, III, 16.

[27] *Dipl. Pap.*, III, 19.

[28] *Germ. Doc.*, 343, p. 303.

General Staff was bending every effort toward obtaining its desire, namely, the immediate execution of general mobilization.

Early in the morning Chief of Staff Yanushkevich felt that he could announce at least the probability of general mobilization to the men in charge of the various military districts, and he therefore sent out a kind of "warning telegram": "July 30th will be announced as the first day of our general mobilization. This information will be confirmed later by another telegram."[29] As a matter of fact, the Tsar did consent before long to place his signature on the *ukase*, although no one knows the exact time or the circumstances of his decision. Dobrorolsky, chief of the department of mobilization, declares that he had this order in his hands toward the end of the morning, before noon.[30]

Early in the afternoon Dobrorolsky set about obtaining the signatures of the three ministers. He has given a vivid and dramatic account of these interviews in his book. The Minister of War, so he tells us, felt that the conflict would demand more strength than Russia possessed, but he gave way before the will of the Chief of Staff, and placed all the responsibility upon his shoulders. Maklakov, Minister of the Interior, already saw signs of a revolution: "In our country the war cannot be made popular for the masses of the people. Revolutionary ideas are much more within the reach of the masses than a victory over Germany. But we cannot escape our destiny . . ." Looking up at the ikons over his desk, he solemnly made the sign of the Cross, and signed the *ukase*. But Admiral Grigorovich, Minister of the Navy, was away and would not be back until seven o'clock. At about five o'clock, therefore, Dobrorolsky returned to Staff Headquarters.

Meanwhile Eggeling, the German Military Attaché, had

29 Hoeniger, p. 100.
30 Dobrorolsky, p. 146.

gone to see the Chief of Staff. Yanushkevich gave him his word of honor "that mobilization had not yet been decreed," and even offered to confirm this statement by writing it out. "I considered that I had a perfect right to put such a statement into writing," said the General later, "for no mobilization had taken place up to that moment. I still had the *ukase* for mobilization in my pocket!"[31]

The situation at this particular moment thus appears to have been somewhat as follows: the execution of *partial* mobilization had been announced by the Ministry for Foreign Affairs, to take effect on the following day; while at the very same moment the General Staff was taking steps to have orders given for *general* mobilization. Nothing definite had actually taken place at all.

The *ukase* for general mobilization did not yet bear all the signatures required by the law.

Here is where an important question enters in: if it is true that the order for general mobilization had been signed by the Tsar at the end of the morning, how did it happen that Sazonov did not know of it, and that he made the declarations to the Central Powers which we have just seen? How could General Yanushkevich declare to Eggeling that the Tsar "did not desire any mobilization" on the fronts along the German border? Of course, as a matter of actual fact, the Tsar's signature did not imply that the order for *general* mobilization would have to be issued, for the sovereign had in all probability signed the order for *partial* mobilization as well.[32] The Russian authorities certainly laid themselves open to the charge of wilfully misleading their future

---

[31] This Eggeling-Yanushkevich interview was described by the German Military Attaché in a telegram on the same day. *Germ. Doc.*, 370, p. 323, and later in his own book, pp. 30-31. It was described by the General in the course of the testimony during Sukhomlinov's trial, as reported in the *Novoe Vremïa*.

[32] Dobrorolsky makes no allusion to this. It is quite likely, however, since the telegram ordering partial mobilization was sent at midnight, without any more signatures having to be secured.

enemies, however, when they gave such definite assurance to the Austrian and German representatives.

IV. *The Decision Made on the Afternoon of 29th July.*

TOWARD the end of the afternoon the Russian Government prepared to take the decisive step. The following is the information which has been gathered as to the details of their proceedings:

Dobrorolsky says that he returned to General Headquarters at about five o'clock. He left again two hours later to go and see Admiral Grigorovich, whom he had been unable to find earlier. This call was thus made at about eight o'clock. Meanwhile—the testimony is not exact as to the hour—Dobrorolsky had received orders from Chief of Staff Yanushkevich to take the order for general mobilization to the telegraph office *without any further word,* as soon as he had obtained Grigorovich's signature. A new element thus entered into the situation. Up till now Dobrorolsky had not been authorized to send the telegram; now, on the contrary, a definite *decision* had been made.

According to the Journal of the Ministry for Foreign Affairs, kept by Baron Schilling, Chief of the Cabinet, a conference had actually taken place between the Chief of Staff and the Minister for Foreign Affairs.[33] The exact hour of this interview is not given. It is probable, however, that it took place between 6.30 and 7.30 in the evening.[34] The result of this deliberation is known, however. "Considering that there is little chance that war with Germany can be avoided, it is necessary to prepare in the requisite time for this possibility. No chance must be taken, therefore, of interfering with general mobilization later on, by executing partial mobilization at the present time." The Tsar was in-

[33] The *Journal,* pp. 49-50, also alludes to the presence of Sukhomlinov, who formally denies having been there.
[34] See, below, note 38.

formed by telephone of these decisions, and gave his approval. Things were thus moving in the direction of *general* mobilization.

Finally, there are a number of witnesses and documents which indicate this new attitude on the part of the Russian Government. "The French Ambassador, Paléologue, received a call from M. Basili, Vice Chancellor for Foreign Affairs, from whom he learned that the Russian Government had decided: first, to issue orders that very night for the mobilization of the thirteen army corps that were to be used against Austria-Hungary; and, secondly, to commence general mobilization *in secret*." The Ambassador was quite taken aback: "Would it not be possible, for the moment, to be content with partial mobilization?" "No," said M. Basili, "the question has just been thoroughly examined by our highest military authorities."[35] At the same time, but in a more ambiguous way, M. Sazonov had wired to Paris: ". . . There but remains for us to speed up our armaments and to face the inevitable fact of a war."[36]

When Dobrorolsky states that he was at the telegraph office at about 9.30, where everything was prepared for the dispatch of the order, his statement would therefore appear to be quite trustworthy.

What reasons were there for holding a conference at this time, and what led the Government to make such a definite decision?

All of the documents agree in attributing great influence to a *démarche* made by Pourtalès.[37] Acting under orders from his Government, the German Ambassador called upon M. Sazonov at about six o'clock.[38] "Further continuation of

[35] *La Russie des Tsars*, I, p. 36.

[36] Tel. 1551, *Livre Noir*, II, p. 289.

[37] M. Paléologue's account, Telegram 1551, *Livre Noir*, II, p. 289, and the *Journal* of Baron Schilling.

[38] Pourtalès received his official instructions at 4.35 P.M., and wired the results of his *démarche* to Berlin at eight. Allowing for the work of codi-

Russian mobilization measures," read Bethmann's instructions, "would force us to mobilize, and in that case a European war could scarcely be prevented."[39] This declaration was not in the nature of an *ultimatum*,[40] but it certainly implied a threat on the part of the German Government,[41] since Bethmann had received word from Ambassador Sverbeïev of the Russian decision about partial mobilization before sending the telegram under discussion.[42] The German Government thus attempted to persuade Russia to abandon a line of action of which she had already notified the other Powers. Pourtalès' move was apparently in answer to the communication made by Sverbeïev. As the Tsar's Government had no intention of yielding to Germany's desire and giving up the measures which it had announced, it must henceforth count on the hostility of Germany. That is why the conference on the twenty-ninth, as soon as it met, immediately faced the necessity of *general* mobilization.

Was it actually planned to carry out general mobilization in secret, without publishing a *ukase?* This would be hard to believe, for such an order cannot be kept confidential. If M. Basili gave that impression to M. Paléologue, it was simply to avoid surprising him too much. And it is altogether possible that the military chiefs used the same strategem in approaching the Tsar.[43]

fication, it is logical to assume that his call was made at about six, despite the statement to the contrary in the *Journal*. He himself said that it was between six and seven.

39 *Germ. Doc.*, 342, p. 302.

40 Although M. Viviani said that it was.

41 Although Pourtalès wrote: "There was no threat involved, as it was simply a friendly declaration."

42 It was on the previous evening, as we have seen, that Sazonov had informed his Ambassador in Berlin of the decision about partial mobilization, and had instructed him to notify the German Government that it would probably be carried out the next day. Ambassador Sverbeïev made this *démarche* during the morning, or at least St. Petersburg had every reason to think so.

43 See below, Ch. XI, p. 209.

V. *The Tsar's Change of Mind.*

JUST as the order was about to be sent out, the Tsar suddenly checked himself. He had given his consent reluctantly, and now, at the last moment, he broke away from the influence of the General Staff and opposed the sending of the telegram.

There is not the slightest doubt about the facts, for the different accounts all agree upon this point.[44] The orders for *general* mobilization were canceled, and it was the order for *partial* mobilization that was sent out the next morning.[45] The charge that the Russian army chiefs "disobeyed" the Tsar, and carried out *general* measures in spite of his formal counter-order, is a lie made up by Sukhomlinov during the trial in 1917, which is contradicted by every other document and every other witness.[46] Sukhomlinov himself has refrained from any further allusion to it in his most recent writings.[47] Only the four districts of Kiev, Odessa, Moscow, and Kazan, therefore, were to be mobilized the next morning.

But the motives which prompted the sovereign to change his mind, and the exact circumstances bearing on the counter-order, are not easy to understand.

The Tsar was extremely anxious to maintain peace. He

[44] Baron Schilling's *Journal,* the testimony of Dobrorolsky, and the memoirs of Paléologue.

[45] The text of the orders sent to Odessa and to Moscow have been published by Hoeniger, pp. 108-109.

[46] During the 1917 trial, Sukhomlinov's statements were not confirmed by Yanushkevich. Dobrorolsky denied them quite categorically; the very idea of disobedience, he said, did not enter anyone's head in 1914. The *secret* execution of general mobilization was impossible, for the Tsar would have learned of it on the very next day. Besides, at 2 A.M. on the morning of the thirtieth, the general in command at Warsaw wired: "The Chief of Staff wired me yesterday that the thirtieth would be indicated as the first day for general mobilization. As this has not happened, we may suppose that there has been some change in the political situation. Would it not be possible to keep me informed as to any such changes?" Hoeniger, p. 40. He had therefore received no orders.

[47] There is no reference to it in his *Erinnerungen.*

communicated his desire to Sazonov in a personal letter on the twenty-seventh.[48] Now, his intimate advisers had felt that the best way to avoid a war between the great Powers might be an exchange of letters between Nicholas II and the German Emperor. Ambassador Pourtalès was informed of this plan and immediately reported it to Berlin.[49] In order to appreciate the Tsar's state of mind, it is necessary first of all to examine this personal correspondence which passed between the two rulers.

The exchange of telegrams began on the night of the twenty-eighth, the first two telegrams crossing each other. The telegram from the Russian Emperor reached the telegraph office of the New Palace at 1.10 A.M. on the twenty-ninth. Nicholas II said that he shared in the "indignation" of public opinion, which could not tolerate the "shameful war" which Austria was conducting against Serbia. He asked the Emperor to restrain his ally. The message sent by William II left the Central Telegraph Office at 1.45 A.M., but was prepared earlier in the evening.[50] It referred to the conciliatory action which the German Government had just taken, with a view to persuading Vienna to agree to "frank negotiations." But of course the Tsar must understand the need for punishing "all the individuals morally responsible" for the Sarajevo crime, and he ought to help the Wilhelmstrasse "to smooth over any difficulties which might arise."

[48] *Livre Noir,* II, p. 283. "For myself, my hope for peace has never died out."

[49] *Germ. Doc.,* 229, p. 226. 8.50 P.M. 26th July.

[50] The Emperor had refused on the twenty-seventh to wire the Tsar, as Bethmann had asked him to do. *Germ. Doc.,* 229, note 3, p. 226. He decided to do so on the evening of the twenty-eighth, and signed the message at 10.15 P.M. The transmission of the telegram was left in the hands of the Wilhelmstrasse, which, when it sent the message to the Central Telegraph Office at 1.45, evidently did not know that a wire from the Tsar had arrived at the telegraph office of the New Palace 35 minutes earlier. The two documents are therefore quite independent of each other. Incidentally, this question is of very little importance, as it is proved that the original *initiative* came from Russian sources, which suggested the whole idea to Pourtalès.

The method of direct "conversation" thus had a definite purpose, and the German diplomats were doubtless planning to profit by it. Many a time in the past William II had entered upon such correspondence with the Tsar. He now hoped that he might exert an appreciable influence upon this weak and timid character, and that his appeals to "monarchical sentiments" might not be without effect. This was precisely the reason for the cordial and conciliatory tone of his telegram, which recalled "the tender friendship which has bound us together so firmly for so many years."

The Tsar was thus led to place absolute confidence, on the afternoon of the twenty-ninth, in the conciliatory intentions of William II. When he learned of the *démarche* carried out on the same day by Count Pourtalès, and of its implications, he was quite surprised. How was this attitude on the part of the Ambassador to be reconciled with the Emperor's message? He decided at once to wire to Berlin:

Thanks for your conciliatory and friendly telegram. Whereas official message presented today by your Ambassador to my Minister was conveyed in a very different tone, I beg you to explain this divergency. It would be right to give over the Austro-Serbian problem to the Hague Conference. I trust in your wisdom and friendship. Your loving,

NICKY.

This message was filed at Peterhof Palace at 8.20 P.M., before Sazonov had seen its text or heard of The Hague suggestion.

Now, at 9.40 P.M. another telegram from William II arrived at Peterhof, which in turn had crossed the Tsar's second telegram.[51]

. . . I think a direct understanding between your Government and Vienna possible and desirable, and, as I already tele-

---

51 *Germ. Doc.*, 359, p. 315, sent at 6.40. The time of its arrival is taken from Schilling's *Journal*, pp. 55-56.

graphed to you, my Government is continuing its exertions to promote it.

Of course, military measures on the part of Russia which would be looked upon by Austria as threatening would precipitate a calamity which we both wish to avoid, and would jeopardize my position as mediator, which I readily accepted on your appeal to my friendship and my help.

WILLY.

Such are the details which enable us to appreciate the Tsar's state of mind. Nicholas II sincerely wished for peace, but he was fearful of compromising Russia's military position. He therefore gave way first to one and then to another conflicting emotion as this famous afternoon drew on. He had absolute confidence in William II. The telegram in which, unknown to Sazonov, he had suggested arbitration, was a proof of that. And yet, almost at the same moment, he gave his approval to the suggestions made by Yanushkevich, under the threat of the statements which had been made by the German Ambassador.[52]

What must his impressions have been when he read the second telegram from Berlin?

William II did not repeat the threat which Count Pourtalès had implied in his remarks to M. Sazonov. He did not say that *Germany* would consider herself threatened by a mobilization directed against *Austria,* and would decide to mobilize in turn. If the Tsar had been irritated by the message which had come from the Ambassador, he was now quite pacified by this second telegram from the Kaiser. He had consented to general mobilization in a moment of anxiety because his counselors had told him that Germany's hostility was no longer a matter of doubt. Now the justification for his action had disappeared.

[52] Perhaps he did not fully realize the importance of his decision, and did not understand that by accepting these suggestions he was ordering general mobilization for *the very next day.* There is no evidence whatever in support of such an idea, however.

Of course, if the Tsar once made a move in this direction, he ought to go still further, and give up even *partial* mobilization. That was what William II asked him to do. But was it sufficient justification for Russia to give up all her plans, now that Germany had spoken in favor of conciliation, and before anyone knew how effective Germany's word would be? Was Germany's promise to intercede at Vienna any guaranty that such intercession would meet with success?[53]

Furthermore, the decision to place thirteen army corps on a war footing had already been communicated to the foreign governments. It followed from the resolutions adopted *in principle* by the Crown Council of 25th July. It would therefore be much more difficult to withdraw that order.

Up to this point the interpretation of what took place has been based upon contemporary documents; now we come to the action taken by the Tsar, judging from the testimony given during the Sukhomlinov trial in 1917.

". . . At eleven o'clock in the evening," said Yanushkevich,[54] "I received a telephone call from the Emperor. He asked me how far mobilization had gone. I replied that it was already under way. He then asked me a further question: Would it be possible not to order general mobilization, but to replace it by ordering partial mobilization against Austria-Hungary? I replied that that would be extremely difficult, that mobilization had already started, and that 400,000 reservists had been called out.[55] The Tsar then

---

[53] I have pointed out already, Ch. VIII, *in fine* that Austria's declaration of war on Serbia hardly increased the confidence which the Russian Government placed in Germany's "efforts" at Vienna, although Bethmann took care to state that the declaration of war "need make no difference." *Germ. Doc.*, 315, p. 284.

[54] Verbatim report from the *Russkoe Slovo*, quoted in *Revue d'histoire de la guerre mondiale*, II, No. 2, p. 54.

[55] According to the *Rietch'*, quoted in *Revue d'histoire de la guerre mondiale*, II, No. 2, p. 54. "I replied that the chief of the department of mobilization was now sending out the telegrams."

declared to me that he had received a telegram from William II,[56] who gave his word of honor that the relations between Russia and Germany would remain friendly if general mobilization were not decreed."

And the witness added:[57]

I begged the monarch not to cancel the orders for general mobilization. I argued in vain that such a counter-order would throw our whole plan into confusion from top to bottom, and that a new mobilization would not only be slow, but impossible. William's word of honor was enough for him, and he ordered me to announce a partial mobilization.[58]

The account given by M. Paléologue confirms these details, which were communicated to him at quarter before one in the morning.[59]

As for Dobrorolsky, his testimony on the whole corroborates what we have already seen, except in one point, namely, the exact hour at which the Tsar changed his mind. According to him, the counter-order reached the Central Telegraph Office "at about 9.30," at the very moment when the telegram was to be sent out. But this is certainly inaccurate, for the message from William II, to which Dobrorolsky himself attributes the Tsar's new decision,[60] did not arrive until 9.40 P.M.

If all these facts are taken into consideration, the order of development becomes somewhat clearer. The Tsar received

[56] Prince Trubetskoi, who delivered the message to Nicholas, told the German Military Attaché on the next day that "the telegram made a deep impression on the Emperor." *Germ. Doc.*, 445, p. 374.

[57] Account in the *Rietch*.

[58] It was at the advice of Sukhomlinov that the Tsar had telephoned Yanushkevich.

[59] M. Paléologue's position was a curious one. He limited himself, so he writes, to informing Paris of *partial* mobilization. Was it not his duty to keep his Government informed of any incidents of which he knew? It is true that, according to Recouly, p. 61, it was an embassy secretary who took it upon himself to modify the tone of the telegram which had already been composed. But M. Paléologue approved of this procedure.

[60] He incidentally quotes the telegram rather inaccurately.

the Kaiser's telegram at about ten o'clock; a few minutes later he canceled the orders for general mobilization, in spite of the resistance of the army chiefs; but he did not touch the orders for *partial* mobilization, which were therefore sent out about midnight.

*   *   *   *   *   *   *

The uncertainty which still persists in part of this account should not dim our eyes to an appreciation of the essential facts, which are: Russia's *decision* to proceed with partial mobilization, announced to Europe on the evening of 28th July; and the *order* to proceed with mobilization, sent out from St. Petersburg on the night of the twenty-ninth. The plans for *general* mobilization might have had a profound effect upon the evolution of the crisis, had they gone through at this time, or had they even been known. *Actually,* however, no one so much as suspected them until the revelations were made in 1917. The sudden shift in the plans of the Russian Government thus could not have had any influence whatever upon the decisions of the Central Powers. And besides, was not the whole question of mobilization being discussed in Germany as well, on the same day, in the Emperor's immediate *entourage?*[61] Only such decisions as were actually carried into effect, or were known at the time, can possibly be taken into account in a consideration of the relative importance of the steps taken by the various governments.

The fact that Russia was proceeding with partial mobilization against Austria now gave to the Austro-Serbian struggle the character of a European conflict. It was therefore a serious step to take, and one which the Tsar's Government did not decide upon without good reasons. The following analysis is intended to determine the true motives underlying this step, in so far as the documents permit us to judge.

[61] See below, Ch. X, I.

Many of the arguments which have been brought up must be rejected at once by the critic of today.

Was Russia right or wrong in thinking that Austria was making ominous preparations along her Galician frontier? The *Orange Book* for 1914 contains an important document upon this point: "The decree has been signed for Austrian general mobilization," M. Shebeko, Russian Ambassador in Vienna, wired to M. Sazonov on 28th July. This statement was quite untrue on that date. The Russian Government, however, considered it as true and deduced the consequences,[62] so it is claimed. But Sazonov made no allusion to it in his interviews with Szápáry and Count Pourtalès. Furthermore, it now appears certain that the document in the *Orange Book* is quite false.

More accurate information, however, was being reported from other sources about the military preparations which Austria was making along the Russian frontier. M. Dumaine, French Ambassador in Vienna, notified the French Government that "troops were being transported and reservists called out in that region." "The cavalry divisions in Galicia are also mobilizing," he said; the Military Attaché confirmed this report,[63] and M. Bronevsky, Russian Chargé d'Affaires in Berlin, brought the matter to the attention of Herr von Jagow. Whether or not this report was true[64] it was quite sufficient to cause great uneasiness at St. Petersburg.

[62] M. Paléologue heard of this rumor on 29th July. Paléologue, I, p. 35.
[63] *Yellow Book*, 90. See also the unpublished telegram from the Military Attaché, given by Bourgeois and Pagès, p. 41.
[64] Its accuracy is debatable. Conrad flatly denies it. The report of the German General Staff dated on 30th July, however, states that in Austria "a third cavalry division has been mobilized, perhaps the 8th DC, Q.G. Stanislau, south-west of Lemberg." *Cf. Dokumente zür Kriegsschuldfrage,* edited by the "Zentralstelle für Erforschung der Kriegsursachen." The English Military Attaché reported on the twenty-eighth that the Galician corps were not mobilized, but that troops of cavalry destined for the Galician frontier had started from Budapest. *Brit. Doc.,* 251, p. 165. On the twenty-ninth he reported the mobilization of the cavalry at Stanislau. *Brit. Doc.,* 290, p. 184.

But all this information is dated on 29th July; now, the *decision* of the Russian Government had already been communicated to Count Pourtalès before noon on that very day.

Was the news of the bombardment of Belgrade the determining factor in Russia's action? This statement is made quite often, but it is also false. The Russian newspapers did not publish this important news until the morning of the thirtieth,[65] and Sazonov himself had not had any word of it until the twenty-ninth, at the time of his interview with Szápáry.[66] The news about Belgrade was therefore a factor which might have *confirmed* the decisions of the Russian Government, but which could not possibly have *determined them.*

On the other hand, there are certain suggestions which merit a more careful examination. Was not the Russian decision facilitated by some word from Paris or London? Before plunging into the conflict, the Tsar's Government must have sounded out the feelings of its ally and its "friend"!

Sir George Buchanan, British Ambassador at St. Petersburg, was strongly urged by Sazonov, on the twenty-fourth, to obtain from his Government a statement of "its solidarity with Russia and France." If England did not definitely take sides "from the very start," she would thus lend encouragement to the hopes of the Central Powers, and would make war "more probable." The Ambassador had declined this request: "We had no direct interests in Serbia, and public opinion in England would never sanction a war on her behalf"; and Sir Edward Grey had approved his declaration, pointing out, at the same time, that the character of Austria's move at Belgrade would lead "almost inevitably" to the mobilization of Austria and Russia against

---

[65] Paléologue, I, p. 37.
[66] *Dipl. Pap.,* III, 19.

each other.[67] Sazonov was notified to this effect on the twenty-sixth, but the attitude of the Foreign Office was somewhat modified as a consequence of his action. In formulating his proposal of the twenty-sixth for a conference, Sir Edward Grey did not preclude the possibility of Russian mobilization, as the wording which he used simply called for the postponement of all *active* military operations.[68] On the following day he told Benckendorff, Russian Ambassador in London, that it must not be taken for granted that England would keep out of the conflict under all conditions; but he added, on the other hand, that this assurance must not be interpreted as a promise to undertake anything more than diplomatic action.[69] The Russian Government could thus notice certain favorable tendencies at London, in spite of the carefully limited promises made by Sir Edward Grey. Although the English Minister did not yet know the extent of Austria's mobilization, he apparently admitted that it authorized Russia to proceed with measures of partial mobilization. At the same time, Sir George Buchanan still urged Sazonov, on the twenty-sixth, to delay the mobilization orders "as long as possible."[70] He could not give this advice in the name of his Government.[71] And when on the twenty-eighth he learned of the imminence of partial mobilization, he merely cautioned Sazonov against taking "any military measures which might be considered as a challenge by Germany." It would have been difficult, to say the least, for the British Government to give Russia any more urgent advice at a time when it neither wished nor was able to promise its

[67] *Brit. Doc.*, 101, p. 80; 112, p. 86.
[68] See above, Ch. VII, p. 107.
[69] *Orange Book,* 42, and *Brit. Doc.,* 177, p. 125.
[70] *Brit. Doc.,* 170, p. 120, and Paléologue, I, p. 32.
[71] Buchanan, *My Mission to Russia,* I, pp. 196-197. These facts have been analyzed, in a spirit hostile to Sir Edward Grey, by Hermann Lutz, "Greys Mitverantwortung für die russische Mobilmachung," *Die Kriegsschuldfrage,* May 1925, pp. 315-322.

eventual support.[72] M. Sazonov made no secret of the fact, during this interview, that "on the day that Austria crossed the Serbian frontier, the order for mobilization against Austria would be issued."[73] Once that order was actually sent out, Sir George Buchanan apparently gave it his approval. "If Russia had not shown that she was in earnest by ordering mobilization, Austria would have believed that she could go to any lengths, and thus trade on Russia's desire for peace," so he told the German Ambassador.[74]

The relations between Russia and France at this time must also be carefully considered. Had M. Poincaré and M. Viviani made any definite promises to M. Sazonov before leaving St. Petersburg? According to a telegram from the British Ambassador, who alludes to confidential statements made to him by M. Sazonov and M. Paléologue,[75] they had come to an understanding upon the following points:

1. Perfect community of views on the various problems with which the Powers are confronted as regards the maintenance of general peace and balance of power in Europe, more especially in the East.

2. Decision to take action at Vienna[76] with a view to the prevention of a demand for explanations or any summons equivalent to an intervention in the internal affairs of Serbia, which the latter would be justified in regarding as an attack on her sovereignty and independence.

[72] As Sir Edward Grey remarks, if the Russian Government had been urged to give up *all* mobilization, it might well have replied that it would be running a serious risk by delaying its military preparation, and might have asked whether the English Government stood ready to guarantee it against such a risk. Now, Sir Edward Grey was not in a position to make such a promise. Grey, II, p. 336.

[73] *Brit. Doc.*, 247, p. 162.

[74] *Brit. Doc.*, 276, p. 177, 29th July.

[75] *Brit. Doc.*, 101, p. 80, 5.40 P.M., 24th July. "The moment has passed," noted Sir Eyre Crowe, "when it might have been possible to enlist French support in an effort to hold back Russia. It is clear that France and Russia are decided to accept the challenge thrown out to them."

[76] These steps had been taken. See above, Ch. V, p. 82.

3. Solemn affirmation of obligations imposed by the alliance of the two countries.

The Russian Government had thus obtained assurance, at the very outset of the crisis, that it could depend absolutely upon having France live up to the terms of their mutual agreement.

The word from Paris still further confirmed these earlier assurances. M. Isvolsky sent his Government an important message on the twenty-seventh: "I was struck with the degree to which the Minister of Justice and his assistants understood the whole situation and had calmly but firmly decided to give us their whole-hearted support, and to avoid the least appearance of a divergence in point of view."[77] On the same day M. Viviani sent instructions to M. Paléologue from on board the cruiser *France*. In carrying them out on the twenty-eighth, the Ambassador gave his formal promise to M. Sazonov that France would live up to "the obligations of the alliance."[78] But he begged the Minister to be prudent: "I beg you not to take any measures on the German front, and to be very careful even on the Austrian front, as long as Germany has not uncovered her real game. The least imprudence on your part would cost us the help of England."[79]

In other words, England and France, although entreating Russia not to alarm *Germany,* did not *definitely* urge M. Sazonov to abandon the mobilization *against Austria.* These shades of difference are all significant. But it does appear certain that neither Paris nor London gave their ap-

[77] *Livre Noir,* No. 195, II, p. 282. The next day Isvolsky reported, No. 198, p. 283, that M. Bienvenu-Martin had never dreamed of exerting "a moderating influence at St. Petersburg." That might be taken as direct encouragement. But the end of the telegram limited the significance of the statement. M. Bienvenu-Martin would not consider "conciliatory action" undertaken at St. Petersburg *alone.* He was willing, however, to have the Powers undertake *simultaneous* action at St. Petersburg and "especially" at Vienna.

[78] These obligations did not require France to mobilize at once if Russia were *the first to mobilize. Cf.* below, Ch. XI, p. 205, note 35.

[79] Paléologue, I, p. 33.

proval in advance to any step whatever, nor gave Russia any direct support, nor urged her on in the slightest degree.

If we then abandon these explanations, no one of which could have accounted for M. Sazonov's action, what motive can be found for the decision of the Russian Government? There is only one left, but that one is beyond all shadow of doubt. It was the news of Austria's declaration of war upon Serbia that decided Russia to proceed with partial mobilization. The German representatives in St. Petersburg clearly recognized this fact. "Up to yesterday," wrote General von Chelius, "all in the *entourage* of the Emperor were filled with the hope of a peaceful outcome; today, since the declaration of war, they consider a *general* war almost *inevitable*."[80] Count Pourtalès' opinion is no less important: "The Minister did not change his mind," he said,[81] "until 28th July, when Russia's threatening attitude failed to prevent Austria from declaring war on Serbia. There is not the slightest doubt that it was this action of the Vienna Cabinet, above all else, which transformed M. Sazonov's whole attitude."

[80] *Germ. Doc.*, 344, p. 304.

[81] In the preface to the German edition of Dobrorolsky's memoirs, *Die Mobilmachung der russischen Armee, 1914*, Berlin, Deutsche Verlagsgesellschaft für Politik und Geschichte, 1922.

CHAPTER X

THE FAILURE OF THE PEACE PROPOSALS
(29th-30th July)

THE orders for Russian partial mobilization were issued quite late on the evening of the twenty-ninth,
but in the afternoon the Central Powers knew of the
decision that had been made, as Sazonov had acquainted
Count Pourtalès with his intentions toward the end of the
morning.[1] It is even probable that Bethmann was formally
notified during the morning by Sverbeïev. Now, intervention by Russia was a factor which transformed the whole
nature of the crisis. Austria would now have sufficient
grounds for mobilizing all the rest of her military forces,
and in two or three days Russian and Austrian troops might
be facing each other in Galicia. It was therefore high time,
and still quite possible, to reach some sort of compromise at
once.

In considering the manner in which Europe reacted to the
idea of Russian partial mobilization, we should start first
of all with Berlin. During the afternoon of the twenty-ninth
and the whole of the thirtieth it was there that the various
lines of diplomatic action intersected, the leading suggestions
up till then being the "seizure of hostage territory," or the
"*Halt im Belgrad*," proposed by William II on the twenty-
eighth, and the maintenance of Serbian sovereignty, which
Russia was strongly supporting.

I. *Bethmann-Hollweg and Military Action.*

BETHMANN-HOLLWEG found himself beset with one great
difficulty on the afternoon of the twenty-ninth, namely, the

[1] See above, Ch. IX, p. 147.

pressure from the military group, who demanded that he should bring matters to an issue as rapidly as possible.

General von Moltke had placed before him a memorandum which outlined the probable course which events would take: Faced with partial mobilization in Russia, Austria would mobilize all her forces. "The moment, however, that Austria mobilizes her whole army, the collision between herself and Russia will become inevitable." Germany would then mobilize, and that would lead to Russian general mobilization, followed by mobilization in France. The German army must therefore be "prepared to take up the war on two fronts." In order that their opponents should not gain a dangerous advantage in their military preparation, "it was of the greatest importance to ascertain as soon as possible whether Russia and France intend to let it come to a war with Germany."[2]

The Austrian General Staff also sent an urgent message to the Chancellor through Ambassador Szögyény. Faced with mobilization in four Russian districts, Austria-Hungary must know at once whether she should retain a considerable part of her strength for use against Serbia, or whether she should direct her main effort against Russia. The General Staff therefore requested Germany to institute "the most extensive counter-measures"—that is to say, general mobilization—as soon as Russia should actually mobilize in the four districts.[3] If Germany agreed to this idea, it might prove useful to point out to Russia that partial mobilization would compel simultaneous counter-measures at Vienna and Berlin. This would be "the best means" to bring her to realize the gravity of the situation.[4]

Both of these statements were prepared when the decisions

[2] *Germ. Doc.*, 349, pp. 306-308, 29th July. Summary of the political situation. No indication is given of the hour at which it was delivered.

[3] It was thus a question of persuading Berlin to make a promise contrary to that which Jagow had given to Russia.

[4] *Germ. Doc.*, 352, p. 310, afternoon of 29th July.

of the Russian Government seemed probable, but were not yet certain. The news which had now arrived from St. Petersburg gave a new significance to the statements issued by the two General Staffs,[5] and offered the military group a chance to exert their direct influence upon the civil authorities. Now, the desire to clear up the situation at once was directly opposed to the exigencies of successful diplomacy.

Actual instances of this clash of interests between the General Staff and the Chancellery cannot be given in any detail, but there is no doubt whatever about the fact. It is attested by Lerchenfeld, the Bavarian diplomat, and by William II himself.[6] A report made by the Bavarian Military Attaché in Berlin, dated on the twenty-ninth, contains some suggestive comments:

I have been under the impression today that there has been a struggle between the Minister of War and the General Staff, on the one hand, and the Chancellor and the Ministry for Foreign Affairs on the other. There is unanimity only upon one point, namely, in their general ill-humor due to the fact that Austria has been so lethargic in her military preparations that it will be another two weeks before she can commence operations.

The Minister of War, supported by the General Staff, strongly desires to take the military steps called for by the strained diplomatic situation, and by the constantly threatening danger of war. The Chief of Staff wishes to go much further; he has thrown all his influence in favor of taking advantage of the exceptionally favorable situation to strike a decisive blow; he points out the fact that France is at the moment in an embarrassing position from the military standpoint, whereas Russia feels if anything too sure of herself; finally, that it is a good

5 Pourtalès' telegram reached Berlin at 2.52 P.M.

6 Lerchenfeld to the Bavarian Government, *Germ. Doc.,* Supp. IV, 15, p. 629, 29th July: "The German Grand General Staff is for counter-measures to correspond, but decision in the matter is still outstanding." *Cf.* also the memoirs of William II, *Ereignisse und Gestalten aus den Jahren 1878-1918,* Leipzig, Koehler, 1922, pp. 210-212.

time of the year, for the harvests are gathered for the most part, and the annual period of military instruction is completed.

The Minister of War and the Chief of Staff had a long conference with the Chancellor this noon, and I hope to learn the results of it this evening.

Faced with these elements urging immediate action, the Chancellor is holding back with all his might, anxious to avoid anything which might lead to similar measures in France and England, and set the whole machine in motion.[7]

It was in Potsdam that the two points of view, representing the military and the civil leaders, clashed in the Emperor's presence on the afternoon of the twenty-ninth. There was no Crown Council on that day, in the sense that the sovereign presided over a gathering of all his ministers. Nor was any decision reached to proceed with mobilization. The rumors echoed by M. Jules Cambon the following day have since been discredited by certain authentic documents.[8] But it is definitely established that the Emperor did receive the Chancellor and the army chiefs (Minister of War Falkenhayn and Chief of Staff Moltke) at 4.30, together with the chief of his Military Cabinet, Lyncker. Later, at 7.15, he received the naval authorities, Admirals Tirpitz, Pohl, and Müller.[9] What took place during these conferences? We can only judge from what followed.

The new situation created by the imminence of Russian partial mobilization was certainly discussed. Tirpitz declares that no question was raised in his presence of decreeing

[7] First published by the pacifist magazine, *Menschheit,* No. 8, and used by R. Grelling, *Revue de Paris,* 15th July 1924, pp. 285-286. The *Bavarian Documents* have confirmed the general tenor of the statement. *Bayerische Dokumente,* Berlin, Oldenbourg, 3rd ed., 1925, pp. 220-221.

[8] Wegerer, "Der angebliche 'Kronrat' der 29. juli 1914," *Die Kriegsschuldfrage,* No. 1, July 1923, pp. 8-12.

[9] These are the hours given in the notebook of Lieutenant-Colonel von Moltke. Admiral Müller also said that the naval chiefs were received separately. Tirpitz has made no statement upon this point.

mobilization or the "state of threatening danger of war." This is also quite possible, for he attended only the meeting of the naval authorities, who may not have known of the divergence of opinion between Moltke and Bethmann. But the matter was certainly taken up at the earlier meeting. The Bavarian Military Attaché knew that the Potsdam conferences were to deal with the question of military action, and he was impatiently awaiting information as to the results of those conferences.

The statements made by Bethmann-Hollweg before the Prussian Council of Ministers the following day enable us to learn approximately what took place. "The military authorities," he said, "expressed the desire that a 'state of threatening danger of war' be proclaimed. But this declaration of a 'state of threatening danger of war' meant mobilization, and that, under present conditions—mobilization on both sides—meant war." Bethmann had therefore "successfully defended before His Majesty the opposing point of view." It was finally decided to confine the immediate action to military protection of the railroads.[10] And the signature of Minister of War Falkenhayn appears at the end of this report of the meeting.

The Chancellor had thus succeeded in carrying his point, for the time being, at least, over the heads of the General Staff.[11] No vital military decision could be made without knowing Vienna's final position with regard to the plans for mediation. "One could not conveniently carry on military and political activities at the same time," insisted Bethmann.

[10] *Germ. Doc.*, 456, pp. 381-382. Minutes of the meeting. *Cf.* also the report by Wenniger, Bavarian military representative in Berlin, 30th July. *Bayerische Dokumente,* 3rd edition, p. 225. He points out that the Emperor was inclined at first to side with the military leaders.

[11] Moltke's insistence is confirmed by Delbrück. *Deutsch-englische Schulddiskussion zwischen Hans Delbrück und J. W. Headlam-Morley,* Berlin, Verlag für Politik und Wirtschaft, 1921, p. 16. The German historian was a friend of the Chancellor's.

Furthermore, the diplomatic situation was also taken into account during the conference at Potsdam. Prince Henry of Prussia had just returned from London, and had sent the Emperor an account of his trip, including King George's remark, ". . . We shall remain neutral. . . ." And the Prince added: "I am convinced that this statement was made in all seriousness, as was also that to the effect that England would remain neutral at the start; but whether she will be able to keep so permanently, I am not able to judge."[12] According to Tirpitz, Prince Henry's impressions were one of the immediate objects for discussion at Potsdam.[13] But they had reference to an interview which was already some days old. It is therefore not surprising that the Emperor's advisers intended to make further advances toward the English Government, to discover more precisely what its actual intentions were.

Certain moves were therefore made in execution of these decisions at Potsdam:

From the military standpoint, Germany contented herself with measures of secondary importance—the recalling of all men on leave, the military protection of railroads, and the construction of emplacements in the fortresses.[14] But the German Government also sent to Brussels, by special messenger, the text of the ultimatum to be handed to the Belgian Government when the time should come.[15] This text was

[12] *Germ. Doc.*, 374, p. 328, 28th July. Prince Henry was also received at Potsdam at 6.10 P.M. on the twenty-ninth.

[13] Jagow was personally inclined to believe that England would stay out of the conflict. *Cf.* Tirpitz, *Erinnerungen*, p. 224.

[14] Germany (Republic), Nationalversammlung, *Beilagen zu den Stenographischen Berichten über die öffentlichen Verhandlungen des Untersuchungsausschusses, I Unterausschuss, zur Vorgeschichte des Weltkrieges, Heft 2, Militärische Rüstungen und Mobilmachungen*, Berlin, Norddeutschen Buchdruckerei und Verlagsanstalt, 1921, p. 12. These measures were identical with some of those implied by Russian *pre-mobilization*. But the English Military Attaché in Berlin reported considerable transportation of troops on the following day. *Brit. Doc.*, 313, p. 198.

[15] *Germ. Doc.*, 375-376. *Cf.* also note 1, attached to this document. The draft prepared by Moltke was slightly altered by Stumm.

drafted by Moltke himself on the twenty-sixth. Instructions were also sent to the Minister at Copenhagen, to be carried out "in the event of the outbreak of war."[16] These instructions had been ready for two days, but it had not thus far seemed urgent to dispatch them. These are a few details which show how the idea of an impending general war was now affecting the attitude of the Wilhelmstrasse.

At the same time, the Chancellor sent for the British Ambassador at about 10.30 p.m., shortly after returning from Potsdam.[17] If war should break out, he asked, could Germany count on the neutrality of England? "We can assure the English Cabinet, on condition of its maintaining a neutral attitude, that we ourselves, in case of a victorious war, seek no territorial acquisitions at the expense of France in Europe." Germany thus reserved the right to annex French colonies. But she gave assurance that she would respect the neutrality of Holland, and she would not penetrate into Belgium unless the operations of French troops compelled her to do so, nor would she violate the integrity of that kingdom. If England should accept this proposal, it might serve as the basis for "a general neutrality agreement in the future, of which it would be premature to discuss the details at the moment."[18] In acknowledging this proposal, Sir Edward Goschen did not conceal his opinion that a favorable response from his Government was highly improbable.[19] This

16 *Germ. Doc.*, 371, p. 324.
17 *Brit. Doc.*, 677, p. 362. Letter from Goschen to Nicolson.
18 *Germ. Doc.*, 373, p. 328. *Brit. Doc.*, 293, p. 185, gives an identical account. It should be pointed out, with regard to the respect for Belgian neutrality, that the German Government stated, in the instructions just sent to the Minister in Brussels, that it had "reliable information relating to the proposed advance of French armed forces along the Meuse, route Givet-Namur." If England had promised to remain neutral, Germany could have fallen back on this argument to justify the entry of her troops into Belgium in the eyes of the British public.
19 *Brit. Doc.*, 293, p. 186.

was the first disillusionment for Germany, which the attitude of the British Government was soon heartily to confirm.[20]

II. *Bethmann-Hollweg and Arbitration.*

"WE are continuing in our efforts with a view to the maintenance of peace," the Chancellor had told the British Ambassador. At that very moment Bethmann found himself presented with a new suggestion. The Tsar's telegram, proposing "to give over the Austro-Serbian problem to the Hague Conference," reached the New Palace at Potsdam at 8.42 P.M.[21]

To tell the truth this proposal had not come altogether without warning. General von Chelius, German Military Attaché at the Russian Court, had had an interview the previous evening with Prince Trubetskoi, who reflected the sentiments of the Tsar's immediate *entourage*. The Prince had made some reference to "the arbitration court at The Hague," and the account of the conversation had reached Berlin early on the twenty-ninth. It was thus evident that the Tsar's suggestion was not the result of a hasty impulse.

The fate of this Russian *démarche*, however, was to be settled at a single stroke. The German Government apparently did not attribute the slightest importance to it whatever. In a note on the margin of the telegram, the Emperor had summed up its value in a single word, "Nonsense!" Upon reading over the Tsar's message, William II jotted down an ironical negative: "Thanks just the same!" Nor was Bethmann any more inclined to accept the proposal. In the instructions sent to Pourtalès during the evening, he

[20] *Brit. Doc.*, 303, p. 193. "You must inform German Chancellor that his proposal that we should bind ourselves to neutrality on such terms cannot for a moment be entertained." This reply was sent from London at 3.30 P.M. on the thirtieth, and reached Bethmann on the morning of the thirty-first.

[21] *Germ. Doc.*, 366, p. 320. See above, Ch. IX, p. 155, for the origin of this suggestion. The question is here considered from the German point of view.

pointed out quite clearly: "Consideration of the Hague Conference would in this case naturally be excluded."[22]

Germany was naturally unwilling to have an international tribunal pass judgment upon the Austrian demands, which would have been hard to defend from a legal point of view. She was therefore averse to any proposal calling for action by The Hague.

She did not have to look far for arguments to justify her attitude. Although Article 38 of the Hague Convention read: "In questions of a judicial nature, and especially in questions concerning the interpretation or application of international conventions, arbitration is recognized by the contracting Powers as the most effective and at the same time the most equitable means of settling difficulties which have not been solved by the means of diplomacy," it had nevertheless been admitted, in discussions at the Hague Conference, that in a case involving the honor or the vital interest of a nation the system of arbitration might be abandoned. Did not this apply to Austria in the present crisis? The Wilhelmstrasse apparently had no intention of allowing the matter to be settled by legal procedure, and Austria consequently took no pains to mitigate the harshness of her rejection of Serbia's reply.

Germany spurned the Tsar's offer with a gesture of disdain.

It was not until much later that she realized the significance of this gesture, and the German historians are still trying today to minimize its importance and true character.

The offer, they say, came from the Tsar alone. The Russian Minister for Foreign Affairs had said nothing about it to Count Pourtalès. That is quite true, but it must also be kept in mind that the German Ambassador had received formal instructions to reject the whole idea, even if M. Sazonov had made any allusion to the offer.

[22] *Germ. Doc.*, 391, p. 342.

The offer came too late, they insist, since it was not made until *after* Russian partial mobilization had been ordered. Quite true, but could not Russia have been asked to give up her plans for mobilization, had the idea been accepted? Even on the following day M. Sazonov declared that he was still ready, under certain conditions, to abandon all military preparations.

Moreover, the German Government, in refusing even to consider the suggestion of arbitration, does not appear to have had in mind any of these objections which have since been raised by the historians.

III. *Bethmann-Hollweg and the "Seizure of Hostage Territory."*

AT the moment when the German Government made this decision, Bethmann had not yet received any reply to the telegram which he had sent to Vienna the previous evening, suggesting the "seizure of hostage territory." He did not know as yet whether Berchtold would be inclined to accept a compromise. But, now that he had succeeded in deferring the measures demanded by the German military group, he was in a position to profit by this delay to bring further conciliatory pressure to bear upon Vienna. After his visit with Sir Edward Goschen, Bethmann realized that it was more important than ever to proceed carefully with regard to England. The news from St. Petersburg, London, and Rome was soon to give him still more reason for apprehension.

The Chancellor knew early in the morning that Austria had not yet followed up the idea of an exchange of views between Vienna and St. Petersburg. Word to this effect had come from Pourtalès.[23] He was thus informed only indirectly

[23] *Germ. Doc.*, 343, p. 303. As a matter of fact, Berchtold had by this time *refused* any exchange of views, but Bethmann did not know that. See above, Ch. VII, p. 117.

of what was taking place at the Ballplatz. Now, according to a telegram from Lichnowsky,[24] Berchtold's attitude had created "a most unpleasant impression" at London. "Unless Austria," Sir Edward Grey had said, "is willing to enter upon a discussion of the Serbian question, a world war is inevitable." And he had gone on to say that it was Germany who should now suggest some plan of mediation.

Furthermore, word had now come from the Serbian Chargé d'Affaires in Rome to the effect that the Belgrade Government was prepared "to accept Points 5 and 6 of the Austrian note," with the reserve that certain explanations should be made "regarding the nature of the participation of the Austrian representatives." This statement had been made to Marquis di San Giuliano on 28th July, and the latter had reported it to London,[25] with the suggestion that the great Powers might interpose to receive Austria's explanation and to advise Serbia to accept "without conditions." Sir Edward Grey had replied to the Italian Government with the request that it should take the matter up with Berlin and Vienna. As far as he was concerned, further diplomatic intervention from London was out of the question, as Berchtold had given him to understand that he would not consider any discussion on the basis of the Serbian note. But the Secretary of State had at once informed the German Ambassador of this new factor in the situation.[26]

Immediately upon the receipt of this news, the German Chancellor sent two telegrams to Vienna, one after the other, asking whether the Austrians were prepared to reply to the

[24] *Germ. Doc.*, 357, p. 313, sent 2.08 P.M., arrived 5.07 P.M. *Cf. Brit. Doc.*, 317, p. 200, in which the phrase used by Lichnowsky does not appear.

[25] *Brit. Doc.*, 231, p. 153, 7.30 P.M., 28th July, arrived 9.45 P.M.

[26] *Brit. Doc.*, 162, p. 116. Sir Edward Grey added a little later that, if mediation were accepted, "he would be able to secure for Austria every possible satisfaction. . . . The Serbs would in any case be punished. . . ." *Germ. Doc.*, 368, p. 322. His attitude was not open to the reproaches made against him by M. Morhardt, pp. 270-273, whose conclusions appear to me entirely false.

proposal he had made on the previous evening.[27] Shortly after midnight he sent off two more telegrams. One informed Tschirschky of the news which had just arrived from St. Petersburg: "Russia claims that neither through Mr. Schebeko nor Count Szapary have the conferences made any headway. Hence we must urgently request, in order to prevent a general catastrophe, or at least to put Russia in the wrong, that Vienna inaugurate and continue with the conferences. . . ."[28] The other repeated Sir Edward Grey's statements, adding: "We consider such compliance on the part of Serbia an appropriate basis for negotiations, if founded on an occupation of a portion of Serbian territory as hostage."[29]

It seems probable, considering the time required for the codification of these messages, that they were drafted at about 10.30. Now, Lichnowsky's telegram was certainly deciphered by about seven o'clock. Why did Bethmann wait for three hours before taking any action? Was it his interview with Sir Edward Goschen that decided him to bring pressure to bear upon Vienna? Upon this point we are reduced to mere conjectures.

When the first pair of telegrams were sent, the Chancellor had just received disturbing news which confirmed the reports that had come to him. From St. Petersburg, word had arrived from Pourtalès that the Vienna Government had replied "with a categoric refusal" to Russia's offer of direct conversations.[30] From Rome, Flotow had reported the complications which were resulting from Austria's obstinacy in regard to compensation for Italy.[31] It was irritating to have

27 *Germ. Doc.*, 377, p. 332, delivered to the Central Telegraph Office at 10.30 P.M.
28 *Germ. Doc.*, 385, p. 340, delivered to the Central Telegraph Office at 12.30 A.M., 30th July.
29 *Germ. Doc.*, 384, p. 339.
30 *Germ. Doc.*, 365, p. 319. Reached the Wilhelmstrasse at 8.29 P.M. The decodification was doubtless completed by eleven o'clock.
31 *Germ. Doc.*, 363, p. 317. Arrived at 8.15 P.M. San Giuliano had declared that "Austria's procedure was against Italian interests."

one's ally so unmanageable! More important still, however, was a second interview which Lichnowsky had had with Sir Edward Grey during the afternoon. The English statesman had repeated his suggestion that Berlin should take a hand in mediation:[32] "It would seem to him to be a suitable basis for mediation if Austria, after occupying Belgrade, for example, or other places, should announce her intentions." This was almost exactly the proposal which William II had made on the morning of the twenty-eighth, and which Bethmann had communicated to Vienna.[33] The Chancellor thus had every reason to feel reassured; England was modifying her views, which were now becoming similar to those held in Germany. But Sir Edward had added a word of grave warning. If Germany and France should become involved in the conflict, "the British Government might, under the circumstances, find itself forced to make up its mind quickly. In that event it would not be practicable to stand aside and wait for any length of time." For the first time, the menace of intervention by England was clearly stated. "England reveals herself in her true colors," exclaimed William II, "at a moment when she thinks that we are caught in the toils, and, so to speak, disposed of! . . . This means that we are to leave Austria in the lurch."[34]

Bethmann did not express his uneasiness quite so vehemently, but he proceeded at once to further negotiations with the Vienna Government. It appears that the Chancellor had already retired when Secretary of State Jagow called to show him the telegrams.[35] He at once wrote out two dispatches, which were sent off at 3 A.M. and which reached Vienna, respectively, at ten o'clock and at noon. He reported

[32] *Germ. Doc.*, 368, p. 321. Sent 6.39 P.M., arrived 9.12 P.M. Also *Brit. Doc.*, 286, p. 182.

[33] It must be kept in mind that when the Wilhelmstrasse informed the Powers of the conciliatory influence which it hoped to exert at Vienna, it had not specified the exact basis of the mediation.

[34] These annotations were not made until 1 P.M. on the thirtieth.

[35] Delbrück, *Deutsch-englische Schulddiskussion*, p. 33.

what Pourtalès had said, and remarked: "The refusal to hold any exchange of opinion with St. Petersburg would be a serious error." He repeated Sir Edward Grey's statements in full, and "urgently and impressively" advised the acceptance of mediation "on the above-mentioned honorable conditions." He also referred to the question of Italy, in regard to which "Vienna seems to disregard our advice." The tone of the telegram had become quite forceful.

"We are, of course, ready to fulfil the obligations of our alliance, but must decline to be drawn into a world conflagration by Vienna, without having any regard paid to our counsel."[36] The Chancellor immediately notified London and St. Petersburg of the steps he had taken. He wired to Lichnowsky:[37] "Kindly thank Sir Edward Grey for his frank explanation, and tell him that we are continuing to mediate in Vienna, and are urgently advising the acceptance of his proposal." To Pourtalès he wired: "Please tell Mr. Sazonoff that we are continuing to mediate; condition, however, would be suspension for the time being of all hostilities against Austria on the part of Russia."[38] Thus he no longer asked the Tsar's Government to abandon partial mobilization, but only "to institute no belligerent conflict with Austria."[39]

Meanwhile a telegram had arrived at the Wilhelmstrasse from Tschirschky. The Austrian Government had finally considered the German proposal of the "seizure of hostage territory," which had been made on the evening of the twenty-eighth, but it could not reply definitely as yet. "So far as the further declaration with reference to military measures is concerned, Count Berchtold says that he is not in a position to give me a reply at once. In spite of my representations

---

36 *Germ. Doc.*, 395, p. 344, and 396, p. 345.

37 *Germ. Doc.*, 393, p. 343, 2.55 A.M.

38 *Germ. Doc.*, 392, p. 343. This telegram confirmed the instructions sent at 11.05 P.M. in response to the news of Russian partial mobilization.

39 This was the result of a correction made by Jagow in the draft of an earlier telegram. *Germ. Doc.*, 380, p. 333.

as to the urgency of the matter, I have up to this evening received no further communication," wired the Ambassador.[40] This was an unpleasant omen.

The Chancellor notified the Emperor on the morning of the thirtieth of what had been taking place. During the night he had taken urgent steps, "in order," he said, "that this episode might be closed one way or another."[41] The Emperor had meanwhile received a telegram from the Tsar confirming the news of partial mobilization in Russia: "The military measures which have now come into force were decided on five days ago for reasons of defense, on account of Austria's preparations." But Nicholas II hoped that these measures would not prevent Germany from exerting "strong pressure" upon Austria.[42] Sazonov had declared to Pourtalès that "the order for mobilization could no longer possibly be retracted."[43] Must these statements be taken to mean that all mediation was out of the question? William II thought so: "I cannot agree to any more mediation, since the Czar who requested it has at the same time secretly mobilized behind my back. It is only a maneuver, in order to hold us back and to increase the start they have already got. My work is at an end!"[44] But the Chancellor still pressed him, urging His Majesty, "so long as no decision has yet been reached at Vienna," not to abandon all thought of mediation. Besides, the *added* fact of Russia's partial mobilization would give Germany a diplomatic advantage of which she should make use. The German Government therefore proposed to undertake new *démarches* at London and St. Petersburg.

The Chancellor telegraphed Lichnowsky at 11.30 on the

[40] *Germ. Doc.*, 388, p. 341. Sent from Vienna at 11.50 P.M., 29th July, arriving at 1.30 A.M.

[41] *Germ. Doc.*, 407, p. 353.

[42] *Germ. Doc.*, 390, p. 342, arrived at 1.45 A.M.

[43] *Germ. Doc.*, 401, p. 349, arrived at 7.15 A.M.

[44] *Germ. Doc.*, 390, p. 342, note.

morning of the thirtieth:[45] "My hope that mediation may still be possible on the basis of the Grey proposal is most seriously imperiled by the Russian mobilization against Austria and by the French preparations for war." Grey must be made to persuade France to give up her war measures, and he must also prevent "any further concentration of Russian troops on the Austrian frontier." What the German Government *now* demanded was the *suspension* of Russian partial mobilization. Incidentally, how was Russia disposed toward the latest English proposal, which called for the "seizure of hostage territory"? This was another point which Sir Edward Grey ought to make quite clear.

At the same time, Prince Henry sent the following telegram to King George, referring to their conversation of the previous Sunday: "If you are really in earnest in your desire to avert this terrible disaster, may I suggest that you use your influence upon France, and also upon Russia, in order to keep those Powers neutral? In my opinion, that would be the most useful thing that could be done."

Now that the first wave of emotion was past, German diplomacy was doing its utmost[46] to draw England over to its side. Sir Edward Grey promised to point out to M. Cambon the natural apprehensions of the German General Staff, although he knew that France was making "no actual war preparations."[47] He also wired at about five o'clock to his Ambassador in St. Petersburg.[48]

On the other hand, the Emperor sent a further personal message to the Tsar early in the afternoon, acting upon the advice of the Chancellor, who had submitted a proposed form

[45] *Germ. Doc.*, 409, p. 355.

[46] Without any great illusions, however, for Bethmann declared before the Prussian Council of Ministers, on the thirtieth, that "any hope based upon England was nil." *Germ. Doc.*, 456, p. 381.

[47] *Germ. Doc.*, 435, p. 370. Sent from London at 4.11 p.m., reaching Berlin at 5.56.

[48] *Germ. Doc.*, 439, p. 371.

for this message.[49] If Russia continued to mobilize against
Austria, the German efforts at Vienna in the interest of
mediation would be "endangered, if not ruined." And William II ended with a strong personal appeal to the Tsar,
over whom he felt that he had a powerful influence: "The
whole weight of the decision lies solely on your shoulders now,
who will have to bear the responsibility for peace or war."[50]

IV. Russia's Attitude.

How did Russia look upon the idea of the "seizure of hostage territory," and of suspending her own preparations in
case Austria should agree to a discussion of the Serbian
affair after occupying Belgrade? M. Sazonov had occasion
to express himself on this very point on the morning of the
thirtieth, during the course of an interview with Count Pourtalès.

Ever since 23rd July Russian policy had been guided by
the following principles: She demanded that the *territorial*
integrity of Serbia should be respected, as well as her *political* integrity, her sovereignty, and her independence.

Upon the first point, the Austrian Government had decided to adopt a conciliatory attitude, after a long period
of hesitation. Szápáry had finally declared the "territorial disinterestedness" of his Government to St. Petersburg on the morning of the twenty-ninth. He had repeated[51]
that Austria did not intend "to annex any Serbian territory."

This declaration did not formally bind Austria. But Germany had decided, on the night of the twenty-ninth, to confirm this promise, and was using her influence at Vienna "to
get the Austro-Hungarian Government to declare formally

[49] *Germ. Doc.*, 408, p. 354. This proposal was considered by the Emperor at about one o'clock.
[50] *Germ. Doc.*, 420, p. 360. The Chancellor notified the Emperor, at 3.30
P.M., that the telegram had been sent.
[51] *Dipl. Pap.*, III, 19.

to Russia once more that it had no idea of territorial acquisitions in Serbia, and that its military measures contemplated solely a temporary occupation."[52]

On the other hand, no progress at all had been made on
the question of Serbian sovereignty. Szápáry had stated
in his interview on the twenty-ninth that his Government
did not wish to make any "attack on Serbian sovereignty."
But Sazonov had argued that the execution of the clauses
of the ultimatum would reduce the kingdom "to the condition of a vassal state."[53] He had also stated his opinion
to Count Pourtalès on the evening of the twenty-ninth:[54]
"Russia's vital interests demanded not only the respecting
of the territorial integrity of Serbia, but also that Serbia
should not sink to the level of a vassal state of Austria, by
the acceptance of Austrian demands that infringed on her
sovereign rights."

M. Sazonov expressed these views once again to Count
Pourtalès in their conversation of the thirtieth. At the Ambassador's request, he decided to formulate in writing the
conditions which he would be inclined to accept.[55] Austria
must recognize that "its conflict with Serbia has assumed the
character of a question of European interest," and must
consent "to eliminate from its ultimatum those points which
infringe on Serbia's sovereign rights." Under such conditions, "Russia agrees to suspend all military preparations."

The idea underlying this formula was the one which M.
Sazonov had so often emphasized. The question of sover-
eignty, in his opinion, was the chief ground of the difference.
No mention was made of the "seizure of hostage territory."
Did this imply a refusal of that idea? It appears not, for

[52] *Germ. Doc.*, 380, p. 333. Instructions sent to Pourtalès before Bethmann knew that London would support his *Halt im Belgrad* formula.

[53] *Dipl. Pap.*, III, 19.

[54] *Germ. Doc.*, 412, p. 356.

[55] *Germ. Doc.*, 421, p. 360. Facsimile in Pourtalès, *Am Scheidewege
zwischen Krieg und Frieden*, p. 52. The statement made by Paléologue, I, p.
37, is incorrect.

M. Sazonov had raised no objection when Count Pourtalès had referred to "a temporary occupation." Furthermore, the formula did not call for the *immediate cessation* of Austrian operations.[56] This was a point, however, which remained to be cleared up, for Russia did not know what "hostage territory" was intended, and did not realize that the Anglo-German proposal called for the occupation of *Belgrade*.

For the rest, M. Sazonov was disposed to promise that Russia "would refrain for the time being from hostilities, in case she receives no provocation from Austria."[57] It is true that, at the very moment when he gave this assurance, M. Sazonov had just got the Tsar to sign the *ukase* for general mobilization.[58] Germany, Austria, and England, however, had not yet learned of this decision, which could not therefore have had any influence whatever upon the replies from those Powers.

How was M. Sazonov's "formula" received in London and Berlin? Ambassador Sverbeïev communicated it to von Jagow at about 5 P.M. on 30th July. The Secretary of State for Foreign Affairs declared at once that he felt it would be "unacceptable" to Austria.[59] At the same hour, Sir Edward Grey expressed his opinion in a telegram to Buchanan.[60] He was no more able than Jagow to give his support to the formula, which called for a direct concession to Russia on Austria's part. He wished the formula to refer to the occupation of Serbian territory, and also to the intervention of the great Powers. He therefore requested Sazonov to alter his wording, and made the following suggestion:

If Austria, *having occupied Belgrade and neighboring Ser-*

---

[56] Pourtalès calls attention to this point.

[57] *Germ. Doc.*, 449, p. 377.

[58] See below, Ch. XI, p. 197.

[59] Bethmann was at first inclined to accept it. *Germ. Doc.*, 421, note 5, p. 360.

[60] *Germ. Doc.*, 460, p. 385; *Blue Book*, 103.

bian territory, declares herself ready in the interest of European peace to cease her advance and to discuss how a complete settlement can be arrived at, I hope that Russia would also consent to discussion and suspension of further military preparations, provided that the other Powers did the same.

The Russian formula was thus set aside, but the German Government did not succeed in persuading Sir Edward Grey to demand an *immediate* cessation of preparations on the part of Russia. In the opinion of the English Government, this concession would not be made by Russia until Austria agreed to the principle of the *"Halt im Belgrad."*[61]

V. *Austria's Attitude.*

AUSTRIA's attitude was uncertain. Bethmann was still waiting for news from Vienna, in spite of the urgent telegrams which he had sent on the night of the twenty-ninth.

The first observation which the German Government had made concerned Austria's refusal to continue direct negotiations with Russia. Berchtold learned of the new German position at about noon.[62] Upon this point he replied that he was prepared to give due consideration to Bethmann-Hollweg's opinion. He had sent instructions "to Count Szapary, for him *to begin* conversations with Mr. Sazonoff."[63] He was going to confer along similar lines with Shebeko, Russian Ambassador in Vienna. He was thus carrying out his promise at once, but upon what terms? He advised Szápáry to ask Sazonov what matters "he would like to have considered"; this exchange of ideas should preferably concern "questions directly touching on Austro-Russian relations" (conse-

61 This was the idea also contained in King George's reply to Prince Henry, sent from London at 8.54 P.M. on 30th July, *Germ. Doc.*, 452, p. 378.

62 Tschirschky's telegram on this subject was sent back to Berlin at 2.30.

63 The italics were inserted by William II, who noted down in the margin: "Begin! Now!"

quently omitting the question of the ultimatum to Serbia).[64] If necessary, the Ambassador was authorized to engage in a discussion "which would not commit him to anything and would deal only with generalities."[65] This did not give evidence of very great earnestness on the part of Berchtold, whose interview with Shebeko was to follow along much the same lines. It was undoubtedly friendly, but it spent itself in a vague way on reminiscences of Austro-Russian policy in the past, without coming to any matter of vital interest.

Early in the afternoon, while Tschirschky was lunching with Berchtold, Bethmann's second telegram, containing the English suggestion about the "seizure of hostage territory," was decoded and handed to the Ambassador. The Austrian Minister listened, "pale and silent," while it was read twice.[66] He replied simply that he would report on it at once to the Emperor. Tschirschky pressed the matter still further, pointing out that this offer of mediation would give complete satisfaction to Austria, and would guarantee her prestige. He renewed his appeal to Forgách and Hoyos, the Minister's confidants. The Austrians did not for a moment question the gravity of the situation; they would agree to promise to occupy only a small portion of Serbian territory *after the conclusion of the peace.*[67] But it seemed out of the question to them "to restrict the military operations which were already under way." Now, the essential feature of the new proposal was, precisely, the *"Halt im Belgrad"!* These replies, however, were merely personal statements, which did not embody the official response of the Government. When would that response be known? Probably after

---

[64] *Cf. Germ. Doc.,* 433, p. 368. As a matter of fact, Austria now considered that even an acceptance of the original note in its entirety would no longer be acceptable. "Now, since a state of war has supervened, Austria's conditions would naturally be different." *Germ. Doc.,* 432, p. 368.

[65] *Dipl. Pap.,* III, 44.

[66] *Germ. Doc.,* 465, p. 387. Tschirschky's account.

[67] *Germ. Doc.,* 433, p. 368.

Berchtold's conference with the Emperor.[68] But it was still felt in Vienna that the question would have to be submitted to the Council of Ministers, and Tisza, head of the Hungarian Government, could not possibly arrive until the following morning.[69] The Austrian decision would thus not be known until noon on the thirty-first, "at the earliest."[70]

The German Chancellor meanwhile made certain declarations before the Prussian Council of Ministers, to show the importance which he attached to Austria's decisions:

"The President of the Council," reads the report of the session, "laid final emphasis upon the fact that all the Governments, including that of Russia, and the great majority of the nations, were peaceable themselves, but control had been lost, and the machine was in motion. As a *politician*, he would *not yet give up his hope or his efforts to maintain peace*, so long as his *démarche* in Vienna had not been repelled. The decision might come in a very short time; then another marching route would be chosen."[71]

It was doubtless at the close of this session that Bethmann was informed, by a telephone message from Tschirschky,[72] of what had taken place at the Ballplatz. He thereupon concluded that Austria would probably reject Sir Edward Grey's proposal, and thus abandon the last hope of settlement by diplomatic means.[73] His fears were well grounded,

---

[68] "Count Berchtold will forward a full and complete answer after receiving the commands of Emperor Franz Joseph," wired Tschirschky at 5.20 P.M. *Germ. Doc.*, 434, p. 369.

[69] *Cf.* Wegerer, *Die Kriegsschuldfrage*, December 1923, p. 133. His opinion might have been asked by telephone.

[70] *Germ. Doc.*, 440, p. 372.

[71] *Germ. Doc.*, 456, p. 382. The session took place between 5 and 7 P.M., according to Montgelas, *Die Kriegsschuldfrage*, September 1925, p. 593.

[72] *Germ. Doc.*, 441, p. 372. This telegram was sent at 9 P.M. and refers to the telephone conversation, which must therefore be fixed at 7 P.M., at the latest.

[73] The reports and telegrams of the Bavarian Military Attaché in Berlin during the day show that it was planned to proclaim a "state of threatening danger of war" at once, in case of a refusal on Austria's part. *Bayerische Dokumente*, 3rd edition, p. 223.

for the Emperor, Berchtold, and Conrad had decided, during the afternoon, to reject the offer of mediation.[74]

Bethmann was most uneasy. Berchtold's obstinacy might easily lead to intervention by England. Grey's statements to Lichnowsky left no doubt whatever upon this point. In spite of the failure of his earlier attempts, the Chancellor decided to make a final *démarche*. At seven o'clock he had the Emperor sign a telegram to Franz Joseph: "I should be honestly obliged to you if you would favor me with your decision as soon as possible."[75] At nine he sent emphatic instructions to Tschirschky:[76]

If Vienna declines to give in in any direction, . . . it will hardly be possible any longer to place the guilt of the outbreak of a European conflagration upon Russia's shoulders. . . . If England's efforts succeed, while Vienna declines everything, Vienna will be giving documentary evidence that it absolutely wants a war, into which we shall be drawn, while Russia remains free of responsibility.

Austria therefore must accept the Grey proposal, "which preserves her status for her in every way."

Hardly had this telegram been sent off when the situation in Berlin was suddenly transformed. The General Staff, who had failed the night before in their attempt to have the "threatening danger of war" proclaimed, now appeared again on the scene. Throughout the day they had been following the progress of Russian military preparations, although they did not yet know that the Tsar had just authorized general mobilization.[77] Early in the afternoon, the *Lokal Anzeiger*, which was known for its affiliation with the military group, appeared with a report of general mobilization in Germany, and, although the statement was immedi-

[74] Conrad, IV, p. 147.
[75] *Germ. Doc.*, 437, p. 371.
[76] *Germ. Doc.*, 441, p. 372, Telegram No. 200.
[77] See below, Ch. XI, p. 197.

ately denied, the news created quite a stir.[78] Austria had announced that she was going to proceed with general mobilization, to offset the partial mobilization in Russia.[79] The diplomats had not pronounced themselves upon the wisdom of such a step, but the German General Staff had advised Conrad von Hötzendorf to make some decision at once.[80] At the very same moment that Bethmann was trying to persuade Vienna to accept the idea of mediation, Moltke was pointing out the necessity of proceeding with military measures, and advising *against* the English proposal.[81]

It was the Chancellor who eventually gave in. At 11.20 P.M. he wired definitely to Tschirschky: "Please do not carry out instructions number 200 for the present."[82] He thus gave up any further attempt to influence the allied government.

To explain to the Ambassador the reasons for his change of attitude, Bethmann prepared another telegram: "I canceled the order of instructions in No. 200, because the Grand General Staff had just informed me that the military reports of our neighbors, particularly on the East, might force us to make prompt decisions, if we did not wish to lay ourselves open to surprises. The Grand General Staff urgently desires to be informed definitely at once about the decisions made in Vienna, especially those of a military character. Please insist on having a reply by tomorrow." But, on thinking the matter over, he never sent the message to Tschirschky.[83]

Now, Prince Henry had just received a reply from King

[78] This false statement was evidently a maneuver to try to force the hand of the Chancellor.

[79] *Germ. Doc.*, 429, p. 367.

[80] See below, Ch. XII, p. 213.

[81] The Austrians were quite conscious of this lack of harmony. *Cf.* Berchtold's remark: "Who *is* in charge at Berlin?" quoted below, Ch. XII, p. 216.

[82] *Germ. Doc.*, 450, p. 378.

[83] In a short review of the first French edition of this work (*Political Science Quarterly*, December 1925, pp. 628-629), Mr. Sidney B. Fay has maintained that Bethmann-Hollweg's change of attitude did not take place

George. It reached the Central Telegraph Office at 11.08
P.M. and was submitted to Emperor William at 11.30, a few
minutes *after* Bethmann had sent his counter-orders to
Tschirschky. "My Government," said the King, "is doing its
utmost, suggesting to Russia and France to suspend further
military preparations, if Austria will consent to be satisfied
with occupation of Belgrade and neighboring Serbian territory, as a hostage for the satisfactory settlement of her demands, other countries *meanwhile suspending their war
preparations.*" In the eyes of the London Cabinet, Vienna's
acceptance of the *"Halt im Belgrad"* principle was the necessary precondition of all efforts at conciliation. The Chancellor simply forwarded the whole telegram to Tschirschky,
to be communicated to Count Berchtold.[84]

during the evening of 30th July. "Bethmann," wrote Mr. Fay, "still held
back successfully against the militarist pressure until the following noon."
I do not share this opinion. Doubtless Bethmann did not yet wish, on the
evening of the thirtieth, to decree the German mobilization *immediately*, but
he completely gave up, on that very evening, insisting at Vienna that
English mediation be taken into consideration. This change on the part of
Bethmann is a fact of the first importance which Herr Kanner has also
brought to light. (*Der Schlüssel zur Kriegsschuldfrage*, Munich, Südbayer-
ische Verlagsgesellschaft, 1926, p. 40.)

This is how I interpret the attitude of the Chancellor. Bethmann was determined, at nine o'clock on the evening of the thirtieth, to bring energetic
pressure to bear on the Austro-Hungarian Government. When Moltke communicated to him the information which he had received on the subject of the
Russian preparations, Bethmann cancelled instruction No. 200. He ceased
then to advise a conciliatory attitude at Vienna. But, a moment later, the
Chancellor realized that the news relating to the Russian general mobilization
was not definite. Even Moltke did not consider it such. It was because of
this that Bethmann did not send the second telegram which he had prepared.
Instead, he adopted a middle course. He rested content with recalling to
Vienna the existence of the English proposal, without insisting again that it
should be accepted.

That the information relating to the Russian preparations had an influence
on the attitude of Bethmann is quite probable. I claim only that so long as
the reports were not conclusive, the Chancellor could, without inconvenience,
continue to urge upon Vienna the English mediation. He did not do so. It is
this that constitutes his change of attitude, determined by the General Staff.

[84] *Germ. Doc.*, 464, p. 386. Bethmann added that he "canceled the order
of instructions in No. 200," in consideration of the telegram from King
George. It is difficult to see exactly how this telegram conflicted with the
instructions in question. Furthermore, the King's telegram arrived at the

This was the situation when the Council of Ministers finally met in Vienna, on the morning of the thirty-first, to take action upon the English proposals. The minutes of this meeting were published in 1919. Count Berchtold stated his position, which had received the approval of the Emperor. The basis of Sir Edward Grey's suggestion could not be accepted. It would be impossible to discontinue hostilities against Serbia. To accept the English proposal would mean that everything thus far had been done "for nothing." In two or three years Serbia would be a source of trouble again.[85] Tisza was of the same opinion; it would be stupid to indicate so soon the conditions which Austria meant to impose upon Serbia. She should simply declare her willingness to negotiate with the Powers, but only after Russia had "countermanded her mobilization." The ministers all agreed that the idea of a European conference was thoroughly distasteful to them. As Berlin had sent word that London must be humored, however, they would show themselves "conciliatory," at least in the *form* of their reply.

In carrying out these decisions, Berchtold informed his Ambassador[86] that he was prepared to "consider" the Grey proposal, but only upon two conditions: "our military operations" against Serbia should be allowed to continue; and "the English Cabinet should persuade the Russian Government to discontinue its mobilization."[87] The attitude of the Aus-

Central Telegraph Office at 11.08 P.M., and was read at 11.30, whereas Bethmann's counter-order was sent to the Central Office at 11.20. It is in any case out of the question to assert, as does Schäfer, "Generaloberst von Moltke in den Tagen vor der Mobilmachung und seine Einwirkung auf Österreich-Ungarn," *Die Kriegsschuldfrage*, August 1926, p. 533, that with the new telegram of Bethmann-Hollweg to Tschirschky "the instructions in No. 200 remained in force (bleibt in Kraft)." It is quite the contrary.

[85] According to the minutes, as they appeared in 1919, Count Berchtold declared that at heart Germany was hoping for the rejection of the idea of mediation. But this significant statement did not appear in the original copy of the minutes, and was only added later by Berchtold himself. *Cf.* H. Martin, *Die Schuld am Weltkriege*, Leipzig, Grunow, 1920, pp. 381-382.

[86] *Dipl. Pap.*, III, 65.

[87] See also Franz Joseph's telegram to William II, sent at 1.06 on the

trian Government thus did not conform in a single point to the principle laid down in the English proposal.

*   *   *   *   *   *   *

Why was the Dual Monarchy so obstinate in refusing the "seizure of hostage territory," when it had been willing to resume its conversations with Russia?

Aside from the argument which Berchtold used during the Council session of 31st July (namely, the desire to have done once for all with the Serbian menace), it is probable that there were two other motives underlying the decision. One of these motives was diplomatic: if Austria, who had set out on a course of energetic action, should give way at the last moment, would not Germany feel, in spite of Bethmann's advice, that her "brilliant second" was incapable of any real action, and would she not tend in the future toward closer relations with England?[88] The other motive was of a technical military nature: the Austrian General Staff had not been planning to attack Serbia on the Danube front, but rather on the Save front. Its troops were therefore not in a position to seize the "hostage" which England had suggested,[89] if the Serbs should resist them by force of arms.[90]

Hardly had these decisions been made when a new report reached first Berlin and then Vienna, which put everything else into the background: Russia had decreed general mobilization![91]

thirty-first: "A rescue of Serbia by Russian intervention at the present time would bring about the most serious consequences for my territories, and therefore it is impossible for me to permit such an intervention. I am aware of the full meaning and extent of my decision. . . ."

88 This is the point of view to be gathered from the remarks made by Hoyos, Chief of the Cabinet under Berchtold, *op. cit.*, p. 86.

89 This they expected to do, however.

90 *Cf.* the references given by Wegerer, *Die Kriegsschuldfrage*, December 1923, pp. 132-133.

91 When Bethmann stated to Goschen "that the communications received from Vienna by telegraph and telephone were *encouraging*, but that Russia's mobilization had spoiled everything" (*Blue Book*, 121), he was badly distorting the facts, since the Austrian decision was made *before* the arrival of the news of Russian general mobilization.

CHAPTER XI

RUSSIAN GENERAL MOBILIZATION

THE decision to order general mobilization in Russia was announced to the public early on the morning of 31st July. Considerable discussion has centered about the circumstances which led up to this decision, before the news was officially published. This discussion has not been fruitless. In order to appreciate the motives underlying the new Russian move, we must consider the reports that were reaching St. Petersburg at this time. Chronological accuracy is in many cases of the greatest importance.

I. *The Tsar's Decision.*

ACCORDING to all the testimony,[1] which varies in matters of detail, but agrees upon the facts as a whole, the Russian General Staff was forced to give up the idea of general mobilization on the evening of the twenty-ninth, upon a formal order from the Tsar. It had, however, decided to make a new appeal to the Tsar as soon as possible.

The General Staff was inspired by motives of a technical military nature. If mobilization were actually carried out in the four districts in the southwest, plans for general mobilization might easily be upset, and it would be impossible to organize the armies destined to operate against Prussia.

Other arguments, however, must be found to convince the Tsar, for these motives of a military nature had failed to win him over on the previous evening. Yanushkevich had argued that partial mobilization was a mistake from the political standpoint, as it would give France reason to feel that Russia was neglecting her duties as an ally. Certainly France, in

[1] See bibliography at the beginning of Ch. IX, p. 139, note 1.

whose eyes the German army alone was to be feared, had
no reason to wish the Russian armies to concentrate their
attack upon Austria. France might well question the possibility of shifting the weight of the Russian offensive, in case
Germany should enter the war (as must be expected), so as
to threaten Prussia on the east. It does not appear that the
French Government actually raised any such argument
against the *ukase* for partial mobilization. This was the
argument used by the Russian General Staff, however, to
bring pressure to bear upon the Tsar. If France were dis-
pleased, would not William II seize the opportunity to obtain a promise of neutrality from her, and then direct his
whole attack against the Russian army, which would be
placed at a great disadvantage by the poor strategy of the
Russian diplomats?[2]

Yanushkevich developed this point of view in a conference
with Sazonov on the morning of the thirtieth, and succeeded
in carrying his point.[3] M. Rodzianko, President of the Duma,
had just returned to St. Petersburg. He too, "speaking as
head of the national representative body," insisted that the
Government should lose no time. He was convinced that Germany was about to declare war. But the Tsar would not
grant the Minister of War's request for an audience, and cut
short all further advances made to him over the telephone
by the General Staff. Finally M. Sazonov asked to be received at Peterhof Palace; it was he who now took it upon
himself to explain the position of the army chiefs and that of
the President of the Duma.[4] Diplomacy, he told the Tsar,

---

[2] Rodzianko, *The Reign of Rasputin: An Empire's Collapse*, London,
Philpot, 1927, p. 108, describes the astonishment of the St. Petersburg army
officers at the delay in ordering mobilization. "If we give up mobilization
now, very serious complications are to be feared." As a matter of fact,
there is no testimony to show that this argument was used with the Russian
diplomats.

[3] *Cf.* Dobrorolsky, p. 150, and the testimony of Yanushkevich during the
1917 trial.

[4] Sukhomlinov, *Erinnerungen*, p. 345. Rodzianko, pp. 106-108. According

had come to the end of its rope. Any further delay in general mobilization would only "dislocate" the army organization, and "disconcert" the Allies.[5] The Emperor was "very pale." He fully appreciated the responsibility which lay on his shoulders. For a time he hesitated.[6] He finally yielded, however, and authorized Sazonov to give the Chief of Staff orders for general mobilization.

The Minister telephoned to Yanushkevich from the vestibule of the Imperial Palace: "Well, carry out your orders, General, and then . . . disappear for the rest of the day." He seemed to fear that the Tsar would change his mind again. The orders were ready. Dobrorolsky, head of the department of mobilization, had been informed of the "favorable turn" which events were taking, and had had time to prepare the new text of the telegram ordering general mobilization. Once again the signatures of the Ministers must be obtained. A special meeting of the Council was being held in the Palais Marie at that very hour, with Goremykin presiding, and Yanushkevich went straight there, accompanied by Dobrorolsky. A few minutes later the telegram was taken to the Central Telegraph Office. The order stated that 31st July would be the first day of general mobilization.[7]

We are in a position to ascertain the exact time when the *ukase* was communicated to the various military districts. According to Dobrorolsky's testimony, the telegram was dispatched to the various district commanders at six o'clock.

to the account in the *Russkaia Volia*, Sazonov's interview with the military leaders lasted just five minutes: "All that was needed was to show Sazonov the map to convince him of the possible results of partial mobilization."

5 Paléologue, I, p. 39. Baron Schilling's *Journal*, pp. 63-66, gives a *résumé* of this interview which substantially corresponds with this account.

6 According to Baron Schilling, General Tatishchev, who was present for a part of the interview, remarked during a moment of silence: "Yes, it is always hard to make up one's mind." This comment irritated the Tsar, who immediately replied: "Then I shall decide!"

7 Certain details are not yet clear. Did Sazonov have a further interview with the military leaders at 4.30 p.m., as some of the documents seem to indicate?

The documents quoted by Hoeniger[8] show that the order actually reached the commanding general in Warsaw at 8.15 P.M., and an artillery brigade at Novgorod at 7.45.

It is not quite so easy to determine the precise hour at which the decision was made. According to Dobrorolsky, it was at one o'clock that Sazonov telephoned the order for general mobilization to Yanushkevich, after obtaining the Tsar's consent.[9] Sukhomlinov claims that he was notified of it at two o'clock at the latest, but he is not absolutely sure.[10] According to M. Paléologue, who was not an eyewitness but was informed the next day by M. Sazonov, "the hands of the clock were pointing exactly to four," and Vice Chancellor Basili makes the same statement. Judging from a report in a German paper in St. Petersburg on 1st August,[11] M. Sazonov did not *arrive* at Peterhof Palace until two o'clock. This would seem to strengthen the statements made by Paléologue and Basili, and Baron Schilling's *Journal* further tends to confirm them, for it states that M. Sazonov was received by the Tsar at three o'clock and that the interview lasted nearly an hour.[12]

The French Ambassador called upon the Minister for Foreign Affairs at about six. As an outcome of this interview, he telegraphed to Paris at 9.15 that the Russian Government "was resolved to proceed secretly with the preliminary measures of general mobilization."[13] This message arrived at 11.30 P.M.

[8] *Zur Vorgeschichte des Weltkrieges*, II, *Militärische Rüstungen und Mobilmachungen*, Anlage 38.

[9] Dobrorolsky has steadily maintained the truth of this statement. *Cf. Die Kriegsschuldfrage*, April 1924, p. 87.

[10] He has finally admitted that the word may not have reached him until 4 P.M. *Die Kriegsschuldfrage*, July 1924, p. 229.

[11] *Petersburger Deutsche Zeitung*, quoted by Hoeniger, in *Zur Vorgeschichte des Weltkrieges*, II, *Militärische Rüstungen und Mobilmachungen*, p. 139.

[12] Schilling, p. 64.

[13] *Yellow Book*, 102. Text published by Appuhn and Renouvin, *Introduction aux Tableaux d'Histoire de Guillaume II*, Paris, A. Costes, 1923, p.

The *ukase* was officially posted the next morning at day-break. M. Paléologue notified his Government by the following brief wire: "General mobilization has been ordered for the Russian army."[14] This telegram, sent from St. Petersburg via Bergen at 10.43 A.M., did not reach Paris until 8.30 in the evening,[15] whereas a similar message sent to the Wilhelmstrasse by Count Pourtalès reached Berlin at 11.40 A.M.[16] Definite word about Russian general mobilization was thus known in Germany nine hours before the French Government learned of it.

II. *The Reasons for the Decision.*

APART from the technical argument which had determined the policy of the General Staff, did the Tsar's Government receive any counsel or any information which might have influenced its decision, and hastened the orders for general mobilization?

1. Did not the Russian Government have good reason to be disturbed over the reports about military preparation in Germany?

M. Sazonov had voiced his apprehensions to M. Paléologue[17] and to Sir George Buchanan.[18] The British Ambassador reported to London on the morning of the thirtieth

xcv. The telegram in which the British Ambassador notified his Government of the decision to order general mobilization was dated at 6.40 P.M., 31st July, but it appears that it was actually sent on the thirtieth. *Cf. Brit. Doc.,* 347, note, p. 218.

14 *Yellow Book,* 118, gives a longer message, Telegram No. 318, which is inaccurate. No reference to the first day of mobilization appeared in the decodification of the official message. *Cf.* also *Cahiers des droits de l'homme,* letter from M. Poincaré, 9th January 1923.

15 This is the hour of its arrival at the telegraph office, and not at the Cipher Bureau. *Cf.* M. Herriot's letter, *Cahiers des droits de l'homme,* 25th March 1925, p. 161.

16 *Germ. Doc.,* 473, p. 391. This wire was sent from St. Petersburg at 10.20.

17 *Yellow Book,* 102.
18 *Blue Book,* 97.

that "the Russian Government had absolute proof that Germany was making military and naval preparations against Russia, more particularly in the direction of the Gulf of Finland." Unfortunately the keepers of the archives for the Soviet Government, who have published so many of the Tsarist diplomatic documents, have not yet brought to light the papers of the General Staff, at least not for this period. Only two of the known documents make any reference to the situation, and they are quite vague. M. Sazonov apparently received "information from the Minister of Marine that the German Fleet is lying at Danzig in a state of mobilization," and he communicated this news to Count Pourtalès.[19] Furthermore, M. Lermontov, Russian Consul-General at Stuttgart, wired on the thirtieth that the German reservists in that city had received their marching orders.[20] These are the only sources of information which we possess at the moment, and they are hardly a sufficient ground for any serious conviction.

One other suggestion must be considered, which has given rise to the most lengthy discussion, namely, the *Lokal Anzeiger* incident.[21]

When the Berlin newspaper published the announcement of German general mobilization, at about 1.30 P.M. on 30th July, M. Sverbeïev, Russian Ambassador in Berlin, was at once notified by Markov, the representative of a telegraph agency, and wired immediately to St. Petersburg: "I learn that the decree has just been issued for the general mobilization of the army and navy." According to the Ambassador's own testimony, it was about 2.30 before this message was

---

[19] *Germ. Doc.*, 459, p. 384. Sent at 8.40 P.M. The German Government emphatically denied the report, but this denial did not reach St. Petersburg until the following evening.

[20] Document published in *Krasnyĭ Arkhiv*, 1922, I, p. 182, reprinted in the *Journal des Débats,* 5th October 1922.

[21] Although for my part I consider that the question has been decided, I feel that I ought to review the essential facts here.

prepared in code and sent off. A few minutes later Sverbeïev learned by telephone from Markov, and also from an official at the Wilhelmstrasse,—Bronevsky, Russian Chargé d'Affaires, having meanwhile been notified to the same effect by Government Counselor Krause—that the news published by the *Lokal Anzeiger* was absolutely false. Sverbeïev at once sent a straight telegram, without code, to St. Petersburg: "Please consider Telegram 142 cancelled. Information follows."[22] A second message followed in code, reporting the formal denial made by the Wilhelmstrasse.[23]

Was it the announcement in the *Lokal Anzeiger* which led to the Tsar's decision, before the arrival of the official denial?

Bethmann-Hollweg was inclined to believe as much on the following day: "I do not consider it impossible that the Russian mobilization can be traced to rumors rife here yesterday —absolutely false and at once officially denied, but which were reported to St. Petersburg as fact—that mobilization was taking place here," he telegraphed to Lichnowsky.[24] Neither Pourtalès nor Szápáry, however, makes any reference whatever to the *Lokal Anzeiger* in his telegrams. As far as the Entente was concerned, no one at all seems to have been notified of the episode.

It was not until November 1916, that the public began to take an interest in the affair. It was then that Sir Edward Grey denounced the *Lokal Anzeiger* for aiding in what he called a ruse of the German General Staff, to bring about Russian general mobilization. The Bavarian Socialist Eisner even goes so far as to declare that the German Government delayed the second and third messages sent by the Russian Ambassador, to prevent the denial from reaching St. Peters-

---

[22] Quoted by Wegerer, "Die verfrühten deutschen Mobilmachungsmeldungen und die russische Mobilmachung," *Die Grenzboten*, 6th May 1922, p. 82.

[23] *Orange Book*, 62, and the *Journal des Débats*, 5th October 1922.

[24] *Germ. Doc.*, 488, p. 403, 31st July. *Cf.* also Lerchenfeld, *Germ. Doc.*, Supp. IV, 26, p. 634.

burg as soon as Sverbeïev had hoped. And a statement by the Kerensky Government, made on 15th September 1917, after the Sukhomlinov trial, also refers to the influence which the false news had upon the Tsar's decision.[25] That is one opinion which is held of the matter.

In Germany, on the other hand, ever since the Armistice the efforts of every student of war responsibility have been directed toward upsetting this claim of the Allies. According to Count Montgelas, inquiries into the records of the telegraph office have proved that Sverbeïev's denial of the rumor was sent off from Berlin, by a series of accidents in transmission, *before* the telegram containing the false report.[26] The latter did not reach St. Petersburg until 7 p.m. at the very earliest. In any case, it could have had no influence whatever upon the Tsar's decision, since the telegram ordering general mobilization had already been sent out by that time.

Personally, I accept Count Montgelas' new explanation as final. To question it would be to charge that the German historian had forged the documents, and he could hardly be accused of that. I therefore do not believe that the German Government delayed Sverbeïev's telegrams, and I believe that the news of the fictitious German mobilization reached St. Petersburg too late to have had any possible influence upon the decisions of the Russian Government. The silence on the part of contemporary witnesses would seem to confirm this point of view. If the message really had the historic interest which tradition has awarded it, how is it possible that neither M. Paléologue, nor M. Basili, nor Sir George Buchanan was accurately informed at once?

25 See Grelling, "Le mystère du 30 juillet," *Revue de Paris,* 1st March 1922, pp. 29-70. Sukhomlinov made similar statements at the time of his visit in Finland.

26 Montgelas, *Deutsche Rundschau,* May 1922, pp. 113-124, gives an abundance of precise details upon this point.

Even though the accidents in transmission mentioned by the German historians seem improbable, and if certain details of the story appear surprising and therefore subject to caution,[27] it is nevertheless impossible to maintain the traditional argument of the Allies. Let us admit that Sverberev's first telegram was composed and transmitted with the greatest speed, while the later ones were delayed: one only has to make allowance for the time required for decodification, and for the difference between German and Russian time to realize that the first telegram could not possibly have reached St. Petersburg *before* five o'clock.[28] How then could the Tsar ever have learned of it at Peterhof Palace by the time when he gave M. Sazonov the orders to proceed with general mobilization?

2. May we attach any greater importance, in explaining the decisions of the Russian Government, to the personal opinions of the Tsar and of Sazonov concerning the diplomatic situation?

M. Paléologue makes two statements upon this point in the telegram which he sent to M. Viviani on the evening of 30th July: M. Sazonov had had an interview with the German Ambassador during the course of the afternoon, and he must have been convinced "that Germany was unwilling to speak the decisive word at Vienna which would ensure peace." Furthermore, "Emperor Nicholas had received the same impression from a personal exchange of telegrams with Emperor William." It remains to be seen whether the documents confirm these statements made by the French Ambassador.

As a matter of fact, M. Sazonov had two interviews with

---

[27] *Cf.* Grelling. It is astonishing that Sverberev should have waited until 4 P.M. to send the second telegram if the denial of the report reached him at 2.30, as M. Jules Cambon's account seems to confirm. He would have been guilty of surprising negligence if this were true.

[28] Taken to the telegraph office at 2.30, transmitted in an hour, decoded immediately, the message could not have been read at the Russian Foreign Office before 4 P.M at the very earliest, which would have been 5 P.M. by Russian time.

Count Pourtalès on the thirtieth, one during the morning and the other toward evening. The former is probably the one alluded to by M. Paléologue. Their exchange of views brought out very clearly the contrast in attitude between Germany and Russia. At the end of the afternoon, however, the Russian Minister for Foreign Affairs did not yet know how the "formula" which he dictated to Count Pourtalès had been received in Berlin.[29]

As for the Tsar, M. Paléologue tells us that he received a telegram from William II which had been "almost threatening." "The whole weight of the decision lies solely on your shoulders now."[30] This telegram must certainly have discouraged the Tsar, since it did not even refer to the offer of arbitration which the Russian sovereign had suggested the night before. But it was not sent from Berlin until 3.30 P.M., and did not reach Peterhof Palace until 6.30.[31] As M. Paléologue himself places the Tsar's decision at four o'clock, the only possible conclusion is that his account, if authentic at all, was somewhat influenced by his imagination.

3. Finally,—and this is an important question—was not the Russian Government encouraged to proceed with general mobilization by news or advice from Paris? "France," says Montgelas, "not only failed to turn Russia aside from general mobilization, but gave her artful advice about the way in which she might continue her preparation in secret, without arousing Germany to take counter-measures within any useful time."[32]

The French Government received a communication from Isvolsky, Russian Ambassador in Paris, at 3 A.M. on the morning of 30th July. It reported the *démarche* made by

29 See above, Ch. X, p. 185.
30 *Germ. Doc.*, 420, p. 360.
31 Schilling, *Journal*, p. 67.
32 Montgelas, p. 166. The same idea is brought out by Morhardt, Ch. III.

Count Pourtalès in St. Petersburg on the afternoon of the twenty-ninth, and announced the intention of the Russian Government to "speed up" its armaments.[33] As Russian *partial* mobilization had already been decided upon, the "*speeding up*" of armaments certainly implied general mobilization.

M. Poincaré at once had an interview with M. Messimy at the Élysée Palace. Official instructions were shortly sent to M. Paléologue as follows:[34]

M. Isvolsky came tonight to tell me that the German Ambassador has notified M. Sazonov of the decision of his Government to mobilize the army if Russia does not cease her military preparations.

The Tsar's Minister for Foreign Affairs points out that these preparations were commenced only after Austria had mobilized eight army corps, and had refused to arrange peacefully her differences with Serbia. M. Sazonov declares that in these circumstances Russia can only expedite her arming, and consider war as imminent, that she counts upon the help of France as an ally, and that she considers it desirable that England should join Russia and France without loss of time.

After thus recalling the object of the Russian *démarche*, the telegram renewed the declaration that "France is resolved to fulfil all the obligations of her alliance."[35] But all hope of peace was not yet lost, for conferences were still taking place between "the Powers less directly interested."

[33] See above, Ch. IX, p. 151. We must not lose sight of the fact that M. Paléologue failed to notify the French Government of the order and counter-order given on the evening of the twenty-ninth.

[34] *Yellow Book*, 101, 7.30 A.M. These instructions were read to the Council of Ministers during the morning.

[35] These obligations were defined in Article 2 of the military pact of 1893: "If Russia is attacked by Germany, or by Austria with German support, France will employ all the forces at her command to defeat Germany." According to Article 3, France undertook to *mobilize* all her forces at once, along with Russia, if the Triple Alliance, or any one of the Powers forming it, should mobilize.

I therefore think it would be well that, in taking any precautionary measures of defence which Russia thinks must go on, she should not immediately take any step which may offer to Germany a pretext for a total or partial mobilization of her forces.

M. Viviani thus advised M. Sazonov to avoid any act which might give Germany the opportunity for a retaliatory measure. Now, orders for general mobilization were necessarily of this character.

But M. Isvolsky, while communicating to his Government the general contents of the preceding instructions, reported at the same time two conversations which might be considered as a commentary on those instructions. M. de Margerie, head of the political division of the Ministry for Foreign Affairs, had told him that the French Government "did not wish to meddle" in Russia's military preparations, but that "it considered it highly desirable, in view of the continued negotiations in the interest of peace, that these preparatory measures should be as private as possible, in order to give no cause for provocation." And M. Messimy, Minister of War, had told Count Ignatiev, Russian Military Attaché, that Russia might easily declare that she was prepared to "slow up" her military preparation for the time being, and still be able to "continue and increase" this preparation, only avoiding so far as possible "any extensive transportation of troops."[36]

The instructions which M. Viviani sent to M. Paléologue at 7.30 A.M. reached St. Petersburg, not at six in the evening, as the French Ambassador incorrectly states in his memoirs, but probably toward the end of the morning. M.

[36] These documents were published for the first time by Romberg, and were reprinted in the *Livre Noir*, II, pp. 290-291. These are merely indirect reports, and may not of course reproduce the actual words of M. Messimy and M. de Margerie.

Isvolsky's telegrams were sent at 9 A.M. and the exact hour of their arrival is not known.

In any case, M. Paléologue sent off at 4.30 the following report of an interview which he had just had with M. Sazonov:[37]

M. Sazonov, whom I acquainted with your desire to see every military measure avoided which might give Germany a pretext for general mobilization, replied that the General Staff had decided to postpone certain secret measures of precaution, whose disclosure might alarm the German General Staff.[38]

The advice of the French Government had therefore been interpreted as it was intended: France did not wish Russia to proceed with general mobilization.

M. Paléologue's *démarche* had been made just in time, before M. Sazonov's visit to Peterhof Palace. According to Baron Schilling's *Journal*, it was about noon that the Minister had an interview with the French Ambassador.[39]

But did not M. Sazonov also receive the two telegrams from Isvolsky almost immediately after his visit with M. Paléologue? This is quite possible, although not a single Russian official makes any allusion whatever to them. Let us therefore admit, in the absence of detailed proof, that these telegrams were known to the Ministry for Foreign Affairs early enough to have had some influence upon the Government's decisions. What conclusion might the Russian diplomats have drawn from a perusal of these documents?

The French Minister of War agreed to the idea that Russia should "strengthen" her military preparations, and con-

[37] This telegram was evidently a reply to M. Viviani's instructions. It was sent at 4.31, and reached Paris at 6.51.

[38] This was a veiled allusion to the Tsar's counter-order.

[39] Sir George Buchanan was received by M. Sazonov at the same time as M. Paléologue. According to his account, which makes no reference to the official advice of the French Government, M. Sazonov declared that general mobilization would certainly follow if Austria rejected the conciliatory formula proposed by Russia. *Brit. Doc.*, 302, p. 192. See above, Ch. X, p. 184.

sequently take steps leading to mobilization in the districts not affected by partial mobilization. On the other hand, he advised against any "large-scale transportation of troops," such as are necessary for the *execution* of mobilization. What did he mean? His suggestion was, in sum, to proceed to call out individual reservists, under the system ordinarily used in the frontier districts at the time of *premobilization,* without going so far as to carry out general mobilization.[40] Such was the half-way measure suggested by M. Messimy, if we are to believe Isvolsky's telegram.

But—and upon this point the statements of M. de Margerie and M. Messimy are in harmony with M. Viviani's instructions to M. Paléologue—there was no question raised of actually ordering, nor even of secretly carrying out, general mobilization.

If this explanation be accepted, the details are easier to understand.

M. Sazonov made up his mind at the end of the morning: he would ask the Tsar to authorize general mobilization. Just at this moment M. Viviani's message was brought to him: the French Government opposed the idea of general mobilization. M. Sazonov did not, however, give up his plan. He proceeded to Peterhof Palace, and the order was signed and sent out.

Now the situation became delicate. Was he to admit frankly to Paris that the advice of the French Government had been ignored?

M. Isvolsky's telegrams offered a possible solution. Since M. de Margerie and M. Messimy had agreed that Russia might proceed with *secret* preparations, M. Sazonov announced to the French Ambassador that *secret* "preliminary measures" were to be taken, without specifying their nature and extent. The very terms of his declaration corresponded with the advice which had come from M. Isvolsky, and did

40 Article 6 of the 1913 decree. See above, Ch. IX, p. 141.

not conflict with the instructions sent to M. Paléologue. Thus the French Government would gain the impression, for the moment at least, that its point of view had been considered.[41]

The Russian Government, however, was somewhat uneasy in its efforts to minimize in the eyes of its ally the significance of the decisions it had made, and to find some easy means of escape from an embarrassing position. M. Sazonov even considered keeping secret the whole order for general mobilization. Baron Schilling noted in his *Journal*, on the thirty-first:[42] "The Minister for Foreign Affairs considers it desirable, in order to avoid any aggravation of the tension between Russia and Germany, to proceed to the stage of general mobilization with as much secrecy as possible, and not to publish a general *order*." This plan was actually arranged on the night of the thirtieth.[43] Upon thinking the matter over, however, says the *Journal*, M. Sazonov realized that it would be impossible from a technical standpoint, and the proclamation of general mobilization was officially posted on the walls of St. Petersburg on the morning of 31st July.[44]

*   *   *   *   *   *   *

After this rather long digression, in which mere hypothesis may have held too large a place, we have now reached the point at which we left off. Since the Russian Government was apparently not influenced by the newspaper reports from Berlin, nor by a disagreeable telegram from William II, nor by advice from Paris,—since the documents at the present time, at least, do not justify a belief in any such

[41] The fact of the matter is that the French Government did not interpret M. Paléologue's message as the announcement of general mobilization. *Cf.* below, Ch. XIII, p. 237.

[42] *How the War Began in 1914,* p. 69.

[43] It would appear that the Tsar, when told of the plan, believed that it would actually be possible. On 1st August, he wrote: "Keep the secret."

[44] But the Russian Government did not send any official word to the foreign governments, nor even, it would appear, to its own ambassadors.

influence,—the sole motive about which there is not a shade of doubt, in the decision in favor of general mobilization, was the technical military argument. This is the only argument even mentioned, for that matter, by the more serious-minded witnesses on the Russian side of the case.[45]

[45] Dobrorolsky, in *Die Kriegsschuldfrage*, May 1925, p. 325, informs us that, during the period of hesitation, he received an order to take steps, "at the close of the present crisis," so that in the future it would be possible to mobilize the various military districts "independently of one another." This would tend to confirm the belief that, at the end of July 1914, the Tsar found himself in the presence of technical military arrangements which actually deprived him of his freedom of action. He did not wish to be similarly restricted again in the future.

CHAPTER XII

AUSTRIAN GENERAL MOBILIZATION

THE Austrian Government had mobilized eight army corps and two cavalry divisions against Serbia. The decree had been issued on 25th July, but the first day of mobilization had been set for the twenty-eighth. The movements of troops in Galcia, to which M. Dumaine referred in a telegram, were at the most those of a single cavalry division. There is thus every reason to believe that no important steps were taken along the Russian frontier until the arrival of the news of Russian partial mobilization.

The Austrian Government felt called upon to reply to this decision by the general mobilization of all its forces. The whole matter was taken up and settled, after some hesitation, on 30th July.

During the morning the Austrian General Staff brought pressure to bear upon the Government, which raised no objections whatever on grounds of principle. Count Berchtold simply wished to be sure that the German diplomats would approve. This was a necessary precaution, since the Ballplatz was aware of Bethmann-Hollweg's desire to bring about mediation. "At this point," noted Tschirschky, "it was determined to mobilize as soon as Berlin should give its consent, and it was quite decided not to tolerate Russian mobilization any longer."[1] Later in the afternoon, after his interview with Forgách and Hoyos, he remarked that[2] "Conrad von Hötzendorf was to submit to the Emperor this evening the order for general mobilization as the reply to the measures already taken on the part of the Russians." And he

---

[1] Tschirschky's note on a telegram which reached Vienna at 6.00 A.M. on the thirtieth. *Official German Documents Relating to the World War*, I, p. 100.

[2] *Germ. Doc.*, 465, p. 387.

added: "They were not quite clear as to whether, in the present state of affairs, the mobilization was called for." *They* doubtless referred to the diplomats, who were uneasy because of the German Chancellor's insistence that they should accept a compromise.

There is still another proof of Austria's indecision at this stage in the development, namely, the interview which took place between Conrad and Berchtold, in the Emperor's presence, at about 3.30 on the afternoon of the thirtieth.[3] The Chief of Staff demanded mobilization. The Minister hesitated: that "would cost millions . . . If the army is in Galicia, we will certainly end in a war with Russia." Upon Conrad's insistence, it was finally agreed that the order for mobilization might be given out on 1st August, but that the question should be reconsidered the next day.

In order to arrive at any decision, it was essential to know how Germany felt, and both the Government and the General Staff set about inquiries in that direction.

Count Berchtold had Ambassador Szögyény approach Herr von Jagow on the subject, stating that "unless the Russian mobilization measures are at once discontinued, our own general mobilization must be at once inaugurated for military reasons." He also tried to obtain a promise that Germany would mobilize along with Austria. The Central Powers should make "a last attempt to prevent a European war" by declaring at St. Petersburg and at Paris that "continuation of the Russian mobilization would have to be followed by counter-measures in Germany and Austria which would inevitably involve serious consequences." But Jagow did not seem disposed to agree to this proposal:[4] "I informed Count Szögyény that we could not coöperate in the move at St. Petersburg, as during the last day or two we had already talked in friendly fashion along this same line, and could not

[3] Conrad, IV, p. 147.
[4] *Germ. Doc.*, 427, p. 365, and 429, note, p. 367.

do it again.[5] Any renewal of such a discussion would have to be an ultimatum." He therefore asked Austria to make the move alone at St. Petersburg, and at 9 P.M. he notified Ambassador Tschirschky of this decision.[6] The German reply did not contain a single word to encourage Austria to declare general mobilization, nor to dissuade her from it.

But the Austrian General Staff had meanwhile, on its own initiative, been consulting the German General Staff.[7] There the tone had been quite different. During the morning of the thirtieth, at about ten o'clock, Major Fleischmann, liaison officer of the Austrian General Staff at Berlin, had an interview with General von Moltke. The Chief of the German General Staff knew of the Russian decision for partial mobilization, although he had not yet received any official communication on this subject. He did not, however, give any promise of immediate German intervention. "Russian mobilization," he said, "is still not a sufficient reason for mobilizing: only when a state of war exists between the Monarchy and Russia. . . . Do not declare war on Russia, but await the Russian attack."[8] When, towards noon, the Russian decision was officially communicated to him, he demanded a knowledge of the intentions of the Austro-Hungarian Government.[9]

During the afternoon, on the contrary, Moltke no longer hesitated to give advice and to make promises. When, about

[5] This was an allusion to the step taken by Pourtalès on the twenty-ninth. See above, Ch. IX, p. 151.

[6] *Germ. Doc.*, 442, p. 373.

[7] On this point see the article by Theobald von Schäfer, "Generaloberst von Moltke in den Tagen vor der Mobilmachung und seine Einwirkung auf Österreich-Ungarn," *Die Kriegsschuldfrage*, August 1926, pp. 514-549, which gives a debatable interpretation of the attitude of the Chief of the General Staff but which produces some unpublished documents from the German and Austrian archives.

[8] This telegram has not been found in the archives. The text of it has been given by Conrad, IV, p. 152, and confirmed by Fleischmann (communication from Fleischmann to the *Reichsarchiv*, Schäfer, p. 524). The exact hour of dispatch is not known. But the telegram arrived at Vienna in the course of the afternoon; in any case before 7.30 P.M.

[9] Telegram sent by Fleischmann at 1.15 P.M., according to Schäfer, p. 524.

two o'clock, he received the Austrian Military Attaché Bienerth, he made certain statements of grave import:[10]

The situation is critical, unless the Austro-Hungarian Monarchy mobilizes at once against Russia. The declaration which Russia has made, on the subject of the mobilization she has ordered, now makes counter-measures necessary on the part of Austria-Hungary, and must figure largely in the official explanation of Austria's motives. That will develop into a *casus fœderis* for Germany. Make some honorable arrangement with Italy, promising her compensation, so that Italy will remain actively in the Triple Alliance. Above all, do not leave a man on the Italian frontier. Decline the renewed advances of Great Britain in the interest of peace. A European war is the last chance of saving Austria-Hungary. Germany is ready to back Austria unreservedly.

Subsequently, probably during the evening, Moltke personally confirmed this advice—at least as regards the mobilization[11]—by means of a message which he sent directly to Conrad:[12]

Resist the Russian mobilization. Austria-Hungary must be saved. Mobilize at once against Russia. Germany will mobilize. Persuade Italy, by offering compensation, to fulfil her duty as ally.

The Austrian General Staff received, at the close of the afternoon of the thirtieth, the telegrams from Fleischmann,

[10] Telegram from Bienerth, Conrad, IV, p. 152. Text confirmed by the *Kriegsarchiv* of Vienna. The telegram was sent at 5.30 P.M. It arrived in Vienna at 9.50 P.M. Ambassador Szögyény, by a telegram sent at 7.40 P.M., which arrived at 10.20 P.M., notified Berchtold of the advice given by Moltke.

[11] Schäfer rightly points out that the telegram sent by Moltke did not reproduce the advice reported by Bienerth: "Decline the renewed advances of Great Britain in the interest of peace." But, in my opinion, this is not a sufficient reason for admitting that the Austrian Military Attaché distorted, on this point, the suggestions made to him during the interview. Moltke, quite evidently, could not, in a telegram *signed by himself,* give advice on a question which lay outside the range of his powers. On the contrary, he could very well give this advice *orally* to the Military Attaché.

[12] Conrad, IV, p. 152.

which did not yet promise German mobilization, but which requested information as to the intentions of Vienna. At 7.30 P.M., Conrad indicated the terms of the reply which should be sent, he said, only *on the following morning* at eight o'clock. "According to the decision of His Majesty it is resolved: To wage war against Serbia. To mobilize the rest of the army and to concentrate it in Galicia. First day of mobilization, 4th August. Mobilization order is released today, 31st July."[13] In truth the decisions of the Vienna Government were not yet *final,* since the question of mobilization had still to be examined the next day. But Conrad was convinced that the decree of mobilization would be issued on the thirty-first. He wished then to give the German General Staff the impression that Austria-Hungary had decided to act. Moreover, in order to take into account the advice of Moltke, he made no allusion to immediate operations *against Russia.* Also, the delay which he foresaw between the order of mobilization (31st July) and its effective realization (4th August) shows that he had no idea of precipitating events. "Await the Russian attack," Moltke had said. In fact, in postponing the dispatch of this telegram until the following morning, Conrad certainly thought that he would receive, by that time, fresh information as to the attitude of Germany.

This information was not long in coming to him. The telegram from Bienerth, which advised the immediate mobilization of the Austro-Hungarian army and announced the German mobilization, arrived in Vienna at 9.50 P.M. It was deciphered in the middle of the night. The message sent by Moltke was seen by Conrad only at 7.45 on the morning of the thirty-first.

The significance of these telegrams is clear. The German General Staff, even before learning of Russian general mobilization, realized that there was a *casus fœderis* for Ger-

13 Schäfer, p. 536, from a communication of the *Kriegsarchiv* of Vienna.

many, and announced the imminence of German mobilization.[14]

When Conrad von Hötzendorf conferred with Berchtold early on the morning of the thirty-first,[15] and when they compared Moltke's advice with that of the Wilhelmstrasse, their first reaction was one of surprise: "Then who *is* running the government at Berlin, Moltke or Bethmann?" asked the Minister. But the firmness of Bienerth's message reassured them. "I have called you together," Berchtold told his colleagues, "because I was under the impression that Germany was holding back, but now we have formal assurance to the contrary from the highest military authority." That was quite enough.

The military and civil leaders of the Dual Monarchy were thus in perfect agreement, and, as the Emperor's sanction had already been granted, there was nothing left but to take the necessary steps to carry out the plan. The order for general mobilization was sent out from the Chancellery at 11.30 on the morning of the thirty-first. It reached General Headquarters at 12.23, and was issued at once. August fourth was to be the first day of mobilization.[16] There is no doubt that this decision coincided with the intentions of Austrian official circles as they had been determined upon during the afternoon of 30th July. It is none the less true that a *final* decision had not yet been made when the advice from Moltke arrived, and that the Austrian Government, before committing an irrevocable act, took into account the encouragement given by the German General Staff.

*   *   *   *   *   *   *

The signature and announcement of the order for general

[14] The importance of these statements has been pointed out by Grelling, *Revue de Paris,* 15th July 1924, pp. 298-299 and by Kanner, *Die Schlüssel zur Kriegsschuldfrage,* pp. 40-41 and 74-79.

[15] This interview must not be confused with the meeting of the Council of Ministers, which occurred at the *end* of the morning.

[16] *Zur Vorgeschichte des Weltkrieges,* II, *Militärische Rüstungen und*

mobilization in Austria occurred definitely later—only by a few hours, it is true—than the order for general mobilization in Russia.[17] But at the moment when the Vienna Government took these steps, it had not yet learned, as the German historians realize,[18] of the decisions and actions of the Government at St. Petersburg. Thus, even if the Tsar had postponed the final organization of his army, Austria would none the less have continued with hers. She had other grounds for her action, since the Russians had started their partial mobilization along the Austrian frontier on the morning of the thirtieth.

Mobilmachungen, pp. 21-23, and Anlagen, 43-44. Also Gooss, p. 307. The Bavarian representative in Vienna notified his Government at 12.30 P.M. on the thirty-first, *Bayerische Dokumente,* Gesandtenberichte, No. 62.

17 At the time, the French Government believed that the Austrian mobilization had come first. *Blue Book,* 134. Sazonov also told Szápáry so, but the latter protested.

18 The telegram from Szápáry announcing general mobilization in Russia was greatly delayed in reaching Vienna.

CHAPTER XIII

GERMANY AND THE DOUBLE ULTIMATUM

THE Tsar's Government had declared, when it ordered general mobilization, that it was still willing to continue negotiations. "We are far from wishing war," Nicholas II wired to William II. "So long as the negotiations with Austria on Serbia's account are taking place, my troops shall not take any *provocative* action. I give you my solemn word for this."[1]

The Austrian Government adopted the same attitude in the message which it sent to its ambassadors:

These measures are of a purely defensive nature. They were taken only because of the pressure of Russian preparations, which we especially regretted since we had no aggressive intentions whatever in regard to Russia. . . . Meanwhile, conferences about the general situation are continuing to take place on a friendly basis between the cabinets in Vienna and St. Petersburg. We hope that they will result in a general peaceful agreement.[2]

Austria would not be able to take the field before 12th August, and Russia certainly mobilized more slowly than any other country. This delay might still leave time for some solution to be found. But did all the governments honestly wish to find such a solution, and did they really believe that it would be possible?[3] Russian general mobilization had gravely endangered all chances for negotiation. It would necessarily provoke a reply in Germany, and that in turn would lead to similar measures in France. Then the power

1 *Germ. Doc.*, 487, p. 402, 2.55 P.M., 31st July.
2 *Dipl. Pap.*, III, 78.
3 Upon this point, see the Conclusion of this volume.

would pass into the hands of the military group. Whether
they realized it or not, the governments were under the guid-
ing sway of the general staffs. And this situation was particularly hopeless in Berlin, where the "war on two fronts"
depended entirely upon lightning successes at the very start.

I. *The Kriegsgefahrzustand and the Ultimatums.*

THE German General Staff was impatiently awaiting word
from Russia. On the evening of the thirtieth Lieutenant-
Colonel von Haeften had an interview with Moltke. "The
situation is becoming quite clear," the Chief of Staff told
him. "We have received two reliable reports from independent sources, stating that general mobilization of all military
forces in Russia has been ordered. . . . .[4] If we postpone
mobilization, our military position will become less and less
favorable. . . . Tomorrow noon the decision will be made in
favor of war or peace. The Chancellor, the Minister of War
and I have an audience together with His Majesty." No
premature move must be made, however: "Before advising
His Majesty to decree mobilization, I prefer to wait for
some further confirmation of the news about Russian mobilization. I expect it early tomorrow morning." In the opinion
of the Chief of Staff, war was inevitable unless a miracle
should take place.[5]

The "confirmation" for which Moltke was waiting and
hoping was slow in arriving. At seven o'clock on the morning of the thirty-first, the Chief of Staff telephoned to General Hell, who was in command at Allenstein: "Have you any

[4] The telegram ordering general mobilization in Russia had been sent out
at 6 P.M. on that very day, but it had not yet been made public. It should
be noted that Moltke's statements correspond closely with the argument
used by Bethmann in canceling his instructions to Tschirschky. *Cf.* above,
Ch. X, p. 190.

[5] Von Haeften's testimony was printed in *Les Études de la Guerre,* by
Puaux, Cahier 8, p. 666. *Cf.* also *Schulthess' Europäischer Geschichtskalen-
der,* 1917, II, pp. 996-997.

reason there on the frontier to think that Russia is mobilizing?" Hell did think so: "The red mobilization posters are stuck up in Mlava," but he had been unable to secure a copy. "You must get hold of this red poster. I must be sure that they are actually mobilizing against us," Moltke repeated. But the General could do no more than assure him that Russia was mobilizing. "I am quite convinced of that."[6]

By noon, when the decisive conference was to take place with the Emperor, Moltke was satisfied. A few minutes earlier the telegram had arrived from Pourtalès with the announcement of Russian general mobilization.[7] At 12.30 the Chancellor summoned Admiral von Tirpitz; he now held in his hands the imperial order declaring "a state of threatening danger of war."

The proclamation of the "state of threatening danger of war" involved[8] precautionary military measures for the protection of the frontiers, for the security of the railroads, the supervision of the postal, telephone and telegraph service, police measures corresponding to what in France is known as "a state of siege," the recalling of all men on leave, and, when necessary, the evacuation of military storehouses in the territory threatened with invasion. It appears that a certain number of reservists were also called out.[9]

This was only a preliminary stage, which could not last long. "The preparatory measures which I have ordered to-

[6] Puaux, p. 678, and *Schulthess*, 1917, II, p. 1000.

[7] It arrived at 11.40 A.M.

[8] *Cf.* Montgelas, Supp. No. 25, pp. 199-200, and the text published in *Die Kriegsschuldfrage*, January 1926, pp. 46-48.

[9] According to M. Puaux, every German military notebook contained the words *Kriegszustand-Mobilmachung*. If the second word were scratched out, the reservist was to report for duty upon the proclamation of the *Kriegsgefahr*. *Strassburg Post*, 1st August 1924. It is true that his statements have been challenged by certain German historians. But they are confirmed by a statement in the report of the session of the Prussian Council of Ministers of 30th July, *Germ. Doc.*, 456, p. 382. "The 'threatening danger of war' went farther than the 'security,'" said Falkenhayn, "if only because of the calling in of the reserves."

day will be followed, with as little delay as possible, by the regular mobilization of my entire military and naval forces.[10] I imagine that 2nd August will be the first day of this mobilization, and I shall be prepared to commence hostilities at once against Russia and France, according to the terms of our alliance," wrote William II to Franz Joseph.[11] It was thus taken for granted that the order for general mobilization would follow within forty-eight hours.[12] "That," declared Bethmann, "would be the signal for the struggle to begin."

The Chancellor admitted to Goschen that he was sorry, "for he knew that France did not desire war."[13]

Since, however, the announcement of mobilization must be followed at once by the opening of hostilities, according to the plan of the General Staff,[14] it was indispensable to proceed first of all to a diplomatic rupture. That is the reason why the German Government decided to issue an ultimatum to St. Petersburg, and another to Paris, at the same time that it proclaimed the "state of threatening danger of war."[15]

It demanded that Russia should cease mobilization at once:[16]

. . . German mobilization must follow in case Russia does not suspend every war measure against Austria-Hungary and

[10] On the previous evening the Prussian Council of Ministers had passed upon the *economic* measures which should come into force in case of mobilization.

[11] *Dipl. Pap.*, III, 81, 31st July.

[12] *Cf.* also *Germ. Doc.*, 479, p. 395.

[13] *Blue Book*, 98. This idea was also echoed by Wenniger, *Bayerische Dokumente,* 3rd edition, p. 229. It was felt, he said, that "France is showing all at once a lack of desire to go to war." 1st August, No. 2700.

[14] This plan called for the entry into Luxemburg during the early hours of mobilization.

[15] Tirpitz, *Erinnerungen*, p. 239.

[16] *Germ. Doc.*, 490, p. 404, 3.30 P.M., 31st July. At the same time, William II wired to the Tsar: "The peace of Europe may still be maintained by you, if Russia will agree to stop the military measures which must threaten Germany and Austria-Hungary." *Germ. Doc.*, 480, p. 399, 2.04 P.M.

ourselves within twelve hours and make us a distinct declaration to that effect.

The telegram reached St. Petersburg at 11 P.M., and the message was delivered at midnight. The time-limit therefore extended until noon on 1st August.

The ultimatum addressed to France informed the French Government of the demand which had just been made of Russia. It added: "Mobilization will inevitably mean war." Did France intend to remain neutral "in a Russo-German war"? An answer must be given within eighteen hours, and was therefore due at 1 P.M. on 1st August.[17]

The replies from Paris and from St. Petersburg thus ought to reach Berlin at about 4 P.M. on 1st August. The orders for mobilization might then be signed at once, and executed on the following day. No one dreamed that the decision would be postponed any longer. "There is no doubt that the replies from Russia and France will be refusals," wrote Lerchenfeld.[18]

The German Government wished to be prepared, however, for the possibility of having France promise to remain neutral. In this case, Ambassador von Schoen was instructed "to inform the French Government that we shall have to demand the turning over of the fortresses of Toul and Verdun as a pledge of neutrality; these we would occupy and return after the completion of the war with Russia."

It is true that this "unfortunate" (the adjective is Schoen's) idea played no part in the course of events, as the Ambassador was not called upon to carry out this clause of his instructions, much to his relief.[19] The details of the telegram were not made public until 1918, and the incident

[17] *Germ. Doc.*, 491, p. 405, 3.30 P.M., 31st July, arrived at 6 P.M.

[18] *Germ. Doc.*, Supp. IV, 24, p. 233, 8 P.M., 31st July.

[19] Schoen, *Erlebtes*, p. 191. "Had I been placed in the position mentioned in the instructions, and had I carried out the orders which were given me, I should have been committing a grave mistake, although of course it would have been no fault of mine."

is only interesting as showing something of the plans of the German Government.[20]

Bethmann-Hollweg himself has made only the following comment:[21] "If France had actually declared her neutrality, we should have had to sit by while the French army, under the protection of a specious neutrality, made all its preparations to attack us while we were busy in the East." This was the fear which was constantly in the minds of the German leaders, and this explains why Germany, according to the Chancellor, felt justified in demanding some security.

But that was not the whole of the matter. Did Berlin really believe that such a guaranty would be practicable under such conditions? That is the interpretation which von Schoen maintains. "The German Government supposed that if France declared her neutrality, which was very improbable, she would allow the occupation of Toul and Verdun." In so thinking, it was committing a grave psychological error, "a blunder,"[22] which proved "its complete misunderstanding of the national feeling in France." But its intention was not to bring on war at any price, by imposing this demand. "The demand to turn over the fortresses was not the result of a desire to provoke a rupture at any cost; it was simply a gross error in judgment."[23]

Ought we not rather to believe, on the contrary, that the German Government was following out a logical plan in making this demand? Its whole plan of campaign consisted in crushing France first. The occupation of Toul and Verdun could hardly take the place of a military victory, and the concentration which had been planned could not be altered at the last moment.[24] Moltke wanted to fight the war

---

[20] The facts were brought to light by M. Pichon, in a lecture given at the Sorbonne.

[21] *Betrachtungen zum Weltkriege,* I, p. 165, note 1.

[22] Schoen, *Erlebtes,* p. 178.

[23] Schoen, *Erlebtes,* p. 179.

[24] See below, Ch. XIV, p. 245.

as he had planned it out; he was not in a position to fight it in any other way. That is why the German Government wished, even had the French Cabinet been tempted to stay out of the conflict, to arouse the public opinion of France to such a degree of indignation that the country would be forced into the war in spite of itself.

II. *The Last Attempts at a Compromise.*
(*31st July-1st August.*)

WHILE the German Government was thus bringing matters to a head, the diplomats once more became very active. Conversations were taking place in several different capitals at once. In order to get a clear idea of what went on, we must examine in turn the moves made by Austria, Russia, and England.

1. The Austrian offers.—At the very moment when she had just proclaimed general mobilization, and refused the proposals made by Sir Edward Grey, Austria suddenly appeared more willing than ever to proceed with negotiations. Both at St. Petersburg and at Paris she took surprising steps in the direction of conciliation.

Count Berchtold had promised on the thirtieth to renew direct conversations with Russia, in order to satisfy the request which Germany had made, and had sent Count Szápáry corresponding instructions, which were incidentally quite vague.[25] The situation had changed by the following day, for both countries had decided upon general mobilization. Szápáry's first reaction was not to carry out these instructions.[26] Upon thinking the matter over, however, he decided on the evening of the thirty-first to enter into "conversation" with the Russian officials.

"I decided to do so," Szápáry wrote,[27] "because, in the

25 See above, Ch. X, p. 186.
26 *Dipl. Pap.*, III, 74, 2.45 P.M., 31st July.
27 *Dipl. Pap.*, III, 75, 11.17 P.M., 31st July.

first place, I did not wish to disavow Emperor William's declaration, which had been to the effect that we were still quite prepared to negotiate; and because, furthermore, for reasons of strategy as well, it seemed to me a good chance to make it quite evident that we were being attacked, and that the whole fault lay with Russia."

The character of the interview was rather curious. The Ambassador declared to Sazonov that Austria was prepared "to negotiate on the most open terms with Russia," and in particular to examine with her the details of the Austrian ultimatum to Serbia, provided it was only a question of their interpretation. The Russian Minister responded eagerly to these advances. His hopes revived, and he attached such "an exaggerated importance" to the interview that Szápáry felt called upon to cool down his ardor by referring to "the recent changes in the situation."[28] The Austro-Hungarian Ambassador was careful not to engage his Government too far, as he did not know what its precise intentions were, and he simply wished to establish "a basis" for future negotiations.

And in Vienna, when Shebeko, the Russian Ambassador, came the next day to pay "a friendly call" at the Ballplatz, and to express the hope that the difference might be settled by direct negotiation, Count Berchtold carefully kept the conversation on general topics, and avoided any direct discussion.[29]

With regard to France, Austria's attitude was quite different. In the course of a conversation with Szécsen, the Austrian Ambassador in Paris, M. Viviani had expressed the hope that the conflict might yet be avoided. Some solution must be found, he had said, which "would assure Russia that Serbia would not be destroyed."[30] The Ambassador did not

[28] *Dipl. Pap.,* III, 97.
[29] *Dipl. Pap.,* III, 99, 1st August.
[30] *Dipl. Pap.,* III, 40. "Russia must be assured first of all that we do not wish the destruction of Serbia."

feel in a position to give the French Government at once
the assurance that it requested, for the Austrian declaration
of "territorial disinterestedness" had been communicated to
him from Vienna "only for his personal information." He
did feel, however, that the time had come for him to pass
this information on informally to M. Viviani.[31] Upon receiving the report of this interview, Count Berchtold wired
at once to Szécsen: "I beg Your Excellency to call M. Viviani's attention at once to the fact that our action in Serbia
has not been taken with a view to any territorial acquisition,
and that we do not wish to attack the sovereignty of that
kingdom."[32]

This promise held good, however, only so long as the war
remained a local affair, that is to say, if Russia did not
intervene.

The declaration of "territorial disinterestedness" thus
seemed to correspond to the desire which the French Premier
had expressed the previous evening. How much confidence
could be placed in it? It must be kept in mind that Austria
had secretly decided to dismember Serbia for the benefit of
Bulgaria and Albania,[33] and that the first proposal made by
Sazonov, referring to "the sovereign rights of Serbia," had
been rejected by Germany.[34]

Count Szécsen carried out these instructions, however, at

[31] According to the Ambassador's own testimony, "Ein vergeblicher Versuch für die Erhaltung des Friedens im Sommer 1914," in *Die Kriegsschuldfrage,* February 1926, p. 66.

[32] *Dipl. Pap.,* III, 62, 31st July.

[33] See above, Ch. IV, pp. 56-57.

[34] *Cf.* above, Ch. X, p. 185. According to a telegram from Isvolsky, No.
223, 1st August, *Livre Noir,* p. 298, Austria insinuated that the Russian
Government had "intentionally" kept silent about the promises made by
Vienna. Now, it is true that Szápáry had declared Austria's *territorial*
disinterestedness to Sazonov, but subject to the reserve that he had never
promised to respect Serbian *sovereignty.*

It was only on 31st July that Sazonov believed that Austria would agree
to any discussion of the essential details of the note, and he at once notified
London and Paris to that effect.

about 11.15 p.m. on the evening of 31st July. M. Viviani
was not then at the Quai d'Orsay, and it was M. Berthelot,
Deputy Political Director of the Ministry for Foreign Affairs, who received the Ambassador. Count Szécsen's remarks
gave the impression that he did not consider "all conciliation
as impossible." He went further than merely presenting the
declaration of his Government, and added, in his personal
capacity, "that it ought to be possible to settle the Serbian
question." Mobilization did not mean war, for it still left
several days for negotiation. "It was up to Serbia to ask
Austria for her conditions." This move might be made
through the good offices of a neutral Power; it should be
based upon a promise to carry out *all* the clauses of the ultimatum. But M. Berthelot had already known for some hours
that both Russia and Austria had ordered general mobilization. He also knew that von Schoen had presented the German ultimatum to M. Viviani that very evening. He therefore replied, "in a strictly private capacity," by saying that
"it seemed rather late for such negotiations, which had now
been superseded by other events."[35] According to the Austrian account of the interview, he added that, "in view of
Germany's *démarche* today[36] the Serbian question was now
pushed quite into the background."

But Count Szécsen did not confine himself merely to his
call at the Quai d'Orsay. At a dinner on that same evening,
the thirty-first, he declared to M. Lahovary, Rumanian
Minister in Paris, that all hopes of a settlement were not yet
lost. "If Serbia should approach Austria, either directly or
through the good offices of another Power," he said, the Vienna Government might perhaps be willing to state what
"complementary demands" it intended to make.[37] M. Laho-

[35] *Yellow Book,* 120, and *Dipl. Pap.,* III, 64.
[36] The ultimatum.
[37] Could Serbia any longer approach Austria directly? It is much more
probable that such negotiations might have taken place through the mediation of another Power.

vary described the conversation to the Swiss Minister, Lardy, who sent at once to Berne for authority to take the initiative suggested. At the same time, Lahovary notified his Serbian colleague, Vesnić, of what had taken place.[38]

The Serbian Minister and the Rumanian Minister, with the knowledge of the Austrian Ambassador, appeared at the Quai d'Orsay between ten and eleven o'clock on the evening of the thirty-first, and informed M. de Margerie of the suggestion which Count Szécsen had made. The Political Director promised to wire at once to Vienna for further light upon the matter. A moment later, as we have seen, Szécsen himself appeared at the Quai d'Orsay.

On the following day, 1st August, Lahovary and Lardy learned the fate of the step they had taken. The answer given them was that the attitude which Germany had now adopted toward Russia (the despatch of the *ultimatum*, and not the *declaration* of war, to which these witnesses refer) made any further discussion impossible.[39] Szécsen had meanwhile been trying in vain to have the Austrian declaration of "territorial disinterestedness" published in the Paris press.[40]

It thus appears that the Quai d'Orsay did not feel that it should carry the matter any further. Late on the morning of 1st August, however, M. Viviani sent a circular letter to all the French ambassadors, describing in a general way

[38] Count Berchtold apparently had not been notified of the remark which his Ambassador had made to Lahovary.

[39] The documents bearing on this *démarche* were made public by M. Victor Basch, in the *Ère Nouvelle*, 27th December 1920. M. Lahovary, in the *Matin* of 4th January 1921, confirmed the statement that his interview with Szécsen, as well as his call at the Quai d'Orsay, took place on the evening of the thirty-first. For further discussion of this whole incident, *cf.* Morhardt, pp. 235-238.

[40] Szécsen says that he made an appeal to this end "to a senator and former minister who was at the head of a well-known newspaper." His request was refused by letter. "The hour for a peaceful settlement is, alas, past!" wrote the senator. *Die Kriegsschuldfrage,* February 1926, p. 68.

the *démarche* of the Austrian Ambassador, and mentioning
the Austro-Russian conversations.

How much importance can be attached to these advances
on the part of the Austrian Government? Was Vienna suddenly struck with terror at the possible consequences of the
imminent conflict? These last-minute changes of mind were
quite characteristic of the Ballplatz.[41] And yet the Austrian
attitude with regard to Russia showed quite clearly that the
Vienna Government did not wish to make more than a mere
gesture, and that the Austrian diplomats did not wish to
bind themselves any more closely. Szápáry simply considered
it necessary from the strategic point of view, in order, as he
said, "to make Russia appear as much as possible in the
wrong." Count Szécsen's efforts to have his statement published in the French press would seem to indicate that he
had a similar purpose in mind.

The *démarche* carried out in Paris was based upon the
possibility of keeping the Austro-Serbian war localized, a
situation which no longer existed, now that Russia and Austria were mobilizing against each other, and now that Europe was faced with Germany's double ultimatum. The Austrian move may therefore be looked upon as an attempt to
discredit Russian mobilization in the eyes of France, and
it was based, like all the earlier Austrian declarations, upon
the equivocal statement concerning "territorial disinterestedness."

As opposed to this interpretation, attention should be
called to a statement which M. Viviani made in the circular
which he sent to all the French ambassadors. The Austrian
attitude, he said,[42] "still allows us to hope for a peaceful
solution." It was Germany's attitude which counteracted all
these efforts! The double ultimatum was doubtless quite

[41] *Cf.* Szilassy, *Der Untergang der Donau-Monarchie,* Berlin, Neues Vaterland, 1921.
[42] *Yellow Book,* 120.

enough to frustrate any attempts at conciliation, but did M. Viviani actually believe the Austrian *démarche* to be sincere? He simply pretended to believe so in order to contrast the Austrian attitude with the German, and thus possibly create ill-feeling between Vienna and Berlin.[43]

2. Russia.—Even before learning of the German ultimatum, the Russian Government had decided definitely not to delay mobilization. "It is technically impossible to stop our military preparations," Nicholas II wired to William II early on the afternoon of the thirty-first,[44] claiming quite erroneously that Austrian mobilization had come first, and had caused that of his own country. Upon receiving the ultimatum from Count Pourtalès, Sazonov also referred to "the technical impossibility of suspending the war measures."[45] But it had been stated in St. Petersburg that the Austro-Russian conversations with regard to Serbia might be continued.

Sazonov seemed to feel that these discussions were still of some importance, as we have seen. He addressed a note to the British Government on the evening of the thirty-first, sending a copy of the same note to the other great Powers:[46]

The Ambassador from Austria-Hungary declares that his Government is ready to discuss the contents of the ultimatum addressed by Austria-Hungary to Serbia. M. Sazonov has replied and expressed his satisfaction. He said that he wished the discussion might take place in London, and with the participa-

[43] There is one fact which would seem to confirm this possibility. On 1st August, M. Dumaine took steps at Vienna to show that Germany was *solely* responsible for the failure of the attempts at a compromise. *Dipl. Pap.*, III, 99. This raises another question: Would it not have been more clever to accept the Austrian proposal, instead of replying that it was "too late"? This might have created considerable ill-feeling between Vienna and Berlin, or at least brought the whole maneuver out into the light of day.

[44] *Germ. Doc.*, 487, p. 402, 2.55 P.M.

[45] *Germ. Doc.*, 536, p. 429.

[46] Romberg, p. 39, and *Brit. Doc.*, 418, p. 249. Shebeko was also optimistic. *Cf. Yellow Book*, 115.

tion of the other great Powers. M. Sazonov hopes that the British Government will assume the direction of the discussion.

The Minister for Foreign Affairs was certainly under illusions as to the meaning and significance of the Austrian declarations. Is there any reason to believe that these illusions were feigned? Count Montgelas does not believe that M. Sazonov could have been under any misapprehension. The German historian feels that his action was simply a maneuver to gain time, in order to permit the Russian army to complete its preparation.[47] This supposition does not appear to me to be justifiable.

A short while beforehand,[48] the Russian Government had modified its "formula" of the previous evening, in such a way as to comply with Sir Edward Grey's request:[49]

If Austria agrees to suspend the advance of her armies upon Serbian territory, and if, recognizing that the Austro-Serbian conflict has taken on the character of a European struggle, she will allow the great Powers to examine the degree of satisfaction which Serbia could give Austria without injuring her sovereign rights or her independence, Russia undertakes to maintain her attitude as an onlooker.

In this second "formula" Sazonov thus did not promise to suspend mobilization, but only to refrain from opening hostilities, as the Tsar had done in his telegram to William II. He proposed a collective intervention by the great Powers; this was the position he had always held, and Austria had refused to accept, up until the recent advances made by Count Szápáry. Would the Russian statesman now agree to the occupation of Belgrade, which had formed the

[47] Montgelas, p. 144.

[48] The time of these two events is not precisely known. But the second "formula" was the object of Telegram No. 1582, whereas the Austrian *démarche* was reported in Telegram No. 1592.

[49] See above, Ch. X, pp. 185-186.

basis of the proposals made by various chancelleries during the last few days? The words "suspend the advance of her armies" might be considered as an implicit acceptance of the idea.[50]

3. England.—The London Cabinet did not yet know, by 31st July, how the idea of the "*Halt im Belgrad*" had been received by the Vienna Government. Moreover, it still maintained that Russia could not be asked to suspend her military preparations so long as Austria had not "set some limit to the advance of her troops into Serbia."[51]

Since Austria had announced, however, that she was willing to renew direct relations with Russia,[52] Grey immediately formulated a new proposal. It was "suspicion," he said, that was blocking any real solution. Could not the four "disinterested" Powers (England, France, Germany, Italy) assure Austria that Serbia would give her "entire satisfaction," and assure Russia that Serbia would not suffer any infringement upon her sovereignty or her integrity? In addition, "all the Powers should suspend preparation and military operations."

This proposal amounted to making a European affair of the conflict, as Sazonov had already offered to do. It meant abandoning the idea of the "seizure of hostage territory," which Vienna had never accepted. It was quite different, too, from the proposal made on the twenty-sixth to hold a conference, for this time the Powers were to bind themselves, in the case of Austria, to see that she received complete satisfaction.

[50] "To suspend the advance" implied that this advance might have begun. In interpreting this formula, the advice which France gave must also be considered. *Yellow Book*, 112. Now, M. Viviani accepted the English idea, "that Austria should stop her advance after the occupation of Belgrade." The interpretation given by Montgelas, p. 150, is therefore inaccurate.

[51] *Blue Book*, 110. Grey did not know at the moment of general mobilization in Russia.

[52] Lichnowsky notified Grey to this effect on the morning of the thirty-first. *Germ. Doc.*, 489, p. 403, 12.15 P.M.

If Germany should agree to a "reasonable solution," Sir Edward Grey added, and if France and Russia should refuse it, the English Government "would not concern itself with the consequences."

This new suggestion reached Berlin on the afternoon or evening of the thirty-first.

On the following morning, Grey learned of the second formula proposed by Sazonov, which agreed in general with his own proposition of the night before. The two schemes differed, however, in one point: Russia did not promise "to suspend all preparation," but only "to maintain her position as an onlooker." In spite of this difference, the English Minister agreed to communicate the Russian formula to the various cabinets, without comment, on 1st August.

Meanwhile word had reached London of Russian general mobilization, which caused considerable surprise. At 3.30 A.M. on 1st August King George telegraphed to Nicholas II: "I cannot help thinking that some misunderstanding has produced this deadlock." He asked that Russia should "leave still open grounds for negotiation, and possible peace."[53]

During the course of the day, the Austrian Ambassador finally delivered his Government's reply to the English proposal of the "Halt im Belgrad," as had been decided upon by the Council of Ministers in Vienna. It was not encouraging. And what would Count Berchtold's position be, now that Russian *general* mobilization was a *fait accompli?* The Ambassador could at least give a definite answer upon this point: ". . . In spite of the Russian mobilization, Austria-Hungary would be prepared to accept mediation and to suspend mobilization in Galicia, if Russia should agree to suspend hers as well."

Sir Edward Grey, who knew nothing of Franz Joseph's

53 *Brit. Doc.*, 384, p. 235.

telegram to William II,[54] and who could not have suspected the real intentions of the Austrian Government,[55] seemed to sense a real desire for conciliation in the present attitude of the Vienna Government. Although Count Mensdorff's reply was hardly satisfactory, the Secretary of State accepted it in a cordial manner, and communicated it to Sir George Buchanan: "You should inform the Minister for Foreign Affairs and say that if, in consideration of the acceptance of mediation by Austria, Russia can agree to stop mobilization, it appears still to be possible to preserve peace."[56]

In his desire to keep the way open for possible negotiations, Sir Edward Grey thus accepted two contrasting suggestions on 1st August. He seemed inclined to accept Sazonov's second formula, although it did not altogether conform to his own point of view, and at the same time he accepted a reply from Austria which did not even promise to limit her military action. After declaring that the suspension of activity in Russia would depend upon Austria's promise to be satisfied with the occupation of Belgrade, he finally intervened at St. Petersburg to demand the suspension of mobilization, without receiving the corresponding promise from Vienna at all. Could the Secretary of State have misinterpreted the meaning of the Austrian reply, or was he annoyed at the suddenness with which Russia had decreed general mobilization?[57] In any case, he seemed to be undergoing a certain change of mind, a change which

[54] See above, Ch. X, p. 192, note 87.

[55] See above, Ch. X, p. 180.

[56] *Brit. Doc.*, 422, p. 251. The British Ambassador was received by the Tsar at 11 P.M. on 1st August. Nicholas II declared to Sir George Buchanan that he would gladly have accepted the English proposals, had it not been for the declaration of war by Germany. *Brit. Doc.*, 490, p. 276.

[57] It should be noted that Bethmann tried to impress Sir Edward Grey with a wholly false idea, by informing him that the news of Russian general mobilization reached Vienna *during* the discussion in the Austrian Council of Ministers, and *before* that body had reached a decision. *Germ. Doc.*, 513, p. 415.

was doubtless modified the next day by more precise information about Austria's real intentions.[58]

*   *   *   *   *   *   *

For any of these suggestions to become a reality, however,
some delay was necessary. Now, the German ultimatums
both expired at about noon on 1st August. Were military
operations to begin at once? Secretary of State Jagow declared to Goschen on the evening of the thirty-first that "it
was impossible for the Imperial Government to consider
any proposal until they had received an answer from Russia
to their communication," that is, to the ultimatum.[59] On 1st
August the British Ambassador communicated another
memorandum to the Wilhelmstrasse to show that it would
be possible to maintain peace, if only there might be a
brief respite before one of the great Powers should start the
war. Jagow replied that Russia "had the weight of numbers
on her side; she might remain mobilized for months without
actually opening any hostilities." With Germany, "the case
was different. Speed was essential for her." The Berlin Government therefore refused either to reconsider or to wait. It
was too late.[60] Military arguments were in absolute control
of the situation.

III. *Mobilization in France and Germany.*

THE German Government received a telegram on the morning of the first stating that the ultimatum had been delivered
to Russia. It knew that Sazonov would refuse to suspend
mobilization, but it was not until noon that the official reply
of the Russian Government was handed to Count Pourtalès.

[58] For his demand about the respecting of Belgian neutrality, see below,
Ch. XIV.

[59] *Brit. Doc.*, 385, p. 236.

[60] It thus became possible for the Tsar, who had been somewhat embarrassed by King George's telegram, to reply by pointing out that war had
actually been declared. *Cf.* Montgelas, p. 146.

The German Government also knew that von Schoen had delivered the ultimatum to France at 7 P.M. on the thirty-first. M. Viviani had replied "that he had received no news of any Russian general mobilization, but only of precautionary measures."[61] As a matter of fact, M. Paléologue's telegram containing the news did not reach Paris, as we have seen, until 8.30 P.M.[62] The French Premier promised a reply on the question of neutrality for 1 P.M. on 1st August, at the latest. Later instructions authorized von Schoen to extend the time limit by two hours, if it should become necessary to ask for a reply to the secret clause.[63]

To tell the truth, it had been the intention at Berlin, ever since the proclamation of the "state of threatening danger of war," to issue orders for general mobilization on the afternoon of 1st August. At five o'clock the ministers and the chiefs of the army and navy were called together at the Imperial Palace. No reply had as yet been received from Paris or St. Petersburg. In spite of that fact, the orders were signed at once.

General mobilization had just been decreed at the same time in France.

Ever since the evening of the twenty-fifth the French Government had begun to take measures of military precaution. It was acting on the principle, according to M. Messimy,[64] of "watching with the minutest attention everything that was going on in Germany," and of having the French army immediately take steps corresponding to those which its intelligence service reported as taking place across the Rhine. Thus it was that the French General Staff ordered

[61] *Germ. Doc.*, 528, p. 423.

[62] M. Viviani had consequently not had word of it by 9 P.M., for time must be allowed for decodification.

[63] *Germ. Doc.*, 543, p. 435.

[64] *Cf.* Recouly, *Les heures tragiques d'avant-guerre*, Paris, La Renaissance du Livre, 1922, p. 61. The German historians question the statement that the measures taken by their General Staff preceded those in France.

all troops engaged in maneuvers to return to their cantonments, recalled all officers on leave on the twenty-sixth,[65] and all enlisted men on the twenty-seventh. It had also decided to have all active military forces, "in so far as it was possible," return from Morocco, and it made provision for the transportation of those troops. On the twenty-ninth General Joffre asked that the frontier troops be allowed to take up their positions. The Cabinet, after considering the matter, gave the Chief of Staff partial satisfaction on the following day. The five army corps which formed the frontier guard might take their places, but without making any special movements by train, and without summoning their reservists. Thus only the units *close* to the frontier were to carry out these orders.

The German proclamation of the "state of threatening danger of war" was reported in Paris on the afternoon of the thirty-first. The Cabinet at once received a message from General Joffre demanding the complete mobilization of all the army corps in the east. "It is essential that the Government should realize that, from now on, every delay of twenty-four hours in calling out the reservists and in sending out the final telegrams for frontier defense will mean a setback in our scheme of concentration, that is to say, an immediate retreat from a part of our territory, of from fifteen to twenty kilometers for each day of delay."[66] At 5.15 P.M. the Cabinet decided that "most extensive measures" should be taken with regard to the five frontier army corps.

General Joffre appeared again at eight o'clock on the morning of 1st August. According to information he had received, Germany could actually proceed with total mobilization under the guise of the "state of threatening danger

[65] The generals were recalled on the evening of the twenty-fifth.

[66] France, Etat-Major de l'Armée, Service Historique, *Les armées françaises dans la grande guerre,* Paris, Imprimerie Nationale, 1923, Tome I, Vol. I, Annex 17.

of war." "I repeat what I told you yesterday. If the Government delays any longer in giving orders for general mobilization, it will be impossible for me to continue to assume the crushing responsibility of the high office in which its confidence has placed me." The General presented a full explanation of his position before the Cabinet at nine o'clock. No objection whatever was raised: "There was not a single protest, not a single remark . . .," wrote M. Messimy. The order was signed and given to the Minister of War, who was to send it out at 4 p.m. At about noon M. Viviani handed von Schoen the reply to the German ultimatum: "France would act in accordance with her interests."[67]

The mobilization telegram was ready to be sent off. General Ebener, Assistant Chief of Staff, received it from M. Messimy at 3.45.[68] A moment later M. Viviani came to the War Office. He wished "to postpone the telegram a bit longer."[69] But the order had already gone out. "The machine was in motion."

IV. *The Ten-Kilometer Withdrawal.*

ALONG the frontier, however, the French and the German troops covering the concentration of the two armies were not to come into direct contact. At the very moment when the French Government ordered the covering troops to take

[67] *Germ. Doc.,* 571, p. 448. 1.05 p.m., 1st August. Reached Berlin at 6.10. According to von Schoen, M. Viviani based the "uncertainty" of this statement on the fact that he regarded the situation as changed. What he had in mind was Szécsen's *démarche,* and Grey's new proposal.
[68] 2.45 German time.
[69] According to M. Messimy, M. Viviani thought that there was still "some hope of a settlement," as the result of an interview with von Schoen. What interview did he mean? There is no light upon this point. Baron von Schoen called upon M. Viviani in the morning, *Livre Noir,* II, p. 295, Tel. No. 218, without renewing his demand for a reply to the ultimatum, nor his threat to leave, but this could not have been the interview referred to. It may have been the interview at noon, for, according to von Schoen's report, M. Viviani showed signs of hesitation at that time. But in that case why should M. Viviani have waited four hours before trying to delay the telegram?

their places, on 30th July, it also made the famous decision which was to keep all its troops back approximately ten kilometers from the frontier for three days.[70]

"The spirit of the order which we gave," declared M. Viviani later,[71] "was not to allow any contact between the German troops and the French troops." The Government wished to prevent any local incidents from occurring, which might bring about war "as the result of an equivocation"; it wanted to be sure to avoid every thoughtless act, every imprudent move. "We realized that everything might turn on some chance incident. A patrol might get on the wrong road and run up against an enemy patrol, a sergeant or a corporal might lose his head, a soldier might think himself in danger and fire off his rifle. . . ."[72] Far better not to expose ourselves to any such contacts, which the enemy might distort into attacks on our part."[73]

In setting up a neutral zone between the two armies, the French Government thus undertook an extreme measure of control over its troops. But at the same time it also had in mind certain diplomatic advantages which might result from the step. It would furnish a proof, in the eyes of the world, that France would not take a provocative attitude; it would also serve as a guaranty that, if some incident should arise between French and German troops, such an incident would be interpreted in favor of the French. The Government was thinking especially of England. "We had to let the English Government know," declared M. Viviani,[74] "that France

[70] On this subject, see *Les armées françaises dans la grande guerre*, Tome I, Vol. I, Annexes; *Procès-verbaux de la Commission d'enquête sur le rôle et la situation de la métallurgie en France*, especially the statements made by M. Messimy, General Verraux, and General Malleterre; and *Débats parlementaires*, Chamber of Deputies, session of 31st January 1919.

[71] Speech in the Chamber of Deputies, 31st January 1919.

[72] *Ibid.*

[73] This was the expression used by General Malleterre before the Briey Committee.

[74] Speech of 31st January 1919.

would not hesitate to uncover her frontiers, in order to give evidence of her good faith, and of her determination not to take the initiative in any attack."

Further light upon the nature and purpose of the measure is cast by the wording of the order itself. At 4.55 P.M. on 30th July the Minister of War wired to the commanders of the frontier troops (the 2nd, 6th, 7th, 20th, and 21st Army Corps) to have their men occupy certain "positions to guard against sudden attack." The order continued: "For diplomatic reasons, however, it is essential that no incident should arise out of any move on our part," and a line was fixed, by naming the different points on the map, which "no troop and no patrol should cross under any pretext."[75]

On 1st August the Government took care to point out that the order for general mobilization did not alter any of the foregoing instructions. The Minister of War made this clear to the general in charge of the frontier troops, and himself telegraphed at 5 P.M. to the various commanders: "With a view to assuring ourselves of the support of our English neighbors, it is still essential not to allow any patrols or detachments to cross the general line fixed by the telegram of 30th July, except in case of a deliberate attack by the enemy."[76] Finally, at 10.30 P.M. the President of the Republic took it upon himself to intervene "for serious diplomatic reasons," and the Minister repeated that "no patrol, no reconnoitring party, no outpost, no detachment," should be allowed to cross the line of demarcation.[77] "Any one crossing the line will be held strictly accountable to the Military Tribunal, and only in case of an obvious attack will any one

[75] *Les armées françaises,* Tome I, Vol. I, Annex 15.
[76] *Les armées françaises,* Annex 25.
[77] *Les armées françaises,* Annex 26. The order adds: "This applies especially to the 20th Corps, which is so close to the enemy. A reliable person reports having been actually face to face with a squadron of Uhlans and a squadron of Hussars."

be permitted to transgress this order, which is being communicated to all the troops."[78]

The French Government not only concerned itself with the details of the order, but undertook also to impress the significance of the measure upon the English Cabinet and upon English public opinion. The Minister for Foreign Affairs wired to M. Cambon on the afternoon of the thirtieth, asking the Ambassador to communicate certain information to Sir Edward Grey concerning military preparation in Germany and France:[79]

> You will draw the attention of Sir Edward Grey to the decision reached by the Cabinet this morning. Although Germany has taken up her position several hundred meters or several kilometers from the frontier, along the whole frontier from Luxemburg to the Vosges, and has brought her covering troops into a strategic position, we have not done so; and this, even though our plan of campaign, drawn up for an offensive, calls for having our covering troops in strategic positions as close to the frontier as the German troops now are. We are thus leaving a strip of French territory defenseless against sudden attack.
>
> We had no reason for doing this, other than to show the British Government and the British people that France, like Russia, did not intend to be the first to open fire.

The execution of the order of course affected the inhabitants of the evacuated area, who were left exposed to attacks by the enemy. From a military standpoint, however, it did not meet with any opposition among the army chiefs. Even though it compelled them to withdraw their "advanced

[78] A previous order, *Les armées françaises*, Annex 29, had forbidden any outpost or patrol to penetrate within a zone of from two to three kilometers along the Belgian frontier, in order "to avoid any incident."

[79] *Yellow Book*, 106, and *Brit. Doc.*, 319 (enclosure in French), p. 201. The French Government took several occasions to point out the nature of the withdrawal to Sir Edward Grey. See, for instance, *Brit. Doc.*, 447, p. 260.

posts," and made cavalry patrols impossible, it did not generally involve an extensive shifting of the "covering troops," who took up their position some distance back from the frontier.[80] Future operations were neither seriously interfered with nor endangered, so long as the withdrawal was temporary.[81] General Joffre simply asked that he should not feel obliged to carry out the order "in absolute strictness." And the Government granted his request.[82] The ten-kilometer limit was set only as a general rule. "They did not draw a line with a ruler," as M. Viviani put it. It was understood, for that matter, that "if a given point were of great strategic importance, the withdrawal would be somewhat less." The customs officials and the forest guards were of course left along the frontier.

The various commanders thus retained considerable freedom in their interpretation of the order. "There are numerous documents in the archives," so M. Messimy told the Briey Committee in 1919, "showing the exact orders sent out to the troops from general headquarters. In these orders, you will see that the line was traced through certain villages about 4 or 5 kilometers back from the frontier."[83] According to all the reports that have been made, the application of the order varied somewhat from sector to sector. "At numerous points," according to M. Messimy, the most advanced posts were only four or five kilometers from the frontier. Whereas the order appears to have been very strictly carried out around Belfort and in the northern Vosges, it appears on the other hand that in the southern Vosges, at one point, at least—at La Schlucht pass—the withdrawal

[80] *Cf.* M. Messimy's statement before the Briey Committee, p. 264. See also p. 313.

[81] General Malleterre, who at first considered the withdrawal "a generous but fatal mistake," admitted in 1919 that he had been misinformed. *Briey Report*, p. 302.

[82] *Briey Report*, p. 260.

[83] Report of M. Engerand on the work of the Committee. Chambre des Députés, *Documents parlementaires,* 1919, No. 6026, p. 2571.

was not executed until the morning of 2nd August, although ordered on the thirtieth.[84] On the front occupied by the 6th Army Corps, General Sarrail limited himself, in carrying out the order, to forbidding all movements within a zone of four kilometers along the frontier.[85] But apart from these local variations, the spirit of the order was apparently felt everywhere. Up until the afternoon of 2nd August the French troops were kept in the positions to which they were assigned on the evening of 30th July.[86]

"Mobilization is not war." Thus read the posters signed by the French Government. Baron von Schoen was still in Paris, although he had referred to his probable departure. No doubt could really have remained in anyone's mind. On the evening of the thirty-first, M. Messimy had declared "in an enthusiastic tone" to the Russian Military Attaché that the French Government had made up its mind to the war.[87]

Certainly the German Government no longer had any doubts. The Emperor had already given his approval to the wording of the declarations of war. The one intended for Russia, sent from Berlin even before the general mobilization order was signed, was soon to be in the hands of Count Pourtalès.

[84] Cf. General Legrand-Girarde, Les opérations du 21e. Corps d'Armée, Paris, Plon, 1922, p. 20. He describes how the order made it necessary for him to evacuate the barracks at Fraize, occupied by the 158th: also the orders given by the general in command at Belfort on 30th July, quoted by R. Puaux; also Le 152e au feu, Nancy, Berger-Levrault, 1920, p. 9.

[85] General Sarrail's memoirs were published by the Revue politique et parlementaire, 10th May 1921, p. 163. The general adds this rather curious remark: "I could not testify under oath to having received this order," but the documents in the Historical Department prove that the order was sent to the 6th Army Corps, which he commanded. His subordinate, General Verraux, had learned of the order, and furthermore, the fact that the General remembers "limiting himself" to forbidding all patrols implies that he must have received instructions concerning the neutral zone.

[86] The order for the "ten-kilometer withdrawal" was rescinded on the afternoon of the second, and the English Government was notified of that fact the next morning.

[87] Livre Noir, II, p. 294, Tel. No. 216.

CHAPTER XIV

GERMANY AND THE DECLARATIONS OF WAR

NOW that the double ultimatum had been sent, and mobilization proclaimed in France and Germany, it may seem that the last page of this story had been written. After all, how important is the actual declaration of war? It is simply a necessary formality; at least, so it was considered by the general staffs and by the various governments, in the privacy of their secret deliberations.

It was still necessary, however, to be extremely careful. The instinctive judgment of public opinion might have serious effects upon the interplay of the various alliances, and the diplomats could not afford to ignore it, as the military leaders wished to do.

The German Government was conscious of the risk it assumed when it took the initiative of declaring war. Many were the discussions and hesitations before it came to a decision. In the last analysis, it was the considerations put forward by the General Staff that dominated the situation. The plan of campaign called for an immediate offensive which should strike at the French army across Belgian territory, and put it completely out of action within six weeks, so that Germany might then turn the major part of her forces against Russia. The campaign in France was to be the deciding factor in the conflict. Did not Moltke's General Staff ever consider the possibility of altering this plan, and of attacking Russia alone? They certainly thought of it, but they considered it altogether "improbable," and did not really take it seriously.[1] "Plan II," although still under con-

[1] Contrary to the opinion held by Schlieffen. *Cf.* Kuhl, *Der deutsche Generalstab in Vorbereitung und Durchführung des Weltkrieges*, Berlin, Mittler & Sohn, 1920, pp. 156 and 171-172.

sideration in 1912, appears to have been wholly abandoned since that time.[2] This fact should be kept in mind as we consider the final steps in the crisis. The German Government was bound by technical military decisions, which had been made some time in advance, and which now dominated the situation.

I. *The Declaration of War upon Russia.*

SINCE the German Government frankly expected a negative reply from Russia on the morning of 1st August, would it not be expedient to accept the consequences at once, and take the initiative in making the break?

Opinion in Germany was divided. "We were not altogether united upon the form which our action should take," writes Bethmann.[3] It is no easy task to analyze in detail the different points of view which were held in Berlin. If we may believe the Chancellor's account, the General Staff intended to cross the Russian frontier at once, not with a view to carrying on a great offensive, but simply to threaten the enemy on that side. For this reason it was essential that war be declared at once. Moltke denies that he had any such intention, but he does not claim to have opposed the immediate rupture; in his opinion, "the declaration of war was a matter of no great importance." The opposition came from Minister of War Falkenhayn and from Admiral von Tirpitz, both of whom considered that it would be a political error to declare war upon Russia at this particular moment. The treaties which bound Austria and Germany to Rumania and Italy were defensive in character. In taking the initiative of making the break, the Central Powers would give their allies a chance to deny the *casus fœderis*. Was not

[2] *Zur Vorgeschichte des Weltkrieges*, II, *Militärische Rüstungen und Mobilmachungen*, p. 47.
[3] *Betrachtungen*, I, p. 156.

this a more powerful argument than the Chancellor's "legal formalism"?[4]

Bethmann-Hollweg's view, however, was finally adopted. Shortly after noon the text of the declaration of war was sent to Count Pourtalès, to be delivered that same evening if the Russian Government, as was to be expected, should reply in the negative.

After alluding to the fact that Russia had ordered general mobilization "without awaiting the results" of German intervention at Vienna, the declaration stated that the duty of the German Government was to protect "the security and the very existence" of the country. This had been the reason for the demand that Russia should at once suspend all the military measures she had undertaken.

As no one in Berlin knew whether Sazonov would *refuse* to agree to the German demands, or would simply *fail to reply* to them, the instructions contained an alternative wording:

Russia having refused to accede to this demand (*or* having believed it unnecessary to respond to this demand), and having made it manifest by this refusal (*or* by this attitude) that her action was directed against Germany, I have the honor, on behalf of my Government, to inform Your Excellency as follows:

His Majesty the Emperor, my August Sovereign, accepts the challenge in the name of the Empire, and considers himself as being in a state of war with Russia.[5]

The telegram did not reach Count Pourtalès until 5.45 P.M., Russian time, and the decodification was not complete until 6.45. The Ambassador at once made a hurried call upon Sazonov, for the order was to have been carried out at five, according to the Chancellor's plan. After receiving the negative reply to the ultimatum that he expected, he handed over

[4] Tirpitz, *Erinnerungen*, p. 240.

[5] *Germ. Doc.*, 542, p. 434. Two other drafts had also been prepared, and appear in the *German Documents*.

248   IMMEDIATE ORIGINS OF THE WAR

the declaration of war, including the alternative wording, either overlooking this detail in his agitation,[6] or because he considered the additional note simply as a "memorandum."[7]

A few hours later the Russian Government suddenly found itself in a most embarrassing position. At about 1.30 in the morning the Tsar received a final personal appeal from Emperor William:

. . . I yesterday pointed out to your Government the way by which, alone, war might be avoided. Although I requested an answer for noon today, no telegram from my Ambassador conveying an answer from your Government has reached me yet. I have therefore been obliged to mobilize my Army. Immediate, affirmative, clear and unmistakable answer from your Government is the only way to avoid endless misery. Until I have received this answer, alas, I am unable to discuss the subject of your telegram.[8] As a matter of fact I must request you to order your troops immediately on no account to commit the slightest act of trespassing over our frontiers.[9]

It is easy to imagine the astonishment of Nicholas II.[10] War had already been declared. William II had doubtless not yet received word from Count Pourtalès by the time he sent the telegram, but he knew that the final interview between the Ambassador and Sazonov had taken place toward the end of the afternoon. And now here he was asking the

[6] According to Paléologue, I, p. 43, who had a direct account of the interview from Sazonov, the German Ambassador burst into sobs as he left the Minister's office.

[7] This is the version of the story given by Count Pourtalès himself, p. 84.

[8] The Tsar had wired the Emperor at 2.06 P.M. on 1st August, *Germ. Doc.*, 546, p. 436: "I understand that you are obliged to mobilize, but wish to have the same guaranty from you as I gave you, that these measures *do not mean war,* and that we shall continue negotiating."

[9] In the *White Book* the Kaiser's telegram was erroneously dated at 10.45 A.M., 1st August. *Germ. Doc.*, 600, p. 463.

[10] Paléologue, I, p. 203, gives an account of the incident which he received directly from the Tsar on 21st November 1914.

Tsar to forbid his troops to cross the frontier! The Minister for Foreign Affairs telephoned to Count Pourtalès at four in the morning to inform him of the curious message which had come, and the Ambassador was quite mystified. He would have liked to believe that the date on the telegram was wrong, and that it had been sent the night before.[11]

To explain this new move on the part of William II, we are left with mere hypotheses. Are we to believe that the Kaiser was "frightened," as M. Palèologue suggests, by the responsibility which he had assumed in declaring war, and that he wished to make a final gesture which should find its way into the *White Book?* Or shall we accept M. Basili's explanation that "he lost his head a bit"?[12] But it was not he who composed the telegram at all. He simply revised a draft which had been submitted to him by the Chancellor![13] If we may believe M. Paléologue's account, the Tsar's first reaction was that the message from William II was intended to make him hesitate or to arouse scruples in his mind, and thus lead him to make some "ridiculous and disgraceful misstep." This is quite possible. For the past twenty years the Kaiser had felt conscious of the influence he was able to exert over "Nicky's" mind. We must consider what immediate interest would have been served by proceeding in this way. Perhaps the incidents which had just taken place in Berlin will furnish the key to the mystery.

II. *Lichnowsky's "Mistake."*

At the very moment when the order for general mobilization had just been signed, and when the declaration of war upon France had received the Emperor's approval, the Wilhelm-

---

[11] Pourtalès, p. 89, and *Germ. Doc.,* 666, p. 497.

[12] This is also the explanation given by Kautsky, *Wie der Weltkrieg entstand,* Berlin, Cassirer, 1919, pp. 141-142. It seems to be further confirmed by the Kaiser's attitude toward Moltke. See below.

[13] *Germ. Doc.,* 599, p. 463.

strasse received a telegram from Prince Lichnowsky which gave an unexpected turn to the whole situation:

> Sir Edward Grey has just had me informed through Sir William Tyrrell that he hopes to be able to give me this afternoon, as the result of a Ministerial Council now in session, some facts which may prove useful for the avoidance of the great catastrophe. Judging from Sir William's hints, this would appear to mean that in case we did not attack France, England would remain neutral and would guarantee France's neutrality.

While awaiting the outcome of the deliberations of the British Cabinet, it was therefore essential, the Ambassador said, not to violate the French frontier.[14]

Sir Edward Grey was, in fact, still wondering at this time whether it would not be possible for the French and German armies, even after mobilization, to remain facing one another without crossing the frontier. "I cannot say," he wired to Sir Francis Bertie, "whether this would be consistent with French obligations under the alliance. If it were so consistent, I suppose the French Government would not object to our engaging to be neutral as long as the German army remained on the frontier on the defensive."[15] But the English Minister apparently understood[16] that in this case Germany would refrain from attacking Russia as well, and would simply remain as a spectator of the Austro-Russian war. There was thus a gross misunderstanding in the whole matter from the outset.[17]

When the Chancellor and the Emperor received Lich-

---

[14] *Germ. Doc.*, 562, p. 444, sent at 11.14 A.M., arrived 4.23 P.M.

[15] *Brit. Doc.*, 419, p. 250. 1st August, 5.25 P.M.

[16] *Cf.* his explanation in the House of Commons on 28th August 1914, reproduced in *Brit. Doc.*, 419 note, p. 250.

[17] It must be admitted that the terms of Sir Edward's message to Sir Francis Bertie were rather curious, and that the Ambassador was somewhat taken aback. *Brit. Doc.*, 453, p. 263. Furthermore, Sir Edward Grey canceled his earlier telegram on the morning of 2nd August. *Ibid.*, 460, p. 266.

nowsky's telegram, they had not learned of M. Viviani's reply to the ultimatum.[18] Without taking time to think over the terms of the message, and without recalling that, if by chance M. Viviani had promised to remain neutral, von Schoen had been instructed to demand the occupation of Toul and Verdun, which might have somewhat discouraged England's good will, William II immediately sent for the Chief of Staff, who had left the New Palace a few minutes earlier, after the signing of the mobilization order.

General von Moltke's memoirs contain a curious account of the discussion which ensued in the Imperial Palace:[19]

The Emperor said to me: "We march, then, with all our forces, only toward the East!"

I replied to His Majesty that this was impossible. The advance of armies formed of millions of men could not be undertaken on the spur of the moment. It was the result of years of painstaking work. Once planned, it could not possibly be changed. If His Majesty should decide to turn his whole force against the East, we should no longer have an organized force, ready to fight, but a mass of armed men, lacking cohesion and lacking provisions.

The Chief of Staff thus rejected the whole plan which had just been proposed by the Emperor! The discussion became more heated:

The Kaiser stuck to his point of view, and became very *stiff*. Among other things, he said: "Your uncle would have given me a different reply." This pained me a good deal, for I have never pretended to be the equal of the great Field Marshal.

Moltke pressed the matter further, however. He explained that Germany could not throw her whole strength against Russia, when France was also mobilizing at her very side:

[18] This reply, which arrived at 6.10 P.M., could not have been decoded before about seven.

[19] *Erinnerungen, Briefe, Dokumente, 1877-1916*, edited by Eliza von Moltke, Stuttgart, Der Kommende Tag, 1922, p. 19.

I finally succeeded in convincing His Majesty that the concentration of our armies, which had been planned with the strongest forces on the French side, and with weak defensive forces on the Russian side, must be allowed to take its course as intended, if we did not want to end in complete confusion. I told the Emperor that after this concentration had been effected, it would be possible to shift the strongest parts of the army to the East, but that the original concentration must be allowed to go through unchanged. Otherwise I could not assume the responsibility.

In replying at once to the word which had come from London, the German Government therefore conformed to the point of view maintained by the General Staff. Germany was prepared to accept the English proposal, so Bethmann wired to Lichnowsky at 7.15 P.M.,[20] but she insisted on three conditions: the mobilization which had been "begun on two fronts" should be allowed to continue; England "should pledge security for the unconditional neutrality of France," until the completion of the Russo-German conflict; finally, Germany should be allowed to carry the war against Russia as far as she pleased. In order to allow the London Government time to make up its mind, the Chancellor promised simply "not to cross the French frontier before Monday, 3rd August."[21]

At the same time, William II wired to the King of England: "On technical grounds, the German mobilization must proceed against two fronts east and west as prepared." If France should remain neutral, however, and if this neutrality should be *guaranteed* by the British fleet and army, "I shall refrain from attacking France," he added, "and shall employ my troops elsewhere."[22]

[20] Oman, *The Outbreak of the War of 1914-1918*, London, H.M. Stationery Office, 1919, p. 103. It is pointed out that Bethmann affected to believe that some *definite* proposal had been made. This was not the case, as is shown even by Lichnowsky's statements.

[21] *Germ. Doc.*, 578, p. 452.

[22] *Germ. Doc.*, 575, p. 451. 7.02 P.M., 1st August.

And the Wilhelmstrasse hastened to notify Baron von Schoen of the English "offer": "Please keep the French quiet for the time being," wired Jagow.[23]

The discussion continued at the Imperial Palace. According to the plan for mobilization, the Grand Duchy of Luxemburg was to be occupied on the first day by the 16th Division of infantry. As the orders for mobilization had been sent out at 5 p.m., the troops were thus supposed to invade the Grand Duchy early the following morning. And now the Chancellor opposed this move! In his opinion, this would constitute "a direct menace against France," which would destroy all hopes of obtaining a "guaranty" from England. Moltke was not even given time to reply to Bethmann's argument:

As I was about to do so [he said], the Emperor turned to the adjutant on duty, without asking me a word, and ordered him to telegraph at once to the 16th Division of infantry, at Trêves, that it was not to penetrate into Luxemburg.

It was a great shock to me, as though something had struck at my heart! Once again I was faced with the danger of seeing our whole plan of concentration upset. In order to understand fully what that means, one must know something of the complexity and detail of the work of concentrating an army. Each train is scheduled to leave on the minute, and any change will have fatal consequences.

I tried to point out to His Majesty that we needed the use of the Luxemburg railways, and that we must assure ourselves the control over them. I was cut short by his reply: all I had to do was to arrange to use other railways in their place!

I was overwhelmed.[24]

23 *Germ. Doc.*, 587, p. 457.
24 What would Moltke have said had he known the true situation? As a matter of fact, while he was bemoaning his situation, the neutrality of Luxemburg had already been violated by a part of this very 16th Division! At about seven o'clock in the evening, some officers and soldiers who belonged, it seemed, to the 69th Regiment, and who were stationed at Trêves,

The General's uneasiness did not last long, however. At 11 P.M. he was again called to the Palace. The Emperor received him in his bedroom, and showed him a telegram which had just come from King George:[25]

In answer to your telegram just received, I think there must be some misunderstanding as to a suggestion that passed in friendly conversation between Prince Lichnowsky and Sir Edward Grey this afternoon when they were discussing how actual fighting between French and German armies might be avoided while there is still a chance of some agreement between Austria and Serbia. Sir Edward Grey will arrange to see Prince Lichnowsky early tomorrow morning to ascertain whether there is a misunderstanding on his part.

It was not even necessary to wait until the next day. After a further call upon Sir Edward Grey, Lichnowsky had just sent a new telegram.[26] The English "offer" was becoming inconsistent. The Minister for Foreign Affairs had simply wondered "whether it would not be possible" for Germany and France to remain facing one another without attacking each other. But he had not carried the idea any further, and, besides, was there any assurance that France would accept this idea? "He would like to inform himself" upon this point. What, then, remained of the news which had caused such a stir in Berlin? Nothing at all. Lichnowsky recognized the mistake he had made. His first telegram was altogether "fruitless," since there was no prospect of "a positive proposal on England's part," and he gave up all idea of taking "further steps."

The following morning he completed his painful expla-

had occupied the Luxemburg station at Ulflingen and had torn up the rails beyond it. The Government of Luxemburg had just filed a protest. Events were progressing even faster than the General Staff had anticipated. *Germ. Doc.*, 602, p. 464. Eyschen, Minister of the Grand Duchy, to Jagow. 9.30 P.M., 1st August.

[25] *Germ. Doc.*, 612, p. 471.
[26] *Germ. Doc.*, 596, p. 460.

nation.[27] "Suggestions of Sir Edward Grey, which were founded on wish to secure France's permanent neutrality, if possible, were made without previous communication with France, and without knowledge of mobilization, and have since been abandoned entirely as hopeless."

But Emperor William had already recognized the futility of the hopes he had formed a moment earlier. The telegram from King George was quite enough. "Now," he said to Moltke, "you may do as you wish." And orders were immediately sent to carry out the movements as planned in the territory of Luxemburg.

The declaration of war upon France, which was already prepared, might now be sent. At least, there was no apparent reason to delay it any longer. A new question arose on the night of 1st August, however, this time at the Chancellery. While Bethmann-Hollweg, according to the memoirs of Admiral von Tirpitz, favored dispatching the declaration of war at once, because the time was ripe to notify Belgium, the Grand Admiral raised another problem. He stressed the position of the Navy, and requested that the "notification" of Belgium, as well as the declaration of war upon France, might be made "as late as possible," so that the Fleet might have time to complete its preparation.[28] Intervention on England's part was now quite probable, but it would certainly not be assured until Germany had openly commenced hostilities. The Admiral requested a little more time. Bethmann-Hollweg yielded, and sent the following note to the Emperor on the morning of 2nd August:[29]

In accordance with understanding with Ministry of War and General Staff, presentation of declaration of war to France not necessary today for any military reasons. Consequently it will not be done, in the hope that the French will attack us.

[27] *Germ. Doc.*, 631, p. 479. 6.28 A.M., 2nd August.
[28] Tirpitz, *Erinnerungen*, p. 242.
[29] *Germ. Doc.*, 629, p. 478.

This whole account gives an impression of confusion and disorder! Friction among the Emperor's assistants, contradictory decisions, general nervousness. We must not, however, mistake the significance of these hesitations. Did William II's impetuous acts during his first interview with Moltke mean that the Emperor was drawing back at the last moment? No. What he had before him was the prospect of a victory without any risks, of a war in two separate phases, which would allow him first to crush Russia, leaving him free to settle with France later. It is easy to understand how such a possibility must have appealed to him. As for the discussions between the Chancellor and the General Staffs, which led to the delay in presenting the declaration of war to France, they can certainly not be taken as an indication that Germany was hoping to avoid the conflict by negotiation, for it was nothing more than the immediate interest of the Fleet which brought about this decision.

Furthermore, German troops actually entered the Grand Duchy of Luxemburg at daybreak on 2nd August. The machine was now in motion, and the violation of Belgian neutrality was soon to follow.

III. *The Violation of Belgian Neutrality.*

THE German plan of campaign called for the entry of troops into Belgian territory at the very outset of operations. In spite of Jagow's declarations before the Budget Committee of the Reichstag on 29th April 1913,[30] the Belgian Government suspected the intentions of the German General Staff. M. de Broqueville had voiced his apprehensions before Parliament during a closed session in 1913. On the other hand, he said, he did not fear a similar encroachment on the part of France. He believed simply that the

30 Belgian *Gray Book,* Annex to No. 12. Jagow had said: "The neutrality of Belgium is defined in international conventions, and Germany is determined to respect those conventions."

French General Staff had considered the possibility of an advance into Belgian territory in case of an attack by Germany. "In order to forestall any possible surprise, we must therefore prepare and be on our guard on both sides."[31]

Upon receiving word of the Austrian declaration of war upon Serbia, the Belgian Cabinet had decided on 28th July to place the army on the "reinforced peace footing," that is to say, to call out three classes of reservists to complete the effective strength of the active divisions. General mobilization was decided upon on the evening of the thirty-first, and was proclaimed the following morning.

The situation was soon to become quite clear. As soon as the English Government heard of the German proclamation of the "state of threatening danger of war," it took identical steps in Berlin and Paris.[32] Would the French and the German Governments "undertake to respect the neutrality of Belgium," so long as no other Power had violated it? At the same time, the English Minister in Brussels had asked the Belgian Government whether it had decided "to do all in its power to maintain its neutrality." This gave reason to suppose that England would intervene if the treaty should be violated.[33]

The French Minister informed the Belgian Government of the reply which had been given to England. "The French Government is resolved to respect the neutrality of Belgium, and it would only be in the event of some other Power violating that neutrality that France might find herself under the necessity, in order to assure the defense of her own security, to act otherwise."[34]

[31] According to a report by Huysmans. *Cf.* also Marsily, *Les chefs de l'armée belge et le respect de la neutralité,* Paris, Payot, 1917, pp. 29-30.

[32] In Paris this *démarche* was made on the evening of the thirty-first, at 10.30.

[33] Bassompierre, "La nuit du 2 au 3 août 1914 au Ministère des Affaires Étrangères de Belgique," *Revue des Deux Mondes,* Vol. 31, 15th Feb. 1916, p. 889.

[34] *Brit. Doc.,* 382, p. 234, and *Gray Book,* 15.

But no reply had come from Germany, who apparently felt that any declaration would be impossible because it might disclose a part of her plan of campaign.

M. Bassompierre called upon Herr von Below, the German representative in Brussels, shortly after noon, in the hope of obtaining some statement from him. The German diplomat could only reply that "personally he was of the formal opinion that Belgium had nothing to fear from Germany." As the Berlin Government had assured Holland on the previous evening, however, that her territory would be respected, its failure to make a similar declaration in Brussels had a very obvious significance. Public opinion and certain political groups in Belgium may, in spite of this, still have been uncertain about Germany's plans. After all, had not Bethmann made it clear in 1911, with regard to the question of Flessingue, that he would refuse to make any public declaration on the question of neutrality, in order to benefit by any possible military surprises? Furthermore, Herr von Below had given a reassuring interview to the *Soir:* "Perhaps you will see your neighbor's roof burn, but the fire will spare your house." The members of the Government, however, could not have had many illusions on the subject. The news which reached Brussels on the second ought to have opened the eyes of any of them who were still cherishing some hope: the territory of Luxemburg had been invaded, and troop trains had left Cologne early in the morning for Aix-la-Chapelle. And yet M. Davignon, the Belgian Minister for Foreign Affairs, declared to the British Ambassador, even on 2nd August, "that there was no reason whatever to suspect that Germany intended to violate the neutrality of Belgium."[35]

At 7 P.M. on 2nd August, von Below called to present the German ultimatum to the Belgian Minister for Foreign Affairs.[36]

[35] *Brit. Doc.*, 670, p. 350.
[36] The text had been sent to him on 29th July. See above, Ch. X, pp. 172-

"The Imperial Government," read the note, "is in receipt of reliable information relating to the proposed advance of French armed forces along the Meuse, route Givet-Namur. This information leaves no doubt as to France's intention to advance against Germany through Belgian territory." As Belgium was not in a position to assure the respect of her neutrality, Germany would therefore be forced to advance her troops into Belgian territory. But this measure was not "an act of hostility against Belgium." If the Brussels Government observed "a benevolent neutrality," Germany undertook "to evacuate the territory of the Kingdom as soon as peace shall have been concluded," to guarantee "the sovereign rights and independence" of the State, and to pay cash for all the necessities required by her troops, and for every damage which they might occasion.[37] On the other hand, if Belgium should resist, she would be treated as an enemy. The reply was demanded within twelve hours.

The note was delivered in German. The Minister's secretaries translated it at once, while word was sent to the Premier. The King was notified and the Cabinet called together in an emergency meeting. The deliberations continued from nine o'clock until midnight. No report of this session has been published. According to Baron Gaiffier, Political Director,[38] there was no divergence of opinion whatever as to the attitude which Belgium should adopt. "One of those present simply showed what the consequences of a different decision might be, merely to prove that it was impossible." The proposed reply, which the Political Director had mean-

173. The order to deliver the note was sent from Berlin at 2.05, with the following comment: "The Belgian Government must receive the impression that all instructions bearing on this affair reached you only today."

[37] The draft of 29th July also offered Belgium "territorial compensation at the expense of France." But this clause was struck out at the last moment (*Germ. Doc.*, 648, p. 486), doubtless out of consideration for England's attitude.

[38] Recouly, p. 136. But the Baron was not present at the meeting, and his statements are simply based on accounts given him by several ministers.

while been preparing, was drawn up on the spot by M. Davignon and M. de Broqueville, assisted by some of the other ministers. It was approved by the Cabinet at two o'clock in the morning.

The German Minister, acting upon the instructions of his Government, had meanwhile made a final *démarche*.[39] He informed the Secretary-General of the Belgian Ministry for Foreign Affairs that the French had opened hostilities by sending a dirigible to drop bombs in German territory; that "eighty French officers, in the uniforms of Prussian officers," had attempted to cross the German frontier by automobile, "to the west of Geldern." These statements had nothing to do with Belgian territory, but Herr von Below pointed out that they showed that France had no great respect for international law. The German Government thus hoped to influence the decision of the Belgian Government by this false information (for neither statement was based on the slightest truth).[40] But all was in vain. Von Below was quite aware of this at the time.[41] "Both commissions executed," he wired at three o'clock in the morning. "Do not believe, however, that this will have any influence on the Belgian reply, which, according to my impression, will probably be in the negative."

He received it, as a matter of fact, at seven o'clock on the morning of the third, from the hands of M. de Gaiffier d'Hestroy. Belgium was neutral, the note said. She had always fulfilled her duties as a neutral "in a spirit of loyal impartiality." There was no "strategic interest" which could justify "a violation of law." "The Belgian Government, if it were to accept the proposals submitted to it, would sacrifice the honor of the nation and at the same time betray its duty

[39] *Gray Book,* 21.

[40] The German Government had accepted these rumors without verifying them.

[41] *Germ. Doc.,* 709, 3.05 A.M., 3rd August.

toward Europe." It had therefore decided "to repel by all the means in its power every attack upon its rights."[42] The German Military Attaché at once carried the text of this reply to Aix-la-Chapelle by automobile.

Early in the morning the Political Director placed a copy of the two documents in the hands of the French Minister in Brussels, M. Klobukowski, and the correspondent of the Havas Agency also made a résumé of them, for use in the British and French press.[43]

M. Klobukowski at once offered M. Davignon the support of the French army. "Without having any official declaration from my Government, I feel that I can tell you, knowing what I do of its intentions, that if the Royal Government should appeal to the French Government as a Power guaranteeing its neutrality, we should respond at once to its appeal."[44] For the moment, however, M. Davignon refused to appeal for the support of the Powers. He wanted to feel that Belgium, in case of aggression, would be able to defend herself, not so much from confidence in the strength of his country, as from a desire not to commit himself irrevocably on either side.[45] King Albert simply sent a message to King George, asking for "diplomatic intervention."[46] That same evening Sir Edward Grey promised that England would enter the war if Belgian neutrality were violated.[47]

At six o'clock on the morning of 4th August von Below notified the Belgian Government that Germany was going

[42] *Germ. Doc.*, 779, p. 554.

[43] *Cf.* Klobukowski, "Les responsabilités de l'Allemagne: Avant l'agression," *Le Temps*, 6th August 1924.

[44] *Gray Book*, 24. M. Klobukowski added that France would doubtless wait until Belgium had made some effective resistance before intervening, unless, of course, the necessities of her own defense led to exceptional measures.

[45] *Cf.* Sir F. H. Villiers, *Brit. Doc.*, 670, p. 350.

[46] *Gray Book*, 25.

[47] *Gray Book*, 26, confirmed by a note on the following day, No. 28.

"to act by force of arms." At eight o'clock the frontier was violated. The news reached Brussels at eleven, just as the Belgian Parliament, after listening to the speech by King Albert, who appealed for "stubborn resistance" and for united action by all loyal Belgians, was passing the most urgent legislative measures.[48] M. Davignon immediately called upon France, England, and Russia for "the aid of their armies." "Belgium," he added, "is happy to be able to declare that she will undertake the defense of her strongholds."[49] In Berlin, on the other hand, where it had been assumed that Belgium would limit herself to a formal protest,[50] the Secretary of State for Foreign Affairs still refused to abandon all hope. He instructed von Below to declare "that Germany was ready at any time to hold out to Belgium the hand of a brother." The basis of a *modus vivendi* would be "the opening of Liège to the passage of German troops, and the cessation of the destruction of railroads, bridges, and artificial structures."[51] But von Below received his passports at 4 p.m. on that same day.

*   *   *   *   *   *   *

When the discovery of the "Brussels Documents" in October 1914, brought to light certain papers bearing on the Anglo-Belgian conversations of 1906 and 1911, Chancellor

[48] *Cf.* Lichtervelde, *Heures d'histoire. Le 4 août, 1914, au Parlement belge*, Brussels, Van Oest, 1918, p. 61. It should be noted that the King still alluded in his speech to the hope "that the terrible events might not take place." The wording had been prepared the night before, and approved that morning by the Cabinet. This sentence was read in spite of the communication which had since come from von Below.

[49] *Gray Book*, 40.

[50] This was Moltke's opinion. *Erinnerungen, Briefe, Dokumente*, p. 17. He even wrote to Jagow, on the afternoon of 3rd August, "I am still counting on the possibility of coming to an understanding when the Belgian Government realizes the seriousness of the situation." *Germ. Doc.*, 788, p. 560. *Cf.* also 849, p. 586.

[51] *Germ. Doc.*, 805, p. 568. Sent from Berlin at 9.20 a.m., 4th August. This *démarche* was renewed, we know, on 9th August. *Cf. Gray Book*, 60 and 62.

Bethmann-Hollweg took the opportunity to declare that Belgium herself "had destroyed her own neutrality for the benefit of England."[52] Morally, Belgium was thus no longer neutral, for she had agreed to study the means of landing English troops in her territory; she had thus taken sides in advance with the Entente. These are arguments which may have seemed useful for war propaganda, but they scarcely deserve a careful examination. The fact is well established that these conversations never got beyond the stage of "an exchange of ideas," and they never resulted in anything like a definite agreement. They were quite compatible with the duties of a neutral, since they dealt only with the case in which Germany might violate the international treaty. They were legitimate, because England was one of the Powers guaranteeing that treaty. The German historians recognize the truth of this fact today.[53] Besides this, did Germany know of these documents at the time when she decided to violate Belgian neutrality?[54] Bethmann-Hollweg himself in 1919 half abandoned the arguments which he had been forced to use during the war. "Certainly," he exclaimed, "the documents compromise Belgium's position, but even if they were much more compromising than they actually are, would they have freed us from the obligation of respecting the neutrality guaranteed in 1839?"[55] According to Montgelas, Bethmann used the single word "appropriate" in addressing the Reichstag on 4th August 1914, when he referred to the "injustice" which had been committed, and added that "necessity knows no law."

[52] These "conversations" were those of Major Ducarne and Colonel Barnardiston in 1906, and of Colonel Bridges and General Jungbluth in 1911. Material upon this question is quite abundant. *Cf.* Langenhove, *Le dossier diplomatique de la question belge,* Paris, Van Oest, 1917; Émile Waxweiler, *Le procès de la neutralité belge: réplique aux accusations,* Paris, Payot, 1916.

[53] Veit Valentin, Ch. XI.

[54] Montgelas, pp. 185-186.

[55] Bethmann, *Betrachtungen zum Weltkriege,* I, pp. 168-169.

IV. *The Declaration of War on France.*

GERMANY declared war upon France at 6.15 P.M. on 3rd August. No doubt had been left in the mind of either Government since 1st August, but each had hesitated to precipitate the actual rupture. The German General Staff believed that France would be obliged "by public opinion" to commit acts of war.[56] The French Government preferred to wait until it could show actual instances of aggression and thus avoid a debate in Parliament on the Franco-Russian alliance, during which unfortunate statements might be made by members of the Extreme Left.[57] The incidents which took place on 2nd and 3rd August are therefore of only secondary importance in the problem of the immediate origins of the war.[58] It is interesting to notice, however, which side was best able to keep its forces under control.

I. Now, there were numerous violations of the French frontier by German troops.[59] M. Puaux's precise and documented account refers to twenty-nine (sixteen on 2nd August and ten before 6 P.M. on 3rd August) in twenty-four different places. Even as early as the afternoon of 30th July, two noncommissioned officers, stationed at Dieuze, crossed the frontier and galloped for two or three hundred meters in French territory, doubtless as an act of bravado. But the later incidents were of quite a different character.

Incursions of German patrols took place on 2nd August, especially in the neighborhood of Belfort.[60] The frontier was crossed at eleven places by cavalry, who collided with customs officers at Suarce, Reppe, and Vauthiermont. The

---

[56] *Germ. Doc.*, 662, p. 495.

[57] Isvolsky to Sazonov, No. 222, *Livre Noir*, II, p. 297.

[58] Although, on both sides, the governments took every opportunity to communicate such information as they had to the English Government.

[59] On the question of the violations of the frontier, see Puaux, *Le mensonge du 3 août*, Paris, Payot, 1917, in which certain documents are published from the historical department of the army.

[60] One, however, was near Sainte Marie, another near Longwy, and a third near Cirey, but without any exchange of shots.

orders for the ten-kilometer withdrawal had been strictly carried out, so that there were no French troops in the frontier area. Only one German reconnoitring party penetrated further into French territory, namely, the one which Lieutenant Mayer led toward Joncherey. It met with an advance post of the 44th Infantry and killed Corporal Peugeot, who was in charge. These facts have been carefully examined, and the very path of the German patrols into French territory has been determined. There is not the slightest doubt about the accuracy of the facts. The Joncherey incident, which was the most serious, was the object of an immediate protest on the part of the French Government.

On 3rd August the patrols became more active in Lorraine. There was only a slight exchange of fire along the Nancy-Château-Salins railroad, and along the Longwy railroad. But at Coincourt, at Réchicourt-la-Petite and at Réméreville, some German cavalry were shot down. One of them, an officer, had patrol orders instructing him to penetrate as far as Saint-Nicolas-du-Port, ten kilometers from the frontier.[61]

To what extent were these violations of the frontier the result of individual initiative? To what extent, on the other hand, were they ordered from headquarters?

The German General Staff itself declared that "on the third of August permission was given to move scouts forward over the border."[62] This discussion is therefore concerned only with the events of 2nd August. The number and the character of the incidents which occurred on the earlier day lead to the belief that regular reconnoitring parties had been planned and ordered. The German General Staff and the Chancellor have formally denied this. The

[61] Finally, at Lunéville an airplane dropped six small bombs at 5.45 P.M., a few minutes *before* war was declared. *Cf.* Puaux, pp. 359-365.

[62] Moltke to Jagow, 4th August, *Germ. Doc.*, 869, p. 596.

Joncherey incident, they say, which is the only complaint they admit to be justifiable, cannot be laid to the charge of headquarters. Lieutenant Mayer was acting on his own initiative, "against express orders." But was the General Staff correctly informed? On the morning of 3rd August, Moltke stated *in person* to the Chancellor that "not a single German soldier had penetrated into French territory." He was obliged to admit his error on the following day. The reconnoitring party at Joncherey and the other patrols near by had doubtless been undertaken by the twenty-ninth Cavalry Brigade, whose mobilization orders called for the immediate execution of reconnoitring expeditions, directly upon the receipt of orders for mobilization, which were assumed to coincide with the declaration of war. The testimony given by one of the men captured at Joncherey confirms this view of the matter.[63] Lieutenant Mayer thus could not have been acting on his own initiative, but it is possible that the actions of the 29th Brigade were not known in detail by the General Army Headquarters. On the other hand, according to a statement made to Sir Edward Goschen on 3rd August, at the request of the Chancellor, by an official of the Wilhelmstrasse, "in some cases as necessary measures of precaution German patrols had crossed the frontier."[64]

These early incidents had a most decided effect in Paris. General Joffre, who had been trying throughout the morning of the second to have the Cabinet countermand the orders

---

[63] This man stated that Lieutenant Mayer, who had been waiting near the telephone in a little inn, suddenly came out and said to his men: "Orders to cross the frontier." *Cf.* Puaux, p. 268. In an address delivered at Joncherey on 17th July 1922, M. Poincaré brought up another argument, which is not so convincing. On 4th August, according to M. Poincaré, the German Consul in Basel, Switzerland, made inquiries of his French colleague concerning Lieutenant Mayer, "who was wounded day before yesterday near Delle, in French territory." But this does not necessarily prove that Mayer was acting under orders from his *superiors*. The surviving members of his patrol may have notified the Army Headquarters in Mülhausen of what had taken place.

[64] *Brit. Doc.*, 553, p. 299.

for the ten-kilometer withdrawal,[65] at last received satisfaction early in the afternoon, as soon as the Minister of War learned of the Joncherey incident. "The French Government," said the instructions telephoned at 2.10 P.M., "considers that the violations of the French frontier are of such a nature as to allow the removal of the earlier order not to penetrate into the zone of ten kilometers on the French side of the frontier. The Government therefore gives the Commander-in-Chief *absolute liberty* of action to carry out his plans, even if it means crossing the German frontier."[66] But the General Staff did not wish to take full advantage of the freedom of action which it had been offered. In communicating the cancellation of the orders for withdrawal to the army commanders, at 5.30 in the afternoon, it added: ". . . The frontier troops will limit themselves to driving any attacking forces back across the frontier, without pursuing them any further, and without themselves crossing into enemy territory." General Joffre renewed his appeal the following morning: "If there are to be any incidents, they must start and finish on French territory."

II. Such was the situation when Baron von Schoen presented M. Viviani with the German declaration of war upon France, at 6.15 P.M. on 3rd August. The letter which he placed in the hands of the French Premier referred, as we know, to "flagrantly hostile acts" committed on German territory by French military aviators, as the justification for the declaration of war:

Several of these have openly violated the neutrality of Bel-

[65] *Les armées françaises dans la grande guerre,* Tome I, Vol. I, Annex 28, an unsigned note from the Chief of Staff. The order given on 30th July, says the note, had made it necessary "to abandon points which had a certain strategic importance for our plan of campaign." The general therefore asked for authorization to reëstablish control over this zone. Otherwise, it would mean considerable losses in order to re-occupy these points later on.

[66] *Les armées françaises dans la grande guerre,* Tome I, Vol. I, p. 85, and Annex 27.

gium by flying over the territory of that country; one has attempted to destroy buildings near Wesel; others have been seen in the district of the Eifel; one has thrown bombs on the railway near Karlsruhe and Nuremberg.

Now, the text which had been telegraphed from Berlin was somewhat longer, and referred to incidents of quite another type:

Up to the present time [read the instructions] German troops have been ordered to respect the French frontier absolutely, and have implicitly obeyed this order everywhere. On the other hand, yesterday, in spite of the assurance of the ten-kilometer zone, French troops had already crossed the German frontier at Altmünsterol and by the mountain road in the Vosges, and are still on German territory. A French aviator, who must have flown across Belgian territory, was shot down yesterday in an attempt to wreck the railroad at Wesel. Several other French airplanes were unquestionably placed over the Eifel district yesterday. These also must have flown over Belgian territory. Yesterday French airmen dropped bombs on the railroads near Karlsruhe and Nuremberg.[67]

The wording as sent from Berlin thus referred, not only to incidents involving airplanes, but also to violations of the territorial frontier. How could the message thus have been transformed *en route?*

Baron von Schoen explains this inconsistency at great length in his memoirs, as he did also upon his arrival in Berlin on 6th August. The text, he said, was *jumbled* during the course of its transmission, "so that, in spite of repeated efforts, it was possible to decode only fragments." Time was flying. "I finally decided to use the little that had been decoded as a declaration of war."

Here is where the discussion begins:

The non-official version of the story given on 7th August

[67] *Germ. Doc.*, 734, p. 530. Sent from Berlin at 1.05 P.M., 3rd August. This text was published by the Wolff Telegraph Agency on 7th August.

by the Wolff Agency was that the telegram had been *muti-lated* by the French Telegraph Service. What could have been the purpose of jumbling the message? Among the reasons for the declaration of war, as stated in the text, some were false, namely, those having to do with "the aviators"; others were more plausible, namely, those concerning the violation of the frontier by detachments of troops. It was claimed that the French Government decided to jumble the embarrassing details of the message, before allowing it to be delivered to von Schoen. It was clever enough to have the war declared on the basis of a lie. This line of argument, however, assumes that the German code was known to the French Government,[68] for otherwise the text would have been jumbled in a haphazard way, and the results might not have been at all those desired by the Quai d'Orsay.

The argument may be turned the other way, and the claim made that the "jumbling" was wholly a makeshift on the part of von Schoen, to meet the new emergency. The Ambassador had just received a protest concerning the Joncherey incident, and now he was to be compelled, without making the slightest explanation, and under instructions from his Government, to declare that not a single German detachment had crossed the frontier! How could he reply to the remarks which M. Viviani would be sure to make upon this point? He thus had a personal interest in omitting the passage concerning the violation of the territorial frontier.[69]

[68] This is scarcely conceivable. Had this been the case, the French Government might have steadily kept the English Government informed of certain details which it might have learned by decoding the German messages.

[69] M. Aulard, who carefully analyzed all the facts in the *Revue de Paris*, 1st May 1922, pp. 28-43, and who has examined certain technical aspects of the "jumbling" of the message, remarks: "It may be considered as an imaginary document prepared by Herr von Schoen or by one of his assistants, to make Bethmann-Hollweg think that the telegram was jumbled, in order to excuse Herr von Schoen from reading the first part of it to M. Viviani."

It goes without saying that von Schoen has formally denied this interpretation of the matter.

The testimony is contradictory on still a further point of fact. Baron von Schoen states that he took care, upon handing the declaration of war to M. Viviani, to call his attention to the change in the telegram. "I pointed out to him," says the former Ambassador, "that a considerable part of the telegram had been impossible to decode, and that it was conceivable that it contained still other grievances, other hostile acts on the part of France."[70] The French Premier, on the other hand, declares most emphatically that the Ambassador never made a single reference to "telegraphic alterations which might have affected the communication."[71] Baron von Schoen has continued to defend the truth of his statement.[72]

There was but a single witness of the interview, M. de Margerie, and he has taken no part whatever in this discussion.

But, even if we accept the simplest explanation—that it was an accident in transmission—von Schoen's position is nevertheless a curious one. Is it not rather astonishing that the Ambassador should have taken it upon himself to declare war on the basis of an uncertain and unintelligible document?

Presented with the mutilated document, he might easily have deferred the declaration of war, and requested further information from Berlin. Baron von Schoen replies that he was instructed to deliver the message to M. Viviani at five o'clock, that he had no authority to postpone this step, and that, furthermore, he already knew that his Government had

70 Schoen, *Erlebtes*, p. 184.

71 Letter to M. Aulard, reproduced in facsimile in *L'histoire politique de la grande guerre*, Paris, Quillet, 1924, p. 42.

72 "Die deutsche Kriegserklärung am Frankreich, am 3 August 1914," *Deutsche Nation*, July 1922, p. 547.

expected to send the declaration of war on that day.[73] His
Austrian colleague had also confirmed this plan. Whatever
Schoen's real motives were, such an explanation is obviously
superficial.

He should at least have notified his Government of the
important action which he had been obliged to take on his
own initiative, and this he did not do. He sent a telegram
to Berlin at 8.30 P.M. on the third, but it has not been reproduced in the *German Documents*.[74] The French Ministry
for Foreign Affairs has the code version of this message,
which apparently makes no reference whatever to any "jumbling" in the text of the declaration of war.[75] Herr von
Schoen seemed perfectly satisfied, and made no mention in
his wire to Berlin of any mutilation in his instructions. "It
would have been useless," he has since declared, "considering
the state of affairs." He considered it sufficient to mention
it in a report after his arrival in Berlin. And yet he had not
hesitated to wire on two other occasions on the same day,
pointing out that another message had been jumbled.[76] It is
at least rather surprising that no such comment seemed
necessary when a declaration of war was at stake.

III. In order to leave no details in the dark, we must
consider the truth of the grievances listed by Bethmann-
Hollweg.

Violations of the frontier were laid to the charge of French
troops in both official and non-official statements in Germany. A dispatch from the Wolff Telegraph Agency on 3rd
August stated that "companies of French soldiers" had been
occupying certain districts in German territory since the
previous evening: Sainte-Marie-aux-Mines, Metzeral, Gott-

---

[73] *Germ. Doc.*, 625, p. 477.
[74] Because it also arrived "slightly jumbled," so Schoen tells us.
[75] This text was published by M. Aulard, *Revue de Paris*, 1st May 1922.
[76] *Germ. Doc.*, 776, p. 553, and 809, p. 569. The jumbled message in this
case, *Germ. Doc.*, 716, p. 521, denied any violations of the frontier, and announced that the rupture of diplomatic relations was imminent.

esthal (Valdieu). It was given to understand that, before any declaration of war, the French General Staff was trying to assure itself the possession of the upper valleys of Alsace. But this was nothing more than a new forgery, doubtless in the habitual style of diplomats. After recounting this grievance in an official telegram, the Chancellor finally decided not to send it out.[77]

What precise information did the German Government have at its disposal? It had a telegram from the commander of the 15th Army Corps:[78] the French had violated the frontier and opened fire first, during the night of 1st August, to the west of Sainte-Marie-aux-Mines, but there had been no casualties. From the Minister of War[79] it also learned that French cavalry patrols had crossed the frontier at Almünsterol in Alsace. A further violation of the frontier near La Schlucht had not been definitely verified.

This was all that Bethmann-Hollweg knew at the moment when he sent instructions for von Schoen to demand his passports. He quite deliberately used the phrase, "the mountain road in the Vosges," which was too indefinite to be disputed.

As the discussion has continued, the German Parliamentary Investigation Committee has tried to look further into the matter. After publishing the "marching reports" of the different regiments, Count Montgelas draws up a long list of grievances.[80] He found, he said, twenty instances in which French *detachments* crossed the frontier, and thirty-six instances in which *patrols* committed the same crime. Shots were exchanged in only eleven cases. Furthermore, it is not

---

[77] *Germ. Doc.*, 717 and note, p. 521. But the Chancellor did bring to the attention of the British Ambassador certain violations of the frontier, which he said had occurred at Altmünsterol and at La Schlucht. *Brit. Doc.*, 553, p. 299.

[78] *Germ. Doc.*, 663, p. 496.

[79] *Germ. Doc.*, 693, p. 510.

[80] *Deutsche Allgemeine Zeitung*, 25th June 1919.

certain that all of the latter engagements took place in German territory. The German historian realizes that certain "errors in detail" are always possible. These statements would have no value unless they were further supported by definite documents. Thus far, to our knowledge, Montgelas has cited only two.

One of these concerned an incident which took place on 3rd August. Two patrols met in the forest west of Sainte-Marie-aux-Mines, and a French *chasseur* fell "twenty meters from the frontier, in German territory." M. René Puaux already knew of this incident.[81] In order to appreciate its true significance, it should not be forgotten that the French posts had just been advanced up to the frontier, in accordance with the Government's new instructions. And this "significant" incident—the adjective is the one used by the German historian—proves at the most that a single patrol overstepped the normal limits of its activity *by a few meters*. Can this incident possibly be compared with the Joncherey affair?

The other document is a telegram from the army post at Saint-Amarin, dated at 11.30 A.M. on 1st August: "Five French infantry soldiers were *seen* in German territory on the Wesserling-Strässel road. They withdrew in the direction of Felseringkopf." Were these five men actually in German territory? The enemy observer may have been mistaken. Did these patrollers belong to some unit which had not yet received or executed the orders for withdrawal? There is nothing to prove it. They may have been a group of forest guards! Much more precise documents than this are needed before we may reach any definite conclusion as to guilt on the French side of the frontier.

In any case, the German archives have not thus far

---

[81] It should be noted that General Legrand-Girarde, who was in command of the 21st Army Corps, formally denies the German claims. *Les opérations du 21me Corps d'Armée*, Paris, Plon, 1922, p. 18.

brought to light a single paper indicating concerted activity by French reconnoitring parties or patrols in Alsatian territory, even as late as 3rd August. Nothing has yet been produced that compares with the regularly planned incursions of German cavalry at Belfort and in Lorraine.

The incident of the French airplanes was entirely in the realm of the imagination. The German Government did not even take time to coördinate its various statements. On the morning of 3rd August, Herr von Jagow told M. Cambon that a French airplane had been flying over Coblenz, but no reference was made to it in the declaration of war. On the other hand, in the official list of grievances the Chancellor pointed out that a French airplane had been flying over Karlsruhe, although no previous mention had been made of the incident. The news was spread about by the Wolff Agency that a French plane "had tried to destroy the railroad" near Wesel, and had been brought down. What was the fate of the aviator? What was his name? Not another word has ever been said on the subject.

The most famous of these incidents is that of the airplane at Nuremberg. At 3.15 P.M. on 2nd August the Wolff Agency announced that "French aviators dropped bombs this morning in the neighborhood of Nuremberg." As the source of this information, it quoted a report from the headquarters of the 3rd Bavarian Army Corps.[82] The newspapers at once appeared with special editions: "As war has not yet been declared between France and Germany, we are now faced with a violation of international law." Quite innocently, even a Nuremberg paper reproduced the dispatch.[83] A second telegram brought further details: the bombs were dropped on the Nuremberg-Kissingen and the Nuremberg-

[82] *Cf.* also *Germ. Doc.*, 664, p. 496. This report was communicated early in the afternoon to Sir Edward Goschen, the British Ambassador. *Brit. Doc.*, 477, p. 271, sent at 2.15 P.M.

[83] *Frankischer Kurier,* quoted by Puaux.

Ansbach railroads, but no report was made of the damage which had been done.

M. Viviani at once denied these statements in his famous speech of 4th August 1914. It was quite possible that a French *commercial* airplane had flown over the Nuremberg district at that time, but it was absolutely certain that no French *military* plane had appeared in the Bavarian skies.[84] On the following day a German newspaper also questioned the accuracy of the news. But the rumor persisted, and for two years the German public continued to believe that the Nuremberg incident was true. It was not until 1916 that Dr. Schwalbe published a denial of the incident,[85] in a modest article in a medical journal, revealing a letter which had been signed on 9th April of that year by the municipality of Nuremberg:

The provisional commander of the 3rd Bavarian Army Corps has no knowledge of any bombs having been dropped on the Nuremberg-Kissingen or the Nuremberg-Ansbach lines, either *before* or *after* the declaration of war. All the newspaper reports on this subject appear to be manifestly false.

It is quite possible that the German Government may have believed at first that the report was true. It is very strange, however, that it should not have taken the trouble to verify its accuracy.[86] But the truth was soon forced upon it. The Prussian Minister at Munich, Treutler, actually wrote to the Chancellor, on the afternoon of the second:

The military report, circulated by the Süddeutsches Korrespondenz-bureau, to the effect that French aviators had dropped

[84] For further information upon this point, *cf.* Oscar Bloch, *La vérité sur les avions de Nuremberg*, Paris, Dangon, 1922.

[85] *Deutsche Medizinische Wochenschrift*, 18th May 1916.

[86] It is likely that the incident appeared extremely opportune to the German military leaders, who were becoming impatient. At least, this is the point made by the Bavarian Wenniger, in his report for the day. The telegram from the 3rd Army Corps, he said, was "quite welcome." *Bayerische Dokumente,* 3rd edition, p. 230.

bombs in the vicinity of Nuremberg today, has so far not been verified. Simply, some unknown aircraft were seen, which were apparently not military planes. There is no evidence of the dropping of bombs, and still less, naturally, that the aviators were French.[87]

How did it happen, then, that the German Government referred in the declaration of war to the dropping of bombs? It is claimed that the denial did not reach Berlin in time. As a matter of fact, according to the editors of the *German Documents*, Treutler's message was not registered at the Wilhelmstrasse until the afternoon of the third. The instructions to von Schoen had just been sent off! But this evidence is hardly conclusive, for the slowness in transmission of the message in this case would be practically incredible. Twenty hours to get a message from Munich to Berlin! And the Prussian Minister certainly had a telephone at his disposal!

*   *   *   *   *   *   *

Germany's declaration of war upon France was thus based on a number of pretexts, some of which were false, and the others uncertain. ". . . The responsibility involved was so grave that irrefutable arguments were needed before any action could be taken. Even if these attacks actually took place, they should not have been considered as having the significance of warlike attacks. . . ." Thus Baron von Schoen passes judgment on the position of his own Government.

[87] *Germ. Doc.*, 758, p. 544.

CHAPTER XV

ENGLAND

THROUGHOUT the whole crisis the attitude of the London Cabinet was being most carefully watched by the other great European Powers. France and Russia were constantly taking precautionary measures to guard against any estrangement of English public opinion. Germany had been steadily trying to avoid the repercussions which her actions might produce at the Foreign Office. The effort was quite marked in both of the rival camps.

The stakes, however, were not quite the same. England already had certain obligations with regard to France, limited and conditional, to be sure, but based upon a precise scheme of military coöperation. The 1912 agreements provided that the two Powers should "act in concert" whenever the general peace of Europe was threatened. The French Government therefore had reason to believe that, if it could convince London of its just rights in the dispute, the interests of England would lead to her intervention. Germany, on the other hand, was solely concerned with obtaining a promise of neutrality from the English Cabinet. Now, the policy which England followed during the crisis was such as to stimulate, alternately, hope and anxiety, in both Berlin and Paris.

Up to 29th July the German Chancellor believed that England's abstention was still a possibility, whatever he may have said, for he approached Sir Edward Goschen as we have seen on that day. The emphatic statements issued by the Foreign Office, however, soon opened his eyes to the truth and considerably upset the Emperor. During the days that followed, the German statesmen revived their hopes on two separate occasions, on the strength of reports which Ambassador Lichnowsky sent from London, although they soon discovered their error.

When the French Government tried, on 30th and 31st July, to obtain a promise of support from London, it felt that England was drifting away, and it feared that intervention would not come until too late. General mobilization was actually declared in France before the policy of the British Government took definite shape.

The importance of these facts is obvious. The hesitating and uncertain policy of the English Government at this time had a very real influence upon the development of the crisis. It is entirely probable that, had Germany been faced in time with a firm decision on England's part, her policy might have evolved toward a compromise. There is no doubt whatever that Germany was encouraged to violent action because of the hesitant attitude which she detected in London. How, then, are we to explain and interpret the actions and intentions of the British Government at this stage in the crisis?

The diplomatic correspondence of the time gives only a superficial or an artificial view of the situation. No light whatever is thrown on the situation by the minutes of the English Cabinet meetings. The statesmen themselves, in publishing their memoirs, have on the whole shown an astonishing degree of discretion.[1] And political passion colors the work of even the best-informed journalist.[2]

---

[1] For example, Asquith, in *The Genesis of the War,* London, Cassell, 1923; Churchill, *The World Crisis, 1911-1914,* London, Thornton Butterworth, 1923; and Grey of Fallodon, *Twenty-five Years,* London, Hodder & Stoughton, 1925, I, pp. 308-348, and II, pp. 1-47, give quite a bit of interesting information, but still maintain a certain reserve.

[2] Leo Maxse, "An 'Aide-Mémoire' to the Historian," published in the *National Review,* July 1919, pp. 659-679. Mr. Asquith has not yet published a single word in reply.

I. *The Attitude of the Foreign Office.*

WHEN the King of England said to Prince Henry of Prussia, on 25th July: "We shall try all we can to keep out of this and shall remain neutral,"[3] he expressed an opinion which was doubtless that of the majority of the English people at the time, and even of the Government. The Austro-Serbian quarrel had not yet become an Austro-Russian conflict, and the reply of the Belgrade Government to the ultimatum had not yet been made public. The Foreign Office then proposed its idea of "four-Power mediation," which did not widely differ in its essential features from the policy advocated by Germany. The London Cabinet thus showed itself ready to take the lead in impartial mediation. It was all the more inclined to do so in view of the recent events in Ireland,[4] which were causing it grave uneasiness, and had occupied all of its attention up to the very day of the Austrian ultimatum to Serbia. "England had a long way to come before she was to take an active part in any continental conflict, so far that one wondered whether she would ever do so, or whether she would not do so when it was too late."[5]

The atmosphere underwent a considerable change after the evening of 26th July, both at the British Admiralty and at the Foreign Office. Austria's intransigency was severely criticized, while the moderate form of the Serbian reply was attributed to Russia's influence. On the evening of the twenty-seventh, Mr. Winston Churchill, First Lord of the Admiralty, instructed the squadron commanders to prepare for possible war,[6] and decided to keep the Fleet concentrated at the end of its maneuvers, instead of allowing it to disperse. Two days later he decided, with Mr. Asquith's ap-

[3] See above, Ch. VII, p. 113.
[4] See above, Ch. V, p. 75.
[5] F. Charles-Roux, "Veillée d'armes à Londres 22 juin-4 août 1914," in the *Revue des Deux Mondes,* 15th August 1926, p. 727.
[6] But the warning telegram was not officially sent out until the twenty-ninth.

proval, to order the Grand Fleet to leave the part of the Channel where the maneuvers were taking place, and to concentrate at Scapa Flow, its wartime base, and this order was at once carried out by night. On the thirtieth he sent instructions to the commander-in-chief of the naval forces in the Mediterranean as follows: "Our first concern must be to help France to transport her troops from Africa." It is true that these decisions were secret, and theoretically should not have had any direct influence upon diplomatic negotiations, but the movements of the British Grand Fleet could hardly escape the observation of the German Government.[7] Moreover, on the afternoon of the twenty-sixth, Sir Edward Grey developed his idea of a conference, contrasting with Berlin's desire for the "localization" of the conflict. Ambassador Lichnowsky informed Berlin of the new plan suggested by the Secretary of State, who now asked Germany to undertake mediatory action at Vienna. On the afternoon of the twenty-ninth, Grey decided to try the effect of a threat: If Germany and France should finally go to war, "it would be impossible for England to stand aside and wait for very long." The next day, with the support of Mr. Asquith, he repelled the advances made by Bethmann in an effort to buy England's neutrality.[8] He realized that the position he had now taken was quite clear.

The attitude maintained by Sir Edward Grey and Mr. Winston Churchill with regard to Germany is significant. Both of them wished to see the peace of Europe preserved, but they were convinced that Great Britain, even in her own interest, ought not to stand aside in the event of a European conflict. The Foreign Office fully realized the importance of letting Germany understand that England would participate in a European war, if it should ultimately come

[7] Szögyény to Berchtold, 31st July, *Dipl. Pap.,* III, 52.

[8] The English reply, *Blue Book,* 101, according to Grey, I, p. 329, was sent off before the meeting of the Cabinet, which, however, approved the telegram on the afternoon of the thirtieth.

to that. The decisions of the Admiralty and the reply to Bethmann's offer showed the intentions of the British Government, and received the approval of the Cabinet. Sir Edward Grey's warning to Prince Lichnowsky, although no more than a personal opinion on the part of the Minister, left still less doubt about England's position. In Berlin there was no mistaking the significance of these actions and these remarks in England. The Wilhelmstrasse now believed "with absolute certainty" that England would intervene, and Emperor William dashed down discouraged and exasperated notes on the margin of Lichnowsky's telegrams: "This means they will attack us."

The British diplomats, however, were still unwilling to take sides to the extent of making any public declaration. Russia and France tried in vain to obtain some manifestation of solidarity from the Foreign Office which would, they said, make the Central Powers reflect more seriously, and would consequently assure the maintenance of peace: "It is only thus that England will succeed in preventing a dangerous disturbance of the European balance of power," wrote M. Sazonov, and M. Poincaré declared to the British Ambassador, Sir Francis Bertie: "If His Majesty's Government announce that, in the event of conflict between Germany and France, England would come to the aid of France, there would be no war, for Germany would at once modify her attitude."[9] Germany and Austria, on the other hand, made it plain to the Foreign Office that the evolution of the crisis depended directly on "whether Russia and France think that they can reckon on the active support of His Majesty's Government in the event of a general complication."[10]

Faced with these conflicting appeals, Sir Edward Grey did not wish to take sides at all. He was not disposed to

[9] *Brit. Doc.*, 318, p. 200.
[10] Rumbold to Grey, 25th July, *Brit. Doc.*, 128, p. 96.

make any promises to Paris or to St. Petersburg, fearing
that they might be encouraged to throw down the gauntlet.
The Under-Secretary, Sir Eyre Crowe, whose sympathies
were obviously on the side of France, had at first advised
Sir Edward Grey to take a definite stand.[11] Upon thinking
the matter over, however, he gradually came to accept the
Minister's point of view in the matter. The British Government, he wrote some days later, "should not by a declaration of unconditional solidarity with France and Russia induce and determine these two Powers to choose the path of
war."[12] This was also the opinion of Sir Francis Bertie: "If
we gave an assurance of armed assistance to France and
Russia now, Russia would become more exacting and France
would follow in her wake."[13]

These two aspects of the policy of the Foreign Office have
been clearly stated by Mr. Winston Churchill, who wrote:
"We had to let the Germans know that we were a force to
be reckoned with, without letting the French and Russians
think that they had us safely in their pockets."[14]

This attitude of reserve on the part of the Foreign Office
was not the result of any deliberate wish, nor of any preconceived plan, but arose rather from circumstances linked with
domestic politics. The views held by Sir Edward Grey and
Mr. Winston Churchill, who felt that British intervention
was practically inevitable, were not yet generally shared,
either in political circles or by public opinion. "We, of
course, living under such conditions as we do here, when no
Government practically can take any decided line without
feeling that public opinion amply supports them, are unable
to give any decided engagements as to what we should or
should not do in any future emergencies." Thus Sir Arthur

11 *Brit. Doc.*, 101, note, p. 81.
12 *Brit. Doc.*, 318, note, p. 201.
13 *Brit. Doc.*, 320, p. 203, 30th July.
14 Churchill, *The World Crisis*, I, p. 200.

Nicolson outlined the English political situation, in a private letter to Sir George Buchanan on 28th July.[15]

The bankers of London were beginning to fear the consequences of a war, and wished to keep their country out of the conflict, "so that it might remain," as M. Paul Cambon put it, "the great market and the commercial standard of the world." Needless to say, they had a considerable influence upon the press. On 29th July the *Daily Chronicle* summarized the arguments of the "neutralists" as follows: "England has no interests vitally endangered. It is an affair which does not concern us, so long as it does not bring about one of two results: the expansion of Russia in Europe, or the defeat of France, followed by the occupation of Belgium and Holland by Germany." Would it not be possible, it asked, "to detach France from the ambitions of Russia at the final critical moment"?

The same opposition was felt within the Cabinet. From the very outset the majority of the members—three-quarters, says Mr. Churchill—had decided "not to allow themselves to be drawn into a European quarrel, unless Great Britain herself were attacked." But if France were plunged into the conflict, would it not be to England's interest to stand beside her? There was a division of opinion within the Cabinet on the question of intervention. Among those opposed to intervention were several ministers who came "immediately after" Mr. Asquith in authority and in their influence upon the Liberal Party, such as Mr. Lloyd George.[16] The partisans of more vigorous action on England's part could not hope to attain a majority, and, besides, any effort on their part to bring matters to a head would involve the risk of "smashing" the Cabinet. Between these two groups wavered the undecided members, one of whom appears to have been Mr. Asquith himself.

[15] *Brit. Doc.,* 239, p. 157.
[16] Grey, I, p. 334.

It may be that the differences within the Cabinet were less clear-cut than they appeared. All the members had of course certain fundamental ideas in common, above all, England's interest in not allowing either of the European belligerents to violate the neutrality of Belgium, nor to occupy Antwerp and the coast of Flanders. The possibility of this danger, however, was viewed differently among the various Cabinet members. Whereas the leaders of the opposition, partisans of intervention, considered a violation of Belgian neutrality by Germany as altogether probable, and won the unanimity of Conservative opinion to their point of view,[17] the Liberal leaders, opposed to all idea of war, were inclined to believe that Germany would not attack France, or at least that she would not encroach upon Belgian territory.[18] Public opinion, according to Benckendorff, the Russian Ambassador, was not yet awake to the situation.

Sir Edward Grey's position at this time was not an easy one. If he should propose to the Cabinet to declare openly that England would enter the war in case Germany attacked France and Belgium, he might be unable to carry the Cabinet with him, and might provoke a ministerial crisis. If, acting on his own authority, he should give encouragement or promises to France or to Russia, he could not be sure that the Cabinet would support him when the time came.[19] He steadfastly believed that England would decide in the end to intervene, but he had to wait until events justified his fears, and until his opponents were won over as a consequence of Germany's action.

It is certain that Berlin was well aware of these diffi-

---

[17] Cf. the letter from Mr. F. E. Smith (Lord Birkenhead) to Mr. W. Churchill on 31st July. Churchill, I, pp. 215-216.

[18] Grey, I, p. 337.

[19] This line of reasoning which Grey followed seems to me quite logical. The great danger to be avoided, as Grey himself said, was "to have France and Russia resist Germany, counting upon our assistance, and then not to have that assistance arrive." Grey, I, 312.

culties and hesitations, and the information reaching the
Wilhelmstrasse may have been even more precise as to the
division within the ranks of the British Cabinet.[20]

II. *The Appeal from France.*

On 30th July, M. Paul Cambon reminded Sir Edward Grey,
in the name of the French Government, of the terms of the
Anglo-French agreement of November 1912. England had
undertaken to join with France if the peace of Europe
were threatened. This threat now existed, as shown by the
German military preparations actually along the frontier.
The time had now come to take sides. This *démarche* of
course accentuated the divergence within the British Cabinet. The Foreign Office was obliged, in view of the uncertainty of the situation, to maintain an attitude of strict
reserve for three days longer, until the morning of 2nd
August, and this attitude naturally stimulated great hopes
in Germany.

At the close of the Cabinet meeting on the thirty-first,
Sir Edward Grey sent his Ambassador in Paris the reply of
the English Government to the French appeal: "Nobody
here feels that in this dispute, so far as it has gone yet,
British treaties or obligations are involved."[21] Furthermore,
the commercial and financial situation was exceedingly serious. England's standing aside might be "the only means of
preventing a complete collapse of European credit," and
that, in the opinion of the Government, was a paramount
consideration. It was therefore impossible for the Cabinet
to give "any pledge at the present time." But, he added,
"further developments might alter this situation, and cause
the Government and Parliament to take the view that inter-

[20] L. Maxse, p. 664, claims that the German Government was informed
by "an emissary who appeared to represent the majority of the Asquith
Cabinet."

[21] *Brit. Doc.*, 352, p. 220; and *Yellow Book,* 110.

vention was justified."[22] As for the objections of M. Poincaré and M. Sazonov, the Secretary of State evaded their criticism by replying: "I think it quite inexact to say that our attitude is a decisive factor in the situation. The German Government is not relying upon our neutrality."[23]

How long was this uncertainty to continue? What would be the new element in the situation that would bring about the decision of the British Government? Would it wait until French territory had been invaded? Sir Edward Grey hinted at a possibility: he would ask France and Germany whether they intended to respect the neutrality of Belgium. The attitude adopted by Germany upon this point might be an "important," even though not a "decisive," factor in the Cabinet's decision. M. Cambon did not conceal his disappointment. He pointed out to Sir Edward Grey that it could not be to England's interest to allow Germany to crush France. Was she going to repeat the great mistake she had made in 1870 by permitting "an enormous increase of German strength"? And the Ambassador concluded by asking that the whole question be submitted to the Cabinet again. Sir Edward Grey did not yield, however, and said that, while the Cabinet might feel called upon to reconsider the question, it would do so only when there was "some new development."

The French Government attempted a new *démarche* at eleven o'clock on the evening of the thirty-first. M. William Martin arrived in London with a personal letter from M. Poincaré to King George,[24] in which the President of the French Republic pointed out the dangers that would be involved in any further delay. "It is, I believe, upon the language and the conduct of the British Government that

22 *Brit. Doc.*, 367, p. 227.

23 Referring to the conversation between Sir Edward Grey and Prince Lichnowsky the previous evening.

24 *Brit. Doc.*, 366, p. 226.

the final hopes for a peaceful solution henceforth depend."
If Germany could be certain of England's neutrality, war
was inevitable; if, on the other hand, she felt that England
would intervene, there were still "the greatest chances" that
peace might be maintained.[25]

When the British Cabinet found itself presented the next
morning with this new appeal, the situation had already
changed. Germany had sent her double ultimatum to Paris
and to St. Petersburg, and had refused to reply to the
question regarding Belgian neutrality. Was not this the new
factor to which Sir Edward Grey had referred the night
before? Not yet, in the opinion of the Cabinet.[26] King George
sent M. Poincaré a lengthy reply, prepared at the Foreign
Office, expressing England's admiration for the attitude of
France, which could in no way be interpreted as provocative. It referred to the efforts already made by the British
Government in the interest of peace, and promised to continue them. But it clearly evaded the essential question: "As
for the attitude of my country," wrote the King, "events
are changing so rapidly that it is impossible to foretell what
their future developments will be."[27] At the same time, after
a lively discussion the Cabinet had refused to order the total
mobilization of the Fleet, as Mr. Churchill had requested.[28]

[25] Furthermore, the French President had already developed these same
ideas in an interview with Sir, F. Bertie on the previous evening. He had
added that if England remained neutral, and if Germany became omnipo-
tent on the continent, "the position of England would be entirely altered
to her detriment as a Great Power." *Brit. Doc.*, 373, p. 231. Sir Francis
Bertie's report upon this interview did not reach London until 1st August.

[26] According to Maxse, Mr. Lloyd George had considerable influence
during these two days, and even brought Lord Rothschild to Downing
Street to defend the position of the bankers who were opposed to intervention. But Maxse produces no evidence whatever. The violent antipathy
he has shown toward Mr. Lloyd George makes it necessary to accept his
statements only with the greatest reserve.

[27] According to M. Paul Cambon, Recouly, p. 54, the King personally
favored intervention. "My shocking letter," he called it later.

[28] This mobilization affected only the oldest units of the Fleet. The
others were already at their war bases.

Upon receiving M. Paul Cambon at the close of this meet-ing, Sir Edward Grey made certain significant statements to him:[29]

I told M. Cambon that the present position differed entirely from that created by the Morocco incidents. In the latter, Ger-many made upon France demands that France could not grant, and in connection with which we had undertaken special obliga-tions towards France. Now, the position was that Germany would agree not to attack France if France remained neutral in the event of war between Russia and Germany. If France could not take advantage of this position, it was because she was bound by an alliance to which we were not parties, and of which we did not know the terms. This did not mean that under no circumstance would we assist France, but it did mean that France must make her own decision at this moment without reckoning on an assistance that we were not now in a position to promise.

I said that we had come to a decision: that we could not propose to Parliament at this moment to send an expeditionary military force to the continent.

The Minister went on, however, to point out that a change in attitude was entirely possible. He intended to declare before the House of Commons on Monday, 3rd August, "that the British Government would not allow a violation of Belgian neutrality." But M. Cambon objected: that was not enough. As a consequence of the Anglo-French naval agreement, France had stripped her Channel and Atlantic coasts of all naval defense. "Will you allow Cherbourg and Brest to be bombarded, when it was by agreement with you, to serve your interests as well as our own, that we concen-trated our ships far away from here?" The Secretary of State promised to inform Germany that the British Fleet would prevent "any demonstration on the French coast."

[29] *Brit. Doc.*, 426, p. 253, 8.20 P.M., 1st August. See also 447, p. 260. M. Cambon said that he could not transmit this reply to his Government.

But would the Cabinet support his decision in the matter? It was not to consider the question for another two days!

Then it was that the German Ambassador again took hope. He urged Sir Edward Grey to formulate "the conditions in return for which" England would promise to remain neutral. He offered to enlarge upon the proposal made by Bethmann-Hollweg on the evening of the twenty-ninth, but Sir Edward Grey refused to make any promises; he wished "to keep his hands untied." The tone of his refusal, however, was apparently not very discouraging, for Lichnowsky thought for several hours that he was about to succeed.[30] This mistake is not hard to understand, when we remember that the Ambassador was fully aware of the dissensions within the Cabinet. Even when he saw through his error, the Prince was still convinced that Germany need not fear an immediate declaration of war on England's part. Had not Asquith said to him: "A war between our two countries is quite unthinkable," and had not the "old gentleman" had tears in his eyes as he referred to the change in public opinion that would almost certainly be caused by the violation of Belgian neutrality?[31]

The atmosphere at the French Embassy was most depressed. England was apparently not going to intervene until it was too late![32]

The intimate colleagues of Sir Edward Grey, less closely in touch with the problems of domestic politics, fully realized the gravity of the situation. They used all their influence during these critical days to impress upon the Secretary of State the necessity for an immediate decision. Sir Arthur

[30] See above, Ch. XIV, p. 250.

[31] *Germ. Doc.,* 676, p. 502.

[32] *Cf.* French, *1914,* Amer. ed., Boston and New York, Houghton Mifflin, 1919, p. 3. He had seen the French Military Attaché, M. de la Panouse, on 1st August, and had assured him that England would remain loyal to her "friendly agreement." But how soon would she do so?

Nicolson, Permanent Under-Secretary of State for Foreign Affairs, urged the immediate mobilization of the army on the thirty-first,[33] and on the same day Sir Eyre Crowe, Assistant Under-Secretary, sent the Minister a personal memorandum, with a pressing, vigorous and far-sighted appeal, to counteract the arguments of the "neutralists."

Was it right for England to stand aside? "The theory that England cannot engage in a big war means her abdication as an independent state. . . . If the theory were true, the general principle on which our whole foreign policy has hitherto been declared to rest would stand proclaimed as an empty futility. A balance of power cannot be maintained by a State that is incapable of fighting and consequently carries no weight."

Was it fair to use "the commercial panic" as an argument? This panic in the city had been "largely influenced by the deliberate acts of German financial houses, who are in at least as close touch with the German as with the British Government, and who are notoriously in daily communication with the German Embassy."

Was the unwritten character of the Entente Cordiale any justification for standing aloof? Certainly there was no "contractual obligation," no "written bond." But "the Entente has been made, strengthened, put to the test and celebrated in a manner justifying the belief that a moral bond was being forged. The whole policy of the Entente can have no meaning if it does not signify that in a just quarrel England would stand by her friends."[34]

It does not appear, however, that this appeal had any immediate influence upon the mind of Sir Edward Grey, for his remarks to the French Ambassador on 1st August

[33] *Brit. Doc.*, 368, p. 227. "If public opinion, at present so bewildered and partially informed, is ready in event of a German invasion of France to stand by the latter, if we are not mobilized our aid would be too late."
[34] *Brit. Doc.*, 369, p. 228.

were even more discouraging than those of the previous day.[35]

III. *The Cabinet's Decision.*

THE change finally came about on the afternoon of 2nd August, sooner than Sir Edward Grey had expected. All the testimony is agreed upon this point. During the morning the situation was still doubtful, and the majority of the Cabinet refused to pronounce in favor of intervention,[36] even though Germany had now definitely declared war on Russia. But Sir Edward Grey was authorized to make the declaration to M. Paul Cambon that had been requested. The following note was sent to the French Ambassador at 2.20 P.M.: "I am authorized to give an assurance that if the German fleet comes into the Channel or through the North Sea to undertake hostile operations against French coasts or shipping the British fleet will give all the protection in its power."[37] It is true that the British Government did not yet promise to intervene, even if France were attacked.[38] The right to make such a promise still lay with Parliament, and Mr. Lloyd George recalled in 1915 that war still did not seem inevitable for England at this stage in the crisis, if Germany should promise not to annex any French terri-

---

[35] The messages reaching Sir Edward Grey from his ambassadors were quite varied. Sir Francis Bertie remained opposed to all military intervention on the continent as late as 3rd August. Sir George Buchanan, on the other hand, wished to see England respond to the appeal of Russia, after the rupture between that country and Germany. To provoke the hostility of Russia for the future was, in his opinion, to endanger the security of India. *Brit. Doc.,* 490, p. 277.

[36] Churchill, I, p. 218. The Government had decided, however, upon the general mobilization of the naval forces.

[37] *Yellow Book,* 137; and *Brit. Doc.,* 487, p. 274. The Secretary of State requested the French Premier to consider this promise as confidential, but Mr. Asquith apparently did not keep it a secret from Prince Lichnowsky. *Brit. Doc.,* 536, note by Sir Edward Grey, p. 293.

[38] *Yellow Book,* 148.

tory.[39] Furthermore, Sir Edward Grey could not afford to ignore the risks that a general war would mean for the whole British Empire, especially for India and Egypt. "It was impossible," he said, "safely to send our military force out of the country" at the outset of such a conflict. Despite these reservations, the promise of naval assistance was, in the opinion of M. Paul Cambon, a decisive guaranty which would lead sooner or later to full intervention.

The causes underlying this change in attitude stand out quite clearly. Word had reached London that German troops had entered the territory of Luxemburg. M. Paul Cambon immediately drew Sir Edward Grey's attention to the treaty guaranteeing the neutrality of Luxemburg. Here was an *opportunity* for the majority of the Cabinet to adopt a more active policy. This motive might not, however, have been sufficient, had not another factor entered into the situation, in this case involving domestic politics. Mr. Asquith received at noon from Mr. Bonar Law a letter which had been composed during the night by Mr. Austen Chamberlain:

Dear Mr. Asquith [read the letter]: Lord Lansdowne and I feel it to be our duty to inform you that, in our opinion, as in the opinion of all of our colleagues whom we have been able to consult, it would be fatal to the honor and the security of the United Kingdom to hesitate in the support of France and Russia in the present situation; and we offer our unhesitating support to the Government for all measures which it may consider as necessary to this end.[40]

[39] Interview given to *Pearson's Magazine*, March 1915, quoted by Maxse, pp. 666-667.

[40] This action on the part of the Conservative Party had been foreseen by Mr. Winston Churchill, after a talk on 30th July with Mr. F. E. Smith (Lord Birkenhead). Mr. Asquith thus knew on 1st August that he might "count upon the support of the Unionist Party." But up till now he had not had any such *direct* assurance. Grey, II, p. 7, questions the influence of this letter as a deciding factor, but he admits that it was read at the Cabinet meeting.

The significance of this letter is beyond all doubt.[41] Faced with a division in his Cabinet, Mr. Asquith had for three days been unable to rally a majority of his own party in favor of intervention. Personally, he was convinced that England had contracted "an engagement of honor" with regard to France. The support of the Conservatives would now make it possible, if need be, to obtain a majority by coalition.

The matter was not altogether settled, however, and the opposition continued in the very heart of the Cabinet. On the afternoon of 2nd August, two members, Lord Morley and Mr. John Burns, handed in their resignations. It was feared that four other members of the Cabinet might resign at the very moment when decisive steps would have to be taken.[42] Germany was prepared to declare that she would not attack the northern coast of France, so long as England remained neutral.[43] Lichnowsky had not yet abandoned all hope.

During the morning of the third, however, word of the German ultimatum to Belgium had reached London, where it was fairly well understood what the reply would be.[44] The Cabinet at once consented to the immediate mobilization of the army,[45] and not a single one of the doubtful members resigned, at least not for the time being.[46] It gave its general

41 Recouly, p. 55, and Maxse, p. 667. Mr. F. E. Smith's remarks to Mr. Churchill had not been nearly so urgent in their tone as Mr. Bonar Law's letter.

42 Lord Beauchamp, Sir John Simon, Mr. L. V. Harcourt and Mr. Masterman.

43 Jagow to Lichnowsky, 9.30 A.M., 3rd August, *Germ. Doc.*, 714, p. 520. This information was communicated to the English Government at about noon. *Germ. Doc.*, 764, p. 546. Also *Brit. Doc.*, 531, p. 291.

44 The text of the ultimatum was not actually known until the afternoon, during the session of the House of Commons.

45 Churchill, I, p. 220. But the Cabinet did not decide to send an ultimatum nor to declare war.

46 Morel, *Truth and the War*, 3rd ed., London, National Labour Press, 1918, p. 298, states that this change on the part of the four members coincided with the violation of Belgian neutrality.

approval to the statement which Sir Edward Grey was to make before Parliament during the afternoon, in which he declared that England would stand behind Belgium and France. Public opinion was now pronouncing itself for intervention: "The House will this evening vote the credit which is asked for," wired M. Paul Cambon. "From this moment its support is assured to the policy of the Government, and it follows public opinion, which is declaring itself more and more in our favor."[47] Sir Edward Grey's speech was enthusiastically applauded in Parliament, where the Government's action was obviously meeting with support. When Lichnowsky read the full text of the speech, he had no further illusions: "Outside the left wing of its own party, the Government will have behind it the overwhelming majority of Parliament in any active policy the purpose of which is the protection of France and Belgium."[48]

The Cabinet had not made the supreme decisions, namely, concerning the ultimatum and the declaration of war, and moreover it never did make them.[49] "They were made necessary by the force of circumstances, and were based upon the authority of the Premier," writes Mr. Churchill. Now, the rapidity of these decisions was of the greatest importance, for any delay in the embarkation of the British expeditionary force might lead to grave consequences from the military standpoint.

Even on 4th August liberal newspapers of the left wing, such as the *Manchester Guardian*, were still trying to delay the rupture: "The question of the integrity of Belgium is one thing; the question of her neutrality is quite another."

[47] *Yellow Book*, 145.

[48] *Germ. Doc.*, 820, p. 574, 10 A.M., 4th August. Lichnowsky had persisted in illusions which were not shared by William II. *Germ. Doc.*, 835, p. 580: "So now he is willing to believe it at last! Poor Lichnowsky."

[49] It simply took occasion, on 4th August, to express its desire to avoid any act of war before the expiration of the time-limit set by the ultimatum, even if, in the Mediterranean, the *Goeben* should attack the French transports. Churchill, I, p. 225.

What difference did the violation of a treaty make, if the territory of Belgium remained intact after the war? Did England's interests demand any more than that? Germany had promised not to annex any Belgian territory whatever.[50]

But Mr. Asquith had decided to act, and to respond to the appeal of the King of the Belgians. Sir Edward Grey instructed his Minister in Brussels on 4th August to declare that England would help Belgium to resist, if Germany should "exert pressure to make her give up her neutrality."[51] At the same time he sent word requesting von Jagow for "an assurance that the demand made upon Belgium will not be proceeded with, and that Germany will respect the neutrality of Belgium."[52] As a matter of fact, German troops were already in Belgian territory. During the afternoon von Jagow replied to the English Ambassador that it was impossible for the German Government "to take a step backwards"; for Germany it was "a matter of life and death."

Toward the end of the day, at about seven o'clock, Sir Edward Goschen again called upon the Secretary of State. He had received fresh instructions from London: the entry of German troops into Belgium had decided the English Government to demand a satisfactory reply from Berlin "by midnight." Otherwise, England would take "all steps in her power" to uphold the neutrality guaranteed by the treaty to which she was a party.[53] Herr von Jagow gave the same reply as before. The Ambassador then went to call upon the Chancellor. "His Excellency at once began a harangue," reported Sir Edward, "which lasted for about twenty minutes. He said that the step taken by His Majesty's Government was terrible to a degree. Just for a word—'neutrality'

50 *Germ. Doc.*, 810, p. 569, sent at 10.20 A.M., 4th August.
51 See above, Ch. XIV, p. 261.
52 *Germ. Doc.*, 823, p. 576.
53 *Germ. Doc.*, 839, p. 582.

—a word which in war time had so often been disregarded—
just for a scrap of paper, Great Britain was going to make
war on a kindred nation who desired nothing better than to
be friends with her."[54] Two hours later Zimmermann, Under-
Secretary of State, asked the Ambassador once more whether
the rupture would amount to a declaration of war. Sir Edward Goschen left no doubt in his mind upon this point. As
soon as the time limit was up, he demanded his passports.

*   *   *   *   *   *   *

The precise nature of the English intervention is thus
quite clear.

From the moment that Austria began, on 26th July, to
manifest an uncompromising attitude, Sir Edward Grey's
colleagues realized that England would be unable to stay
out of a European conflict. If the Central Powers should
emerge victorious, should crush France and occupy the
Channel, "with the willing or unwilling coöperation of Holland and Belgium," what would be England's position,
friendless on the continent? And if France and Russia should
triumph, what would be their attitude toward British interests? "What about India and the Mediterranean?"[55] Although his colleagues leaned in the direction of France and
Russia, Sir Edward Grey still hesitated, for he knew what
was going on within the Cabinet. He was therefore careful
not to take sides openly. But, under constant pressure from
Sir Eyre Crowe and Sir Arthur Nicolson, he did not want
to encourage Germany's hope that England would stay out
of the conflict, although that was, to tell the truth, still a
possibility. It was to dispel such a hope that he interviewed
the German Ambassador on 29th July. It was easier for Sir
Edward to express his personal point of view in talking
with the ambassadors than in his official *instructions*, which

[54] *Brit. Doc.*, 671, p. 351. The Chancellor spoke in English. *Cf.* note 4 of
the document.
[55] *Brit. Doc.*, 101, note by Sir Eyre Crowe, p. 82.

had to be submitted for the approval of the Cabinet. Now, the plans of the Foreign Office can hardly be said to have coincided with the all too vague intentions of the Government.

There actually came a moment when the Cabinet refused to follow the lead of the Foreign Office. When M. Paul Cambon called upon England to fulfill the provisions of the 1912 agreement, the English statesmen were undecided. Sir Edward Grey recoiled at the idea of English military intervention on the continent. It was the message from Mr. Bonar Law that put an end to all this hesitation, and Germany, in refusing to promise to respect Belgian neutrality, still further helped to convince the Cabinet. The decision made on 2nd August was only a partial one, and modest enough in outward appearance, but it was really of fundamental importance, for it showed for the first time that England felt bound by her earlier naval agreement. It therefore seems fair to say, with Morel,[56] that England's intervention was decided upon *before* the neutrality of Belgium was violated, and even before the German ultimatum was presented in Brussels. It was determined by "the general interests of England." Even if England should stand aside at the outset, would she not be driven to intervene during the course of the war, in order to avoid the consequences of a German victory? Now, the longer this intervention was postponed, the more costly it would be, and with less assurance of success.

Does this mean that the defense of Belgian neutrality did not play an important part in the evolution of England's attitude? On the evening of 2nd August the mind of the Cabinet had evolved to a point beyond that of the general public. Mr. Asquith could not and did not wish to act *immediately*, by sending an expeditionary force, unless pub-

[56] *Cf.* also Blunt, *My Diaries,* London, Secker, 1919-1920, 2 vols., II, pp. 449-451.

lic opinion was heartily in favor of it. And yet it was essential that some sort of military action should take place at once. The violation of Belgian neutrality produced in the mind of the English people the wave of emotion which made that intervention possible. It was this act on Germany's part which decided the Cabinet to give the Prime Minister full powers to make emergency decisions. Mr. Asquith was now in a position to go as far as he wished, and to do so at once.

These are the elements in the situation which successively led up to England's intervention. The hesitation on the part of the English Cabinet was by no means a feint to lure Germany on, as it has often been thought. It was thus no crafty premeditation which led to the buoying up of Germany's hopes. England's hesitation was the outcome of a rivalry of opposing influences within the Cabinet.

The significance of these renewed hopes in Germany should not, however, be too greatly exaggerated. Even if Germany was encouraged from time to time to believe that England would remain neutral, there was at least one moment when she had a more accurate view of the situation. On the evening of 30th July and on the morning of the thirty-first, at the very moment when she sent her double ultimatum to France and Russia, she had every reason to think that England *would* intervene. And *that* is the hour when Germany made her vital decision.

CHAPTER XVI

ITALY

ENGLAND'S intervention in the struggle was a great
disillusionment for Germany. The abstention of
Italy, on the contrary, was by no means a complete
surprise for the Chancellor and the General Staff. The conflicting interests of Italy and Austria in the Balkans and
on the Adriatic made it impossible for those two Powers to
reach anything more than a temporary solution of any of
their problems. Each successive renewal of the Triple Alliance had been marked by an effort on Italy's part to guard
against any disturbance of the equilibrium that might endanger her interests, and Article 7 of the Treaty made specific reference to the principle of compensation. In Vienna
it was so generally believed that the Triple Alliance would
break up in case of a general European war that one rest-
less group argued for a *preventive* war against Italy. Nor
had Germany in recent years had any illusions about the
strength of the Alliance. The Government in Rome had, it
is true, given indications of a more favorable attitude,[1] but
the German General Staff was not counting upon any decisive military support from that direction.[2]

During the course of the negotiations of July 1914, however, Germany made every effort to keep Italy within the
Alliance. The fact that the conflict had originated in the
Balkans at once gave Italy the chance to appeal to Article
7, and to begin talking of *compensation*. That was a question
which Vienna and Rome would have to settle directly between
themselves, but Germany kept an eye on the negotiations,

---

[1] It appears that Germany sensed this change in attitude in May 1914.

[2] Conversation between Moltke and Conrad, 12th May 1914, Conrad, III,
pp. 670-671. For French trans. *Cf. Revue d'histoire de la guerre mondiale,*
II, No. 3, pp. 154-155.

and it may be added that she did not find Count Berchtold as tractable and docile as she would have liked.[3]

I. *Berlin's Advice.*

THE early interviews were lengthy and rather painful. Even before the Austrian ultimatum was handed to Serbia, the Italian Government knew what the intentions of the Ballplatz would probably be. Its Ambassador in St. Petersburg did not hesitate, on 15th July, to draw the attention of the Russian Government to the dangers that were involved.[4] Marquis di San Giuliano had been careful to make it plain, to Berlin rather than to Vienna, that he could not support the Austrian claims against Serbia.[5] "If Austria had the design of suppressing the Serbian struggle for nationalism by violence," he told Flotow, the German Ambassador, "it would be quite impossible for any Italian Government to accompany her along this path; all the traditions of the nationalist idea and of the principles of liberalism compelled Italy to keep off this road. . . . To believe in the supreme power and efficiency of police measures in such national questions is Austria's old mistake. Italian history of the last century offers an example of it. The analogy of the two cases is so striking that, for this reason alone, no one should dare to expect any Italian sympathy for the Austrian procedure." Flotow had no illusions about the difficulty of the situation: "Unless Austria," he wrote Jagow, "compels herself to recognize plainly, in view of the danger, that in case she intends to take anything in the territorial line, she will have to compensate Italy, I consider the situation hopeless."[6]

    [3] The sources which have been drawn upon for this account are almost wholly German and Austrian. This is a point which must be borne in mind while reading the chapter.

    [4] *Cf.* Schilling's *Journal,* pp. 25-26.

    [5] Flotow to the Wilhelmstrasse, 14th July, *Germ. Doc.,* 42, p. 106; also 64, p. 125, on the sixteenth; and 73, p. 133, on the sixteenth.

    [6] *Germ. Doc.,* 75, p. 134. Personal letter.

Jagow frankly recognized the danger on 15th July, and acted at once upon the information which he had received. "It is of the greatest importance that Vienna should come to some understanding with the Cabinet at Rome regarding its aims to be sought in Serbia in case of war, and should retain Italy on her side, or—as a conflict with Serbia alone would not mean a *casus fœderis*—keep her strictly neutral."[7] With this in mind, he had already thought of suggesting to Austria that some offer of compensation for Italy would be necessary; what he had in mind was the Trentino.

Count Berchtold would not hear of this. When Tschirschky carried out his instructions on 20th July, he was met with a flat refusal.[8] The Vienna Cabinet, Berchtold said, had no intention of annexing any Serbian territory whatever, and every valid ground on which Italy could lay claim to compensation was thus removed. After all, what was Austria asking of Italy? "Neither coöperation nor support, but simply abstention from any hostile procedure against an ally." This was really not too much to hope for, for Italy, "both for military reasons and for those connected with the domestic political situation," would be quite incapable, in Berchtold's opinion, of intervening actively against the Central Powers.

From this time on it was taken for granted both at Berlin and Vienna that Italy would not follow her allies into the war. But whereas Vienna was quite satisfied with the prospects, Berlin, fearing that Italian neutrality could not long remain passive, wished to tempt Rome with the bait of territorial gain.

Marquis di San Giuliano did not officially learn of the Austrian ultimatum until 24th July, at the same time that it

---

[7] Jagow to Tschirschky, *Germ. Doc.*, 46, p. 110.

[8] *Germ. Doc.*, 94, p. 145. Prince Stolberg, adviser to the Ambassador, had already sounded out the possibilities on the eighteenth. The attitude of Count Hoyos, Chief of the Cabinet, had been reserved, but not unfavorable.

was communicated to the Entente Powers. He at once made a protest. Why had Austria entered upon such action "without first advising the other allies?"[9] Germany demanded an explanation from the Ballplatz, which had promised to notify the Italian Government in time. It appears that von Mérey, Austrian Ambassador in Rome, was taken suddenly ill, and had therefore been unable to reach Marquis di San Giuliano.[10] But the Italian Minister used this incident as the excuse for declaring that "Italy did not consider herself involved." He immediately raised the question of compensation, notifying Jagow that Italy desired at once to have "certain detailed information as to the interpretation of Article 7 of the Treaty." In a conversation with the German Ambassador, he even hinted at a threat: "Marquis di San Giuliano did not directly give expression to the possibility that Italy might eventually turn against Austria, but it could be heard in gentle hints. I took no notice of these hints, as I thought it best not to admit such a possibility in any way."[11] The warning could not be ignored, however. It would no longer be possible to count on the active assistance of Italy in case of a European conflict; she must at least be prevented from adopting an attitude of open hostility.

On this same day the Italian Government addressed itself for the first time directly to Vienna. If the Austro-Serbian conflict should lead to the occupation of Serbian territory— even a *temporary* occupation—Italy reserved the right to claim compensation. By virtue of Article 7, negotiations in this matter should take place "before the proposed occupation," and this point was insisted upon by the Duke of Avarna in his conversation with Count Berchtold.[12]

William II was irritated by these Italian claims: "The

9 Flotow to Jagow, 24th July, *Germ. Doc.*, 136, p. 171.
10 Tschirschky to Jagow, 25th July, *Germ. Doc.*, 187, p. 204.
11 *Germ. Doc.*, 244, p. 235, 25th July.
12 *Dipl. Pap.*, II, 46.

little thief must always have his swallow, too," he jotted down on the margin of one of Flotow's telegrams.[13] But he hardly gave it another thought at the time: "That is all bosh, and it will come out all right in the end of itself, in the course of events." On the twenty-sixth, however, Tschirsch-ky spoke to Count Berchtold in quite a different tone:[14] it was time "to drop the theoretical contention over the inter-pretation of Article 7." The German Government declared itself firmly in support of the Italian Government, and considered that the text of the Article did justify Mar-quis di San Giuliano's claims. Some practical agreement must therefore be reached. The Ambassador met with no success, however, in spite of support from Conrad von Hötzendorf. Berchtold replied that military operations did not amount to a temporary occupation, and "as it is not yet certain that we shall be obliged to proceed with a temporary occu-pation of Serbian territory, any discussion on this subject appears to me to be premature, and I shall make every effort to have it temporarily adjourned." This was con-trary to the will of the German Government,[15] but it corre-sponded with the advice sent by Mérey, Austrian Ambassa-dor in Rome, who had a considerable influence over Berch-told.[16]

The Italians were becoming impatient. Marquis di San Giuliano declared to Ambassador Flotow on the twenty-sixth that he had no faith in "the Austrian promises not to lay claim to any Serbian territory." If Count Berchtold would not grant some measure of compensation, "Italy would be forced to *stand in the way* of Austria." The Italian diplo-

[13] *Germ. Doc.*, 168, p. 193.

[14] *Germ. Doc.*, 326, p. 290, and 328, p. 293. Also *Dipl. Pap.*, II, 63, and II, 51.

[15] According to Tschirschky, *Germ. Doc.*, 326, p. 290, it would seem that Italy hoped to obtain more through Berlin than she was demanding for herself at Vienna.

[16] He advised Berchtold to let the Italian Government and press make their outcry, but to stick to his point. *Dipl. Pap.*, II, 50.

mats had had good reason to approach Berlin first, for the
mutual distrust between Vienna and Rome made any direct
negotiations extremely difficult.[17] Von Jagow would not consent to undertake any official intervention: "Italy will have
to negotiate the compensation matter with Vienna direct."[18]
But he was too clearly aware of the danger to let the matter
go unheeded. On the twenty-seventh, after William's return,
the Wilhelmstrasse sent urgent instructions to Tschirschky
to persuade Berchtold to negotiate. "His Majesty considers
it to be absolutely necessary that Austria come to an understanding with Italy on the compensation question *in time*,"
the Chancellor noted.[19]

For fifteen days Berlin had been hoping that Vienna
would do so, and Vienna had turned a deaf ear to all such
requests.

II. *The Concessions Made by Count Berchtold.*

UNDER pressure from Berlin, Count Berchtold finally decided to make a promise, but a promise that did not lead to
any immediate settlement of the matter. He did not intend
to occupy any Serbian territory, he said, but he admitted
that such an occupation might become necessary "during the
course of the war." In case such occupation should be more
than transitory, Austria-Hungary would be prepared "to
enter upon an exchange of views with Italy on the question
of compensation." This was the declaration which he made
to the Duke of Avarna, and instructed Mérey, his Ambassador, to make to Marquis di San Giuliano. He conceded this
much in view of the "solemn and urgent appeal" of the
German Government.[20] In the mind of the Austrian Govern-

---

17 *Germ. Doc.*, 211, p. 217.

18 *Germ. Doc.*, 239, p. 232, evening of 26th July.

19 *Germ. Doc.*, 244, note 3, p. 235; see also 267, p. 248; and 269, p.
249. Italy was notified that Germany was supporting her demands. *Germ.
Doc.*, 287, p. 265.

20 Count Berchtold thus tried to account for his action in the eyes of

ment, however, it was assumed that any eventual compensation would be granted *at the expense of one of the Balkan States*, and not at the expense of Austro-Hungarian territory. "The partition of any part whatever of the Monarchy cannot even be considered as a subject for discussion."[21]

Austria thus promised to negotiate the matter—at some later date. Emperor William was thoroughly dissatisfied: "They should do it at once!"[22] It is quite surprising that Under-Secretary of State Zimmermann should have expressed his approval of the Austrian proposal, as Szögyény claims that he did.[23] In any case, Bethmann-Hollweg considered it quite insufficient and, what was worse, clumsy: "Vienna's declaration that in case of the permanent occupation of parts of Serbian territory, she will come to an arrangement with Italy is, furthermore, in direct opposition to the assurances of her territorial disinterestedness given at St. Petersburg. As her ally we cannot support any double-faced policy." Austria must be given a severe warning: "If Vienna threatens in this fashion to blow up the Triple Alliance on the eve of a possible European conflagration, the whole alliance will begin to totter."[24]

The Chancellor sent fresh instructions to Tschirschky that same evening.[25] He expressed, in strict confidence, a certain degree of uneasiness over the conduct of Austria, who was keeping her plans secret even from her own ally. He instructed the Ambassador to inform Count Berchtold

Mérey, who carried out the *démarche* on the evening of the twenty-ninth. *Dipl. Pap.*, III, 36.

[21] Berchtold to Mérey and to Szögyény, *Dipl. Pap.*, II, 87.

[22] *Germ. Doc.*, 328, p. 293. William II's note on a telegram from Tschirschky to Jagow.

[23] *Dipl. Pap.*, III, 2.

[24] Note from the Chancellor to Jagow, *Germ. Doc.*, 340, p. 301. He added that Germany must not become "completely entangled in Vienna's towrope." *Cf.* also his note on *Germ. Doc.*, 301, p. 277.

[25] *Germ. Doc.*, 361, p. 316, 8 P.M., 29th July. These instructions were thus sent before the arrival of Flotow's telegram.

that some satisfactory proposal must be made at once to Rome, instead of putting off the Italians any longer with "meaningless phrases."

Austria could surely have no doubt this time about the opinion of the German Government. Szögyény himself noticed a good deal of uneasiness in Berlin on the afternoon of the thirtieth, which he attributed to the fear that Italy would break away from the Triple Alliance. As a matter of fact, the concessions made on the twenty-eighth were quite insufficient, and the Italian Cabinet was by no means satisfied with them.[26] Szögyény now pronounced himself in favor of the policy recommended by Germany, namely, to enter *at once* into negotiations with Italy.[27] Emperor William made a personal appeal the next day to Franz Joseph: "I beg you to do everything to persuade Italy to participate, making every possible concession. All else must be made subordinate, in order that the Triple Alliance may unitedly enter upon the war."[28]

Count Berchtold took his own time about responding to these appeals. On the thirtieth he merely asked Mérey for "his point of view." The latter remained absolutely firm, and still felt that the declaration of 28th July had been an error. It would be useless to make any further concession. "I am convinced," he wrote, "that the question of Italy's participation in the war does not really depend upon compensations, but above all upon the view taken by the Cabinet here of the situation in Europe as a whole, and upon military considerations." At the most, some promise might be made to Italy of compensation—without specifying its nature—at the end of the war, if she should have fulfilled her obliga-

26 Berlin had evidence of this from Flotow's telegram, *Germ. Doc.*, 363, p. 317. With regard to Szögyény's error, *cf. Germ. Doc.*, 443, p. 374.

27 *Dipl. Pap.*, III, 32. This telegram was in marked contrast with his earlier statements, except upon one point: "Naturally, every one here is convinced that it could not be a question of the Trentino."

28 *Germ. Doc.*, 503, p. 411.

tions as an ally, and if Austria herself should have occupied certain new territory.[29]

Before this advice reached Vienna, the Council of Ministers had already met and taken up the general question of compensation. Not a single one of the Ministers seems to have had any fear of driving Italy into the arms of the Entente. It was for them simply a question of determining whether or not Italy's *active assistance* would be of vital importance. The German General Staff thought that it would. Two opinions were expressed at the meeting of the Council. Bilinski felt that if Italy's coöperation were so valuable, "they should certainly consent to purchasing it by making the necessary sacrifices." He apparently favored *immediate* compensation. Tisza, on the other hand, along with Burian and Stürgkh, declared "that it would be impossible to decide upon any concessions unless Italy actually did coöperate in case of a great war." This was the opinion that finally won out. Count Berchtold was authorized, in case Austria should proceed to the annexation of a portion of Serbia, "to disclose to Italy the prospect of some compensation." What would it be? Valona, and not Trieste. Moreover, Italy must first of all perform her duties as an ally.[30]

The Minister for Foreign Affairs at once entered into negotiation with the Duke of Avarna, the Italian Ambassador. He thought that he was on the point of reaching an agreement. A note which the German Ambassador had helped to prepare was presented to the Duke of Avarna, who accepted it. It stated that if Austria-Hungary were led to make certain territorial acquisitions in the Balkans: "The Imperial and Royal Government stands ready to come to an agreement with Italy upon the compensation to be awarded the latter, whether Italy lends her assistance to Austria in case of the occurrence of the *casus fœderis* as provided by

[29] *Dipl. Pap.*, III, 61, arrived 11 A.M., 1st August.
[30] *Dipl. Pap.*, III, 79.

the Treaty, or whether she grants her assistance without the occurrence of the *casus fœderis*."[31] It was assumed that this was the note which would be sent to Rome the next day. As a matter of fact, the declaration which Count Berchtold made to the Italian Government on 1st August was quite different indeed:

I accept the interpretation given by Italy and Germany to Article 7, on condition that Italy shall maintain a friendly attitude with regard to the military operations undertaken by Austria-Hungary against Serbia, and that she shall fulfil her duties as an ally in case the present conflict leads to a general conflagration.[32]

The word *compensation* thus did not appear at all, nor did the message contain any formal promise of negotiations. At the same time, this note amounted to a considerable concession. But by the time it reached Rome, the Italian Cabinet had already made its first important decisions.

III. *Italy's Declaration of Neutrality.*

THE Italian Cabinet adopted the principle of neutrality for Italy at its meeting of 31st July. It considered, as Marquis di San Giuliano told Flotow,[33] "that Austria's procedure against Serbia must be considered as an act of aggression, and that consequently a *casus fœderis*, according to the terms of the Triple Alliance treaty, did not exist." The Government reserved to itself, however, the right to determine "whether it might be possible for Italy to intervene later in behalf of the allies," on condition that Italy's interests should be well protected. Did this constitute an invitation to offer further important compensation? Flotow thought so, but he also feared that the attitude adopted by England might eventually weaken the position of those in Italy who favored neutrality.

31 *Germ. Doc.*, 573, p. 450.
32 *Dipl. Pap.*, III, 87.
33 *Germ. Doc.*, 534, p. 427.

When Count Berchtold's declaration reached Rome, Marquis di San Giuliano consented to call the Cabinet together again to reconsider the matter, but it simply confirmed its earlier decision. In the opinion of the Italian Government, the Austrian proposal was insufficient because it did not suggest "any agreement as to the nature and importance of the eventual compensations," and because it made the interpretation of Article 7 dependent upon "the attitude which Italy should adopt during the present crisis."[34] These were not, however, the only reasons underlying the decision of the Italian Government. San Giuliano himself pointed out to the German Ambassador two reasons of a very different character, namely, the fear of domestic trouble—"our participation in a war contrary to Italian interests in the Balkans might, under certain circumstances, sweep away the whole Monarchy here"; and, secondly, the fear of a naval attack by England—"the Italian coasts and harbors could not be exposed to English cannon."[35] Of course, the Italian statesman may have been all too glad to conjure up these excuses, in his embarrassment in justifying his Government's decision! Perhaps, say the Austrians, he was exaggerating these fears more than he had a right to do. This is not likely, however, since all the information that reached the German Ambassador confirmed the Minister's official statements.

The German diplomats made one final, futile effort, but without much hope as to its success.[36] They communicated to Rome the news of the declaration of war on Russia, and added: "The war with Russia will unquestionably result in an attack upon us by France. . . . We expect from Italy the fulfilment of the obligations of her alliance."[37] In

[34] Dipl. Pap., III, 108 and 109.

[35] Germ. Doc., 614, p. 472; 675, p. 501; 745, p. 538.

[36] Moltke, Germ. Doc., 662, p. 494, stated that he would be satisfied if Italy would show her sympathy for the Triple Alliance by sending a single division, "one division of cavalry."

[37] Germ. Doc., 628, p. 478, 6 A.M., 2nd August; and 694, p. 511, 12.25 A.M., 3rd August.

order to support his statements, the Chancellor reported to
Rome several instances of French "aggression" the next
evening. "Use all your influence to convince the Italian
Minister that these provocations, made against all good faith
and honor, stamp the war thereby forced upon us as an
aggression by our enemies, which affords a *casus belli*." Marquis di San Giuliano replied that these acts of France "were
nothing but the consequences of Austria's first aggressive
act."[38]

In vain did Count Berchtold try at the last minute to
resort to a policy of intimidation. He informed the Italian
Ambassador in Vienna that the declaration he had made
about the interpretation of Article 7 held good only "if
Italy should from the beginning perform her obligations
as an ally."[39] The Duke of Avarna received this warning
on the second.

In vain did Lieutenant-Colonel von Kleist, William II's
special envoy at Rome, attempt to use his personal influence
with the King. "The King replied that personally he was
whole-heartedly with us," wrote Kleist, "but that, unfortunately, he had merely influence, and no power!"[40] Italy made
her official declaration of neutrality on 3rd August.

Would Italy, however, content herself with mere neutrality? It was feared in Berlin that Italy's estrangement
from the Triple Alliance might be carried still further. The
King had not concealed from Kleist that "the incredible awk-
wardness of Austria had reacted upon Italian sensibilities."
It was thus altogether possible that the Italian Government
intended to profit by this general conflict to realize some of
her cherished ambitions at Austria's expense. "*At present
the King was not figuring on anything of the sort being
done*," wrote Kleist, after a further interview with the

38 *Germ. Doc.*, 745, p. 538, 2 P.M., 3rd August.
39 *Germ. Doc.*, 668, p. 498.
40 *Germ. Doc.*, 771, p. 550. Emperor William had also wired to the King
on the thirty-first. *Germ. Doc.*, 530, p. 424.

King.[41] This was hardly reassuring for the German Government. William II noted on the margin of the telegram: "Vienna must under all circumstances make binding promises and offer big compensation, which will be so alluring to Italy that they will work." Vienna had by this time received a direct warning from Rome. Marquis di San Giuliano had declared to von Mérey, in referring to the Trentino, "that that would be the only compensation which could be considered."[42] The Minister's remark takes on its full significance when compared with a communication from General Cadorna to General Conrad von Hötzendorf: "If Austria-Hungary does not occupy the Lovćen, and does not disturb the equilibrium on the Adriatic, Italy will never take action against Austria-Hungary."

Italy thus allowed it to be understood through innuendoes that she might side with the Entente, pointing out at the same time that, if Austria decided to offer her the territory she claimed, she might throw her weight on the side of the Triple Alliance. William II was quite prepared to insist that Austria should make these concessions. But Count Berchtold considered this policy as nothing short of blackmail; he would not give in, and he would not admit that the question of the Trentino was in any way involved.[43] But he could not run the risk of "breaking off all possible ties," and he therefore promised Italy, on 5th August, that Austria would not attack Montenegro.

The negotiations with Italy bring out very clearly, once again, the obstinacy of the Austrian Government.[44] It is true that Germany had the easier part to play. She was quite prepared to offer compensation which would cost her nothing herself. It is not surprising that Vienna should have taken

[41] *Germ. Doc.*, 850, p. 587.
[42] *Dipl. Pap.*, III, 127.
[43] *Dipl. Pap.*, III, 142.
[44] It is quite possible that Count Szögyény contributed to some extent, by the error committed in his telegram of 27th July, to encourage certain false

a different view of the matter. If, however, Austria wished to carry out her plans against Serbia in order to avoid domestic difficulties, would it not have been to her own interest to assure herself the support, or at least the benevolent neutrality, of Italy? Now that she had embarked upon a struggle in which her very existence was at stake, ought she not concede the impossible, for the sake of maintaining the Triple Alliance? This was certainly William II's view of the matter.

The Austrian statesmen, it is true, had powerful arguments in support of their case. If they should give up a piece of territory peopled by Italians, would it not establish a dangerous precedent, which might encourage similar claims in other neighboring states, like Rumania? It was the lot of the Dual Monarchy never to succeed in ridding itself of this danger. It evaded it in one direction, only to have it crop up again in another. Since Austria could not possibly afford to give in, would it not therefore be better to let Italy face the facts? "If Berchtold," writes Hoyos,[45] "had disclosed his plans to the Italians as straightforwardly as he did to the Germans, Italy would at once have demanded the Trentino as compensation. Under the existing circumstances, this demand would have been rejected as unacceptable, and the result would have been a quarrel, which would have thrown Italy even sooner into the arms of our enemies."

All of which goes to show that the attitude of the Ballplatz was not dominated by any question of prestige or of *amour-propre*, but by the very same interplay of powerful forces which had condemned the whole Austrian Empire to perish.

hopes in Count Berchtold's mind. It is certain that the presence in Rome of a man like Mérey, who was ill at the time, irritable, and uncompromising, was a most unfortunate circumstance, the more so as the Ambassador was on extremely bad terms with San Giuliano. *Cf. Germ. Doc.*, 363, p. 318, *et al.* Flotow even accused him of failing to carry out the instructions sent to him from Vienna.

[45] Hoyos, p. 65.

CHAPTER XVII

THE BALKAN STATES

EVEN as early as 5th July, the Central Powers had already begun a diplomatic campaign in the Balkans. The memorandum which Count Hoyos presented to William II on that date had suggested the reconstitution of a strong Balkan "bloc" under the patronage of Vienna.[1] In the opinion of the Austrians, the full execution of this plan involved the conquest of Serbia as a prerequisite step. In order to bring this about, however, as much immediate support as possible should be obtained among the various Balkan States.

This policy of the Central Powers called first of all for preliminary efforts in the direction of Rumania, who was wavering at this time in spite of being bound to them by a defensive alliance.[2]

Would it be possible to secure her active coöperation? The Ballplatz hardly thought so, but the Wilhelmstrasse was confident, because of the fact that King Carol was a Hohenzollern.

The second effort should be directed toward Bulgaria, in order to bring about her entry into the Triple Alliance. This would be an extremely difficult task, for Bulgaria and Rumania had been enemies as recently as 1913.

[1] See above, Ch. III, pp. 35-36.

[2] The Austro-Rumanian Treaty had been renewed in February 1913. Article 2 read as follows:

"If Rumania is attacked without any provocation on her part, Austria-Hungary is bound to render her aid and assistance against the aggressor within time to be of service.

"If Austria-Hungary is attacked under the same circumstances, in a part of her territory in the vicinity of Rumania, the *casus fœderis* will be considered to have arisen for the latter State."

But Czernin, Austrian Minister in Bucharest since 1913, considered the Treaty as "a dead letter."

Finally, it was hoped to bring about a *rapprochement* between Bulgaria and Turkey, whose mutual relations were much more favorable.[3]

These efforts were by no means abandoned between 5th July and 4th August 1914,[4] but the results obtained by the beginning of the European war fell considerably short of the hopes of the Central Powers.

I. *Rumania.*

WALDBURG, German Chargé d'Affaires at Bucharest, had an interview with King Carol on 10th July. He told the sovereign that Germany and Austria desired to further "any attempts at a *rapprochement* between Bulgaria and the Triple Alliance,"[5] and he came to ask the King whether, "in view of the serious nature of the situation, he would not be able to break away from Serbia." The King did not think that it would be possible for Rumania to consider, for the moment, an alliance with Bulgaria, whose Government had no authority, and might "be swept away at any moment."[6] He seemed disposed, however,[7] to undertake some sort of action against the movements in Rumania which were hostile to Austria,[8] and to detach himself from Serbia, in whom he really "took very little interest." Might the King be called upon to do even more? In the case of an Austro-Serbian conflict, he said, Rumania would "be under no obligations."

[3] A treaty had actually been drawn up between them before the Sarajevo crime, but not signed.

[4] They were continued long after that date.

[5] According to *Germ. Doc.*, 21, p. 88, Berchtold considered on 9th July that for the present it might be wiser not to press these attempts too far.

[6] *Germ. Doc.*, 28, p. 92; 41, p. 102; and 66, p. 127. Three reports from Waldburg, each in quite a different tone, upon his interview with the King.

[7] At least, Waldburg felt that he could "deduce" this from the statements which the sovereign made.

[8] These movements were largely connected with the problem of Transylvania. Upon this point King Carol asserted "that he would never consent to taking Transylvania by conquest."

When he had received Count Czernin on the previous evening, the King had also "avoided expressing himself on the attitude to be assumed by Roumania in the event of a conflict."[9] It was therefore impossible for any one in Berlin to foretell what the future would bring forth.[10]

The news of the Austrian ultimatum caused a considerable stir in Bucharest. "Austria has gone mad!" people said. Count Czernin remarks that he felt a growing "wave of hatred" all about him.[11] The King remained the one source of hope for the Central Powers, but he had no illusions about the gravity of the situation, and was fast losing confidence. When Austria officially asked Rumania, on 28th July, for her loyal coöperation in case of aggressive action by Russia, he told Czernin "not to count too definitely" upon military support. "The King was moved as he has never been before as he spoke to me," wrote the Minister.[12] "He assured me that his army would certainly fight on the side of the Triple Alliance if he could follow the guidance of his own heart, but that it was not possible. So many things had changed during the past year that it would be impossible for him to adhere to the Treaty."

The German Government, however, made further advances to the King. It pointed out on the twenty-ninth that Rumania had nothing to fear, as it might feel quite assured of Bulgaria's neutrality. But King Carol had his doubts about this point; when the conflict started the present Gov-

---

9 *Germ. Doc.*, 39, p. 100.

10 According to Conrad, IV, p. 79, Czernin favored settling the question once for all by putting the decisive question to King Carol *before* sending the ultimatum to Serbia. Certain diplomats in Vienna, however, preferred to take Rumania by surprise, by facing her at once with a *fait accompli*. Conrad himself was trying to obtain definite information through his Military Attaché at the earliest possible moment.

11 Czernin, *Im Weltkriege*, Berlin and Vienna, Ullstein, 1919, p. 110.

12 *Österreichisch-ungarisches Rotbuch, Diplomatische Aktenstücke betreffend die Beziehungen Österreich-Ungarns zu Rumänien in der Zeit vom 22 Juli 1914 bis 27 August 1916*, Vienna, Manz, 1916, No. 3.

ernment would be swept away by Russian influence, and "Bulgaria would at once go over to the Russian camp."[13] On 30th July Jagow requested the King to send a telegram to the Tsar, "in which the obligations of Roumania should be made plain." This would, he said, be a means of stopping the conflict. He hoped thus to induce the Rumanian Government to make a public stand, but Carol refused,[14] and referred once more to "the great difficulties in the way of his living up to the obligations of his alliance." On the following day William II himself took a hand in the matter: "I trust that, as a King and as a Hohenzollern, you will stand faithfully by your friends. . . ." He also sent word to offer Rumania the annexation of Bessarabia if she should take part in the war.[15] But Bratianu, the Rumanian Premier, attached no great importance to this promise. "It would only be of value to Roumania in the event that Russia had to surrender further territories also to Austria and to Germany, and should become so weakened that Bessarabia would actually remain a possession of Roumania permanently."[16]

Now, the Rumanian Government was also receiving advice and offers at this same time from St. Petersburg.

Sazonov sent word to Bucharest on 26th July that he could not abandon Serbia to her fate, and he asked to be notified of the attitude which Rumania proposed to adopt.[17] "We are convinced that all of Rumania's sympathies and hopes point the way to a community of interests with Serbia. If Austria today is attacking Serbia in order to punish her irredentism, tomorrow Rumania will find herself in the same

---

[13] *Germ. Doc.*, 379, p. 332.

[14] *Germ. Doc.*, 389, p. 342; and 463, p. 386.

[15] *Germ. Doc.*, 472, p. 391; and 506, p. 412.

[16] *Germ. Doc.*, 582, p. 454. According to *Germ. Doc.*, 868, p. 595, political circles in Bucharest at the time considered that Bessarabia would be "nothing but a second Alsace-Lorraine."

[17] Sazonov to the Russian Minister in Bucharest, Tel. No. 1506, Schilling, *Journal*, p. 91.

position, and she will have to abandon forever the realization of her national ideal."

Sazonov thus brought the problem of Transylvania to the forefront in order to influence the Rumanian Government. In spite of this fact, Diamandi, Rumanian Chargé d'Affaires at St. Petersburg, did not hesitate to show that his country would be in a most delicate situation if the Austro-Serbian quarrel led to general war, however friendly he may have been personally to Russia.[18]

Disturbed by certain information which had reached him, Sazonov became quite insistent on the twenty-ninth. A "categorical" question should be put to Rumania. On the following day he decided to offer Transylvania to Rumania, if the latter would consent to intervene on the side of Russia:[19] "You may formally declare to Bratianu that we are prepared to favor the annexation of Transylvania by Rumania." This step was to be taken only if the Russian Minister in Bucharest thought it wise. In replying to Poklevsky's *démarche*, the Rumanian Premier simply stated that his country's intervention on the side of Russia "was not impossible." But would Russia's future allies, especially England, consent to taking such a large piece of territory from Austria-Hungary?[20]

Up until 31st July, Bratianu thus maintained an attitude of strict reserve, and his position caused no little uneasiness in St. Petersburg and in Paris.[21]

[18] He had been invited by Sazonov on the twenty-fourth to attend the conference which the Minister held with the English and French Ambassadors. *Journal*, p. 29. On the same day, the Russian Minister in Bucharest felt that Rumania would not abandon her neutrality. *Cf.* the Russian documents translated into German, *Die Kriegsschuldfrage*, February 1926, p. 100.

[19] Nos. 1541 and 1556, *Journal*, pp. 96 and 98. The initiative taken by Russia thus preceded the similar suggestion made by M. Poincaré. Isvolsky to Sazonov, No. 224, *Livre Noir*, II, p. 298.

[20] Poklevsky's telegram, No. 174, 31st July, *Die Kriegsschuldfrage*, February 1926, pp. 103-105.

[21] Sazonov to Poklevsky, No. 1579, *Journal*, p. 99; and No. 224, *Livre Noir*, II, p. 298.

On 1st August the Rumanian Government learned of Italy's decision to remain neutral, on the strength of the fact that the war was the result of *provocation* on Austria's part. Now, Rumania's position was identically the same as Italy's; she was bound by the same treaty obligations. This was an essential factor in the ultimate decision of the Bucharest Government. Furthermore, the decision could not be postponed any longer, for Germany had decided to demand "the immediate mobilization of the Rumanian army and its advance against Russia." Bratianu immediately requested the King to call together a Crown Council, which was set for 3rd August.[22]

At five o'clock on that day there were gathered together in the King's Palace the Ministers, the party leaders, among them Marghiloman, leader of the Conservatives, and Jonescu, leader of the Democrats, Carp and Rosetti, former Premiers, and the President of the Rumanian Parliament. In all, about twenty persons were present.[23] The King knew in advance the opposition he was to encounter. Jonescu had told him on the previous evening that a victory of the Germans and Hungarians "was incompatible with Rumanian independence." The sovereign did not hesitate, however, to state his case:

"For thirty years the policy of Rumania has bound her to the Triple Alliance; during this time we have been bound to it by a formal treaty, which was signed by our most important statesmen, and supported by all parties. It is a matter of honor for the whole country to keep the pledge it has given." Public opinion could hardly have been said to share this feeling, but what difference did that make?

[22] The meeting was delayed until the third by the absence of Take Jonescu, who was on his way from London. Take Jonescu, *Souvenirs*, Paris, Payot, 1919, p. 40.

[23] *Cf.* the very detailed and accurate account of this gathering by Lindenberg, *König Karl v. Rumänien*, Berlin, Hafen-Verlag, 1923, p. 306. The author does not state his sources, but his description is certainly based upon direct testimony.

"Despite these violent currents of opposition, I am firmly convinced that the day will come when the country will approve of the policy which it now seems necessary for us to pursue."

Carp, former Premier, was the next speaker, and he too pronounced himself for the Central Powers. Everyone else present favored giving up the alliance. One of the speakers, Rosetti, did not think that the country was in any condition to take part in a war. Another, Marghiloman, recalled the wording of the Treaty: ". . . without any provocation," and concluded that Rumania had no obligations in the matter. Bratianu, who had been making efforts to calm the fears of the Central Powers, also pronounced for neutrality. The discussion grew more lively: "You are forcing the King to break his word," exclaimed Carp, and Marghiloman replied: "The King's word is not in question. On the contrary, by our action we are protecting the King. If we fought, people would say: 'It is the King's war.'" In the end, Jonescu did not hesitate about going even further: "We might even enter the war on the side of France without the consent of the King." The King at once rose to his feet: "So, you have come to that! I thank you! But before I should draw my sword against my own allies, I should prefer to pack up my trunk and return whence I came. Gentlemen, good afternoon!" and he left the room.

With one exception, the Council gave its unanimous support to Bratianu. Rumania would remain neutral, but without making a formal declaration of her neutrality, so as not to play into the hands of the Entente. She would even, if need be, permit the intervention of Bulgaria against Serbia, so that Austria might withdraw some of her troops from the southern front. This was the most that the Rumanian Government could promise the Central Powers. Czernin was not surprised, but he did not believe that this neutrality could stand as final. "Only our success in the theater of war will decide if and when Rumania will join us."[24] But what would happen in case of a defeat? Rumania must then be expected to join the other side. The King would resist, as he told the German Minister the next day, but he might be forced to abdicate![25]

For the moment, the Central Powers were compelled to declare themselves satisfied. Bratianu had intimated that it would be desirable for them to do so, for the promise that he had given concerning Bulgarian intervention held good only "if the two Empires should consider this attitude on the part of Roumania as one corresponding to a state of friendly relations."[26] And von Jagow had at once complied with this request.

II. *Turkey.*

WHILE Rumania was thus gradually detaching herself from the Central Powers, the Austrian and German diplomats found some consolation in the attitude of Turkey. The first conversations were undertaken only with the greatest difficulty. Although the governments in Berlin and Vienna had agreed to seek for an alliance with Turkey, they had apparently neglected to issue very precise instructions to their representatives in Constantinople. Thus it happened that while Marquis Pallavicini, the Austrian Ambassador, was planning on 16th July to work toward the conclusion of an agreement, Wangenheim, his German colleague, was actually opposing the plan.[27] This *faux pas* very nearly ruined the whole situation.

"Turkey," concluded Wangenheim in his report to the

[24] Austrian *Red Book,* 1916, 7.

[25] King Carol died on 10th October 1914. At the end of September the Council of Ministers had been upon the point of deciding to intervene against Austria; that would have meant abdication.

[26] *Germ. Doc.,* 841, p. 583; and 864, p. 593.

[27] Here is further proof that Wangenheim was not present when the decisions were made in Potsdam on 5th July.

Wilhelmstrasse, "is today still worthless as an ally." She would only be a burden to the Central Powers, without being able to guarantee them the slightest advantage in return.[28] And with that, he proceeded to oppose all idea of such an alliance among the Turks themselves.

On 22nd July, Enver Pasha made direct advances to the Ambassador: Turkey could not remain isolated, for "she needed the support of one of the groups of Great Powers." Only a minority of the Turkish National Committee favored the Entente, which held the strongest position in the Mediterranean. The majority was favorable to the Triple Alliance, "which was more powerful from the military point of view." Turkey must make a choice. Enver Pasha decided to seek at once for an agreement with Bulgaria, as the first step toward the Triple Alliance. Would the Central Powers be willing to grant Turkey their patronage? If they refused, "the friends of the Triple Entente on the Committee would gain the upper hand." Turkey thus came and offered herself as an ally![29]

Ambassador Wangenheim received these offers with surprising coolness. He considered them dangerous from the point of view of Turkey herself: "The economic recuperation of the country would be put at stake by an alliance." And furthermore, the political considerations were even more serious, for Turkey would have to defend her eastern frontier against an attack by Russia. The Ambassador felt that "the Triple Alliance Governments would presumably be reluctant to burden themselves with obligations in return for which Turkey as yet was able to offer no satisfactory equivalent."[30]

In Berlin, however, the Emperor became quite irritated: "Rot!" he noted down in the margin of the report. "A re-

28 *Germ. Doc.*, 71, p. 130.
29 *Germ. Doc.*, 117, p. 157.
30 Pallavicini in turn adopted the same attitude, under Wangenheim's influence. *Germ. Doc.*, 149, p. 178.

fusal or a snub would amount to her going over to Russo-Gallia, and our influence would be gone for once and all!" Would the burden be too heavy? "Let him first join them to us, the rest will take care of itself!" And the Emperor concluded with a definite order: "Wangenheim must express himself to the Turks in relation to a connection with the Triple Alliance with unmistakably plain compliance, and receive their desires and report them! Under no circumstances at all can we afford to turn them away."[31] The Emperor's personal intervention was the occasion for a special message from Jagow to the Ambassador on 25th July.[32]

Upon receiving these "peremptory orders," Wangenheim yielded. He accepted the Turkish offer, and began negotiations on the twenty-sixth. On the following evening the Grand Vizier proposed to give the alliance the character of a secret treaty, both defensive and offensive, "between Germany and Turkey against Russia." The secret would be kept even from the other Turkish Ministers. Upon this basis, the German Chancellery at once prepared the draft of a treaty, in five articles: Germany guaranteed Turkey her territorial integrity "as against Russia"; she left her military mission in Constantinople, and it was to be assured "the actual exercise" of the supreme command in Turkey in the event of war.[33] But Bethmann took care not to assume any unnecessary obligations; the treaty would become inoperative "in case no war should take place between Germany and Russia" as a result of the Austro-Serbian conflict. This last point was rejected by the Grand Vizier. After incurring the displeasure of Russia by engaging in these negotiations, he did not wish to run the risk of finding himself alone against her. He therefore asked that the treaty should be

[31] *Germ. Doc.,* 149, p. 178.

[32] Jagow had advised in an earlier telegram, *Germ. Doc.,* 144, p. 175, not to undertake any too "far-reaching obligations."

[33] *Germ. Doc.,* 320, p. 286.

concluded for a period of at least four years. Berlin acceded to this request on 31st July.[34]

Nothing was now lacking but the exchange of signatures.[35] Wangenheim became more insistent, for he feared lest the news of Russian general mobilization might disturb the Turks and lead them to change their decision.[36] Authorization to sign the treaty reached him on the morning of 1st August, subject to the condition, however, that Turkey should undertake some "action against Russia worthy of the name." The treaty was signed on the following day, and was to be ratified within a month.[37]

Hardly had the decision been made when the whole question was reopened. Enver Pasha had felt obliged to disclose the secret to several of his colleagues, who protested against the extent of the obligations, and who demanded a promise of some sort of compensation.[38] Germany consented. On 6th August, in an additional clause, she promised to obtain for Turkey at the end of the war the abolition of the Capitulation Treaties, a war indemnity, and a rectification of her boundaries in Asia.

The Russian diplomats, who knew as early as 27th July that negotiations were taking place, nevertheless did not suspect on 2nd August that an agreement had already been reached. Turkey was doubtless "hoping for the success of our enemies," as the Russian Ambassador wrote on that day, but she would await the outcome of the initial military encounters before making any final decision. There was in his opinion no cause for uneasiness on account of the Turkish military preparations. The Bulgarian representative in

[34] *Germ. Doc.*, 411, p. 355; and 508, p. 412.
[35] Vienna was not informed of these negotiations until the thirty-first.
[36] *Germ. Doc.*, 517, p. 416, 3.10 P.M., 31st July.
[37] *Germ. Doc.*, 726, p. 526; and 733, p. 529.
[38] The Turkish Government pointed out, furthermore, that it had not yet received any assurance of Bulgarian support. *Germ. Doc.*, 854, p. 589.

Constantinople had, it is true, given the Russian Ambassador to understand "quite clearly" that an agreement had been reached between Turkey and Germany. But Giers did not let this remark trouble him: "I do not deny the possibility of such an agreement, but, given the unprepared condition of the Turkish army, it certainly cannot come into effect very rapidly."[39]

The execution of the treaty should not, in Wangenheim's opinion, take place at once. He felt that it would be better, in attacking Russia, to wait for the coöperation of the Bulgarians. But Liman von Sanders, head of the German Military Mission to Turkey, wished to see Turkey enter the war as soon as possible, so as to profit by Enver Pasha's friendly attitude. This was also the feeling in Berlin, where only limited confidence was placed in a mere exchange of signatures. Was there not the danger that England's intervention might lead the Turkish Government to reconsider? "In order to prevent the Porte from escaping us at the last moment under the influence of England's action, the declaration of war on Russia by Turkey, today, if possible, would appear to be of the greatest importance."[40]

The German diplomats did not, however, gain their point. The Turkish Government did not wish to take sides publicly before completing its military preparations. Three days after the signing of the treaty with Germany, Enver Pasha declared to the Russian Military Attaché that Turkey had no engagements with any foreign Power. He gave the impression that if Russia should succeed in forming a "Balkan bloc," and if she should offer the Porte compensation in the Aegean Sea or in Western Thrace, the Turkish Government would not hesitate to send the German Military Mission

[39] The telegrams from Giers have recently been translated into German and published, *Die Kriegsschuldfrage,* January 1926, in particular, pp. 9-14.

[40] *Germ. Doc.,* 836, p. 581, 6.08 P.M., 4th August.

back to Berlin.[41] On 4th August he had notified England
that he intended to maintain "strict neutrality in the present
conflict."[42] Even on 10th August, when it opened the Dar-
danelles to the German cruiser *Goeben*, the Porte succeeded
in avoiding a rupture with the Entente, with whom it continued to negotiate. It was not until the end of October, after
securing a loan from Germany, that Turkey carried out the
promise she had made on 2nd August.

Only then was the German Government able to proceed
with the political scheme which was, in its opinion, the chief
advantage of the Turkish alliance: "To excite the fanaticism
of Islam . . . to send out a Mussulman call to arms in the
English colonies . . . to foment insurrection in India, Egypt
and the Caucasus."[43] On 5th August Moltke wrote to Jagow:
"By means of the treaty with Turkey, the Foreign Office
will be in a position to bring this idea to realization."

III. *Bulgaria and Greece.*

THE Central Powers planned to follow the Turkish alliance
by an alliance with Bulgaria. Furthermore, in order to iso-
late Serbia more completely, it was important that she should
be deprived of the support of Greece, who had been bound
to her since 1913 by a defensive treaty of alliance. It was not
an easy task to obtain the support of both Sofia and Athens,
for the bait which might be held out to lure each of them was
precisely the same—Serbian Macedonia. Besides this, up
until 3rd August, Germany and Austria had not abandoned
all hope at Bucharest, so that Rumania must also be kept in
a favorable mood. Now, while the purpose underlying the
Austro-German policy is easy to understand, the plan of

41 Note from Giers to Sazonov, 5th August, *Die Kriegsschuldfrage*,
January 1926, pp. 11-12. Sazonov replied the next day that it seemed to him
desirable to continue the conversations, "if only to gain a certain amount of
time." He was unwilling, however, to make any promises. *Ibid.*, p. 14.

42 *Brit. Doc.*, 598, p. 316.

43 *Germ. Doc.*, 751, p. 541; 767, p. 548; 876, p. 599.

action of the Central Powers is not so clear, at least in the light of our present knowledge. It should be remembered that their efforts encountered not only the difficulty of rival claims among the Rumanians, Greeks and Bulgars, but that they also had to contend with the diplomatic maneuvers of the Entente in the same field.

I. The influence of the Central Powers in Sofia was rather slow in making its appearance. Berchtold, who had at first been anxious to settle the whole thing at once, hesitated on 8th July to conclude "the prospective alliance with Bulgaria," for it might disturb Rumania. He therefore decided to suspend all negotiations with the Bulgarian Government for the time being.[44] During his later dealings with the Bulgars, he still kept in mind the dangers that were involved.

It was from Sofia, moreover, that the first advances apparently came. On 25th July, Radoslavov, the Bulgarian Premier, declared to the German Minister, after a loan had been concluded with the German financiers, that "his Government was now firmly established, and could begin to follow a line of conduct of its own, by seeking to become attached to the Triple Alliance."[45] King Ferdinand "was overjoyed," and had commissioned him to draw up a proposed treaty.

For several days the plan was under consideration, but Bulgaria's attitude meanwhile began to take more definite shape. Her representatives in Vienna gave "the most binding assurances" of neutrality on 28th July;[46] on the thirtieth she made an official statement in Athens of her neutrality in the Austro-Serbian conflict; she sent word to Bucharest that she would make no efforts to reconquer the Dobrudža, so long as Rumania "placed no obstacles in the way of Bulgarian aspirations in Macedonia." This was to add further strength to the efforts which the Central Powers were making

[44] Germ. Doc., 17, p. 80; 19, p. 82; and 21, p. 88.
[45] Germ. Doc., 162, p. 190.
[46] Germ. Doc., 305, p. 279; and 318, p. 285.

to gain King Carol's support. At the same time, Bulgaria rejected the advances of the Entente, who had given her to understand that she might hope for the annexation of a portion of Serbian Macedonia,[47] and stated to the Russian Minister that "Bulgaria would not lift a finger for the benefit of Serbia."[48]

The Bulgarian Premier made new advances on 2nd August. He proposed a definite scheme "for the accession of Bulgaria to the Triple Alliance." The Central Powers were to guarantee the territorial status of the Kingdom, and to help her to expand toward the *west*, "at the expense of a country not belonging to the Triple Alliance." In the event that Rumania should take sides with the Triple Alliance, she would have nothing to fear from Bulgaria.[49]

Bethmann-Hollweg authorized his Minister in Sofia to proceed with the negotiations. Up until the morning of the third the German Government may have hesitated between the friendship of Greece and that of Bulgaria, but now it knew pretty well the attitude of the Greek Government. Furthermore, the Turkish Government had expressed its desire to be certain of support from Bulgaria. These are doubtless the reasons which led to the Chancellor's decision. He requested Austria to take corresponding action, and two days later he sent detailed instructions and full authority to his own representative in Sofia.

The tardy efforts of the German Government, however, were all in vain. The Austrians were in no particular hurry

[47] *Germ. Doc.*, 794, p. 562. Serbia would have received compensation in Bosnia-Herzegovina. On 31st July Sazonov tried to prepare Serbia for the idea of giving "territorial compensation" to Bulgaria, *Journal*, p. 71, Telegram No. 1574. On 5th August he asked the Serbian Government to make Bulgaria definite promises: Ištib and Kočana, as the price of neutrality; still more, as the price of intervention, *Die Kriegsschuldfrage*, January 1926, p. 18.

[48] *Germ. Doc.*, 318, p. 286.

[49] *Germ. Doc.*, 673, p. 500.

to accede to Bethmann's request.[50] Three days slipped by. Meanwhile the Bulgars learned that the Rumanians had declared their neutrality, and they asked to be allowed to reconsider the matter. When the general war finally broke out, the efforts of the German diplomats in Sofia had not led to any tangible results.

These efforts, however, were not abandoned. In spite of the appeals of the Entente, Bulgaria gave her adherence in principle to the Central Powers early in September. The news of the battle of the Marne made her hesitate once again, and it was not until 6th September 1915, that she finally decided to throw in her lot with that of Germany and Turkey.

II. Germany's relations with Athens were of quite a different character. It was a question of separating Greece from Serbia, in the hope of then attracting her, if possible, to the Austro-German group. Now, Venizelos had replied to the appeals from Belgrade, on the twenty-fourth, that he would maintain a "benevolent neutrality," and would protect Serbia against an attack by Bulgaria. If Germany still hoped to win over the Greek Government, she must therefore count solely upon the personal influence of King Constantine. Even then, could she expect to succeed when she was seeking the friendship of Bulgaria at the same time? Constantine brought this fact to the attention of William II on 27th July: if a Turko-Bulgarian *rapprochement* were brought about, the results of the Treaty of Bucharest and the balance of power in the Balkans would be upset. "In this case I would not take the side of Austria against the Slavs."[51]

Thus the King also indicated in this message that he might still turn toward the Central Powers if his wishes in this matter were taken into consideration.

[50] *Germ. Doc.*, 798, p. 564; and 857, p. 590. The Austrian Government announced on the fourth that it would accept the proposal, but the German representative in Sofia wired, later on that same day, that his Austrian colleague had as yet received no instructions.

[51] *Germ. Doc.*, 243, p. 235.

But the German Government would not commit itself to any agreement whatever. William II replied to Constantine on 31st July, demanding a prompt decision one way or the other. If a general conflict should come about in Europe, "all the Balkan nations will have to make their choice." It was altogether to the interest of Greece, said the German Emperor, "under the mighty shield of the Triple Alliance," to shake off the hegemony which Russia was endeavoring to impose upon the Balkans. By turning toward the Entente, she would expose herself at once to attack from Turkey and even, William added, from Bulgaria and Italy! "Our personal relations would probably have to suffer forever as a result."[52]

Constantine's reply was hardly such as to satisfy the Emperor: "It seems to me that the interests of Greece demand her absolute neutrality." But this neutrality was linked, in the mind of the Greek Government, with "the preservation of the *status quo* in the Balkans," and she was consequently opposed to Germany's plans. Bulgaria's intervention in Macedonia would be a blow to the balance of power in the Balkans, and Greece decided to oppose it.

Once again German diplomacy had not for the moment succeeded in obtaining anything. William II became irritated, and wished to warn Greece that she would be "treated as an enemy" if she refused to support the idea of a Turko-Bulgarian alliance, which was uppermost in the mind of Berlin. If this threat was ever officially communicated to the Greek Government, it does not appear to have had any effect upon its line of conduct.[53]

* * * * * * *

On 2nd August, Moltke wished to bring matters to an issue

[52] *Germ. Doc.*, 466, p. 388.

[53] William expressed himself forcibly to Theotoky, Greek Minister in Berlin (marginal note of William II, *Germ. Doc.*, 702, p. 515), but, according to the *German Documents*, there is no reason to suppose that the Chancellor officially communicated the threat to Athens.

in the Balkans as soon as possible.[54] The diplomacy of the Central Powers had certainly not met with success. In Sofia, Athens, and Bucharest, it had counted upon the personal influence of the sovereigns, who were linked to Germany either by tradition or by family ties. None of the three kings had had sufficient power to carry out the German plan. Rumania's decision to remain neutral had been a particular blow to William II: "Our allies are already before the war falling away from us like rotten apples! A total collapse of both German and Austrian foreign diplomacy. This should and could have been avoided."[55]

The Entente had not been any more successful in the Balkans. It had succeeded, it is true, in detaching the Bucharest Government from the Austro-German alliance. But Rumania, like Bulgaria and Greece, was waiting until the fortunes of war had decided between the two groups of Powers, before throwing in her lot with either side.

The diplomatic struggle in the Balkans had only just started. This was but the first clash of interests. Not a single one of the doubtful Balkan States, not even Turkey, in spite of her treaty obligations, took up arms at the outset of the world conflict.

[54] *Germ. Doc.,* 662, p. 494.
[55] *Germ. Doc.,* 811, note by William II, p. 570.

CONCLUSION

BEFORE drawing together the essential features of this account in a summary, whose apparent finality may be misleading, it is my duty to point out its weaknesses. Although the documents are numerous enough to permit us to outline the whole course of events, to ascertain their exact dates, and to show their intimate relation one to another, they still leave room for a degree of uncertainty in matters of detail.

Although the interpretation of the documents enables us to pierce the minds of the statesmen and reveal their intentions, such a study leads by its very nature to frequent divergence of opinion. This volume has given many an instance of such divergence.

It should be added, furthermore, that historical criticism would be far too easily satisfied if it considered each government as a homogeneous unit, in which the rôle of different individuals was wholly absorbed. To say that a given policy originated at the Wilhelmstrasse is far too general and superficial. There were, as a matter of fact, three men in that office whose intentions, tendencies, and illusions were by no means identical—Bethmann, Jagow, and Zimmermann. An Italian historian, Barbagallo, has made an interesting study and comparison of the contrasting tendencies of each of these three men, indicating the share of influence which each had upon German policy as a whole. A similar study of the Foreign Office or of the Quai d'Orsay would be of no small interest.

The personal rôle of certain ambassadors would also be worthy of analysis. The attitude of Tschirschky, the German representative in Vienna, for instance, is of particular importance. Did he or did he not use his influence with the Vienna Government to encourage it to take brutal action

against Serbia? The representatives of the Entente at the
Ballplatz were all of the opinion that he had spurred on
Count Berchtold. Furthermore, the manner in which the
Ambassador carried out his official instructions from Berlin
have also given rise to rather disturbing statements. In the
light of these observations, the testimonial of honesty accorded to Tschirschky by the witnesses before the German
Parliamentary Investigation Committee may be nothing
more than a kindly affirmation of friendship for him. The
importance of Tschirschky's case is quite obvious. Although
not of equal interest, the personal opinions of Prince Lichnowsky, the advances made by Baron von Schoen and Count
Szécsen, and the reticence of M. Paléologue are by no means
to be ignored. These are all problems which cannot yet be
definitely settled.

On the other hand, there are certain cases in which tradition has greatly exaggerated the rôle played by a given individual in the development of the crisis. The example of William II is most typical.

It is true that the character of the sovereign was clearly
expressed in the notes which he jotted down in the mar-
gins of telegrams. In his opinion, moral forces counted for
nothing: "He might offer Persia to England."[1] He would
shout out a triumphant declaration, and then suddenly give
way to overwhelming discouragement, often culminating in a
fury of anger. Thus it was, during the final days of the
crisis, that he was subject to moments of hesitation and
regret, when he was dominated by the fear of England's
intervention, and by the imminent threat of defection on the
part of Italy. At the outset, on the other hand, he had constantly urged vigorous methods; up until 28th July he
wanted nothing less than the complete crushing of Serbia,
he was going to strike a death-blow to Russian prestige, the

[1] Marginal note of William II on a telegram from Lichnowsky, *Die
deutschen Dokumente zum Kriegsausbruch*, I, 157.

present crisis was going to lead directly to the great conflict from which he would emerge victorious.

The Emperor's influence upon German policy, however, was neither continuous nor was it always effective. No doubt he made many suggestions, and he sometimes issued special orders of considerable importance; but any one who reads through his famous marginal annotations will find it difficult to trace in them any precise policy, any succession of general orders, which could in any way have determined the action of his ministers. Besides, both the Chancellor and the Secretary of State lacked confidence in the impulsive acts of their sovereign, and feared the consequences of his hasty gestures. During the Emperor's cruise in the North Sea they refrained from sending him certain telegrams, or took great care to see that certain passages were omitted from the original texts before forwarding them to the Imperial Chancellery. It was not the Emperor, then, who had control of the situation.

Such an analysis as this is certainly worthy of our consideration.

The limits of such criticism, however, are quite definite. It is certain that, as new information is brought to light, the historian will be able to clear up certain doubtful facts, and to analyze more carefully the personal divergences of opinion among the various statesmen; it is doubtful whether he will be able to throw any more light than we now have upon the underlying intentions of the different leaders. We might even go so far as to say, in all modesty, that the idea of these critical events, taken as a whole, which we are now in a position to give, will not be sensibly modified by his efforts.

* * * * * * *

I. The Sarajevo crime was the occasion for marshaling the opposing forces of Austria and Russia for the third time within a period of ten years.

Austria had by no means resigned herself to the consequences of the Treaty of Bucharest. She was conscious of having lost the prestige she once possessed in the Balkans, and she was firmly determined, even before the crime, to oppose "energetically" any further extension of Russian influence. The murder of the Archduke decided Count Berchtold to adopt brusque methods, to act forcefully and, if need be, by violence. Was the Austrian Government really driven by *vital* necessity to undertake such action, and in such a way? He believed so, and with good reason. The Dual Monarchy was hovering on the very brink of disintegration, and the national aspirations of the South Slavs together with the Pan-Serbian propaganda were nothing less than a menace to the existence of the Empire—only one among many, perhaps, but still the most serious. The Government did not have the courage to try out such a thoroughgoing solution of the problem as the Archduke had proposed, namely, the establishment of a kind of federation which would perhaps have led to the assimilation of the South Slavs. It therefore found itself in a constant struggle with this spirit of irredentism, and it did not feel strong enough to succeed in overcoming that spirit by peaceful methods. It saw no other solution but to undertake violent action against the center of nationalism toward which the hopes of the Serbs within the Monarchy were directed, namely, "the elimination of Serbia as a factor of political importance." This was, for example, the conviction of General Conrad von Hötzendorf, who had for years been urging a "preventive" war against his troublesome neighbors. The leaders of Austria-Hungary saw before them the choice between war and revolution, and they felt that there was no other alternative. They chose war. Only one of them, Count Tisza, had a clearer view of the situation. His advice was disregarded.

Germany shared the convictions of Berchtold and Conrad. She was at this moment, according to a German historian, passing through "a crisis in her position as a world power," and she was irritated and disturbed by Austria's weakness. In her own interest, she felt the necessity of buoying up her ally. Here was an opportunity which must not be passed by. This explains why, on 5th July, the Emperor and the Chancellor gave their full support to the Austrian program. This support was the deciding factor, for without it the Vienna Cabinet could never have carried out any of its plans.

The united action of the Central Powers was thus not the result of a wave of indignation or impatience; it followed logically from a policy which had been worked out in advance with the greatest care. Even though Germany had nothing to do with the details of the action against Serbia, and even though she affected to know nothing whatever about them, Austria knew in advance that she could count upon Germany's support. Now, Austria wished to settle the whole matter by force of arms, and the wording of the ultimatum to Serbia was such as to provoke a war. If the Belgrade Government had accepted all the demands in the note, Count Berchtold would have been greatly disappointed, for it was not his intention to be satisfied with a mere diplomatic victory. He also reserved to himself the possibility of renewing the quarrel by exercising "considerable latitude" in carrying out the clauses of the note. The Austrian documents supply many formal proofs of this desire for a war. Now, Germany gave the Austrian demands the sanction of her approval, and thus took the responsibility for them in the eyes of Europe, whatever her private opinion may have been.

In the opinion of the Central Powers, this war was an affair exclusively between Austria and Serbia, and it was both possible and desirable to keep it localized. This was the fundamental idea contained in the statement sent by Germany to the other great Powers on 24th July. There is nothing, to tell the truth, to prove that Germany and Austria actually *wanted* to bring on a general war at this time. There is every reason to think, on the contrary, that they would have been satisfied with only a limited degree of success, which would have been sufficient to strengthen their position and to reëstablish their prestige. But they did demand that Europe should keep her hands off, that she should stand by and watch Serbia being crushed. Was this probable or even possible, when Russia was so obviously hostile, as Berlin and Vienna well knew? She would not be very apt to let the advantages which the double Balkan war had brought her slip through her fingers quite so easily. It was inconceivable that she should abandon the Balkan Slavs, who were her special protégés. The great question was whether the St. Petersburg Government would limit itself to a diplomatic protest, or whether it would proceed to armed intervention. Vienna believed that war with Russia was altogether likely. Opinion in Berlin was divided; one group, including Bethmann-Hollweg, recalled that Russia had been satisfied with mere threats on two occasions already. She might easily withdraw a third time. Others, like Ambassador Lichnowsky, were convinced that the Tsar's Government could not help intervening; in his opinion, the whole idea of localization was "an idle fancy." But whether Russian intervention was a *probability* or only a *possibility*, it could not fail to have an important influence on the plans of the Central Powers, and a vital factor it certainly turned out to be.

Through the interplay of the elaborate system of alliances, however, action on Russia's part would doubtless lead to a general war. This was a further risk to be run, and it must be run. After carefully weighing the pros and the cons, the Austrian Council of Ministers concluded that a general war would find Austria better prepared in 1914 than she would be later on. Furthermore, the German General Staff knew that the Russian armament program would not reach its full completion until 1917. "The moment is so favorable

from the military standpoint that, according to all the fore-
casts, there will never be another like it," said Moltke several
months before the Sarajevo crime.[2] It looked dangerously as
though his one desire were to forestall the enemy by an
attack. The diplomats, it is true, were more reserved. "I do
not want to fight a preventive war," Jagow said, but he did
not object to the idea of an immediate conflict. If the conflict was to come, it would be better to have it come now.
The leading statesmen in Berlin and Vienna were thus united
in favor of the plan of action adopted on 5th July, even
at the price of a European conflict. In case of such a conflict, be it said, they were counting upon the neutrality of
England, and they hoped for the support of Italy and
Rumania.

Between the alternatives of localization and military intervention by Russia, there was room for still another solution,
namely, diplomatic action. Sazonov was quite ready to negotiate with Austria. The other Powers might also have taken
a hand in the solution of the Austro-Serbian dispute, in order
to avoid Russian intervention. But the Central Powers
blocked both of these possibilities. They clung persistently
to the line of action as they had planned it out in advance;
just as Austria refused to enter into direct negotiations
with Russia, so Germany also rejected the proposal to hold
a conference. *Localization* was holding out firmly against
Europeanization. "In vital matters," said William II, "one
does not consult others."

There was a moment, therefore, when the Central Powers
were offered the choice between two solutions: either the
entire execution of their plan, which meant the likelihood
of a *general* European war, or a compromise. And they
refused the compromise. In order to cut short all attempts

[2] This opinion on the part of the Chief of Staff was drawn to the
attention of the Bavarian Government by Lerchenfeld, 31st July 1914, *Cf.*
Bayerische Dokumente, 71.

at mediation, Count Berchtold decided on 28th July to declare war upon Serbia. His action was altogether unnecessary
from the military standpoint, for the army, which had only
just mobilized a part of its forces, was not in a position to
commence operations for another ten days. The declaration
of war had no other purpose than to face Europe with a
fait accompli, and to show clearly that Austria had no intention of allowing herself to be checked by any diplomatic
game. And Germany, fully aware of what the consequences
might be, allowed her ally to proceed with the declaration
of war.

In taking this step, Germany accepted of her own free will
the possibility of Russian intervention and of general war,
doing so the more readily because she persisted in counting
upon the abstention of England. But perhaps, one hears it
said, Germany would have preferred to avoid the war, even
though she gave the appearance of urging it on! It is a good
deal, in such a case, to have the appearances against one.
How could Germany's opponents possibly be expected to
judge her intentions other than by her gestures? And even
if this attitude on Berlin's part was nothing more than an
attitude, was it not quite enough to justify the decisions
of the Entente Powers? In my opinion, however, appearance
and reality were intermingled. I do not believe that Germany
decided, early in the crisis, to provoke a general war *at any
cost.* So far as we are able to judge, Germany would have
been satisfied, on 27th July as on the fifth, with a diplomatic
victory. But she knew that a reaction on Russia's part was
becoming more and more probable, and she even admitted the
likelihood of Russian partial mobilization, for Jagow said
that Germany would not take up arms "so long as Russia
mobilized only on the Austrian frontier." The general conflict was drawing near, and still she refused to abandon the
path she had taken. Did she still believe that Russia was
bluffing? Did she imagine that the Russian Government

would back out at the last minute? There is nothing in any
of the documents to justify such an opinion.

By 27th July, Germany and Austria had brought about,
by their concerted action, all the "conditions" for a European war.

II. The Austrian declaration of war upon Serbia led in
turn to military intervention on the part of Russia.

1. On 29th July, after notifying the great Powers, Russia
issued orders for partial mobilization against Austria. These
orders affected thirteen army corps. They had been agreed
upon in principle five days earlier, in case Austria should
carry out her threats against Belgrade. Nevertheless, it was
a serious step to take, for Russia was thus the first nation
to threaten the use of force to prevent the Vienna Government from carrying out its plan.

In taking this step, Russia was not only responding to
a sentimental appeal from Serbia, but she was also defending
her own interests. Had Count Berchtold succeeded in this
scheme of reducing Serbia to the level of a vassal state, and
of reconstructing a Balkan League favorable to Austria,
the results of the Treaty of Bucharest would have been seriously affected, Russia's position in the Balkans would have
been greatly weakened, and her prestige in Europe would
have received an overwhelming blow.[3] It is true that Austria
had assured St. Petersburg of her *territorial disinterestedness;* she would not annex any Serbian territory. But this
promise, which held good only for the time being, did not
imply that the balance of power in the Balkans would be
maintained. As a matter of fact, Austria was secretly intend-
ing to hand out strips of Serbia to Bulgaria and to Albania. An imprudent remark by one of her diplomats in
Rome or London had doubtless been picked up by the repre-

---

[3] Sazonov was receiving most urgent warnings in this regard from his
representatives in the Balkans. *Cf.* the telegrams from Giers and from
Savinsky, *Die Kriegsschuldfrage,* January 1926, pp. 7 and 16.

sentatives of the Entente, and it is quite likely that its echoes had already reached the ears of Sazonov.

Even if he did not suspect the sincerity of this "disinterestedness," the Russian Minister for Foreign Affairs felt that the Austrian demands constituted a severe blow to the independence and to the sovereign rights of Serbia. He repeatedly emphasized this point. There was thus no question about the interests which determined the attitude of the Russian Government. M. Sazonov was not faced with so imminent a danger as Count Berchtold, for he did not have the same reasons to fear the rapid disintegration of the Empire he was serving if he failed to take immediate action. At the same time, he did have to face an element of discontent among those who had not forgotten the events of 1908 and 1912. It is therefore hardly surprising that he should have wished to block Austria's path, and that he should have rejected outright the idea of localization. How could he be expected to agree to any settlement of a conflict involving the vital interests of his country, without his having any voice in the negotiations? Could any one think for a moment that he would content himself with the rôle of a spectator?

He did resort to direct military action, it is true, to oppose what was only an indirect threat, for Austria had not yet mobilized her forces against Russia. Russian partial mobilization would lead to Austrian general mobilization, and millions of men would thus be drawn up against each other along the Galician frontier. The initiative in this case did come from Russia, but how could it be otherwise? Austria had clearly shown, in declaring war upon Serbia, that she would reject all efforts at conciliation. Sazonov could thus no longer count upon any effective intervention by the great Powers. Austria, on the other hand, was left quite free to crush Serbia at her will. Sazonov had no other alternative but to make a show of force, if his own vital interests were to be maintained.

Russian partial mobilization was thus in the nature of a reply.

2. But the decision to proceed with partial mobilization was followed, on the afternoon of 30th July, by the signature of orders for general mobilization. This was a much more serious step to take. Germany had already taken the occasion to point out, on the twenty-seventh, that "if Russia mobilized in the north," she would be obliged to do the same. The *ukase* for general mobilization, if signed by the Tsar, was thus sure to provoke an immediate reaction in Germany, which would lead in turn to mobilization in France. The situation was now becoming more clearly defined, greatly to the satisfaction of the military leaders in Berlin, and Russia had now furnished them with the excuse for carrying out their plans.

Why did Russia decide to hurry along her plans for general mobilization? The news that had reached St. Petersburg was not such as to compel the Russian Government to make an *immediate* decision, and to issue the orders on that particular day. After his interviews with the German Ambassador, however, Sazonov was convinced that it would be impossible to maintain peace. The *démarche* carried out by Count Pourtalès on the twenty-ninth showed a distinct change in the German point of view: the Chancellor would not tolerate "the continuance of any military measures," even of a partial nature. But was this conviction on Sazonov's part sufficient justification for his taking a step which might precipitate the whole conflict? Here is where the technical military arguments entered in. Russian mobilization was a much slower affair than German mobilization, and if there were really no hope of maintaining peace, it was to Russia's interest to begin as soon as possible to summon her reservists and to arrange for the transportation of troops. Furthermore, the plans of the Russian General Staff had not admitted the possibility of partial mobilization, and the mobilization of only thirteen army corps against Austria might seriously damage the whole technical military machinery. That is why the army chiefs were so insistent in their appeals to the Tsar for general mobilization, and why they ultimately overcame his resistance. In Germany, too, the General Staff had greatly restricted the Government's freedom of action by appealing, at the critical moment, to a prearranged plan of campaign.

This action and this gesture were unquestionably *Russian* decisions, as can be seen from the attitude adopted by France and England. Of course, after M. Poincaré's visit to St. Petersburg, and after the reassuring statements made by M. Paléologue, Russia knew that France would live up to "the obligations of the alliance." And, according to the reports from her Ambassador in London, regarding the personal sympathies of Sir Edward Grey, she knew that she might also count on a friendly attitude on the part of England. It is entirely possible, and even quite likely, that this knowledge about the other members of the Entente served as a kind of encouragement at St. Petersburg. Neither France nor England had raised any fundamental objection to the idea of Russian *partial* mobilization. But did that mean that she was now free to proceed to more extensive measures? The English Ambassador had advised Sazonov to avoid going as far as general mobilization, and the French Ambassador expressed the desire of the Paris Cabinet, on the thirtieth, that Russia should guard against taking any measure which might furnish the pretext for a reply on Germany's part. Sir Edward Grey and M. Viviani thus certainly did not want Russian general mobilization. There was no objection in Paris to Russia's developing the measures of "*pre-mobilization*" that she had been taking ever since 25th July, so long as she did not proceed to the extensive transportation of troops, and so long as she did not begin strategic concentration. But the Russian Government went even further; it refused to adhere to the limits set by the French Government. It is now our task to attempt to determine the practical significance of this decision.

Is it strictly true to say that Russian general mobilization came at a time when an understanding had almost been reached, and that she thus broke off the thread of negotiations at the very moment when it was about to be strengthened?

It is quite true that Germany's attitude had undergone a considerable change during the days when these military decisions were being made in Russia. Her Government had made a real effort to obtain concessions from Vienna; it had tried to act as a kind of check. The same Government which, up to 27th July, had firmly adhered to the principle of "localization," and had allowed Austria to declare war upon Serbia, was now willing to accept a compromise. Upon the Emperor's suggestion, the Chancellor had insisted on the twenty-eighth that Berchtold should consider a new proposal, namely, the seizure of Serbian territory as a hostage. On the night of the twenty-ninth, the tone of the Wilhelmstrasse had become still more urgent, even quite forceful. But we should make no mistake about the character of this "reversal of policy" and about the motives which inspired it. This new effort on Germany's part was, in the first place, not spontaneous. As far as Germany was concerned, the fear of England was the beginning of wisdom. The tone of the Serbian reply and the clumsiness of Austrian diplomacy in regard to Italy were, I admit, contributing causes which irritated the Emperor and the Chancellor; but each successive step they took was determined by news received from London. So long as Germany had felt entirely certain of England's abstention in case of a general war, she had been unwilling to alter her original plan in the slightest degree. Now, however, the risks which she had so calmly accepted were beginning to take on larger proportions, and it was time to give up her uncompromising attitude. The threat of English intervention, which had been hinted at for two days, became of decisive importance on the twenty-ninth, in the minds of the German statesmen, and it was during the course of that very night that the advice sent to Austria became so urgent.

In what spirit was this counsel given to Vienna? What the Chancellor feared most of all was not war. He would have liked to avoid it, he said, had that been possible without having to abandon "the aims pursued by Austria." What he did desire above all was that, if war should become necessary, it should not be started under unfavorable conditions. Now, Austria's uncompromising attitude caused him no little uneasiness, because of the direct effect which it might have upon the position of England and of Italy. If the conflict were extended, "it was imperative that the responsibility should fall upon Russia," wrote Bethmann on the twenty-eighth.[4] And on the thirtieth he drew attention to the untenable situation in which he would be placed if Russia should remain "free of responsibility," while Vienna continued to refuse all concession. "It was of the greatest importance to put Russia in the position of the guilty party," he explained to his colleagues of the Prussian Ministry. In his opinion, it was one of "the factors determining the attitude of Germany toward the present conflict."[5] What was uppermost in the Chancellor's mind was that the war should be a struggle of the Central Powers against Russia and France, and not against the Triple Entente.

Now, it was not Russian general mobilization that caused the failure of Bethmann-Hollweg's efforts. Even before the Tsar's decision was known in Berlin, Germany had again changed her mind, and the whole of the Chancellor's policy had been brought to naught.

[4] *Germ. Doc.*, 323, p. 288.
[5] *Germ. Doc.*, 456, p. 380.

The understanding which Bethmann was urging upon
Vienna might have been brought about either by direct Austro-Russian conferences, or by Austria's acceptance of the
idea of "the seizure of hostage territory." Now, the negotiations started by Sazonov on the twenty-sixth were broken
off on the twenty-eighth by Count Berchtold. It is perfectly true that, upon Germany's insistence, the Ballplatz
decided on the thirtieth to renew these negotiations. But
the instructions which Count Berchtold sent to his Ambassador in St. Petersburg were rather strange, to say the least.
What he had in mind was "an academic discussion, dealing
with vague generalities." The intentions of the Austrian Government were thus highly questionable. In any case, the plans
for these negotiations were not carried out until the thirty-
first, *after* Russian general mobilization. As for the plan to
occupy "hostage territory," the *"Halt im Belgrad"* idea, it
met with no success whatever in Vienna on the decisive day
of 30th July. Ambassador Tschirschky tried in vain to obtain a favorable reply from Count Berchtold; that evening
the Wilhelmstrasse felt convinced that Austria would refuse
any concession. The very next day, in fact, the Austrian
Council of Ministers decided to reject outright all mediatory
proposals. At the hour when this decision was made, word
of Russian general mobilization had not yet reached Vienna.

The situation was somewhat analogous in Berlin. The
Chancellor had been encountering steady opposition for two
days from the General Staff, who were anxious to make a
final decision at once. Bethmann had at first resisted their
pressure. On the evening of the thirtieth he yielded. He
canceled the forceful instructions which he had sent that
very evening to Tschirschky, and contented himself with
sending to Vienna, somewhat later, a copy of the telegram
from the King of England, which could hardly have been
said to take the place of direct admonition. Who, then, was
responsible for this new change of mind on Germany's part?

It was the General Staff. It was out of consideration for Moltke's wishes that Bethmann refrained from carrying out the energetic step at Vienna that he had planned. And furthermore, the German army chiefs had approached Conrad directly, urging him to mobilize, and promising him that Germany would do the same. Berlin was no longer waiting for diplomatic decisions on the part of the Austrian Government, but for military decisions.

By the time the Tsar's Government decided upon general mobilization, the idea of mediation had thus been discarded. The publication of the Russian *ukase* had nothing whatever to do with the rejection of the idea by the Central Powers.

Is it historically accurate, then, to say that the orders for general mobilization marked the Russian Government as the "aggressor," and that the execution of these orders led "without fail" to the outbreak of hostilities?

There is no doubt that, in the minds of the negotiators of the Franco-Russian alliance, certain elements of danger were involved in the possibility of Russian *general* mobilization against Austria alone: "Russia would appear before Europe in the rôle of the aggressor, and a difficult situation would be created with regard to the neutral Powers," wrote General Boisdeffre in 1892. It is also certain that in the opinion of the French and British statesmen in 1914, the fact that Austrian general mobilization was decreed first, as they believed, constituted one of the elements in the indictment of the Central Powers. The state that mobilized first gave the impression of wanting the war to come. During the negotiation of the Franco-Russian military convention, it had been agreed that mobilization on the part of either Germany or Austria would be considered as the sure sign of approaching hostilities. "Mobilization is the declaration of war!" This did not imply that, in the eyes of France, *Russian* mobilization amounted to a declaration of war, and that the French Government was consequently obliged, in 1914, to commence hostilities, nor even that Russia considered herself bound to commence hostilities at once. The phrase simply meant that the French generals and political leaders in 1892 and 1893 considered that any mobilization of their potential *enemies* would be looked upon as the manifest sign of an aggressive intention. Was it not fair, however, that the same reasoning should be applied to Russia in 1914?

M. Sazonov was extremely careful to avoid showing any such aggressive intentions. On the contrary, he declared over and over again that, in his opinion, mobilization would not necessarily lead to an immediate declaration of war, and that the Russian army could remain for a long time "with rifles stacked," without commencing hostilities. If his statements are to be believed, the decision of the Russian Government did not imply the slightest desire for war. "I shall continue to negotiate up to the very last minute," he told M. Paléologue. And he did negotiate. On the day following the orders for general mobilization he consented to modify the "formula" which expressed his point of view. He entered into a conversation with the Austrian Ambassador with such enthusiasm that Count Szápáry tried to restrain his excessive optimism. Austria had expressed a willingness to negotiate. This proved that mobilization had not put an end to all diplomatic relations, and had not made hostilities inevitable. It had created an atmosphere of suspicion, of course, and had led to military "counter-measures" which lessened the chances for an understanding and reduced the time, which was always such an asset. But it did not imply that war must follow "without fail."

Naturally, such last-minute negotiations could hardly be expected to inspire much confidence. Some one has said that diplomacy always tries to make "peace signals" whenever a war is near. It is hard to believe that the *démarches* carried out by the Austrian representatives in Paris and in St. Petersburg proceeded from any very sincere desire to preserve peace. Was the case different with Russia? She had every reason to prolong the discussion as much as possible, in order to gain time and to complete her preparation. "It may seem desirable to complete our strategic concentration without commencing hostilities, in order not to destroy irrevocably the enemy's hope that the war may still be avoided," said a Russian document in 1912. "Our military measures must consequently be masqued by a semblance of diplomatic negotiations, in order to lull the fears of the enemy." The question therefore comes down to this: were the steps taken by Sazonov on 31st July sincere, or were the negotiations in which he took part nothing more than a sham?

It is hard to ascertain his true intentions, inasmuch as the wording of his second "formula" was not perfectly clear. The Russian Government was not, however, opposed to the "seizure of hostage territory," which had been suggested as the basis for mediation; it was thus disposed to make certain concessions. If Austria, on her side, had agreed on that day to limit her military activity to the occupation of Belgrade, an understanding might well have been reached. There is nothing in any of the documents which would lead us to believe that Sazonov would have given up the idea of negotiations at the last minute.

III. War, however, was to follow *at once*. The plan of the German General Staff demanded it. Moltke had prepared for a war on two fronts. He was convinced that victory would never be possible without a rapid offensive in the west, without a swift enveloping movement across Belgium. He felt that it was imperative to complete this offensive as early as possible, in order to be in a position then to turn the main body of his forces against Russia. The longer the delay in commencing hostilities, the less the certainty of success, since it would allow the Russian General Staff to develop its preparatory measures more fully in advance. That was the justification for the urgent action which he took. That explains why he was so insistent, on 29th July, that the Chancellor should reach a decision at once, for from that time on he felt, as did the Russian General Staff, that war was sure to come. That is why he saw to it that the wording of the ultimatum to Belgium was prepared as early as the twenty-sixth; that, again, is why he inspired the famous clause concerning "Toul and Verdun" in the ultimatum sent to France. It is evident that he was uneasy about the news from Russia, where preparations were being made of whose extent he could not be sure. Russian general mobilization brought him face to face with a definite situation. He was not sorry, and he at once set about the execution of his pre-arranged plans. In the face of such exigencies, the Government yielded. It even precipitated the rupture. It did not attempt to leave the respite of twenty-four or forty-eight hours which the military chiefs could, without great difficulty, have granted.

The critic should pause once more over this last point. The German General Staff had prepared a plan which could not be altered in any respect. It was *obliged*, if it was to carry out that plan under the most favorable conditions, to declare war upon Russia, and to break with France and attack her. But this plan of campaign was not unknown to the civil authorities. The Chancellor knew that it was essential for German troops to pass through Belgium. He was acquainted with the methods and the principles of German strategy, as well as with the general plan to be followed in case of a military concentration. The Government thus assumed the responsibility for a plan which would *inevitably* force it to take the initiative in any attack. Why did it not bear this in mind when it provoked the diplomatic crisis of 1914?

Germany had thus decided, after 31st July, that she would

pay no attention to any further mediatory proposals which might be made. She expected a reply to her double ultimatum by about noon on 1st August; she anticipated a refusal of her demands, and she had decided to declare war at once. When the English Ambassador made a final offer of mediation in Berlin, von Jagow replied, without questioning the sincerity of the English attempt: "It is too late!" In the opinion of the Emperor and the Chancellor, however, the oncoming struggle was not to be "fresh and joyful"! The optimism which they were obliged to display to those around them by no means reflected their own personal convictions. "If we do not respect Belgian neutrality, England attacks us and Italy deserts us. That is the situation in a nutshell! So there is betrayal of the Allies, as well!" wrote William II on 1st August. The conditions of the conflict were hardly those he had hoped for.

*   *   *   *   *   *   *

World opinion in 1914, on the question of war responsibility, pronounced a spontaneous judgment which was based upon instinctive sympathies. French diplomacy had shown its self-control and its desire to avoid any aggressive gestures; the "ten-kilometer withdrawal" was one of the most significant steps which it took in this direction. The German and Austrian diplomats have themselves often testified to the calm and peaceful aspect of French public opinion in July 1914. The Austro-German diplomacy, on the other hand, had been responsible for a series of clumsy blunders, of gestures marked by brutality, and of instances of violence. It had cynically declared its contempt for treaties, it had tried the effect of threats, it had apparently taken delight in arousing the national loyalties of its enemies. And that explains, better than any efforts of propaganda, the preference of the masses in Europe and all over the world. Preference must not, however, be allowed to take the place of reason.

A steady stream of German propaganda has attempted in a methodical way to alter the world's judgment in this matter, by emphasizing certain facts, quite true in themselves, by isolating them from the sequence of events as a whole. Its error lies in its exaggeration and distortion of the significance of those facts. It has tried to draw attention to the secret aims of the great Powers, and it has been suggested that, whereas Germany was too clumsy to conceal her intentions, as she certainly was, the Entente Powers were far too clever about concealing theirs. To resort to such methods is to shift the emphasis in the discussion, rather than to face squarely the fundamental question at issue. Sane judgment looks for its basis neither to instinctive preferences, nor to these one-sided artifices. The important thing is to determine what is meant by an act of aggression.

This definition is indeed a delicate one. It is extremely rare, in any conflict, to find all the elements of provocation laid to the charge of a single state; it is rare indeed if the opponent has not laid himself open to some criticism as well. Some choice is therefore necessary to determine the precise acts which imply the will to aggression in a given instance.

1. There are some who would lay the emphasis upon outward signs:

The aggressor, they say, is the nation that declares war; the aggressor in 1914 was therefore Germany, who took the initiative of the double ultimatum and the actual rupture.

But a nation might well be driven to a declaration of war by a diplomatic maneuver, by a combination of circumstances which the enemy has succeeded in turning to his advantage. *To have war declared against oneself* might be simply an artful trick, like that of Bismarck in 1870. During the crisis of 1914, the statesmen did not at heart consider the declaration of war as fundamental.

Or again, it might be maintained that the aggressor is the nation that mobilizes first. Now, among the great Powers, Russia was the first to order general mobilization.

In this case, it must be considered whether the state that mobilizes is not responding to clever provocation on the part of its enemies, who are thus inciting the state to make hasty decisions and thus to put itself in the wrong.

According as one attaches more importance to mobilization or to the declaration of war, the decisive responsibility will be attributed, in the first case, to Russia, and, in the second, to Germany. But it is important to take into account all the possible and plausible excuses that may be offered, and to consider the mutual reactions of the various nations upon each other. It would appear that any one who confines himself to these outward signs, taken as a whole, and apart from all contributing elements and events, must conclude that the responsibility is divided.

2. Others, questioning the value of these outward signs, seek rather to determine the inherent will to aggression, taken by itself.

The aggressor, they say, is the nation which refuses to take into account the views of its opponents, which does not lend itself to any discussions or concessions, and which rejects the proposed conditions of peace. The idea of aggression is tending more and more at the present time, in the conscience of the various peoples, to become identified with the refusal of arbitration. Now, arbitration implies that a State will submit what it believes to be its own particular right or vital interest to the judgment of a third party; it involves discussions and concessions. Which nation systematically discarded all ideas of compromise in 1914? It was Austria. And Germany, although aware of the danger at the last moment, came fully to her support notwithstanding. The basis for a compromise might easily have been found in a recognition of the territorial integrity and the sovereignty of Serbia. Not once did Vienna *fully* accept these principles as the basis for a possible settlement.

Here, then, are two contrasting points of view, one limiting itself to a consideration of outward signs, the other attempting to get at the underlying intentions of the various nations. One is summary and inadequate; the other seeks the more profound truth.

During a diplomatic crisis there are certain feelings and certain forces which play upon the various statesmen and determine all their actions.

One of these *feelings* is that of mutual suspicion, which always enters in and affects their independence of judgment. When a diplomat notices, at these moments of sharp tension, a tendency toward conciliation on the part of his opponent, his first act is a kind of defense reflex. He suspects some artful maneuver, some ruse, and he strives to uncover some deep and dark motive. Or perhaps—if he does not attempt to detract from the importance of his opponent's new attitude—he does exactly the opposite, and exaggerates it; his opponent is at last becoming reasonable—because he is afraid! Why, surely, the moment is ripe to push the advantage still further and win real success. All diplomacy is based upon calculations of precisely this character.

One of the *forces* is the entangling complication of alliances. Take the case of Germany and Austria: from 28th July on, Bethmann-Hollweg was out of sympathy with Count Berchtold's obstinate intransigency, but he did not dare to express his opinion direct to Vienna. He vented his ill-humor in little notes which were spicy enough, but reached only his immediate colleagues! His tone softened down when it came to wording an official telegram; or, perhaps, a qualifying phrase at the end of the message greatly diminished its significance. A nation does not dare frankly to oppose the wishes of its ally. France may well have felt this same hesitancy in her dealings with Russia.

The influence of the military leaders is a factor of still greater importance. The Chief of Staff, responsible for the mobilization of the forces and for the conduct of the war, knows the value of a single day. He is watching the enemy closely, for he fears that he may be anticipated and caught off his guard. He naturally is anxious that military preparations may be started as soon as possible; this was precisely the attitude of both the German and the Russian General Staffs, the one because its whole plan of offensive depended upon the speed and effectiveness of the first shock; the other because it feared the upsetting of a mechanism which was so delicate and so slow. The exigencies of the "Plan" dominated the entire attitude of the German Government after 31st July. They also explain the Russian decisions in favor of mobilization which were made between 28th and 31st July.

Now, all these forces did not make their appearance during the early days of the crisis, but during its final phase. By that time the freedom of the various governments was no longer absolute; they were constrained to make hasty decisions; they were hopelessly entangled.

In order to formulate a precise judgment upon the question of war responsibility, it is essential to return to the time when the governments were still able to call themselves the masters of their own actions. More attention must be paid to the deliberate steps which created the conditions of the conflict—to the decisions which were thoughtfully arrived at in the quiet of the various chancelleries during their moments of greater leisure.

The military provocation of July 1914 was determined by a diplomatic provocation. The connecting link between them was furnished by the Austrian declaration of war upon Serbia. Now, Germany and Austria were *alone* in desiring this provocation. It is true that they had reason to feel uneasy; nationalistic movements were threatening the very existence of the Dual Monarchy, and, indirectly, the position of the German Empire. But they would not consent to any solution other than that of violent action. They had agreed upon the program after careful deliberation, having coolly considered all the possible consequences of their action. So far as the *immediate* origins of the conflict are concerned, that is the one fact which dominates all the others.

A BRIEF BIBLIOGRAPHY

I. COLLECTIONS OF DIPLOMATIC AND PARLIAMENTARY DOCUMENTS.

GENERAL, AUSTRIA-HUNGARY, BELGIUM, FRANCE, GERMANY, GREAT BRITAIN, RUSSIA, SERBIA.

II. MEMOIRS.

III. SECONDARY WORKS.

IV. PERIODICAL LITERATURE.

I. COLLECTIONS OF DIPLOMATIC AND PARLIAMENTARY DOCUMENTS

GENERAL

SCOTT, James Brown, *ed.* Diplomatic documents relating to the outbreak of the European war. New York, Oxford University Press, American Branch [etc.], 1916. 2 vols.
Published by Carnegie Endowment for International Peace, Division of International Law.

NEW YORK TIMES. Why England, Germany, Russia and Belgium went to war . . . "White Papers" of England and Germany, the "Orange Paper" of Russia, and the "Gray Paper" of Belgium, and other diplomatic correspondence and documents relating to the European war. New York [etc.], New York Times Co., 1914.

GREAT BRITAIN. *Foreign Office.* Collected diplomatic documents relating to the outbreak of the European war. London, H. M. Stationery Off., 1915. (Miscellaneous, no. 10, 1915.) Parliament. Papers by command. Cd. 7860.

MACH, Edmund Robert Otto von, *ed.* Official diplomatic documents relating to the outbreak of the European war, with photographic reproductions of official editions of the documents (Blue, White, Yellow, etc., Books) published by the governments of Austria-Hungary, Belgium, France, Germany, Great Britain, Russia, and Serbia. New York, The Macmillan Company, 1916.

BEER, Max, *ed.* "Das Regenbogen-Buch"; deutsches Weissbuch, österreichisch-ungarisches Rotbuch, englisches Blaubuch, französisches Gelbbuch, russisches Orangebuch, serbisches Blaubuch und belgisches Graubuch. Die europäischen Kriegsverhandlungen; die massgebenden Dokumente, chronologisch und sinngemäss zusammengestellt, übersetzt und erläutert von Dr. Max Beer. Bern, F. Wyss, 1915.

AUSTRIA-HUNGARY

AUSTRO-HUNGARIAN MONARCHY. *Ministerium des K. und K. Hauses und des Äussern.* Diplomatische Aktenstücke zur Vorgeschichte des Krieges, 1914. Wien, Hof- und Staatsdruckerei, 1915.

—— [English translation] The Austro-Hungarian Red Book (no. 1). (*In* SCOTT, J. B., *ed.* Diplomatic documents relating to the outbreak of the European war. New York, 1916. Part I. pp. [1]-346.)

AUSTRO-HUNGARIAN MONARCHY. *Ministerium des K. und K. Hauses und des Äussern.* Österreichisch-ungarisches Rotbuch. Diplomatische Aktenstücke betreffend die Beziehungen Österreich-Ungarns zu Rumänien in der Zeit vom 22. Juli bis 27. August 1916. Wien, Manz, 1916.

AUSTRIA (REPUBLIC) *Staatsamt für Äusseres.* Diplomatische Aktenstücke zur Vorgeschichte des Krieges 1914; Ergänzungen und Nachträge zum österreichisch-ungarischen Rotbuch. Wien, Staatsdruckerei, 1919. 3 vols.

—— [French translation] Pièces diplomatiques relatives aux antécédents de la guerre de 1914 publiées par la république d'Autriche. Suppléments et additions au livre rouge austro-hongrois, tr. par Camille Jordan. Paris, A. Costes, 1922. 3 vols.

—— [English translation] Austrian Red Book; official files pertaining to pre-war history [An addendum and supplement to the Austro-Hungarian Red Book, 1914]. London, G. Allen & Unwin, Ltd. [1920.] 3 vols.

"PHAROS." Der Prozess gegen die Attentäter von Sarajewo, nach dem amtlichen Stenogramm der Gerichtsverhandlung aktenmässig dargestellt. Berlin, R. von Decker, 1918.

BELGIUM

BELGIUM. *Ministère des affaires étrangères.* Correspondance diplomatique relative à la guerre de 1914. (24 juillet-29 août.) Anvers, Impr. et publicité Flor Burton, Société Anonyme [1914.]

—— [English translation] The Belgian Grey Book (no. 1). (*In* SCOTT, J. B., *ed.* Diplomatic documents relating to the outbreak of the European war. New York, 1916. Part I. pp. [347]-416.)

LANGENHOVE, Fernand van, *ed.* Le dossier diplomatique de la question belge; recueil des pièces officielles, avec notes. Bruxelles et Paris, G. van Oest et Cie, 1917.

FRANCE

FRANCE. *Ministère des affaires étrangères.* Documents diplomatiques 1914. La guerre européenne. I. Pièces relatives aux négociations qui ont précédé les déclarations de guerre de l'Allemagne à la Russie (1er août 1914) et à la France (3 août 1914). Déclaration du 4 septembre 1914. Paris, Imprimerie Nationale, 1914.

—— [English translation] The French Yellow Book. (*In* SCOTT, J. B., *ed.* Diplomatic documents relating to the outbreak of the European war. New York, 1916. Part I. pp. [531]-767.)

FRANCE. *État-major de l'armée.* Les armées françaises dans la grande guerre. Tome I, 1er vol. and Annexes. Paris, Imprimerie Nationale, 1922. 2 vols. Copyright, 1923, by Le Ministère de la Guerre.

FRANCE. *Assemblée nationale. Chambre des députés.* Rapport fait au nom de la Commission d'enquête sur le rôle et la situation de la métallurgie en France (1) (Question de Briey . . .), par M. Fernand Engerand, député. [Paris, Martinet, imprimeur de la Chambre des députés, 1919.] 2 vols. in 1. 1. ptie. Concentration de la métallurgie française sur la frontière de l'est. 2. ptie. La perte de Briey.

—— —— (*In* FRANCE [Journal Officiel] Chambre des députés . . . Documents parlementaires. Annexes aux procès-verbaux des séances. Projets et propositions de loi. Exposés de motifs et rapports. 11e legislature, session ordinaire de 1919. pp. 225-236; 2566-2591) Annexe no. 6026, session de 1919. 2e séance du 16 avril 1919.

FRANCE. *Assemblée nationale. Chambre des députés.* Procès-verbaux de la Commission d'enquête sur le rôle et la situation de la métallurgie en

BIBLIOGRAPHY 361

France. Défense du bassin de Briey . . . réunis au nom de la Commission par M. Maurice Viollette, président de la Commission. Paris, Imprimerie de la Chambre des députés, Martinet, 1919. 2 vols. (Chambre des députés. 11. législ., sess. de 1919, no. 6026 (annexe); annexe au procès-verbal . . . 16 avril 1919.)

—— Procès-verbaux de la Commission d'enquête sur le rôle et la situation de la métallurgie en France (1) (Bombardement du bassin de Briey) réunis au nom de la Commission par M. Maurice Viollette, président de la Commission. [Paris, Martinet, imprimeur de la Chambre des députés, 1919.] 2 vols. (Chambre des députés. 11. législ., sess. de 1919, no. 6026 (2.-3. annexe); annexe au procès-verbal . . . 16 avril 1919.)

GERMANY

GERMANY. *Auswärtiges Amt.* Aktenstücke zum Kriegsausbruch. [Berlin, G. Stilke, 1915.]

—— [English translation] The German White Book. (*In* SCOTT, J. B., *ed.* Diplomatic documents relating to the outbreak of the European war. New York, 1916. Part II. pp. [769]-860.)

DIRR, Pius, *ed.* Bayerische Dokumente zum Kriegsausbruch und zum Versailler Schuldspruch, im Auftrage des Bayerischen Landtages. München und Berlin, R. Oldenbourg, 1922.

—— —— 3.erw.Aufl. München, R. Oldenbourg, 1925.

GERMANY (REPUBLIC) *Nationalversammlung.* Beilagen zu den Stenographischen Berichten über die öffentlichen Verhandlungen des Untersuchungsausschusses. (I. Unterausschuss) Zur Vorgeschichte des Weltkrieges. [Heft I] Schriftliche Auskünfte deutscher Staatsmänner. Berlin, Verlag der Norddeutschen Buchdruckerei, 1920.

—— [English translation] First Sub-committee report. (*In* Official German documents relating to the world war, tr. under the supervision of the Carnegie Endowment for International Peace, Division of International Law. Vol. I. New York, Oxford University Press, American Branch, 1923. pp. [1]-120.)

—— Beilagen zu den Stenographischen Berichten über die öffentlichen Verhandlungen des Untersuchungsausschusses. (I. Unterausschuss) Zur Vorgeschichte des Weltkrieges. Heft II. Militärische Rüstungen und Mobilmachungen. Berlin, Verlag der Norddeutschen Buchdruckerei, 1921.

KAUTSKY, Karl, *ed.* Die deutschen Dokumente zum Kriegsausbruch; vollständige Sammlung der von Karl Kautsky zusammengestellten amtlichen Aktenstücke mit einigen Ergänzungen, im Auftrage des Auswärtigen Amtes nach gemeinsamer Durchsicht mit Karl Kautsky hrsg. von Graf Max Montgelas und Prof. Walter Schücking. Charlottenburg, Deutsche Verlagsgesellschaft für Politik und Geschichte m.b.H., 1919. 4 vols.

—— [English translation] Outbreak of the World War; German documents collected by Karl Kautsky and edited by Max Montgelas and Walther Schücking, tr. by the Carnegie Endowment for International Peace, Division of International Law. New York [etc.], Oxford University Press, American Branch, 1924.

GREAT BRITAIN

Great Britain. *Foreign Office.* Great Britain and the European crisis. Correspondence, and statements in Parliament, together with an introductory narrative of events. London, H. M. Stationery Off., 1914.
—— British diplomatic correspondence. (Collected diplomatic documents relating to the outbreak of the European war. London, 1915. Part II.)
—— [American edition] The British Blue Book (no. 1). (*In* Scott, J. B., *ed.* Diplomatic documents relating to the outbreak of the European war. New York, 1916, Part II. pp. [861]-1054.)
Great Britain. *Foreign Office.* British documents on the origins of the war, 1898-1914. Edited by G. P. Gooch . . . and Harold Temperley . . . London, H. M. Stationery Off. Vol. XI. The outbreak of war, Foreign Office documents June 28th-August 4th 1914. Collected and arranged . . . by J. W. Headlam-Morley, 1926.

RUSSIA

Russia. *Ministerstvo inostrannykh diel.* Recueil de documents diplomatiques. Negociations ayant précédé la guerre. 10/23 juillet-24 juillet/ 6 août, 1914. Petrograde, Imprimerie de l'État, 1914.
—— [English translation] The Russian Orange Book (no. 1). (*In* Scott, J. B., *ed.* Diplomatic documents relating to the outbreak of the European war. New York, 1916. Part II. pp. [1329]-1382.)
Romberg, Konrad Gisbert Wilhelm, *Freiherr* von, *ed.* Die Fälschungen des russischen Orangebuches, der wahre Telegrammwechsel, Paris-Petersburg bei Kriegsausbruch, hrsg. von Freiherrn G. von Romberg . . . Mit Genehmigung des Auswärtigen Amts. Berlin und Leipzig. Vereinigung wissenschaftlicher Verleger, W. de Gruyter & Co., 1922.
—— [English translation] Falsifications of the Russian Orange Book . . . edited by Baron G. von Romberg. New York, B. W. Huebsch, Inc., 1923.
Russia. *Ministerstvo inostrannykh diel.* Materialy po istorii franko-russkikh otnoshenii za 1910-1914 gg. Moscow, G I Z, 1922.
Edited for the People's Commissariat for Foreign Affairs by René Marchand.
Un livre noir, diplomatie d'avant guerre d'après les documents des archives russes, novembre 1910-juillet 1914, préface par René Marchand. Paris, Librairie du Travail [1922-1923.] 2 vols.
Schilling, Moritz Fabianovich, *Baron.* Nachalo voiny 1914 g., Podennaia zapis' b. Ministerstva inostrannykh del. (*In* Krasnyi Arkhiv, Moscow. vol. 4, 1923. pp. 3-62.)
—— [German translation] Der Beginn des Krieges 1914, Tages-Aufzeichnungen des ehemaligen russischen Aussenministeriums; vollständige Uebersetzung der Veröffentlichung aus dem Archiv der Sowjetregierung (Krasny-Archiv, Heft IV, Moskau, 1924 [sic.]), mit einem Vorwort von Alfred von Wegerer. Berlin, Deutsche Verlagsgesellschaft für Politik und Geschichte m.b.H., 1924. (Beiträge zur Schuldfrage hrsg. von der Zentralstelle für Erforschung der Kriegsursachen, 2. Hft.)

—— [English translation] How the war began in 1914, being the diary of the Russian Foreign office from the 3rd to the 20th (old style) of July 1914, published by the "Red Archives" department of the Russian Soviet Government in their "Historical Journal," Vol. IV, 1923. Tr. from the original Russian by Major W. Cyprian Bridge . . . London, G. Allen & Unwin, Ltd. [1925.]

SERBIA

SERBIA. *Ministarstvo inostranikh dela.* Le livre bleu serbe. Négociations ayant précédé la guerre (16/29 juin-3/16 août 1914). Parïs, Berger-Levrault [1914?]

—— —— (*In* MACH, E. R. O. von, *ed.* Official diplomatic documents relating to the outbreak of the European war. New York, 1916.)

Photographic reproduction of *Pages d'histoire, 1914-1915.* No. 22. Les pourparlers diplomatiques 16/29 juin-3/16 août. IV.

—— [English translation] The Serbian Blue Book. (*In* Scott, J. B., *ed.* Diplomatic documents relating to the outbreak of the European war. New York, 1916. Part II. pp. [1439]-1490.)

II. MEMOIRS

ASQUITH, Herbert Henry (*Earl of Oxford and Asquith*). The Genesis of the War. London, New York [etc.], Cassell and Co., Ltd., 1923.

BETHMANN-HOLLWEG, Theobald von. Betrachtungen zum Weltkriege. Berlin, R. Hobbing, 1919-1921. 2 vols.

—— [English translation] Reflections on the World War . . . Tr. by George Young. New York, Harper & Bros., 1920.

BILIŃSKI, Leon. Wspomnienia i Dokumenty. Warszawa, 1924-1925. 2 vols.

BLUNT, Wilfrid Scawen. My Diaries, being a personal narrative of events, 1888-1914. London, M. Secker, 1919-1920. 2 vols.

—— —— [American edition] New ed. New York, A. A. Knopf, 1923. 2 vols.

BUCHANAN, *Sir* George William. My Mission to Russia and Other Diplomatic Memories. London, New York [etc.], Cassell and Co., Ltd., 1923. 2 vols.

CHURCHILL, Winston Leonard Spencer. The World Crisis, 1911-1914. London, T. Butterworth, Ltd. [1923.]

—— —— [American edition] New York, Scribner's, 1923.

CONRAD VON HÖTZENDORF, Franz, *Graf*. Aus meiner Dienstzeit, 1906-1918. Wien [etc.], Rikola Verlag, 1921-1925. 5 vols.

CZERNIN VON UND ZU CHUDENITZ, Ottokar Theobald Otto Maria, *Graf*. Im Weltkriege. Berlin und Wien, Ullstein & Co., 1919.

—— [English translation] In the World War. New York and London, Harper & Bros. [c1920.]

DELBRÜCK, Clemens Gottlieb Ernst von. Die wirtschaftliche Mobilmachung in Deutschland, 1914; aus dem Nachlass hrsg., eingeleitet und ergänzt von Joachim von Delbrück. München, Verlag für Kulturpolitik, 1924.

DOBROROLSKY, Serge. Die Mobilmachung der russischen Armee 1914. Mit Beiträgen von Graf Pourtalès . . . Oberst a.D.von Eggeling . . . Graf Montgelas . . . und einem Vorwort von Dr. Ernst Sauerbeck. Berlin, Deutsche Verlagsgesellschaft für Politik und Geschichte m.b.H., 1922. (Beiträge zur Schuldfrage hrsg. von der Zentralstelle für Erforschung der Kriegsursachen, 1. Heft.) Translation by M. and Mme. C. Appuhn of an article in VOÏENNY SBORNIK [MILITARY REVIEW], 1. fasc. Belgrade, 1921.

—— La mobilisation de l'armée russe en 1914. (*In* REVUE D'HISTOIRE DE LA GUERRE MONDIALE, Paris. 1. année, nos. 1-2, Jan.-Apr. 1923. pp. [53]-69; [144]-165.) Translation by M. and Mme. C. Appuhn of the article in VOÏENNY SBORNIK, 1. fasc., together with a second article by Dobrorolsky, in VOÏENNY SBORNIK, 2 fasc.

FRENCH, John Denton Pinkstone (*Viscount Ypres*). 1914, by Field-Marshal Viscount French of Ypres. London, Constable and Co., Ltd., 1919.

—— —— [American edition] Boston and New York, Houghton Mifflin Co., 1919.

GREY (of Fallodon), Edward Grey, *Viscount*. Twenty-five Years, 1892-1916. London, Hodder & Stoughton, 1925. 2 vols.

—— —— [American edition] New York, Frederick A. Stokes Co., 1925. 2 vols.

JONESCU, Take. Souvenirs. Paris, Payot & Cie, 1919.

—— [English translation] Some Personal Impressions. New York, Frederick A. Stokes Co. [c1920.]

KÜHL, Hermann Joseph von. Der deutsche Generalstab in Vorbereitung und Durchführung des Weltkrieges. 2. neubearb. Aufl. Berlin, E. S. Mittler und Sohn, 1920.

—— [French translation] Le grand état-major allemand avant et pendant la guerre mondiale. Analyse et traduction [par Général Douchy]. Paris, Payot & Cie, 1922.

LEGRAND-GIRARDE, Émile Edmond. Opérations du 21e corps d'armée (1er août-13 septembre 1914). Paris, Plon-Nourrit et Cie [1922.]

LICHTERVELDE, Louis de, *comte*. Heures d'histoire, le 4 août, 1914, au Parlement belge. Bruxelles et Paris, G. van Oest et Cie, 1918.

—— [English translation] August the Fourth, 1914, in the Belgian Parliament. London, Wightman & Co., Ltd., 1918.

MOLTKE, Helmuth Johannes Ludwig von. Erinnerungen, Briefe, Dokumente, 1877-1916 . . . Hrsg, . . . von Eliza von Moltke . . . Stuttgart, Der Kommende Tag A.-G., 1922.

MORGENTHAU, Henry. Secrets of the Bosphorus: Constantinople, 1913-1916. London, Hutchinson & Co., 1918.

—— [American edition] Ambassador Morgenthau's Story. Garden City, New York, Doubleday, Page & Co., 1918.

MUSULIN VON GOMIRJE, Alexander, *Freiherr*. Das Haus am Ballplatz; Erinnerungen eines österreich-ungarischen Diplomaten. München, Verlag für Kulturpolitik, 1924.

PALÉOLOGUE, Georges Maurice. La Russie des tsars pendant la grande guerre. Paris, Plon-Nourrit et Cie [c1921-.]

—— [English translation] An Ambassador's Memoirs . . . Tr. by F. A. Holt. New York, George H. Doran Co., 1924-1925. 3 vols.

POURTALÈS, Jakob Ludwig Friedrich Wilhelm Joachim, *Graf* von. Am Scheidewege zwischen Krieg und Frieden; meine letzten Verhandlungen in Petersburg, Ende Juli 1914. Charlottenburg, Deutsche Verlagsgesellschaft für Politik und Geschichte m.b.H., 1919.

RODZÍANKO, Mikhaïl Vladimírovich Krushenïe Imperïï (Zapiski predsĭedatelĭa Russkoï gosudarstvennoï dumy) [The break-up of the empire (Memoirs of the president of the Russian Duma)]. (*In* ARKHIV RUSSKOÏ REVOLIÛTSII, Berlin. Vol. 17, 1926, pp. 5-[169].)

—— [German translation] Erinnerungen. Berlin, R. Hobbing, 1926.

—— [English translation] The reign of Rasputin: an empire's collapse . . . Tr. by Catherine Zvegintzoff. London, A. M. Philpot, Ltd., 1927.

SCHOEN, Wilhelm Eduard, *Freiherr* von. Erlebtes; Beiträge zur politischen Geschichte der neuesten Zeit. Stuttgart und Berlin, Deutsche Verlags-Anstalt, 1921.

—— [English translation] The Memoirs of an Ambassador; a contribution to the political history of modern times . . . Tr. by Constance Vesey. London, G. Allen & Unwin, Ltd. [1922.]

SUKHOMLINOV, Vladimír Aleksandrovich. Erinnerungen. Deutsche Ausg. Berlin, R. Hobbing, 1924.

Szilassy, Gyula, *báró*. Der Untergang der Donau-Monarchie; diplomatische Erinnerungen von Baron J. von Szilassy . . . 1. Aufl. Berlin, Verlag Neues Vaterland, E. Berger & Co., 1921.

Tirpitz, Alfred Peter Friedrich von. Erinnerungen . . . Neue durchgesehene Aufl. Leipzig, K. F. Koehler, 1920.

—— [French translation] Mémoires du grand amiral von Tirpitz. Paris, Payot & Cie, 1922.

(Collection de mémoires, études et documents pour servir à l'histoire de la guerre mondiale.)

—— [English translation] My Memoirs. New York, Dodd, Mead and Co., 1919.

Wilhelm II, *German Emperor*. Ereignisse und Gestalten aus den Jahren 1878-1918. Leipzig, K. F. Koehler, 1922.

—— [French translation] Mémoires de Guillaume II. Paris, Librairie Hachette, 1922.

—— [English translation] The Kaiser's Memoirs . . . English translation by Thomas R. Ybarra. New York and London, Harper & Bros., 1922.

III. SECONDARY WORKS

APPUHN, Charles, and RENOUVIN, Pierre. Introduction aux Tableaux d'histoire de Guillaume II, Paris, A. Costes, 1923.

AULARD, François Victor Alphonse. 1914-1918. Histoire politique de la grande guerre, publiée sous la direction de A. Aulard . . . avec la collaboration de E. Bouvier . . . et A. Ganem. Paris [etc.], A. Quillet [1924.]

BARNES, Harry Elmer. The Genesis of the World War; an introduction to the problem of war guilt [second revised edition]. New York and London, A. A. Knopf, 1927.

BARTULIĆ, Rudolf. Ungarns Rolle im Weltkrieg; eine historisch-politische Studie nebst Enthüllungen über den österreichisch-ungarischen Geheimdienst und die Sarajewoer Verschwörung auf Grund von persönlichen Erlebnissen des Kroaten Rud. Bartulitch; bearb. und hrsg. von Gottfried Beck. Lausanne, Payot & Cie, 1917.

—— [French translation] La responsabilité de la Hongrie; étude historique et politique, suivie de renseignements sur le service de sûreté austro-hongrois et sur la conjuration de Serajevo, d'après les révélations du Croate R. Bartulitch, par G. Beck. Paris, Payot & Cie, 1917.

BLOCH, Oscar. La vérité sur les avions de Nuremberg. Étude sur les responsabilités de la guerre. Paris, J. Dangon, 1922.

BOURGEOIS, Émile, and PAGÈS, Georges. Les origines et les responsabilités de la grande guerre; preuves et aveux. Paris, Hachette, 1921.

BÜLOW, Bernhard Wilhelm von. Die Krisis; die Grundlinien der diplomatischen Verhandlungen bei Kriegsausbruch . . . 3.ergänzte und erweiterte Aufl. Berlin, Deutsche Verlagsgesellschaft für Politik und Geschichte m.b.H., 1922.

CHOPIN, Jules, pseud. Le complot de Sarajevo (28 juin 1914), étude sur les origines de la guerre. [By Jules E. PICHON.] Paris, Éditions Bossard, 1918.

DELBRÜCK, Hans. Deutsch-englische Schuld-Diskussion zwischen Hans Delbrück . . . und J. W. Headlam-Morley. Berlin, Verlag für Politik und Wirtschaft g.m.b.H. [1921.]

DENIS, Ernest. La grande Serbie. Paris, Delagrave [c1915.]
(Bibliothèque d'histoire et de politique.)

DURHAM, Mary Edith. The Serajevo crime. London, G. Allen & Unwin, Ltd. [1925.]

EGGELING, Bernhard Friedrich O. von. Die russische Mobilmachung und der Kriegsausbruch, Beiträge zur Schuldfrage am Weltkriege. Oldenburg i.Gr., Berlin, E. Stalling, 1919.

FRANTZ, Gunther. Russlands Eintritt in den Weltkrieg; der Ausbau der russischen Wehrmacht und ihr Einsatz bei Kriegsausbruch. Berlin, Deutsche Verlagsgesellschaft für Politik und Geschichte m.b.H., 1924.

GOOCH, George Peabody. Recent Revelations of European Diplomacy. London, New York [etc.], Longmans, Green and Co., Ltd., 1927.

GOOSS, Roderich. Das Wiener Kabinett und die Enstehung des Weltkrieges. 2.Aufl. Wien, L. W. Seidel und Sohn, 1919.

HOENIGER, Robert. Russlands Vorbereitung zum Weltkrieg auf Grund un-veröffentlichter russischer Urkunden. Berlin, E. S. Mittler und Sohn, 1919.

Hoyos, Sándor, *gróf*. Der deutsch-englische Gegensatz und sein Einfluss auf die Balkanpolitik Österreich-Ungarns. Berlin und Leipzig, Vereinigung wissenschaftlicher Verleger, 1922.

HULDERMANN, Bernhard. Albert Ballin. Oldenburg i. O., Berlin, G. Stalling, 1922.

—— [French translation] La vie de Albert Ballin . . . Tr. par H. Simondet. Paris, Payot & Cie, 1924.

—— [English translation] Albert Ballin . . . Tr. from the German by W. J. Eggers. London, New York [etc.], Cassell and Co., Ltd., 1922.

KANNER, Heinrich. Kaiserliche Katastrophenpolitik, ein Stück zeitgenös-sischer Geschichte. Wien [etc.], E. P. Tal & Co., 1922.

—— Der Schlüssel zur Kriegsschuldfrage. Ein verheimlichtes Kapitel der Vorkriegsgeschichte. Nebst polemischen Artikeln von General Graf Max Montgelas. München, Südbayer. Verlagsgesellschaft m.b.H., 1926.

KAUTSKY, Karl. Wie der Weltkrieg entstand; dargestellt nach dem Akten-material des deutschen Auswärtigen Amts. Berlin, P. Cassirer, 1919.

—— [French translation] Comment s'est déclenchée la guerre mondiale. Paris, A. Costes, 1923.

—— [English translation] The Guilt of William Hohenzollern. London, Skeffington & Son, Ltd., 1920.

Der KRIEG zur See, 1914–1918, hrsg. vom Marine-Archiv. Berlin, E. S. Mittler & Sohn. Der Krieg in der Nordsee, bearb. von O. Groos. 1920–1925. 5 vols. Der Kreuzerkrieg in den ausländischen Gewässern, bearb. von E. Raeder. 1922–1923. 2 vols.

LINDENBERG, Paul. König Karl von Rumänien, ein Lebensbild dargestellt unter Mitarbeit des Königs, Berlin, Hafen-Verlag g.m.b.H., 1923. 2 vols.

MARGUTTI, Albert Alexander Vinzenz, *Freiherr* von. Vom alten Kaiser. Per-sönliche Erinnerungen an Franz Joseph I. Kaiser von Österreich und Apostol. König von Ungarn. 1. Aufl. Wien, Leonhardt-Verlag, 1921.

—— [English translation] Emperor Francis Joseph and his Times. New York, G. H. Doran Co., 1922.

MARSILY, William Henry. Les chefs de l'armée belge et le respect de la neutralité. Paris, Payot & Cie, 1917.

MARTIN, Hermann. Die Schuld am Weltkriege. Leipzig, F. W. Grunow, 1920.

MONTGELAS, Maximilian Maria Karl Desiderius, *Graf* von. Leitfaden zur Kriegsschuldfrage. Berlin und Leipzig, De Gruyter & Co., 1923.

—— [English translation] The Case for the Central Powers, an impeach-ment of the Versailles verdict. New York, A. A. Knopf, 1925.

MOREL, Edmund Dene. Truth and the War . . . [3d ed.] London, National Labour Press, Ltd., 1918.

MORHARDT, Mathias. Les preuves; le crime de droit commun, le crime diplo-matique. Paris, Librairie du Travail [1924.]

MÜHLON, Wilhelm. Die Verheerung Europas; Aufzeichnungen aus den er-sten Kriegsmonaten. Zürich, O. Füssli, 1918.

—— [English translation] The Murder of Sarajevo; translation of an article [entitled "After Vidov Dan, 1914"] . . . published in Krv Slovenstva [The Blood of Slavdom], Belgrade, 1924. [London] The British Institute of International Affairs [1925.]

Klobukowski, A. W. Les responsabilités d'Allemagne avant l'agression. (In Le Temps, Paris. Aug. 6, 1924. p. 2.)

Lajusan, H. Les origines de la guerre. Nouvelles données sur l'état d'esprit des milieux officiels allemands en 1914. (In Revue d'histoire de la guerre mondiale, Paris. 4. année, no. 2, April 1926. pp. [141]-143.)

Lutz, Hermann. Greys Mitverantwortung für die russische Mobilmachung. (In Die Kriegsschuldfrage, Berlin. 3. Jahrgang, no. 5, May 1925. pp. 315-322.)

Mandl, Leopold. Zur Warnung Serbiens an Österreich. (In Die Kriegsschuldfrage, Berlin. 2. Jahrgang, no. 4, Apr. 1924. pp. 108-111.)

Maxse, Leopold James. An "Aide-mémoire" to the historian. (In The National Review, London. No. 437, July 1919. pp. [659]-679.)

Montgelas, Maximilian Maria Karl Desiderius, Graf von. Der Grundirrtum Professor Pekars. (In Die Kriegsschuldfrage, Berlin. 3. Jahrgang, no. 9, Sept. 1925. pp. 590-596.)

—— Der Zusammenbruch der Ententelegende über die russische allgemeine Mobilmachung. (In Deutsche Rundschau, Berlin. Jahrgang 48.8, Bd.191, May 1922. pp. 113-124.)

Mousset, Albert. L'attentat de Serajevo. (In Revue d'histoire diplomatique, Paris. 39. année, no. 1, 1925. pp. [44-68].)

Ostrymiecz, August Urbański von. Mein Beitrag zur Kriegsschuldfrage. (In Die Kriegsschuldfrage, Berlin. 4. Jahrgang, no. 2, Feb. 1926. pp. 70-87.)

Schäfer, Theobald von. Generaloberst von Moltke in den Tagen vor der Mobilmachung und seine Einwirkung auf Österreich-Ungarn. (In Die Kriegsschuldfrage, Berlin. 4. Jahrgang, no. 8, Aug. 1926. pp. 514-549.)

Serge, Victor. La verité sur l'attentat de Serajevo. (In Clarté, Paris. 4. année, no. 74, May 1925. pp. [205]-212.)

Seton-Watson, Robert William. L'archiduc François Ferdinand. (In Le Monde slave, Paris. Nouv. sér., 2. année, no. 4, April 1925. pp. 1-18.)

—— The Murder at Sarajevo. (In Foreign Affairs, New York. Vol. 3, no. 3, April 1925. pp. [489]-509.)

Steed, Henry Wickham. The Pact of Konopisht, Kaiser and Archduke: June 12, 1914. (In The Nineteenth Century and After, London. No. 468, Feb. 1916. pp. 253-273.)

—— The Quintessence of Austria. (In The Edinburgh Review. Vol. 222, no. 454, Oct. 1915. pp. [225]-247.)

Szécsen de Temerin, N., gróf. Ein vergeblicher Versuch für die Erhaltung des Friedens im Sommer 1914. (In Die Kriegsschuldfrage, Berlin. 4. Jahrgang, no. 2, Feb. 1926, pp. 66-70.)

Weber, A. Graf Tisza und die Kriegserklärung an Serbien, von Dr. A. Weber. (In Die Kriegsschuldfrage, Berlin. 3. Jahrgang, no. 12, Dec. 1925. pp. 818-826.)

Wegerer, Alfred. Der angebliche "Kronrat" der 29. juli 1914. (In Die Kriegsschuldfrage, Berlin. 1. Jahrgang, no. 1, July 1923. pp. 8-12.)

—— Der Anlass zum Weltkrieg. Ausschnitte zum Attentat von Sarajevo. (*In* DIE KRIEGSSCHULDFRAGE, Berlin. 3. Jahrgang, no. 6, June 1925. pp. 353-405.)

—— Der Halt in Belgrad. (*In* DIE KRIEGSSCHULDFRAGE, Berlin. 1. Jahrgang, no. 6, Dec. 1923. pp. 130-134.)

—— Die verfrühten deutschen Mobilmachungsmeldungen und die russische Mobilmachung. (*In* GRENZBOTEN, Leipzig; Berlin. 81. Jahrgang, no. 17, May 6, 1922. pp. 79-84.)

INDEX

Adelt, L., 14 n
Adriatic Sea, 15, 299, 311
Aegean Sea, 324
Africa, 280
Agram, 16, 118 n
Aggression, act of, definition of,
351-353
Aix-la-Chapelle, 258, 261
Albania, 57, 90, 128, 129 n, 227, 339
  See also Balkans
Albert, King of the Belgians, 259,
261, 262, 262 n, 295
Alexander, Crown Prince, Regent
of Serbia, 93
Alexander, King of Serbia, 22
Allenstein, 220
Alliances, entangling, 73, 336, 353
Allied Powers, 3, 10, 11, 202, 203
  See also Triple Entente
Alsace, 272, 274
  See also Alsace-Lorraine
Alsace-Lorraine, 106, 316 n
  See also Alsace; Lorraine
Altmünsterol, 268, 272, 272 n
Antwerp, 284
Appuhn, Charles, 8 n, 198 n
Arbitration, aggression and, 352;
  honor or vital interest and, 175
Armaments, 11
Artamanov, Vassili, Russian Mili-
  tary Attaché in Belgrade, 24, 24 n
Asia, Turkey in, 323
Asquith, Herbert H., British Prime
  Minister, 278 n, 279, 280, 283, 289,
  291 n, 292, 292 n, 293, 294, 295,
  297, 298; and intervention, 293
Athens, 326, 330; authorities at, 325,
  328, 329 n
Atlantic Ocean, 288
Aulard, F. V. A., 269 n, 270 n, 271 n
Austria (Monarchy), 117; aristoc-
  racy of, 16, 17
  See also Austria-Hungary
Austria (Republic), 5, 7 n, 30 n,
  132 n

Austria-Hungary, 5, 10, 11, 13, 16-
  20, 22, 27, 29, 31, 111 n, 132 n,
  135 n, 281; alliances of, 41, 246,
  313, 313 n (see also Triple Alliance, Treaty of); archives of, 5,
  7 n, 29, 30, 30 n, 36, 213 n; Balkan
  policy of, 10, 35-36, 35 n, 38-41,
  42, 54, 56-57, 83, 84, 89-90, 116,
  128, 145, 299, 313-315, 320, 325,
  327-328, 328 n, 330, 334, 339; Cabinet of, 35, 35 n, 63 n, 89, 165, 301,
  335; Council of Ministers of, 5,
  17, 44 n, 53, 54, 56, 56 n, 57, 59-62,
  82 n, 128, 188, 191, 192, 216, 234,
  235 n, 307, 336, 345; and France,
  80, 81, 82 n, 84, 226-227, 227-228,
  230, 346; General Staff of, 18,
  30 n, 31, 40 n, 168, 169, 192, 211-
  216; German support for, 11, 35,
  37-38, 38 n, 40-44, 40 n, 48, 51,
  53, 56, 57, 63, 64, 67, 67-69, 73, 76,
  78, 83, 84, 86, 113, 120, 130, 133,
  136, 137, 145, 179, 180, 211-216,
  222, 305-306, 331, 334-335, 343,
  346, 352, 353 (see also Austria-
  Hungary and Serbia, German attitude towards; Ultimatum, Austrian, German note concerning);
  Government of, 15, 27 n, 30, 37,
  42, 50, 53, 58, 59, 60, 62, 74, 133,
  134, 211, 212; and guilt of Serbian
  war, 67, 119, 123, 136, 310, 318,
  335; intelligence service of, 30-31;
  intransigency of, 91, 97, 110, 112,
  129, 131, 133, 136, 175, 177, 189,
  192, 279, 296, 311, 344, 345, 353;
  and Italy, 178, 178 n, 180, 214,
  299-312, 343, 344; military operations of, 107, 108, 109, 118, 119,
  120, 122, 124, 127, 129, 130, 131,
  136, 141 n, 143, 160, 163, 168, 169,
  185, 187, 192, 211, 232, 233, 233 n,
  235, 303, 308, 319, 348; Ministry
  of, for Foreign Affairs, 92; mobilization of, 58, 97, 101, 118, 118 n,

Bach, Aug., 5 n

Balance of power, in Balkans, 328, 329, 339; in Europe, 10-11, 123, 163, 281, 290

Balkans, 10, 15, 35-36, 39, 41, 42, 53, 54, 73, 75, 78, 116, 128, 139, 145, 305, 307, 329, 339 n; balance of power in, 328, 329, 339; Italy and, 299, 309, 329; wars in, 10, 15, 25, 56 n, 94

See also Austria-Hungary, Balkan policy of; Central Powers, Balkan policy of; Russia and Balkans

Ballin, Albert, General Manager of the Hamburg-American Line, 75, 76 n, 113, 114, 114 n

Baltic Fleet, 142

Baltic Sea, 84

Barbagallo, Corrado, 331

Barnardiston, Nathaniel Walter, Colonel, British Military Attaché at Brussels in 1906, 263 n

Barnes, Harry Elmer, 1 n

Barrère, Camille, French Ambassador at Rome, 112; quoted, 112

Bartulić, Rudolph, a Croat in the Austrian Army, 15-16, 15 n, 16

Basch, Victor, 229 n

Basel, Switz., 266 n

Basili, N. A., Vice Chancellor at the Russian Ministry for Foreign Affairs, 146 n, 151, 152, 198, 202, 249

Bastaić, Paul, Member of the *Mlada Bosna* (Young Bosnia) Society, 21 n

Bassompierre, de, Chief of Department of the Belgian Ministry for Foreign Affairs, 257 n, 258

Bavaria, 275; Government of, 6, 6 n, 169, 337 n; Third Army Corps of, 274, 275, 275 n

Bavarian Documents, 8, 170 n

Beauchamp, William Lygon, Earl, Member of the British Cabinet, 293 n

Beck, Gottfried, 15 n

Behncke, Paul von, Vice Admiral, Acting Chief of the German Admiralty Staff, 75 n

Belfort, 243, 244 n, 264, 274; General in command at, 244 n

Belgium, 172, 242 n, 245, 283, 296, 348, 349; Cabinet of, 257, 259, 260, 262 n; compensation offered, 259, 259 n; defensive measures of, 256-257, 261 n, 262; and England, 114, 236 n, 257-258, 261, 262, 262-263, 284, 286, 288, 289, 294, 295, 297, 297-298, 350; and France, 242, 256-257, 261, 261 n, 262, 267-268, 268, 286; German ultimatum to, 172-173, 172 n, 255, 258-259, 258 n, 259 n, 293, 293 n, 297, 349; integrity of, 173, 294-295; mobilization of, 257; neutrality of, 114, 173 n, 236 n, 256-263, 267-268, 268, 284, 286-289, 293 n, 294-295, 297, 297-298, 350; Parliament of, 256, 262; public opinion in, 258; reply of, to ultimatum, 259-261

Belgrade, 14, 20, 21, 24, 25, 26, 28 n, 30, 32, 62, 65, 66, 74, 94, 96, 127; authorities at, 30, 54 n, 57, 61, 63, 64, 64 n, 82, 92, 93, 94, 97, 101, 107, 108, 124, 141, 177, 279, 328; bombardment of, 161; bridgehead at, 57 n; Government withdrawn from, 96; occupation of, 122, 127, 129, 136, 143, 167, 179, 183-187, 191, 193, 232, 233, 233 n, 234, 235, 339, 345, 348; police of, 33

Below-Saleske, Herr von, German Minister at Brussels, 173 n, 258, 260-262

Benckendorff, Alexander, Count, Russian Ambassador at London, 108, 109 n, 147, 162, 284, 342; quoted 109 n

Berchtold, Leopold, Count, Austro-Hungarian Minister for Foreign Affairs, President of the Austro-Hungarian Ministerial Council, 28, 29, 35 n, 37, 38, 38 n, 39 n, 41 n, 43, 45, 53 n, 55 n, 56 n, 57, 58, 59, 59 n, 63, 64, 64 n, 67 n, 68 n, 69, 69 n, 70, 75, 82 n, 83, 92, 97, 117 n, 118, 119, 119 n, 124, 125 n, 130, 132, 134, 135 n, 136, 180, 187, 188, 188 n, 191, 191 n, 192 n, 212, 214 n,

Public opinion, 1-4, 36, 154, 245, 350; Austro-Hungarian, 40; Belgian, 258; British, 145, 161, 173 n, 242, 277, 279, 282, 284, 289, 290 n, 294, 297-298; European, 59, 130, 350; French, 224, 225, 264, 350; Rumanian, 318-319; Russian, 86, 144, 148; Serbian, 33
See also Press, the

Radoslavov, Dr. V., Bulgarian Premier, Minister for Foreign Affairs and of the Interior, 326
Railways, German, 171, 172, 221; Russian, 144
Réchicourt-la-Petite, 265
Recouly, Raymond, 139 n, 144 n, 146 n, 158 n, 237 n, 259 n, 287 n, 293 n
Red Book, 5, 320 n
Réméreville, 265
Renouvin, Pierre, 198 n
Reparations, 3
Reppe, 264
Reval telegram, 82 n
Revolutionary governments, 3
Revolutionists, Bosnian, 21; Russian, 21
Rhine, R., 237
Ritter von Grünstein, O., Baron von, Bavarian Chargé d'Affaires at the Vatican, 101 n
Rodd, Sir R., British Ambassador at Rome, 107 n, 112 n
Rodzianko, Mikhail V., President of the Russian Duma, 139 n, 196, 196 n
Roedern, Friedrich, Count von, German Secretary of State for Alsace-Lorraine, 106
Romberg, K. G. W., Baron von, 6 n, 105, 105 n, 106 n, 206 n, 231 n; quoted, 106
Rome, 101 n, 176, 178, 339; Austrian embassy at, 5; authorities at, 109, 110, 112, 299, 301, 304, 308-311
Rosetti, Former Rumanian Premier, 318, 319
Rothschild, Lord Alfred de, London banker, 287 n

Rumania, 24 n, 312; alliances of, 35-36, 41, 246, 313, 313 n, 315, 316, 318, 319; and Bulgaria, 39, 54, 313-316, 319, 320, 326, 327, 328; Council of Ministers of, 320 n; Crown Council of, 318-319; and Entente, 319, 320, 326; and France, 317, 317 n, 319; Government of, 37, 39; and nationalism, 314-318; and neutrality, 317 n, 319, 328, 330; parties in, 318; public opinion in, 318-319; and Russia, 316-317, 318; and Serbia, 57, 314, 316, 319; and Triple Alliance, 35-36, 39, 41, 55, 313, 314-316, 318-320, 320 n, 325, 326, 327, 330, 337
See also Balkans
Rumbold, Sir Horace, Counselor to the British Embassy at Berlin, temporarily Chargé d'Affaires, 107 n, 281 n
Rummerskirsch, K., Baron von, Master of Ceremonies for Archduke Franz Ferdinand, 29
Russell, Hon. Alick, Lieutenant Colonel, English Military Attaché at Berlin, 172 n
Russia, 7, 24; and Asia, 54; and Austrian ultimatum, 58, 74, 75, 80, 81, 83 n, 87-90, 112 n, 115, 116, 139, 184, 300, 340; and Balkans, 10, 36, 37, 39, 41, 54, 56, 73, 88, 116, 139, 145, 147, 316-317, 321-324, 329, 334, 336, 339, 340 (*see also* Russia and Serbia); Belgian appeal to, 262; Cabinet of, 104; Council of Ministers of, 141, 142, 142 n, 145, 157, 197; and England, 10, 74, 94, 111, 115, 123, 143, 145, 161-165, 182, 191, 205, 277, 281-284, 284 n, 291 n, 292, 296, 342; "formulas" of, 184-186, 204, 207 n, 232-235, 347, 348; and France, 11, 58, 63, 74, 80, 88, 103, 106, 111, 113, 115, 137, 142, 163-165, 163 n, 204, 205, 205 n, 223, 250, 264, 283, 288, 309, 342, 346, 353 (*see also* France and Russian mobilization); general mobilization of, 144-153, 156-159, 168, 185, 189,

279, 343; time limit on, 66, 91-92, 94

"Union or Death," 22
See also "Black Hand"

United States of America, 1, 1 n, 64 n

Valdieu, 272

Valentin, Veit, 108 n, 263 n

Valona, 307

Vatican, 101, 101 n; Cardinal Secretary of State at, 101 n

Vauthiermont, 264

Venizelos, Eleutherios, Greek Premier, 328

Verdun, 223, 224, 251, 349

Verraux, Martial Justin, French General, 240 n, 244 n

Versailles, 2

Versailles, Treaty of, 2, 3

Vesnić, Dr. M. R., Serbian Minister at Paris, 93, 229

Victor Emmanuel III, King of Italy, 310, 310 n

Vienna, *passim;* archives in, 3, 7, 30, 31 n; British embassy in, 135 n; British Military Attaché at, 160 n; Bulgarian representatives in, 326; French Military Attaché at, 160, 160 n; German embassy in, 70; Russian Chargé d'Affaires at, 89, 128 n; Serbian legation in, 27

Villiers, Sir Francis H., British Minister at Brussels, 257, 261 n, 295

Viviani, René, French Premier and Minister for Foreign Affairs, 79, 82, 83, 84, 86, 104, 105, 152 n, 163, 164, 203, 206, 207 n, 208, 226-231, 233 n, 237, 237 n, 239, 239 n, 242, 243, 251, 267, 269, 269 n, 270, 275, 291 n, 342; quoted, 82, 205, 206, 230, 240, 240-241

Volga, R., 143

Vosges Mountains, 242, 243, 268, 272

Waldburg, Heinrich, Count von, Secretary of Legation to the German Legation at Bucharest, tem-

porarily Chargé d'Affaires, 314, 314 n

Waldersee, Fr. Gustav, Count von, Major General, First Chief Quartermaster on the German General Staff, 51, 51 n, 78; quoted, 50-51, 78

Waldthausen, Dr. Julius, Baron von, German Minister at Bucharest, 320

Wangenheim, Baroness von, 46

Wangenheim, Hans, Baron von, German Ambassador at Constantinople, 46-47, 78, 320-322, 320 n, 323, 324; quoted, 320-321

War, localization of, *see* Localization of war

War of 1914-1918, 1, 2, 3, 6, 6 n, 10, 11 n, 47, 64 n; responsibility for, *see under countries and individuals*

Warsaw, city of, 153 n, 198; district of, 143, 144

Waxweiler, Émile, 263 n

Weber, A., 37 n

Wedel, Dr. Botho, Count von, Reporting Counselor in the German Foreign Office, 61 n

Wegerer, Alfred, 13 n, 27 n, 30 n, 170 n, 188 n, 193 n, 201 n

Wendel, Hermann, 14 n

Wenniger, Bavarian military representative at Berlin, 169, 171, 171 n, 188 n, 222 n, 275 n; quoted, 169-170, 222 n, 275 n

Wesel, 268, 274

Wesserling-Strässel road, 273

White Book, 4, 248 n, 249

Wie der Weltkrieg entstand, 9, 249 n

Wiesner, Friedrich von, Counselor to the Austro-Hungarian Ministry for Foreign Affairs, 29 n, 31, 31 n, 32, 33; quoted, 31

William, Crown Prince of the German Empire and of Prussia, 76-77; quoted, 77

William II, Emperor of Germany, King of Prussia, 9, 24, 38, 40, 40 n, 41, 45, 68, 70 n, 71, 74, 88,